CW00601552

At Home and Under Fire

Although the Blitz has come to symbolize the experience of civilians under aerial attack, Germany first launched air raids on Britain at the end of 1914 and continued them during the First World War. With the advent of war in the air, civilians far removed from traditional battle zones became a direct target of war rather than a group shielded from its impact. This study examines how British civilians experienced and came to terms with aerial warfare during the two world wars. Memories of the First World War's air raids shaped British responses to the various real and imagined war threats of the 1920s and 1930s, including the bombing of civilians during the Spanish Civil War and, ultimately, the Blitz itself. The responses of the government and of many contemporary observers to the arrival of air power emphasized the significance of civilians – by which they meant the gendered category of women and children – to the waging of modern war.

Susan R. Grayzel is Professor of History at the University of Mississippi. She is the author of *Women's Identities at War: Gender, Motherhood, and Politics in Britain and France during the First World War* (1999), which was awarded the 2000 British Council Prize by the North American Conference on British Studies, and *Women and the First World War* (2002). Her more recent work appears in *Gender, Labour, War and Empire: Essays on Modern Britain* (2009), co-edited with Philippa Levine.

At Home and Under Fire

*Air Raids and Culture in Britain from
the Great War to the Blitz*

SUSAN R. GRAYZEL

University of Mississippi

CAMBRIDGE
UNIVERSITY PRESS

CAMBRIDGE UNIVERSITY PRESS
Cambridge, New York, Melbourne, Madrid, Cape Town,
Singapore, São Paulo, Delhi, Mexico City

Cambridge University Press
32 Avenue of the Americas, New York, NY 10013-2473, USA

www.cambridge.org
Information on this title: www.cambridge.org/9780521874946

© Susan R. Grayzel 2012

This publication is in copyright. Subject to statutory exception
and to the provisions of relevant collective licensing agreements,
no reproduction of any part may take place without the written
permission of Cambridge University Press.

First published 2012
Reprinted 2013

A catalog record for this publication is available from the British Library.

Library of Congress Cataloging in Publication Data

Grayzel, Susan R.
At home and under fire: air raids and culture in Britain from the Great War to the Blitz /
Susan R. Grayzel.
 p. cm.
Includes bibliographical references and index.
ISBN 978-0-521-87494-6 (hardback)
 1. Civil defense – Great Britain – History – 20th century. 2. Civil defense – Social aspects
– Great Britain – History – 20th century. 3. Bombing, Aerial – Great Britain – History
– 20th century. 4. Bombing, Aerial – Social aspects – Great Britain – History – 20th
century. 5. Civilians in war – Great Britain – History – 20th century. 6. Civilian war
casualties – Great Britain – History – 20th century. 7. World War, 1914–1918 – Aerial
operations, German. 8. World War, 1939–1945 – Aerial operations, German. 9. Great
Britain – History, Military I. Title.
D810.C69G68 2011
363.350941′09041–dc22   2011012050

ISBN 978-0-521-87494-6 Hardback

Cambridge University Press has no responsibility for the persistence or accuracy of URLs
for external or third-party Internet Web sites referred to in this publication and does not
guarantee that any content on such Web sites is, or will remain, accurate or appropriate.

In memory of my mother,
and above all, for Joe

Contents

Acknowledgments

To some extent, I have been working on this book since I first came across accounts of bombs dropping on the streets of London while researching women during the First World War. As I began this project in earnest at the end of the 1990s and certainly after the events of 9/11 and the responses to them, I became convinced that the air raid and the new understanding of the state, the civilian, and the home at war that it produced needed a history. Along the way, I was sidetracked by two enormous sets of challenges – the arrivals of my daughters and the serious illnesses faced by my parents. The commingling of the labor of teaching, researching, and writing while attending to growing children and a dying parent definitely shaped the book that has emerged. Given the long gestation of this project, I have numerous debts to old mentors and new colleagues, to archivists and librarians, and to a variety of audiences that listened to me deliver my work-in-progress. And I offer the usual but no less sincere apologies to anyone I may have inadvertently left out and for any errors, which remain mine alone.

Like many others who study Britain's twentieth-century wars, I am indebted to the staff at several departments of the Imperial War Museum, especially Rod Suddaby in the Department of Documents and Mary Wilkinson in the Department of Printed Books, as well as to those of the Film and Video Archive, the Photography Archive, and the National Inventory of War Memorials. I am grateful to the trustees of the Imperial War Museum for granting permission to quote from letters and diaries for which the museum holds copyright and to Lavinia Anson, Judith Baines, Tony Bull, Bruce Gordon-Smith, Jean Hale, William King and family, A. T. Lockwood, Charles Mattison, David Moore and Christine Citron Moore, Keith Nicholson, Andy Spatcher, June Troy, and Esther Wells for granting permission to quote from the papers of their family members entrusted to the Imperial War Museum. Every effort has been made to trace copyright holders of all material held at the Imperial War Museum, and both the Imperial War Museum and I would be grateful for any information that might facilitate getting in touch with those whose identities or addresses are not currently known.

Staff members at the British Library, the National Archives, the National Library of Women, the Mass Observation Archives, and the Women's International League British Section Archives at the British Library of Political and Economic Science aided my research in Britain, and those at the New York Public Library, Widener Library at Harvard University, and especially the Interlibrary Loan Office of the J. D. Williams Library at the University of Mississippi helped me enormously stateside.

I am so thankful that Tom Laqueur has never stopped offering his support and critical eye. Along with Laura Mayhall and Lucy Noakes, he took on the burden of reading the entire manuscript in draft form. Comments from all three vastly improved the final book, and I am ever in their debt. In addition, Tami Davis Biddle, the late Gail Braybon, Deborah Cohen, Laura Doan, Martin Francis, Adrian Gregory, Nicky Gullace, Mo Healy, Isabel Hull, Kali Israel, Helen Jones, Jon Lawrence, Fred Leventhal, Philippa Levine, Molly Nolan, Maura O'Connor, Susan Pedersen, Tammy Proctor, Paul Saint-Amour, Peter Stansky, Penny Summerfield, Chris Waters, and Mary Wilkinson offered timely comments, references, and/or encouragement. Sonya Rose and Bob Moeller have been especially stalwart supporters and role models.

I owe audiences (and the organizers of these events noted in parentheses) my deep gratitude for stimulating feedback as I presented my work-in-progress at the Institute for Historical Research's Centre for Metropolitan History Conference on Metropolitan Catastrophes (Stefan Goebel and Derek Keene); the Massachusetts Historical Society's Conference on Women, War and Work (Ondine Le Blanc); the Mershon Center of the Ohio State University (Mark Grimsley); Harvard University's Minda de Gunzburg Center for European Studies British Studies Group (Jim Cronin) and its Conference on Gender and Postwar Reconstruction (Laura Frader); the Society for First World War Studies Conference in Lyon (Pierre Pursiegle and Jenny McLeod); the University of Alabama at Huntsville (Molly Johnson); the University of Cincinnati's Conference on Europe in Cross National Perspective (Maura O'Connor and Deborah

Cohen); and the University of North Carolina at Chapel Hill's workshop "Gender, War, and Nation in 20th-Century Europe" (Karen Hagemann and Chad Bryant). I am also grateful for the questions posed by participants at the American Historical Association Annual Meeting in 2004, the Anglo-American Historical Meeting in 2007, the Berkshire Conference on the History of Women in 2008, and several annual meetings of the North American Conference on British Studies.

I also remain enormously indebted to Lew Bateman for his ongoing interest in my work and to Eric Crahan and others, including the anonymous readers, at Cambridge University Press who helped transform my research into this volume.

I consider it a privilege to teach at a publicly funded university that serves a diverse student population, but such institutions rarely have abundant resources. I am honored that the College of Liberal Arts under Dean Glenn Hopkins and the Department of History at the University of Mississippi repeatedly chose to invest in my work. I am also grateful for the comradeship of past and present history department colleagues, especially members of several writing groups (Nancy Bercaw, Erin Chapman, Deirdre Cooper-Owens, Angela Hornsby-Gutting, Theresa Levitt, Amy Randall, and Noell Wilson). A final reason that I count myself lucky to teach at the University of Mississippi has come from students who have inspired me with their own work, particularly Dr. Nick Brown, Dr. Emily Machen, and soon-to-be Dr. David Speicher. The last two also served as wonderful research assistants.

I owe a special debt to my fellow moms in academia for inspiration, advice, and empathy, including those who were close at home, like Julie Anderson, Nancy Bercaw, Beth Boyd, Chiarella Esposito, Katie McKee, and Susie Pedigo, and those farther away, like Nicky Gullace, Laura Mayhall, Dana Rabin, Jessica Weiss, Marcia Yonemoto, and, above all, Simone Davis. I remain awed by the love and care that babysitters, coaches, and teachers have given my daughters. Fara Shook stands in her own category as a nurturing presence in all of my children's lives since their infancy; my gratitude to her is incalculable.

I cannot imagine my life and that of my family over the period of time that I have been writing this book without the presence of Kirsten Dellinger and Jeff Jackson, Deborah Barker and Ivo Kamps, Chuck Ross and Val Ross, Karen Raber and Doug McPherson, Marc Lerner and Nina Rifkind, Julie Anderson, Annie Quinney, Laura Schwemm, Katie Gibson, Jessica Beels, Branwen Gregory, Lisa Hunter, and the incomparable Muriel McClendon.

My friends in England (and increasingly their families) have provided a range of welcome support – cups of tea, lovely meals, spare beds, and, above all, timely encouragement – over many years, so I extend my deepest gratitude to Clare Collins, Andy Fellows, Judith Higgin, Susan Morrissey, Lucy Noakes, and Etta Logan, who has provided all of the above and more.

And at long last, I offer my infinite appreciation of my family. Jon Grayzel and Julia Gallagher, Dave Grayzel and Courtney Dickinson, my nephews Connor, David, and Benjamin, and my niece Annabelle have been sources of solace for the long haul. On our annual visits north, Tim Ward and Susan Ward, and Tom Ward and Tess McDonough-Ward have welcomed me into their family. I have vivid memories of my father, Arthur Grayzel, reading books like Richard Crossman's *Diaries of a Cabinet Minister* at the beach during family vacations when I was growing up. I am pretty sure that I did not become the kind of historian he would read by choice, but his enthusiasm for the study of the past has been inspirational. I am grateful to him and to Claire Lieberwitz for their ongoing interest not only in my children, but also in my work. And my daughters – Sarah, Rebecca, and Miranda – have enriched and changed my life. I am awed to share my home with all three of these unique women-in-the-making and empowered by their energy, imagination, smarts, and love.

I dedicate this book to two extraordinary people. I was in the long middle of this project when my mother, Estherann Grayzel, was diagnosed with amyotrophic lateral sclerosis (ALS). Her resiliency and valiant struggle against this incurable illness, which slowly deprived this dedicated physician of her speech, breath, and motion, taught me truly to understand courage in the face of death. Finally, there is Joe Ward. For nearly twenty years, he has been both my best friend and closest colleague; since that time, he has read (and edited) virtually every word I've written, shared all the challenges and delights of raising our children, comforted me, provoked me, made me laugh, and given me the gift of his abiding faith and love; this book is his.

Introduction

Modern War and the Militarization of Domestic Life

THE STATE AND THE HOME

By the summer of 1917, the horrific losses incurred during the First World War had helped forge a stronger alliance between the state and the home, between government officials and British feminists, over a shared interest in reproduction to sustain the nation.[1] A concrete manifestation of this aspect of total war occurred in late June 1917 when Great Britain celebrated its first National Baby Week, the culmination of wartime initiatives to promote infant welfare. Shortly thereafter, Ida O'Malley wrote an editorial – "Bombs and Babies and Reconstruction" – for the feminist paper the *Common Cause*, remarking on the startling set of circumstances that occurred during Baby Week. O'Malley began:

> Last Saturday morning as Baby Week was drawing to a close, Londoners suddenly saw a flight of invaders appearing out of the blue, and the streets that had been decorated in honour of the babies were shaken by the noise of bombs and by London's guns, as she defended herself against the foe. After the battle in the air was over, or had moved away

---

[1] For more on this comparatively, see Ann Taylor Allen, *Feminism and Motherhood in Western Europe, 1890–1970: The Maternal Dilemma* (New York, 2005); and Gisela Bock and Pat Thane (eds.), *Maternity and Gender Policies: Women and the Rise of the European Welfare States, 1880s–1950s* (London, 1991). For Britain, see Deborah Dwork, *War Is Good for Babies and Other Young Children: A History of the Infant and Child Welfare Movement in England, 1898–1918* (London, 1987); and Susan Pedersen, *Family, Dependence and the Origins of the Welfare State in Britain and France, 1914–1915* (Cambridge, 1993), in particular on the expansion of welfare state policies around motherhood during wartime. A classic articulation of state interest in maternity remains Anna Davin, "Imperialism and Motherhood," *History Workshop Journal* (Spring 1978), 9–35.

from her immediate vicinity, thousands of London women and girls finished off their week's work in offices and shops and factories and hurried home to see whether their own dwellings were standing and their
own families alive.... The day with all its contrasts, its blue sky, and
sunshine, and babies, and menace of swift death, was altogether very
characteristic of the strange times in which we live, and, very unlike anything we could have imagined before nineteen hundred and fourteen.

This experience prompted O'Malley to reflect on the changing nature of
war and its implications for the future. She encouraged her readers to
appreciate that since the start of the war:

things which used to be separate in fact, or in our minds, have been
violently thrown together, and, as it were, mixed up. In former days it
used to be possible to arrange things in categories. One could still, if one
wished, think of the state as separate from the home, of men as separate
from women.... [T]hings which used to be thought as only interesting to men, such as military defences, are now perforce of immediate
interest to women.[2]

The air raids that fell upon Londoners in broad daylight changed
matters intensely and irrevocably. As O'Malley observed, the arrival of
air warfare blurred boundaries between home front and frontline. Air
raids transformed the relationship between combatants and civilians and,
more important, between the state and the home. Those whom air raids
affected had to confront an essential feature of modern and total warfare:
every home could now come under fire. As a result, civilians mattered in
wartime as never before.

Although "the Blitz," a shorthand term used here, as it has so often
been, for the extensive aerial campaign that Germany waged against the
United Kingdom in 1940, has come to symbolize *the* twentieth-century
experience of British civilians under attack, Germany first launched air
raids on Britain in 1914 and continued them throughout the First World
War. With the advent of aerial warfare, civilians – which contemporaries
usually signified as women and children – decisively became targets of
war rather than a group shielded from its impact. Denounced initially
as atrocities precisely because they attacked such innocents, by the end
of the Second World War air raids had become an ever more acceptable
military practice. Indeed, as the century progressed, air power came to
be seen as a most effective way to conduct war, despite the certainty that
aerial attacks invariably killed non-combatants.

[2] I[da] B. O'M[alley], "Bombs and Babies and Reconstruction," *Common Cause*, 13 July 1917.

War has always had consequences for civilians, but something profoundly new happened during the First World War.[3] As I have emphasized in previous work, the war gave rise to the expression "home front," dividing the necessary labor of civilians (gendered feminine) from that of "war front" soldiers (gendered masculine).[4] The air raid shattered this sense of separateness between the two fronts, forcing the state (albeit gradually) to acknowledge both its inability to isolate civilians from war's dangers and its urgent obligation, central to the national ability to wage war, to protect them from this new threat (or at least to attempt to do so). The air raid potentially brought all civilians into the war zone and thus made their ability to survive vital to sustaining the war effort.

The massive scale of attacks on civilians during the Second World War has to a great degree obscured the significance of the smaller scale, though still terrifying, raids of its predecessor. In his otherwise persuasive and fascinating study of the Blitz, Angus Calder overlooks the fact that many in Britain had been introduced to the idea of air raids, and the need for civilians to be stoical in their face, twenty years earlier.[5] More recently, Sonya Rose has discussed the rise of wartime civic republicanism as the essence of citizenship constructed during the Second World War.[6]

---

[3] Accounts of war from Herodotus and Thucydides to the present make this point. Recent work has tried to argue that the nature of warfare dramatically changed for Europeans with the Napoleonic wars; see, e.g., David A. Bell, *The First Total War: Napoleon's Europe and the Birth of Warfare as We Know It* (Boston, 2007). See also the discussion of parallels between 1792–1815 and 1914–1945 in Karen Hagemann, "Home/Front: The Military, Violence and Gender Relations in the Age of the World Wars," in *Home/Front: The Military, War and Gender in Twentieth-Century Germany*, ed. Karen Hagemann and Stefanie Schiller-Springorum (Oxford, 2002). Some of the critical response to Bell and others has suggested the limits to Bell's approach in terms of thinking about totalizing warfare; see, e.g., Peter Paret, Review of Bell in *American Historical Review* 112:5 (2007), 1489–1491. In a brief study of aerial attacks against Germany during the First World War, Christian Geinitz asserts that "bombing thus fulfilled a major prerequisite for total warfare: ... eradication of the boundary between military and civil society." See Christian Geinitz, "The First Air War Against Noncombatants: Strategic Bombing of German Cities in World War I," in *Great War, Total War: Combat and Mobilization on the Western Front, 1914–1918* (Cambridge, 2000), 224. For more on the concept of "militarization" to decribe war's impact on non-military affairs see John Gillis, "Introduction," in *The Militarization of the Western World*, ed. John Gillis (New Brunswick, NJ, 1989), and Michael Geyer, "The Militarization of Europe, 1914–1945," in *The Militarization of the Western World*, ed. Gillis.

[4] Susan R. Grayzel, *Women's Identities at War: Gender, Motherhood, and Politics in Britain and France during the First World War* (Chapel Hill, NC, 1999).

[5] Angus Calder, *The Myth of the Blitz* (London, 1991), ch. 1, quote from 2.

[6] Sonya O. Rose, "Sex, Citizenship, and the Nation in World War II Britain," *American Historical Review* 103:4 (October 1998), 1147–1176. This argument is elaborated in Sonya O. Rose, *Which People's War? National Identity and Citizenship in Wartime*

Her work makes significant contributions to our understanding of British identity during this war, but the influence of the changing nature of warfare itself on that identity falls outside the range of her study. This book engages constructively with the works of Calder and Rose by showing how the experience of air raids during the First World War prompted the construction of a type of civil identity during that war and in the interwar period that could be resurrected in the Second World War. Technology itself demanded new ways of thinking about the state and the home, producing a newly militarized yet democratic civilian citizen.

State agents sought to direct the process of identity construction and the manufacturing of consent to further state expansion into the domestic realm as they came to understand that modern warfare placed the security of every man, woman, and child among the highest national priorities. Complicating this process were notions developed prior to the First World War, and advanced by feminist pacifists during the war, that the "physical" force of men was distinct from the "moral" force of women but that each could form the core of separate but equal claims to citizenship. By virtue of their wielding a physical force, that is, by serving or even potentially serving in the military, men performed a vital, gender-specific task that earned them the right to participate in the nation's affairs, particularly by voting.[7] This argument was crucial to those who opposed the extension of the franchise to women. Feminists responded less by demanding the right to take up arms than by insisting that they offered the state a comparable, gender-specific, and vital moral force, because a world run by physical force was a dangerous thing. This moral force was expressed by their domestic and especially maternal duties (which were also of national interest), and this implied, moreover, that granting the vote to women and thereby empowering this moral force could lead to a world without war.

The First World War shifted this debate in somewhat unexpected ways. In 1916 military conscription was introduced, albeit in piecemeal form, and over the course of the war, women in Britain for the first time became official members of the armed forces in newly created women's services such as the Women's Army Auxiliary Corps.[8] Members of such

---

Britain, 1939–1945 (Oxford, 2003). More recently, Helen Jones has looked at the class-based responses of workers and the question of wartime productivity in light of air raids, in her *British Civilians in the Front Line: Air Raids, Productivity and Wartime Culture, 1939–45* (Manchester, 2006).

[7] That such arguments came into play despite Britain's lack of a conscript army in stark contrast to other European rivals is itself noteworthy.

[8] For a comprehensive study of this, see Lucy Noakes, *Women in the British Army: War and the Gentle Sex, 1907–1948* (London, 2006).

organizations, as well as nurses serving in military hospitals and ambulance drivers near traditional battle zones, sometimes found themselves in harm's way, and some lost their lives to enemy attacks. The performance of such dangerous national service by women raised questions about the presumed linkage of war service and citizenship. In addition, ongoing efforts to identify and acknowledge the essential contributions of female war workers, particularly in the munitions industry, as a kind of military service prompted claims that such women deserved special recognition. After all, some of these women died in industrial accidents and a few were killed by aerial warfare. As the war progressed, it thus became increasingly difficult to consider either military service or the potential to die for the national cause as belonging exclusively to men.

The linkage of service to the military (or to the state's military ends) and citizenship figured prominently in legislative debates about enfranchising women that began midway through the war.[9] Wartime discussions of the franchise focused on the need to ensure that all men serving in the military could vote and on the possible disenfranchisement of conscientious objectors. Women inserted themselves into these debates.[10] The question of women's service to the nation played a key role in the parliamentary discussions of franchise reform in 1917 and 1918. As one member of Parliament put it, the vote should go to "women who have not only suffered and died for their country in many of the fields of war, but, let there be no mistake, without whose heroism, self-denial, skill and physical strength and endurance, this country would never have successfully faced the crisis."[11] Initially, however, the expansion of the franchise to women was linked to maternal service and sacrifice; the final legislation of 1918 gave the vote only to women over thirty, thus excluding the generation of young women that had literally worked for the war effort

---

[9] Nicoletta F. Gullace, *The Blood of Our Sons: Men, Women, and the Renegotiation of British Citizenship During the Great War* (New York, 2002).

[10] Material here and in the previous paragraphs is drawn from Grayzel, *Women's Identities at War*; chs. 1, 5, and especially 6 for a general overview of debates over suffrage in Britain. For other accounts of debates over citizenship, particularly the franchise, during the First World War, in addition to Gullace, see Susan Kingsley Kent, *Making Peace: The Reconstruction of Gender in Interwar Britain* (Princeton, NJ, 1993), ch. 4; Martin Pugh, *Women and the Women's Movement in Britain, 1914–1959* (Houndsmills, 1992); Sandra Holton, *Feminism and Democracy: Women's Suffrage and Reform Politics in Britain, 1900–1918* (Cambridge, 1986); Martin Pugh, *Electoral Reform in War and Peace, 1906–1918* (London, 1978). For prewar links between patriotism and women's service to the nation, see Anne Summers, *Angels and Citizens: British Women as Military Nurses, 1854–1914* (London: 1987), 287–288.

[11] *Parliamentary Debates (Commons)*, 28 Mar. 1917, Vol. 92, cols. 517–518.

in munitions factories and elsewhere. British women would only receive the same voting rights as men a decade later.[12]

The arrival of aerial warfare further complicated such debates because the inclusion of the home in the battle zone gradually forced the state to consider what happened in the domestic sphere to be of central concern to a national war effort. The air raid came to be seen as producing a *new* kind of non-gender-specific civic virtue, the core in many ways of a transcendent wartime national civil identity. After the dust literally and figuratively settled on the First World War, participant states and their inhabitants had to come to terms with this particular aspect of its legacy. As recent studies of interwar Britain by Susan Kent and Richard Overy have asserted, the Great War bequeathed to its survivors a world of trauma and anxiety.[13] And clearly, we can find the influence of such moods on interwar culture and politics. Yet the argument that follows here offers a somewhat different exploration of the paradox of Britain between the wars by focusing on how the concrete experience of aerial warfare shaped interwar culture and politics, inspiring both its deepest anxieties and fears and its more idealistic impulses for remaking the world.

This book therefore seeks to enhance the understanding of both world wars as well as the period that separated them. It traces the effects of the air raid from its origins in the First World War, through the efforts both to prepare for and to prevent its usage in the interwar period, to its more widespread reappearance in World War II. The argument insists that ideas about gender were crucial to how this new type of war was imagined, experienced, remembered, and, crucially, anticipated. In particular, it analyzes how women and men alike attempted to determine what meanings could attach to a citizenry in which all people – regardless of gender, age, or class – could lay down their lives for their nation at war. It also emphasizes that the foundation of this transformation was an altered relationship between the state and the home. With the onset of air raids, the state could fulfill its commitment to protecting its citizens only if all of them – every man, woman, and child – engaged actively in the process. The state's ability, indeed its obligation, to intrude into the home in the name of national security was the air raid's primary consequence, and this became evident from the First World War onward.

---

[12] See Grayzel, *Women's Identities at War*, ch. 6, for elaboration.
[13] Susan Kingsley Kent, *Aftershocks: Politics and Trauma in Britain, 1918–1931* (Houndsmill, 2009); Richard Overy, *The Twilight Years: The Paradox of Britain Between the Wars* (New York, 2009).

NON-COMBATANTS, AERIAL ATTACKS, AND THE
LAW OF WAR BEFORE 1914

With the arrival of the air raid, a state could guarantee the safety of no space and no one. Women and children – a category of people that had come by the nineteenth century to be one that warring societies were obligated to protect from the worst excesses of warfare – could come under direct fire even if they were far removed from the primary battle zone. At the outset of aerial warfare, propaganda highlighted the fact that those killed in air raids included civilians. Such attacks undermined the responsibility of the state, and especially the role of men as principal state actors, to protect women and children. For example, the destruction of private homes and of a school in London's East End during the daylight airplane raids of Baby Week 1917 contributed to feelings ranging from unease to panic to outraged indignation. Air raids also helped to inspire new political claims for and by women, including new demands on the state. Before examining further how changes in the technology of war altered the relationship between the state and the home, it is important to consider the origins of the militarization of domestic life in the decades before the war.

Historically nations have turned their male citizens – and their men alone – into warriors, and this, in turn, supported the association of military service with the rights and privileges of citizenship. Yet if we go back to one of the first great modern European calls to arms for all citizens, the *levée en masse* of 1793, we see truly an appeal to "tout Français" – all the French – not all "Frenchmen," as Carla Hesse has rightly insisted.[14] In this injunction, the state commanded some form of military service from all. However, the tasks associated with such service are divided along lines not only of gender but also of age – "young men" are to "go forth to battle" while "married men" are to "forge weapons and transport munitions." Meantime, women must supply them with "tents and clothing" while children "make bandages from old linen."[15] Thus did the revolutionary French state incorporate its entire population into that presumed masculine realm of warfare. The significance of this change was not lost on contemporaries. As Carl von Clausewitz observed in 1832,

[14] Carla Hesse, "Silences and the History of Representations of War: Comment on Peter Paret, 'Justifying the Obligation of Military Service,'" and Michael Howard, "World War One: The Crisis in European History," *Journal of Military History*, Special Issue 57 (1993), 143–144.

[15] All excerpts from the *levée en masse* as quoted in Hesse, "Silences," 143.

the Napoleonic wars had "shown what an enormous factor the heart and sentiments of a Nation may be in the product of its political and military strength."[16] Clausewitz was not merely talking about the need to sway hearts and minds in order to carry out war successfully; he was acknowledging the significance of a shift noted by the *levée en masse* – the state's ability to deploy a nation in its *totality* in the waging of modern war.

Great Britain did not immediately grasp the consequences of this development. Unlike most of its European counterparts, whose citizens had experienced the devastating effects of foreign invasion, it did not maintain a standing army. Perhaps to a greater extent than other nineteenth-century nations, Britain engaged in wars between 1815 and 1914 that did not drastically alter the lives of its non-combatant citizens, because they were set almost entirely either in the imperial theater or in distant European war zones such as the Crimea. To be sure, imperial wars encouraged the expansion of the economy and state in ways that touched the lives of perhaps the majority of Britons, but they were largely shielded from many of the immediate consequences of such warfare. The mainstream media paid little attention to the collateral damage inflicted on non-combatants until the South African or Boer War at the end of the century, but then their focus fell largely on the suffering of "white" colonial populations.[17]

In the late nineteenth and early twentieth centuries, concerns about the potential consequences of warfare led the major European powers to adopt the Hague Conventions in the hope of establishing rules for war between major powers and protecting non-combatants.[18] The Conventions acknowledged the aggressive military role of the modern

---

[16] Carl von Clausewitz, "On the Character of Modern War," *On War* (1832, Rpt. and trans. Harmondsworth, 1982), 295. I am grateful to Joe Ward for this citation.

[17] See Laura E. Nym Mayhall, "The South African War and the Origins of Suffrage Militancy in Britain, 1899–1902," in *Women's Suffrage in the British Empire: Citizenship, Nation, and Race,* ed. Ian Christopher Fletcher, Laura E. Nym Mayhall, and Philippa Levine (London, 2000), 3–17; and Paula M. Krebs, *Gender, Race, and the Writing of Empire: Public Discourse and the Boer War* (Cambridge, 1999), for information on domestic campaigns over the British treatment of Boer civilians. For a compelling case study linking imperial warfare – in the German case – with the First World War, see Isabel V. Hull, *Absolute Destruction: Military Culture and the Practices of War in Imperial Germany* (Ithaca, NY, 2005). For a brief narrative overview of nineteenth-century conflicts, see Lawrence James, *Warrior Race: A History of the British at War* (London, 2002), pt. 4.

[18] For a summation of the Hague Conventions and other aspects of international law on the eve of World War One, see Nicoletta F. Gullace, "Sexual Violence and Family Honor: British Propaganda and International Law during the First World War," *American Historical Review* 102:3 (1997), 714–747.

state (and perhaps of the brutal practices of imperial warfare that might have to be curtailed), recognized that this could foster future conflict between nations, and reflected the desire to discriminate between legitimate and illegitimate military tactics. Among other challenges, the Conventions had to grapple with probable as well as existing military techniques and weaponry. The potential of bombardment from the air as a new means of attacking civilians was discussed in terms of the rules of engagement set forth in the Convention of 1899, which prohibited "the throwing of projectiles from a balloon or an airplane on cities, villages, habitations or buildings that were not defended." Such "open" cities were to be protected from violence "even for the purposes of reprisal."[19]

Following upon the Russo-Japanese War and recurring tensions between the Great Powers over their imperial holdings, the Second Hague Convention of 1907 took place against a backdrop of heightened potential for international conflict. At the outset, the British were cautiously optimistic about the Convention's potential to curtail war. The *Times* celebrated "the remarkable spectacle of a gathering of very eminent representatives of all the sovereign States of Europe, Asia, and in the present instance, of South as well as North America ... assembled not to discuss any acute question of international relations but to examine general principles and, if it may be, to decide upon regulations which may help to prevent international conflicts, and, in the event of their outbreak, to mitigate their ferocity."[20] As one of the opening speeches further asserted, international opinion could only favor decisions that reasoned that "[i]n order to ensure that wars shall be short and of rare occurrence ... the nations engaged must be made to bear the whole burden thereof." At this time, "the whole civilized world" felt a "sentiment of international amenity" that fostered the idea of limiting war's effects and reducing the chance that a state might be thoroughly destroyed by modern warfare.[21]

Such hopes found expression in the petitions and proposals brought forward by peace societies and other extra-governmental organizations excluded from addressing the conference and partaking in its

---

[19] See Articles 62 and 63 of the Hague Conventions of 1899. It is worth noting that the declaration was binding for only five years in the case of war between signatory parties. For an overview of this and other laws concerning aerial warfare, see Tami Davis Biddle, "Air Power," in *The Laws of War: Constraints on Warfare in the Western World*, ed. Michael Howard, George J. Andreopoulos, and Mark R. Shulman (New Haven, CT, 1994). For a contemporary overview, see Harold Hazeltine, *The Law of the Air* (London, 1911).

[20] "Latest News: The Second Peace Conference," *Times* 15 June 1907.

[21] Speech of President Nelidoff, "The Hague Conference," *Times*, 17 June 1907.

discussions. A notable exception was made to such rules in order to permit delegates of the International Council of Women to offer their support for "universal peace and disarmament." The exception was justified both because this group represented "millions of women all over the world" and because "the Conference wished to reduce as much as possible the suffering which war entailed upon all, and especially upon women."[22] Nonetheless, discussions at the Convention focused very little direct attention on such issues, concerning themselves instead with such questions as whether obligatory arbitration could be used to settle disputes.[23]

In terms of the bombardment of civilians, the agreements approved at The Hague in October 1907 embodied only a few modest changes to the 1899 Convention.[24] For instance, the restriction on throwing objects from a balloon was maintained. However, modifications to Article 25 of the Land Warfare Convention stressed that attack "by whatever means, of towns, villages, dwellings or buildings which are undefended is prohibited."[25] Significantly, the Naval Convention of 1907 differed from its Land Warfare counterpart, and while it prohibited the bombing of "undefended ports, towns, villages, dwellings, or building" by naval forces, it permitted the naval bombardment of "military works, military or naval establishments, depots of arms or war materiel, workshops or plants which *could* be utilized for the needs of the hostile fleet or army, and the ships of war in the harbor."[26] In other words, one aspect of the agreement protected "undefended" locales, but another made anything that even potentially served a military purpose – anything that helped the army or navy – a legitimate target.

---

[22] Quoted in "The Peace Conference," *Times*, 19 June 1907. It is relevant to this discussion that Bertha von Suttner, author of the popular and widely translated novel, *Die Waffen Nieder* (1889), or *Lay Down Your Arms*, won the Nobel Peace Prize in 1905 for her work on disarmament. Part of the appeal of her fiction was her emphasis on the war-induced suffering of wives and mothers.

[23] See the press coverage summarizing the Second Hague Convention in *Times*, October 1907.

[24] "The Second Peace Conference: Its Results and Lessons," *Times*, 21 Oct. 1907.

[25] Amendment of Article 25, Hague Convention 1907, in "The Laws of War," at "The Avalon Project at Yale Law School, www.yale.edu/lawweb/avalon/lawofwar/hague04, and in E. A. Whittuck, *International Documents: A Collection of International Conventions and Declarations of a Law-Making Kind* (London, 1909); see also Biddle, "Air Power," 142.

[26] "Article 1 and Article 2," "Bombardment by Naval Forces in Time of War (Hague IX), 18 October 1907, in "The Laws of War," at "The Avalon Project at Yale Law School, www.yale.edu/lawweb/avalon/lawofwar/hague09, Whittuck, *International Documents*, and also quoted in Biddle, "Air Power," 143. Emphasis mine.

The Foreign Office subsequently clarified the British position on this issue. Sir Edward Grey asserted that as far as naval warfare was concerned:

> His Majesty's Government consider that the objection, on humanitarian grounds, to the bombardment of unfortified towns is too strong to justify a resort to that measure, even though it may be permissible under the abstract doctrine of international law. They wish it, however, to be clearly understood that any general prohibition of such practice must not be held to apply to such operations as the bombardment of towns or places used as bases or storehouses of naval and military equipment and supply, or ports containing fighting ships.[27]

If places that stored "military equipment" or were put to use as "bases" constituted legitimate targets for naval bombardment, the protection of such areas from aerial bombardment would seem moot. Furthermore, these Hague Conventions also stated that "family honor and rights, the lives of individuals and private property ... must be respected," although again with a great deal of leeway over what this might mean.[28] The intent of such measures was to ensure the protection of civilians from both traditional and novel means of waging war. The strong humanitarian objection to attacking "unfortified" venues reflected the views that civilians deserved protection from the horrors of war. Aerial bombardment certainly had the potential to attack directly the lives and property of all non-combatants and to subject groups such as women and children to war's barbarism. However, whether air raids had been classified by the Hague Conventions as a forbidden form of warfare remained open to political interpretation; in the realm of the popular imagination, the question was not if but when aerial attacks against civilians would occur.

WAR IN THE AIR

The Hague Conventions provide a glimpse into how governments imagined states must conduct war against one another, but they were hardly

[27] Edward Grey to Edward Fry, "General Instructions to the Secretary of State," 12 June 1907, in "Appendix: Instructions to British Plenipotentiaries," in Whittuck, *International Documents*, 240.

[28] "Article 46," Section III of the "Convention Respecting the Laws and Customs of War on Land (Hague IV)," 18 Oct. 1907, in "The Laws of War," at "The Avalon Project at Yale Law School, www.yale.edu/lawweb/avalon/lawofwar/hague04 and in Whittuck, *International Documents*. See the discussion in Gullace, "Sexual Violence and Family Honor"; the quote from Article 46 appears in note 74, 733.

the only agents undertaking such imaginative work. Perhaps the most famous evocation of aerial warfare before its full-scale usage was a novel that appeared a year after the Second Hague Convention, H. G. Wells's *The War in the Air* (1908). There were other contemporary examples. French novels by Emile Driant and more popular imperial adventure tales for boys appeared between 1908 and 1914, such as Herbert Strang's *The Air Scout* (1912), which stressed the dangers that might come from ignoring one's enemies' acquisition of air power. In these representations, white Europeans and their descendants inevitably triumph over their non-white, colonial counterparts; it is thus noteworthy that this was not the case in *The War in the Air*.[29] However, Wells's depiction of the indiscriminate destruction of New York City by German airships captured the imagination of readers at the time and has been viewed as prophetic ever since.

The War in the Air's hero is a scrappy Englishman, Bert Smallways, who finds himself accidentally involved in a great German offensive, led by the novel's arch villain, a German crown prince. The novel may have inaccurately predicted the predominance of airships instead of airplanes, but the book's emphasis first on Germans and then on the "Asiatics" as the primary enemies of Britain (and of France and the United States by extension) must have resonated with contemporary audiences.[30] Moreover, the novel reaches a climax when the despotic prince orders the destruction of the civilian population of a great city, in this case New York:

> Something had dropped from the aeroplane.... [B]linding flames squirted out in all directions from the point of impact.... The people running out into the road took preposterous clumsy leaps, then flopped down and lay still, with their torn clothes smouldering into flame.... [B]lack smoke came pouring into the street ... presently shot with red flame....
>
> As the airships sailed along they smashed up the city as a child will shatter its cities of brick and card. Below, they left ruins and blazing conflagrations, and heaped and scattered dead. (135–136)

---

[29] H. G. Wells, *The War in the Air* (Lincoln, NE, 2002 [1908]). See also the discussion of Wells's *The War in the Air* and French novelist Emile Driant's *L'Aviateur du Pacifique* and *Au dessus du continent noir*, among other works, in Robert Wohl, *A Passion for Wings: Aviation and the Western Imagination, 1908–1918* (New Haven, CT, 1994), ch 3; H. Strang, *The Air Scout: A Story of National Defence* (London 1912). Wells's novel receives a brief mention in I. F. Clarke, *Voices Prophesying War*, 2d ed. (Oxford 1992), 88–89. Novels about more conventional invasions of the British Isles also appeared in the decades before 1914, and some of these are discussed in Clarke.

[30] Wells, *The War in the Air*. All references to the 2002 reprint edition are made parenthetically in the text.

Global war ensues, and the novel recounts the full-scale destruction of civilization that follows the use of comprehensive air power.

One of the book's most troubling messages appears toward the end, when Smallways learns that following the destruction of New York, the whole world is at war – Berlin, London, Hamburg, Paris, all burning – "fighting in the air all over Europe – all over the world." Tellingly in Wells's vision, Europeans and their civilization are threatened from Asia and the East. As the book's one sympathetic German explains, the world itself has changed: "No place is safe; no place is at peace. There is no place a woman and her daughter can hide and be at peace. The war comes through the air, bombs drop in the night. Quiet people go out in the morning and see air-fleets passing overhead – dripping death – dripping death!" (159).

As a consequence of such swift, unprecedented, widespread destruction, "there was not a city or town in the world outside China, however far from the actual centres of destruction, where police and government were not adopting special emergency measures to deal with a want of food and a glut of unemployed people" (162). Unlike earlier forms of battle, aerial warfare leads in this account to "social disorganization" – the peculiar plight of "a modern urban population under warlike stresses" (163). It takes the world by surprise that "war became perforce a universal guerilla war, a war inextricably involving civilians and homes and all the apparatus of social life" (165). It is a world that may never experience "peace" again (222–223) and a world where everything associated with modern, European life becomes something imaginary and lost. Wells's novel served as a chilling warning of what the stakes might be like if full-scale war returned to Europe, indicating as it did that the state itself could offer no protection.

Wells's tale inspired mixed reviews. As George Calderson summed up in the *Times Literary Supplement*: "The book is powerful, terrifying, and suggestive; but there is no argument for or against armaments to be deduced from it. It is merely a boisterous piece of fiction.... [W]ith all its qualities of imagination, it cannot be reckoned as a serious piece of artistic work."[31] A review in *Punch* began, "I am tired of stories of the German invasion of England," and thus the reviewer was pleased to find a book in which German aggression is taken out on America. Although the book "does not quite hit the mark," it is "an immensely interesting story."[32] A brief review in the *Bookman* found it entertaining but

[31] "Fiction" [George Calderson], *Times Literary Supplement*, 5 Nov. 1908.
[32] "Our Booking-Office," *Punch*, 6 Jan. 1909.

didactic: "We admit the possibility of airships on a large scale, and full of deadly armaments, making havoc of our civilisation, but we can't swallow the notion of all the powers of the earth engaged in war at the same time, and Mr. Wells does not convince us."[33] Interestingly, a transatlantic perspective found Wells's visions more credible. A prominent American review described it as a "pamphlet against war," conveying the message that "the world is shrinking" and "no nation is so aloof … it is safe from the deadly resources of science."[34] The stage was set for a new cultural understanding of the stakes of modern war.

THE AIR RAIDS THAT FOLLOW

In both diplomatic arrangements and cultural work, the idea of civilians fundamentally remaining a protected group in nations at war was being called into question well before the introduction of air raids into Europe. A number of important implications follow from this changing cultural context that have ramifications for the militarization of domestic life, for the "mixing up" of state and home, and of the roles of men and women. Even as representatives of the International Council of Women brought a message urging peace and disarmament on behalf of *all* women to the Second Hague Convention, their status continued to be that of outsiders on the world stage. It remained uncertain that their potential suffering in future wars could be curtailed by international laws created without their participation.[35] In addition, as the cultural evidence of the prewar era made plain, a new war that left all civilians vulnerable to air power meant that there would no longer be a "place a woman and her daughter can hide and be at peace." If the possible expansive vulnerability of women and children was imagined in 1908, the emergence of attacks on civilian targets after 1914 brought this into greater public recognition.

This book begins by exploring the air raids of 1914–1918, first as lived experiences and then as memory and representation. As its early chapters demonstrate, both in reactions to air raids during the First World War and in the memoirs, fictional accounts, and political arrangements that followed, the sense that the home and its inhabitants were no longer safe

---

[33] "The War in the Air," *Bookman*, December 1908.
[34] "Mr. Wells in His Earlier Manner," *New York Times*, 14 Nov. 1908.
[35] See Olive Schreiner, "Women and War," in *Woman and Labour* (London, 1911), for a potent prewar evocation of feminist pacifism based on the suffering of women over the loss of their loved ones during war and their exclusion from any say in the governments that could declare and wage war on their behalf.

and had thus become actively engaged in the state's survival of warfare entered into British culture and society in highly significant and highly gendered ways. As the middle section of the book reveals, both interwar disarmament campaigners and those actively engaged in planning for the next war used a shared notion of the potential, new vulnerability of the entire civil population either to argue for curtailing new forms of war, especially after aerial bombs began to fall on European soil in the Spanish Civil War, or for preparing to face these threats. The final part of the book traces these developments as the imagined next war became reality, and as air raids once again threatened and devastated British homes and lives.

Chapters 2 and 3 take us through the raids of the First World War. Combining firsthand accounts from diaries and letters with the discussion of aerial warfare in the media and in the halls of government, they uncover a variety of responses to the new civilian experience of being under fire from the sky. By examining the responses of both men and women, civilians and combatants, unofficial and state-sanctioned voices, these chapters reveal how much the idea of "women and children" being under attack fueled resentment that had to be carefully managed to make sure that it was aimed against the barbarous enemy rather than against a state that could no longer protect its own civilian population. These case studies also trace the evolving official response, particularly in Chapter 3, as the government debated how to protect newly vulnerable inhabitants. Both chapters trace the state's growing realization that what it termed alternatively morale, character, and psychology had as much to do with defeating the enemy – given the new conditions posed by modern weaponry – as did more practical measures designed to counter the air raid, including retaliation and reprisals. This realization helped create a model of wartime civil identity, one that emphasized a universal stoicism potentially available across class and gender lines.

The core of the book then carefully examines the legacy of the Great War's raids throughout the interwar period. It focuses especially on interactions between the state (which at least until the mid-1930s engaged largely with the prospect of aerial warfare by developing what would become Air Raids Precautions as a mode of civil defense), and various agents of civil society (the news media, political groups especially feminists and pacifists, theorists, commentators, and writers of all sorts). Before the state could prepare for another war, it had first to determine the contours that such a war would entail. The emergence of civil defense planning relied on a greatly expanded notion of state power as well as on a developing consensus about the *voluntary* nature of wartime participation by civilians. In order to win the next war, one that would surely be waged against women and children, against schools and homes as well as factories and battle zones, the state would have to make use of civilians as never before.

Some of the reactions to air raids – based on direct witnessing or indirect knowledge from other sources of their destructive power against non-military targets – painted them in the worst possible light. The very existence of aerial warfare, for many in the interwar period, served as a formidable warning that the postwar world must curtail these new forms of warfare or risk annihilation. Visceral evidence of this appears in the memoirs, autobiographies, and fictional accounts of aerial warfare as well as in the rhetoric of various peace campaigns that focused explicitly on the need to abolish aerial and chemical weaponry. At the same time, state agents also engaged extensively in imagining not only destruction but also survival in order to prepare civilians for what was to come. The end result was a cultural awareness that civilians mattered as never before in sustaining war. Thus, state programs worked hard to engage in a process of making the prospect of attacks on homes normal and part of everyday life – in other words, in domesticating the air raid itself.

During this time, responses to aerial warfare were based on the memory of what had occurred and fearful speculation as to what might come. Chapter 4 thus delves into the portrayal of air raids, first in interwar memoirs, then in interwar culture, especially fictional works that imagined the war of the future. Chapter 5 then analyzes the imaginative work of the state by looking at the initial secret debates and plans of the Committee of Imperial Defence's Sub-Committee on Air Raid Precautions. Those meeting in secret to consider the civilian population and the war to come drew on the lessons learned from the damage sustained during the First World War. These government planners debated the measures to be undertaken to prepare an entire society for the threat of aerial warfare, a threat that included the possibility of chemical attacks via air power. Chapter 5 also pays close attention to how new and sometimes gendered assumptions about the significance of morale played a role in preparations to protect and effectively mobilize nearly every non-combatant.

While preparations for dealing with future air raids proceeded, some British politicians along with activists outside the government began to work for disarmament. Many pacifist and feminist groups, often working together, called for the banning of aerial warfare precisely because it was a menace to women and children. Chapter 6 investigates the rationale behind campaigns that eventually coalesced around the League of Nations Conference on Disarmament in Geneva in 1932–1934; the rhetoric and strategy of feminist pacifists, such as the analysis put forth by Helena Swanwick; and the ultimate failure of proposals that tried to internationalize air power or ban the military use of aircraft altogether. In order to explore more fully what animated these campaigners, Chapter 7 examines reactions to the use of air power in overseas conflicts, including unrest in the British Empire, Italy's campaigns in Ethiopia, and Japan's attacks in Asia. It then focuses on the widespread, readily accessible depictions of the return of air raids to Europe after the outbreak of the Spanish Civil War, and finishes with an analysis of Virginia Woolf's 1938 *Three Guineas*, an anti-patriarchal and anti-fascist treatise that begins with a meditation on photographs from the war in Spain, as a culminating articulation of anti–aerial warfare efforts.

Following these discussions of campaigns against air power, Chapters 8 and 9 investigate how various constituencies, including individuals and state agents, intensified their planning for the "next war" in the middle to late 1930s. The various international crises of the 1930s made clear that the much-anticipated dangers of a future war were close at hand, and the first of these chapters uncovers the development of government efforts to offer concrete measures to protect all civilians, even those women and children who could make no useful contribution to the war effort. Additionally, it looks at how all civil defense planning – conducted largely in secret – became increasingly public with the passage of Air Raids Precautions (ARP) legislation in 1937 and the issuing of instruction manuals and even training and propaganda films by the decade's end. Chapter 9 then provides a case study of one of the most obvious emblems of the changing nature of warfare: the baby gas mask, a protective device that acknowledged how truly horrific and indiscriminate the next war might become.

With total war again on the horizon, efforts to ensure civilians' participation and awareness of their role in national defense intensified. Chapters 10 and 11 thus analyze civilian responses to ARP and the potential, and then actual, return of air raids. Chapter 10 starts with the Czechoslovakian Crisis of September 1938 and the first test of ARP in action through the declaration of war in September 1939, to the so-called Phony War of late 1939 and early 1940, and finally to the Blitz itself. In an encapsulated form, this chapter explores some of the limits of the state as it sought both to protect and to mobilize its civilian population, while looking at the intense private and public reactions of men and women to war and the prospect of war that once again made every British home a potential target. The book then concludes in Chapter 11, with a kind of coda that offers an analysis of the cultural climate in which world war and air war returned to Britain. It suggests that popular culture, both literary and cinematic, helped to market to an expanded audience the basic ingredients – both material and moral – required to face the air raid. The aim of these final chapters is to show how the political developments and cultural work of a variety of actors from the arrival of aerial warfare in 1914 made the unthinkable acceptable.

The widespread recognition that the home front and war zone were now one and the same inspired the invention of civil defense as well as a new kind of civil identity, one both transcendent and hopefully universal. What follows here is not, by any means, a complete account of aerial attacks on Britain during the world wars, nor is it a straightforward chronology of the evolution of civil defense measures. It offers a preliminary attempt to make sense of these crucial developments but remains, I hope, the first of several interventions, for among other things, there are important regional and transnational dimensions to these transformations that this book only intermittently addresses.[36] Scotland, and especially Northern Ireland, unfortunately proved beyond the bounds of this study, as did a truly in-depth look at the effects of these developments on local communities. Nor is there sufficient space here to examine fully the compelling imperial aspects of the rise of the civil defense state, especially in terms of interwar planning and implementation during the Second World War. What this book offers is a layered narrative that explores how the air raid redefined the civilian experience and expectations of warfare itself and that addresses some of the critical cultural and political implications of this fundamental change.

The advent of the air raid decisively altered the boundaries of modern warfare, and between 1914 and 1945, Britain was clearly one of the most important sites of this development. The First World War ushered in an era when no place could claim immunity from war and when civilians could be "terrorized" from the air; the Second World War made attacks

---

[36] I address some of the effects and implications of aerial warfare during the First World War for France in "'The Souls of Soldiers': Civilians Under Fire in First World War France," *Journal of Modern History* 78:3 (2006), 588–622, and some of the theoretical issues in "Across Battle Fronts: Gender and the Comparative Cultural History of Modern European War," in *Comparison and History: Europe in Cross National Perspective*, ed. Deborah Cohen and Maura O'Connor (New York, 2004), 71–84. I hope that some of the issues raised here and in what follows will lead to more research into these crucial aspects.

on homes and civilians ever more tangibly felt. The Cold War era, with the nuclear threat of mutually assured destruction, and the post–Cold War world of wars of ethnic cleansing and terrorism, have demonstrated how lasting such changes have been. What follows returns us to the origins of this modern transformation. By recovering the history of the air raid from its place in accounts of military strategy, we may be better able to understand its influence on the twentieth-century world and, perhaps, beyond.

2

Destroying the Innocent

The Arrival of the Air Raid, 1914–1916

INTRODUCTION

On 22 October 1917, British soldier Jack Mudd sent a letter to his wife days before he would be reported missing in action. The letter reveals his fears not for his own safety but for that of his family at home in England: "I guess you have been worried with the air raids you know dear its hard to be out here fighting & yet your wife & children cant be safe still dearest dont worry you have a 20,000 to 1 chance & God will watch over you as he has been with me ever since I have been out here."[1] The odds against Lizzie Mudd being killed in an aerial attack were greater than her husband calculated, and in the end, her survival of this new form of warfare and his death on a more traditional battleground mirror the statistics for civilian and military casualties during the war. The consequences of the raids of the First World War have been almost completely overshadowed by the enormous combatant death tolls of this war and the damage done by the air raids of the Second World War. Certainly, one gets this impression from most histories of the two world wars.[2] However, Jack Mudd's letter suggests the need to consider the profound changes in the

[1] Imperial War Museum (IWM), Department of Documents, Papers of J W Mudd (82/3/1), Jack Mudd to Lizzie Mudd, Letter, 22 Oct. 1917. In all citations from documents in this chapter and elsewhere unless other noted, spelling and grammar have been unaltered from the original in order to preserve the integrity of tone and language.

[2] For one recent attempt that pays some attention to the First World War's raids, see Tammy M. Proctor, *Civilians in a World at War, 1914–1918* (New York, 2010). Still, the focus of studies of air power remains the post–World War One era; see, e.g., Yuki Tanaka and Marilyn B. Young (eds.), *Bombing Civilians: A Twentieth-Century History* (New York, 2009), which discusses the First World War's air raids only in a few pages.

common understanding of warfare's consequences for civilians that followed the invention of the air raid.

As this chapter and the next demonstrate, Mudd was not alone in feeling disturbed by this important alteration in the previously assumed "natural" order of things – that men would face danger and risk their lives precisely in order to protect women and children from the horrors of war. Such a change in the status of civilians, and the gradual recognition by the state of the need to incorporate them into a new form of defense against war making that made the home its target, eventually led to the invention of civil defense. First, however, came the realization that air war had finally arrived.

If aerial warfare, as we have seen, had been anticipated since the development of aeronautics, its actual deployment was both worse and oddly less traumatic than predicted in the decade before 1914.[3] Nonetheless, the air raids of the First World War literally hit home. The British government recorded official statistics at the war's end and, significantly, broke casualties down by gender (men and women are listed separately), age (children had their own category), and status, with deaths of soldiers and sailors (a much smaller group) listed separately from those of civilians. Thus the air raids of the First World War in Britain killed 1,239 civilians (of whom 366 were women, 252 children) and injured 2,886 (1,016 women, 542 children), with material damage totaling £3,087,098.[4]

---

[3] Some attempts to curtail the potential use of aerial bombardment against non-military targets had been made in the Hague Conventions of 1899 and 1907, as discussed earlier. For an overview of these measures and other laws concerning air warfare, see Tami Davis Biddle, "Air Power," in *The Laws of War: Constraints on Warfare in the Western World*, ed. Michael Howard, George J. Andreopoulos, and Mark R. Shulman (New Haven, CT, 1994). See also her *Rhetoric and Reality in Air Warfare: The Evolution of British and American Ideas about Strategic Bombing, 1914–1945* (Princeton, NJ, 2002), ch. 1, for more on prewar attitudes to aerial bombardment.

[4] See the Official Return of Casualties printed as "Air and Sea Raids on Great Britain," *Times*, 13 Jan. 1919, and "Record of Bombardments," vols. 1 and 2, TNA HO 45/10783. For a record that compares civilian and military casualties, see *The Times Diary & Index of the War*, apps. I and X. Compared with the 851,117 military dead and 2,067,442 wounded, there were a total of 1,508 civilians killed by air or naval bombardments and 3,490 wounded (the vast majority from aerial attacks). An overall discussion of the air raids of the First World War can be found in Lee Kennett, *The First Air War, 1914–1918* (New York, 1991); John H. Morrow, Jr., *The Great War in the Air: Military Aviation from 1909–1921* (Washington, DC, 1993); Dominick Pisano et al, *Legend, Memory and the Great War in the Air* (Seattle, 1992); and Robert Wohl, *A Passion for Wings: Aviation and the Western Imagination, 1908–1918* (New Haven, CT, 1994). A discussion of the raids of 1917–1918 can be found in Raymond H. Fredette, *The Sky on Fire: The First Battle of Britain, 1917–1918* (1966, rpt. Washington, DC, 1991), and Andrew Hyde, *The First Blitz: The German Bomber Campaign Against Britain in the First World War* (Barnsley, 2002).

It was relatively simple to calculate the losses in the war's aftermath, but despite prewar predictions of the possibility that aircraft could bring war to the British Isles, much of the government response was improvised and often criticized by the civilian population as deeply inadequate.

This chapter and the next investigate the reactions to zeppelin and airplane raids in wartime Britain by examining responses in the news media, government pronouncements and actions, and popular culture, as well as firsthand accounts of aerial warfare in letters and diaries. One compelling aspect of these accounts is that they reveal how those in the traditional battle zones reacted to the news of their families under fire at home. This chapter covers the years from 1914 to 1916, exploring responses to the initial arrival of the air raid. It compares the use of "innocent" victims of raids in government-sponsored atrocity propaganda with the other ways in which public media reacted to attacks that killed or injured women and children. While showing how air raids came to Britain, it also investigates the creation and early maintenance of a consensual and non-gender-specific kind of civil behavior represented mainly as stoicism. The next Chapter delineates both this development and the expansion of the state as it began to accept that it had a direct role to play in preparing civilians fully for modern war. Such transformations accelerated during the last years of the war, which witnessed more devastating raids on England, especially during the summer of 1917. As aerial warfare continued, public commentary came to identify which true Britons (e.g., not immigrants) could display this new form of civil heroism, and the state more directly responded to the threat of, and damage caused by, air raids. By the end of the war, a multiplicity of voices had begun to suggest that air raids had created an equivalency between soldiers and civilians, and between home front and front line.

THE WAR COMES HOME

The technological changes accompanying the First World War – particularly the use of zeppelins and airplanes to bomb civilian areas – helped challenge the idea that the home front and war front were naturally separated and thus that only men could claim an authentic experience of battle, of warfare. From the start, such novel methods seemed to undermine the consensus over what was a legitimate war target and what constituted the acceptable realm of war. They materially closed the divide between the fronts. This occurred first outside of Britain when its ally France was attacked from the air in August 1914, an event that made many prewar fears newly real and that led to public condemnation of this bombing raid on Paris as violating the Hague Conventions and being an act "against humanity."[5] When Paris was bombed again in September, media coverage emphasized that while the raid was intended for the Eiffel Tower, "an old man ... was killed on the spot, while his little granddaughter had one leg terribly injured," and that Parisians "have exhibited no fear."[6] This emphasis on the lack of fear and the injury of civilians deemed the most vulnerable because of age and/or gender presaged responses to the advent of raids in Britain.[7]

The war's first attacks on Britain's homeland came from the sea. The population was shaken by naval incursions on the coast in mid-December 1914 when German cruisers shelled British coastal towns, particularly Scarborough and Hartlepool. Media responses to this naval bombardment were extensive, and the headlines made clear how the *Times*'s readers were meant to respond: "The German Aim: Attempts to Create Panic in England." While calling attention to the lack of a "redeeming feature" in hurling shells at peaceful watering places, the accounts acknowledged that the attacks indicated that "war is getting nearer to us."[8] Another article reported "unhappily" that fifty people were killed, listing them as "soldiers, and civilians, men, women and children."[9] Headlines focused on "Scarborough's Ordeal" and also noted that it would be "good for recruiting."[10] Media coverage consistently emphasized that "the enemy achieved no useful purpose by their visit of destruction."[11]

Hartlepool and Scarborough became watchwords for German aggression and provided the first wave of what became iconic images of attacks on civil spaces: bombed-out homes and female and youthful casualties.

---

[5] See "Bombs Dropped In Paris," *Times*, 31 Aug. 1914, and coverage of what was described as a pathetic exodus from the city, "Exodus from Paris," *Times*, 3 Sept. 1914. The quote is taken from "The Paris Bombs," *Times*, 4 Sept. 1914. For a fuller discussion of these raids and other attacks on France, see Susan R. Grayzel, " 'The Soul of Soldiers': Civilians Under Fire in First World War France," *Journal of Modern History* 78:3 (2006), 588–622. Attacks on Paris would receive ample British media attention throughout the war.

[6] "More Bombs Dropped on Paris," *Times*, 28 Sept. 1914.

[7] Little attention was paid to Allied raids on German targets. For an account of such raids – which also began in September 1914 – see Christian Geinitz, "The First Air War Against Noncombatants: Strategic Bombing of German Cities in World War I," in *Great War, Total War: Combat and Mobilization on the Western Front 1914–1918*, ed. Roger Chickering and Stig Förster (Cambridge, 2000), 207–225.

[8] "The German Aim," *Times*, 17 Dec. 1914.

[9] "Hartlepool under Fire," *Times*, 17 Dec. 1914.

[10] "Scarborough's Ordeal" and "War and Temper: Good for Recruiting," *Times*, 17 Dec. 1914.

[11] "The Attack on Whitby," *Times*, 17 Dec. 1914.

These quickly found their way into military recruiting posters.[12] The bombing of non-military targets and attacks on British residential areas, especially on "women and children," provoked shock at the outset. In an editorial immediately following the Scarborough and Hartlepool bombings, the *Times* began: "For the first time for many centuries the coast of England has been directly and seriously attacked.... The loss of life among the civil population was considerable, and the wounded numerous.... The raid of yesterday resulted in the loss of some innocent lives, and the destruction of some amount of property. It had one greater result.... It has indelibly impressed upon the British nation a consciousness of the manner in which Germany wages war." Such views, by insisting on the lack of "surprise" and the naval attacks as renewals of older forms of warfare, implied the ability of civilians to counter such assaults. The editorial defended the government against critics who blamed it for not preventing these raids; the role of the navy, it pointed out, was to engage and destroy enemy ships, not to stand guard to repel attacks or invasion. The "duty" of repelling "rests upon the manhood of the nation." What could be criticized was the failure to "have explained collectively to the civil population what they ought to do in certain emergencies."[13] This would be a crucial point when aerial attacks commenced.

Shortly after the naval raids, Britain faced the arrival of attacks from the air. Public accounts of such incursions coincided with continual updates on the fate of the victims in Scarborough and Hartlepool. For instance, a small notice in the *Times* on 24 December recorded that Stanley Stewart, aged six, had died from injuries received at Hartlepool, bringing the death toll to 101.[14] A few days later, the *Times* informed its readers that "the threatened German air raid has to some extent become an accomplished fact," noting that a German plane dropped a bomb "in the garden of a local residence" near Dover on Christmas Eve and returned to the skies on Christmas Day, 1914.[15] While this early foray caused no damage, it did prompt the commissioner of police to offer a public notice that "the civil population are warned to keep under cover, preferably in basements, upon hearing the sound of firing by guns or of explosion," and there was also public notification that the police were preparing

---

[12] See "Men of Britain Will You Stand This?" In IWM, Department of Art, PST 5119.
[13] "The Raided Coast Towns," *Times*, 17 Dec. 1914.
[14] "More Hartlepool Casualties," *Times*, 24 Dec. 1914.
[15] "Aeroplanes at Dover and over the Thames," *Times*, 26 Dec. 1914.

for the possibility of attacks on London.[16] Less publicly, the commissioner instructed the London County Council Education Authorities and the Board of Education as well as the general manager of the London Underground as to the appropriate measures that should be taken both in case of a warning and in the event of an actual aerial attack.[17]

THE WAR IN THE AIR ARRIVES

When zeppelin raids began in January 1915, details of the human suffering produced by the attacks accompanied official reports describing the hostile actions. Thus media coverage emphasized, for example, that a boy had been "killed as he lay in bed," while his mother, father, and a baby sibling were "seriously injured."[18] From the start, such accounts also noted that despite official admonitions to the contrary, in places like Yarmouth (one site attacked on the night of 19 January) "the majority of people seem to have left their houses at once and gone into the streets to see what was the matter."[19] While critical of this reaction, news coverage of the assault on King's Lynn explained that "the populace showed the most complete composure in this trying ordeal."[20] Later accounts of the raids listed the dead but also explicitly called attention to their attackers' violation of appropriate military conduct, describing them as causing "damage to *open* towns."[21]

The reaction to the more widespread introduction of air raids associated the attacks with "barbarism" and described them as brutal assaults on civilization and innocent life. As the *Times*'s editorial reflecting on these early raids concluded:

> As for the gross violation of international law implied by dropping bombs upon undefended towns and villages, that is now an old story. The German Government and the German people alike have made it clear ... to the whole world that they are ready to commit any outrage and do not propose to obey any of the laws of GOD or man. They practise ruthless and inhuman destruction of the weak and helpless.... [W]e

---

[16] See "Notice to the Public," signed by E. R. Henry, 28 Dec. 1914, in TNA HO 45/11192. For the public dispersal of this information, see "Police and Air Raids," *Times*, 19 Jan. 1915.

[17] Memorandum Regarding Aircraft Attack on London, 14 Jan. 1915, in TNA HO 45/11192.

[18] "Seven Bombs on King's Lynn: Boy Killed in Bed," *Times*, 20 Jan. 1915.

[19] "A Zeppelin Raid," *Times*, 20 Jan. 1915.

[20] "Seven Bombs on King's Lynn."

[21] "The Zeppelin Raid," *Times*, 21 Jan. 1915. Emphasis added.

are confronted with a recrudescence of brutality such as the world has not witnessed for a thousand years.... [The airships] will come again to destroy on a larger scale, and it is well we should know it. [But] when we strike home against Germany we will not soil our hands with these shameful crimes. We will fight honourably, in the assurance ... that the earth will be purged of these relapses into barbarism.[22]

While the "honourable" conduct of war would seem to preclude retaliation in kind, further proof of German "barbarity" was implied by reports that news of the zeppelin raid "caused the wildest delight and satisfaction throughout Germany."[23]

A letter to the editor of the *Times* concurred that the most recent raids were indefensible violations of international law. "No ingenuity can suggest that the raid had any military purpose whatever," it stated, but "the sole intention was to inflict injury on non-combatants in order to create a panic.... The claim that belligerents are entitled to take action against non-combatants for such a purpose is of the gravest importance." The letter writer emphasized the larger, more chilling implications of aerial warfare, "for if it is to be permitted to attack a civilian population in order to frighten the Government of the country in which they live, then there would seem to be no limits to the devastation and destruction of life which may be inflicted."[24] The letter concluded by urging neutral states to call Germany to task for this outrage. Toward that end, the *Times* let its British audience know of American "indignation" and condemnation of German "savagery."[25]

Civilians and government officials across southern England struggled to comprehend the meaning of the raids. An inquest held to account for the deaths of four individuals in these early coastal raids returned a verdict of death "by an act of the King's enemies." This was despite the sentiment of some members of the coroner's jury that in the cases of Percy Goate, aged fourteen, and Mrs. Gazeley, a recent war widow of twenty-six, the verdict should have been "murder."[26]

---

[22] "The Air Raid in Norfolk," *Times*, 21 Jan. 1915.

[23] "The Zeppelin Raid." The notion of this war as one of savagery has been examined by several recent studies, notably Stéphane Audoin-Rouzeau and Annette Becker, *1914–1918: Understanding the Great War*, trans. Catherine Temerson (New York, 2002), and Alan Kramer, *Dynamic of Destruction: Culture and Killing in the First World War* (Oxford, 2007).

[24] H. Erle Richards, Letter to the editor, *Times*, 21 Jan. 1915.

[25] See "American Indignation," *Times*, 21 Jan. 1915, and "Pure Savagery," *Times*, 21 Jan. 1915.

[26] "The Air Raid: Evidence at the Inquests," *Times*, 22 Jan. 1915.

Zeppelin raids ceased for some months after the attacks of 19 January and then commenced again along the coastal areas, particularly in the east, in April. These early experiences of attacks could prompt some to assert their fortitude. Red Cross worker Georgie Fyfe wrote to her mother in February that "I am afraid you are anxious about me when you read of Bombs and Bombardments in the newspapers, but you mustn't be. We all have to take our chance at this work and we take no unnecessary risks, so I hope we shall all 'win through.' "[27] Responding to later raids in April in his diary, Frank Lockwood attested that they did relatively little harm: "Zeppelin made a futile raid on the English Coast to-night. Newcastle & district was visited. Result, 2 persons slightly wounded. Fancy coming 350 miles to do such trifling damage."[28]

At the end of May 1915, outlying areas of London experienced their first raids, during which six people were killed.[29] Among these, the death that received the most attention was that of Elsie Lilian Leggett, aged three, who died from suffocation and burns; her sister Elizabeth, aged eleven, would die from injuries inflicted in the same attack about a week afterward.[30] An article covering the inquest for Elsie Leggett began by noting that "a bomb crashed right through the children's bed" and that "the father is now in hospital suffering from shocking burns sustained in rescuing his four other children." At the inquest, Elsie's mother testified about the heroic actions of Mr. Leggett, who had tried to save all five children:

> 'My husband got four of the children out,' added the witness, with emotion, 'but the other was left. He thought he had got them all out. They were all very badly burned,' she said tearfully. 'I went straight from my bedroom into the street and screamed for help, and as I went I saw flames in the back bedroom.'

[27] IWM, Department of Documents, Papers of G S Fyfe (86/64/1), Georgina Fyfe, Letter to mother, 10 Feb. 1915. Fyfe says in the next line that "as I never say anything that has not already been mentioned in the papers, I do not understand why my letters have not reached you" – this provides a sense of the raids as public knowledge.

[28] IWM, Department of Documents, Papers of F T Lockwood (96/52/1), Frank Taylor Lockwood, Diary, 14 Apr. 1915. A few days later, he offered this condemnation of German methods of warfare in general: "The Germans are indeed a barbaric & brutal enemy. They care nothing about the laws of warfare. All they care for is to win, whether the means be fair or foul & they seem to prefer the latter. The latest rule they have broken is the use of appliances & shells that give of asphyxiating gases." See Lockwood, Diary, 19 Apr. 1915.

[29] For the official report, see "The Air Raids," *Daily Chronicle*, 7 June 1915.

[30] "Death of a Child," *Times*, 2 June 1915, and "Death of Another Child Victim," *Times*, 10 June 1915.

Mrs. Leggett repeated that due to the excitement, her husband thought he had rescued all the children. As the headline reminded the public, this killing of small children in their beds epitomized the "tragedy of the Zeppelins" and its horror.[31]

In his summing up at the inquest of a married couple, both of whom died in the same attack, the coroner denounced the "entirely new and barbarous practice" of using armed airships "as weapons of aggression against defenceless civilians in their beds in the undefended suburbs of our cities, seaside and health resorts, and country villages." Yet, he added, "however resentful we may feel at the manner and methods authorised by the German army, we cannot properly and legally put into the verdict any matter that is not capable of being proved by the evidence before you." The jury concluded that Henry Thomas Good and Caroline Good "died from suffocation and bombs, having been murdered by some agent of a hostile force."[32] Other newspapers emphasized the "innocence" of these victims by calling attention to the position of their bodies: "man and wife found dead kneeling at bedside."[33]

Newspapers such as the liberal *Daily Chronicle* highlighted the tragic deaths of two other innocent victims under the heading "Children Killed by Zeppelins ... Tragic End to Visits to a Picture Palace." It reprinted the "pathetic stories" that emerged during the inquests held for Samuel Reuben, aged eight, and Lily Lehrman, aged sixteen, both of whose parents went out searching for them on the night of the raid, only to find them in hospitals. The victims had gone out to seek the simple diversion of a "picture palace" and had instead suffered "terrible injuries" from flying metal when the bomb fell, according to the coroner. He added that while the jury could not return a verdict of murder, "[t]here is no doubt from a moral point of view that it is murder, and murder of a most despicable character.... There is no law for it except to get more recruits who can oppose from which this contemptible means of warfare arises." Even retaliation in kind would not stop this, for "[t]hey would still be dropping bombs all over the country and be destroying life."[34]

---

[31] "Tragedy of the Zeppelins," *Daily Chronicle*, 3 June 1915.

[32] "The Zeppelin Raid on London," *Manchester Guardian*, 3 June 1915. The coverage in other papers was more sensational; the *Daily Chronicle* described the couple as having been killed "while in an attitude of prayer." See "Tragedy of the Zeppelins," *Daily Chronicle*, 3 June 1915.

[33] "Inquest Stories of the Air Raid," *Pall Mall Gazette*, 2 June 1915.

[34] "Children Killed by Zeppelins," *Daily Chronicle*, 4 June 1915. More sober coverage can be found in "Young Victims of the Air Raid," *Times*, 4 June 1915, and "Child Victims of the Air Raid," *Pall Mall Gazette*, 3 June 1915.

It is clear from the press coverage of the inquests held for those killed by this zeppelin raid that many felt them to be victims not merely of war but of something entirely illegal, of "murder." The manner in which they were killed was itself "immoral" and "illegitimate." Several editorials were quick to stress this point. The *Times* explained that the "lesson of the Zeppelins" was "a very old one ... the Germans mean to prosecute the war with every resource at their disposal, legitimate and illegitimate." It made clear that it considered the zeppelin raids the latter.[35] The right-wing *Pall Mall Gazette* weighed in by asserting "that is the worst of frightfulness: it can never be frightful enough to accomplish its purpose," adding that the killing of babies would only bring "larger armies against you and more resolute."[36]

Other news outlets similarly condemned the morality of an enemy who would use this method of waging war. The *Manchester Guardian*, a leading liberal voice, proclaimed that the raid on London marked "one further stage in the moral isolation of Germany. Military value, in the proper sense of that term, it had none.... No soldier was killed or wounded, but an infant, a boy, a man, one woman, and it may be another, have lost their lives. This is not war as it had been understood by civilised nations. It is simply an attempt to produce an impression by terror." The *Guardian* made direct reference to the provisions in the Hague Convention of 1907 prohibiting the attack "by any means whatsoever" against "undefended towns," but added that it was "characteristic of the German method ... that having attacked unfortified places and so compelled defences to be erected, they make of these defences an excuse for their proceedings." It further made an explicit connection between atrocities committed by Germany elsewhere and in Britain:

> [B]y a succession of acts of violence beginning in Belgium in the first days of the war Germany has abrogated the distinction between combatant and non-combatant on which all civilised warfare has depended for its relatively humane conduct. Perhaps we should rather say that instead of abrogating it she has turned it to the disadvantage of the civilian. For the armed soldier at least had belligerent rights.... But the civilian is liable to attack and is held guilty if he defends himself....
>
> In all this and in her other outrages on the laws of war Germany reaps more or less temporary advantage. What she does not appear to recognise is that, step by step, she is consolidating the world against her.[37]

[35] "The Lesson of the Zeppelins," *Times*, 2 June 1915.
[36] Editorial, *Pall Mall Gazette*, 6 June 1915.
[37] "Moral Isolation," *Manchester Guardian*, 2 June 1915.

Thus was Germany held responsible for destroying the ethos by which "civilised" nations conducted war and shockingly placing civilians in an even *worse* position than combatants.

A perspective from a more left wing political persuasion was far less comfortable letting Britain off the hook. In the aftermath of the raid, the *Daily Herald* equated the "evil duty" carried out by the zeppelins over London with that of other aircraft over "Germany, France, and Italy." It proclaimed that "splendid isolation exists no more, and if ... [we continue] on meeting fell science with science more dire then the planet promises to be a mundane and visible hell." The "natural moral" instead was to demand "reason and peace" in place of the "wild competition of destruction." Instead of "hurl[ing] forth charges as to those who began the destruction or those who are the most destructive," it was important to recognize that all powers were equally to blame for maintaining themselves on "a basis of force and might ... on their capacity for destruction."[38]

And the raid had still other deadly effects. The *Times* reported that an inquest held to determine the cause of death of "prematurely born twins of a Jewess" found it to be the woman's having "become extremely apprehensive and scared over the Zeppelin raid." This had caused her to give birth prematurely and led to her infants' deaths. The jury accepted this explanation.[39] Thus, while the official death toll was listed as one man, one woman, and four children, it included neither the deaths of these twins nor two other deaths attributed to "shock" caused by the raid.[40]

In addition to condemnation of the Germans, this early raid on London provoked public responses that celebrated British forbearance. The *Pall Mall Gazette* was happy to reprint a letter written to Count Zeppelin by thirteen-year-old Dorothy Perkins, a student at a school for the "physically defective." This "little crippled girl" informed the count that

> England is not Zeppelin-proof – you know that – but England's people are. I do not mean that the bombs from your airships can do no harm, but I mean you create no fear in their hearts when you send your aircraft over here. You do not make them cower under the bedclothes (for, of course, you send them by night), neither do they hide in cellars,

[38] "Zeppelins and a Moral," *Daily Herald*, 5 June 1915.
[39] See "Young Victims of the Air Raid," *Times*, 4 June 1915.
[40] For the two related deaths, see "After the Zeppelin Raid: How an Old Man and Woman Died," *Pall Mall Gazette*, 4 June 1915.

but their first impulse is to run to the streets to 'have a look.' I thought I would let you know it is no good to send them, to save some of your men a perilous midnight journey.[41]

Perkins signed herself a "British Subject," and the reprinting of her letter seemed destined to show its readers the steadfast quality with which all British civilians – even those young, female, and disabled – could face these raids.

The first substantive air raid on London also unleashed anti-German attacks. As the *Pall Mall Gazette* reported, "[P]robably as a consequence of the air raid acute anti-German feeling broke out again to-day in London." It described angry mobs surrounding shops suspected of being owned by Germans in Shoreditch.[42] Nor were such sentiments restricted to the "mob." A letter to the editor of the *Pall Mall Gazette* following the 31 May attacks of 1915 declared that "if one thing is proved beyond a doubt by the recent attack on London, it is – the vital urgency of wholesale German internments at once." It was clear to the writer that Germans in England had helped to signal the zeppelins.[43] Other public voices warned of the danger of retaliating locally against Germans. An editorial in the *Manchester Guardian* cautioned that the only thing that could prevent universal condemnation of Germany would be the spectacle of "attacks on the helpless people of German birth of technically German nationality who live amongst us … who in many cases came to live among us as a free people among whom they might escape the odious burden of German militarism." It condemned such "misdirected … vengeance" as "unpatriotic" and urged that the "true answer to every act of frightfulness is to increase our efforts to meet the enemy in the field and show ourselves unmoved in our homes."[44]

---

[41] "Schoolgirl on Zeppelins," *Pall Mall Gazette*, 12 June 1915.

[42] "Anti-German Outbreak," *Pall Mall Gazette*, 1 June 1915. A month earlier, in May 1915, anti-German riots also occurred with the news of the sinking of the *Lusitania*. For more on this and other anti-German outbreaks during the war, see Adrian Gregory, *The Last Great War* (Cambridge, 2008); Nicoletta F. Gullace, "Friends, Aliens, and Enemies: Fictive Communities and the Lusitania Riots of 1915," *Journal of Social History* (2005), 345–67; and Panikos Panayi, *The Enemy in Our Midst: Germans in Britain during the First World War* (Oxford, 1991). For a more contemporary account of other anti-German actions, see E. Sylvia Pankhurst, *The Home Front: A Mirror to Life in England during the First World War* (London, 1932; rpt. 1987).

[43] "Zeppelin Murders," Letter signed "Royal Naval Air Service" to the editor, *Pall Mall Gazette*, 5 June 1915.

[44] "Moral Isolation," *Manchester Guardian*, 2 June 1915. This still distinguishes between the fighting front (fields) and the home, despite the damage sustained on both.

Personal accounts of the raids that struck the coast reveal some of the tensions between the new kind of fear and the exhortation to stay "unmoved in our homes." Living in Grimsby, Jeanne Berman described her experience of a raid in her diary in June 1915 with a hint of disbelief:

> We lay awake listening to the noise of the engines, but we were at first incredulous as to its being a Zeppelin, so were disinclined to move. At last we heard the shooting, so all doubt was removed.... We got up & roused the children. We all dressed. We felt faint.... I felt my teeth chattering a little, but soon became calm. Mother came in and took the few shillings out of the drawer & the silver. We peeped out of the window & saw a red glow in the sky, & guessed that buildings were burning somewhere. I dressed very calmly & without hurry, can't think how I did it. All the time we could hear the engines throbbing, the noise of the bombs, & the shooting. We came down afterwards all was still. We went out & heard that the Zeppelins had gone & that some buildings on the docks had been set on fire.... It was a most lovely night, the sky clear, lit with stars & the air scented.... Who would imagine that amongst so much beauty & peace there had been death & destruction.

Berman's matter-of-fact account exudes a sense of a natural, indeed beautiful, peacetime world disturbed by aerial attack. There was some initial fear – teeth chattering – but she soon became calm; in the end, she was left with the sense of the unreality of it all. This personal account demonstrates, too, a sense of an entire domestic scene, of the family, under attack, something that more public accounts were also quick to emphasize.[45]

In addition to the deaths inflicted on civilians, especially children, another element that made early air warfare so unsettling was the sense of not knowing precisely what was about to occur and, after mid-1915, what had in fact taken place. While this was seemingly as public an act of warfare as could be committed against a civilian population (people could easily see the airships and later planes and hear the guns), government efforts to keep exact information out of the papers led to many aspects of the incidents being kept from the media. It was shortly after the late May raids that an official announcement forbade the publication of details of the routes taken by aircraft or the locations where bombs had fallen in order "to secure the public safety."[46] The *Pall Mall Gazette*

---

[45] IWM, Department of Documents, Papers of H Miller (02/38/2), Jeanne Berman, Diary, 8 June 1915. She describes this raid as passing over Hull on Sunday night.

[46] See Memorandum, 8 May 1915, in TNA HO 45/11192 and the public announcement of this in "Detailed Reports Forbidden," *Times*, 1 June 1915, and "Statement by the Press Bureau," *Manchester Guardian*, 1 June 1915.

applauded this decision, claiming that the raids had given "the people of London a rare opportunity to show their discipline and obedience" and urged its readers to be "neither clamouring for news nor retailing gossip. We shall hear in good time all that is necessary for us to know."[47] In contrast, the *Times*'s editorial objected to the prohibition on publishing details of the raids in some measure, insisting that the number of casualties needed to be made public as quickly as possible in order to prevent the spread of "wild rumours."[48]

Despite placing restraints on public discussion of the air raids, the government in the form of the Home Forces General Headquarters was quickly assembling secret circulars under the auspices of its Intelligence Section. These contained detailed information, complete with maps that showed the paths taken by raiders and the places where their bombs had fallen. A general introduction to a report on the attacks of 1915 began by noting that "its contents are strictly secret ... [as] there is every reason to believe that the enemy is often in ignorance as to the courses that his airships have followed, and as to the result of the raids." Therefore, all such information had to be kept out of enemy hands. Part of the reason for this was the shift in the nature of attacks during the course of 1915. The raids of the spring were described as "experimental," but with the fall, they demonstrated "for the first time the existence of a well thought-out and progressive programme."[49]

The sense of air raids becoming both "thought out" and less infrequent prompted some visible public responses by mid-1915. Commercial enterprises were quick to take advantage of growing anxiety about air raids. Advertisements for both the Kyl-Fire Fire Extinguisher and the Minimax Fire Extinguisher highlighted their efficacy in fighting fires caused "by hostile Aircraft" in June.[50] Playing on fears of potentially even more destructive aerial warfare, the Hospitals and General Contracts Co. advertised a new respirator (gas mask) in early June, offering protection against "asphyxiating gases" under the heading "Be Prepared for Zeppelin Bombs."[51] Insurance companies offered to safeguard property

[47] "Notes of the Day," *Pall Mall Gazette*, 1 June 1915.

[48] "The Lesson of the Zeppelins."

[49] Home Forces General Headquarters, Section I, *Air Raid Secret Circulars*, 1914–1916, Collection of IWM.

[50] Advertisement for Kyl-Fyre Fire Extinguisher, *Times*, 2 June 1915, and Advertisement for Minimax Fire Extinguisher, *Times*, 5 June 1915. Quote is from the latter. Such advertisements continued throughout 1915; see Advertisement for the Pyrene Fire Extinguisher, *Daily Chronicle*, 10 Sept. 1915.

[51] Advertisement for Hospitals and General Contracts Co. Ltd., *Pall Mall Gazette*, 9 June 1915.

as well as lives. Property owners in coastal areas had already sought to insure homes and business establishments, but after the first set of naval raids, insurance premiums went up; the *Times* reported that, despite this, several underwriters remained vulnerable to claims based on the early damage that had occurred in Scarborough and Hartlepool.[52]

When aerial raids intensified in 1915, newspapers themselves began to offer financial assistance to subscribers who were victims of raids.[53] Both the popular *Daily Mail* and *Daily Chronicle* offered their readers sums of money for losses sustained in raids. After the June 1915 raids, the *Daily Chronicle* offered its readers the following sums: £150 for damage to homes and their contents by a hostile aircraft, £100 for fatal injuries, £30 for damage inflicted by the enemy but not by air power, and £10 to cover medical fees for non-fatal injuries.[54] The *Chronicle* also ran large advertisements by firms such as the British Dominions General Insurance Company under the heading "Zeppelin Raids," offering a new, "special aircraft policy" that would insure property against damage or loss not only from the raids themselves but also from defensive measures taken against them.[55] The *Pall Mall Gazette* reported that the government was considering some kind of state insurance or pension for air raid victims, while noting that it had previously granted aid to compensate those who suffered losses from enemy attack and would do so for victims of the recent raids on the East Coast.[56] Its editorial page praised these efforts to secure insurance and thus facilitate commercial interests in the City.[57]

The state's ongoing need to balance a variety of interests was evident in how it recorded what it took to be the main details of the raids. Thus, the government's secret circular for the raid of the night of 9–10 August commented that the dead were all "civilians" and included one man, nine women, and six children. Yet when information about the raid appeared in public forums, it was more alarmist, under headlines such as "Forty-Six Civilians Killed and Injured"; only more careful reading revealed that

---

[52] "Bombardment Risks," *Times*, 17 Dec. 1914.
[53] An official scheme for insuring against damages due to aerial bombardment was promulgated in September 1917. See discussion in the following chapter.
[54] "Zeppelin Insurance," *Daily Chronicle*, 2 June 1915.
[55] Advertisement for the British Dominions General Insurance Company Ltd., *Daily Chronicle*, 2 June 1915.
[56] "State Insurance Against Zeppelins," *Pall Mall Gazette*, 8 June 1915.
[57] "Air Raid Risks," *Pall Mall Gazette*, 9 June 1915. A more thorough exploration of how to calculate these risks appeared about ten days later; see "Air Raid Policies," *Times*, 19 June 1915.

ten people had died and thirty-six had been injured.[58] An editorial in the *Manchester Guardian* after a mid-August raid insisted that while such attacks were "trying to tempers and very cruel in their incidence of suffering," they could have no direct influence on the outcome of war, for "we have it in our power to turn every air raid into a failure simply by taking as little notice of it as possible."[59] A few days later, the secret circular noted that a zeppelin raid had killed a man, woman, and child and that while the Germans had reported that it had reached London, the airship had not in fact succeeded in doing so. Instead, this raid inflicted significant damage on the coast, a fact readily grasped by locals. Writing from the trenches in mid-August and describing the sensation of being under German shell fire, Jimmie Soames nonetheless told his wife that he heard from his mother "& they [his parents] were in the air raid at Lowestoft [a coastal area] & a good deal of damage appears to have been done to property & nearly all the visitors have cleared out ... as a result so the local people will suffer pretty heavily."[60]

The Germans had more success on the night of 7–8 September, when they hit the London port districts of Deptford, Southwark, and Woolwich. The circular noted, "[T]he number and nature of the bombs thrown shows that the chief intention was to do as much damage by fire as possible, without the slightest regard to human life," given that the attacks launched 300-kilogram bombs.[61] Even in these secret reports, a tone reminiscent of the popular press in condemning these methods of war emerges. Publicly, the news media announced that the attack of the night of the 8th had killed twenty in greater London and the eastern counties, including two women and six children.[62] The *Pall Mall Gazette* editorialized about these raids under the heading "Man and Beast," proclaiming them "expeditions of massacre – undertaken partly to terrify our non-combatants into a desire for peace and partly because Germans enjoy killing for its own sake." It praised the recent actions of the Trades Union Congress (TUC) to support the war and squelch dissenting voices,

---

[58] See "Last Night's Air Raid," *Pall Mall Gazette*, 18 Aug. 1915.
[59] "The Air Raids," *Manchester Guardian*, 19 Aug. 1915.
[60] IWM, Department of Documents, Papers of G H Soames (88/44/6), James [Jimmie] Soames, Letter to G. H. Soames (wife), 15 Aug. 1915.
[61] Home Forces General Headquarters, Sections II and III, Appendix on Raid, 7/8 September 1915, *Air Raid Secret Circulars*, 1914–1916, Collection of IWM.
[62] See the official announcement reprinted under "A Record of the Raids," *Times*, 19 Aug. 1915, and details of the September raid as part of "Air Raid on Wednesday," *Times*, 10 Sept. 1915.

adding that "an indecisive suspension of hostilities means a compact with crime – a compounding of the greatest and vilest felonies by which the rights of humankind have been assailed." The air raid thus revealed the true nature of the enemy and thereby called upon "the whole manhood of a proud and honest people" to reject any calls for peace.[63] The *Daily Chronicle* concurred, condemning the "air assassins" in one editorial that accused the Germans of "breaking all laws, human and divine" and promising in return a "terrible reckoning."[64]

A second editorial in the *Daily Chronicle* denounced the Germans for waging "war on non-combatants." The piece directly compared several actions by Germany that it deemed atrocities: those committed by its army in Belgium, by its navy in shelling Scarborough and initiating submarine warfare, and by its zeppelins. It spoke directly of Germany's violation of the "chivalrous" conduct of war, of the downing of the ocean liner *Lusitania*, and of "the terrible report of Lord Bryce's Commission," which had "placed on record for all time the atrocious crimes committed by the German army during its passage through Belgium." In Belgium, then, as on the high seas and as in England, "nearly all their victims are civilians, most of them women and children." The acts of the zeppelin raider are "not war: they are murder pure and simple.... Its crimes produce no military object; they produce no moral effect ... [except] to stimulate recruiting and to keep alive in the hearts of our people the flame of an inextinguishable hate for Germany."[65] This editorial was immediately followed by a short poem entitled "The Zeppelin Harvest," in which the damage inflicted by the raiders is described as returning to them:

> And the frightful seed they scattered
> reaped a harvest there and then
> Every cradle burned and battered
> raised a squad of khaki men.[66]

According to such imagery, the German raiders burn and murder babies, and the response of outraged British men demonstrates their courage and defiance by joining the army. Thus is the air raid ultimately self-defeating, and thus is what might be read as male weakness – the inability to defend infants in cradles – turned into proof of male valor – the "squad

[63] "Man and Beast," *Pall Mall Gazette*, 9 Sept. 1915.
[64] "The Air Assassins," *Daily Chronicle*, 9 Sept. 1915.
[65] "War on Non-Combatants," *Daily Chronicle*, 10 Sept. 1915.
[66] A. W., "The Zeppelin Harvest," *Daily Chronicle*, 10 Sept. 1915.

of khaki men" who, in the poem's final stanza, will in turn "scatter seeds of terror."[67]

Here is a clear articulation of the view that air raids were an atrocity, one that reveals the outrage that accompanied their introduction. Images of bombed-out homes and female casualties quickly found their way into many aspects of popular culture. Propaganda and the media coverage highlighted how attacks on civilians violated international codes of war. One of the best-known posters condemning aerial bombardment features a cartoon of the Kaiser and Hindenburg discussing Germany's "knights of the air," while burning hospitals, which are clearly marked with a red cross, as well as the destruction of a town may be seen in the distance. The sarcastic use of the word "knight" reminds us that this is no form of chivalry.[68] As did the *Daily Chronicle's* editorial, it calls into question the German nation's claim to masculine bravery tied up in heroic military feats if it is waging war against the unarmed and the helpless.

Recruiting propaganda made use not only of bombed-out homes but also of the dramatically altered skyline of zeppelins against the backdrop of the capital city's most notable landmarks. One vivid poster features a zeppelin passing Big Ben while the text states: "It is far better to face the bullets than to be killed at home by a bomb. Join the Army at once & help to stop an air raid."[69] Clearly this was meant to channel male frustration over the inability to do anything about air raids into action by suggesting that facing bullets was preferable to being bombed and killed at home. What the poster ignores is that this was not an option for those represented as predominant among the raids' victims: women and children.

An image by artist Frank Brangwyn for the *Daily Chronicle* suggested a connection between the hapless victims of zeppelin raids and those suffering from other forms of German aggression in occupied Belgium. Entitled "The Zeppelin Raids: The Vow of Vengeance," the drawing features a Tommy raising his fist to a passing airship. He stands above a prostrate body, and next to this body, a mother and child mourn the dead. The woman's head is covered and bowed; the child wipes his eyes.[70] This is strikingly similar to images of prostrate bodies and grieving women and

[67] A. W., "The Zeppelin Harvest."
[68] "Knights of the Air," IWM Department of Art, PST 13561.
[69] "It Is Far Better ... ," IWM Department of Art, PST 12052.
[70] "The Zeppelin Raids: The Vow of Vengeance," IWM Department of Art, PR 464. The drawing also served to advertise the "air raid insurance" offered to readers by the *Daily Chronicle* discussed earlier.

FIGURE 2.1. "It Is Far Better to Face the Bullets." First World War recruiting poster. Reproduced by permission of the Imperial War Museum.

children that accompanied propaganda about the German invasion of Belgium and its subsequent atrocities and sought relief for Belgian refugees. A poster for the Belgian & Allies Aid League also featured an illustration by Brangwyn depicting refugees, including suffering men, women, young children, and infants. Here, too, a man in the center of the image raises his hand in a gesture of futility.[71] Placing the two images alongside one another, one is struck by two things: the powerful suggestion of victimization epitomized by visible civilian distress in both posters and the fact that the soldier in the "Vow of Vengeance" is as helpless (and hapless) as the male refugee in the appeal for aid for Belgium. Far from being able to protect (feminine) civilian life, the British soldier – the epitome of masculinity – can only promise revenge.

[71] "Belgian & Allies Aid League," IWM Department of Art, PST 6299. See other examples depicting civilian, especially female, victims in the posters "In Belgium Help" and "Belgian Canal Boat Fund," IWM Department of Art, PST 10909.

In the aftermath of this first wave of sustained damage, new attention to the state and behavior of civilians under fire also appeared. The *Times* weighed in with an editorial on "Zeppelins and psychology":

> No doubt the Germans believed that with their Zeppelin war upon civilians they would cause a panic among civilians. It is part of their theory of war that civilians are generally contemptible in war. They exist but to be frightened.... It takes little to throw civilians into a panic in peace; it was natural, therefore, to expect that bomb-dropping would throw them into a panic in war. Consider, for instance, the panic that was caused by the Jack the Ripper murders. If Germany became a Jack the Ripper among the nations, might she not expect to have her way with them? She did expect that, and she has been disappointed. The Zeppelins appear to cause wonderfully little panic at the moment of murder, and no permanent panic afterwards. Their effect is, not a demand for peace, but a demand of the whole nation to help in the war. The Germans do not understand human nature, and they have never understood it less than in this matter.

Why have they so miscalculated? Fundamentally, the editorial continues, because they assume that civilians are different from soldiers, but they are not. Soldiers are merely "the civilian trained and specialized."[72]

This statement, coming as it does at the end of the war's first year and in response to the innovation of the air raid, is striking for several reasons. First, its reference to the lack of panic shown by civilians and its insistence on the equivalence of soldiers and civilians highlights "total" war as a cultural phenomenon. In effect, it claims that bombing the "home front" has helped create a situation where "the whole nation" demands to help. Not only are civilians involved in war because they are, like those in the military, literally under fire, but they have also become like soldiers because they know how to face death and destruction without "panic." Second, the implication of comparing Germany to Jack the Ripper – the sexually violent predator – underscores the repeated idea of German militarism as embodying a deviant masculinity. Faced with a savage, barbaric, voracious enemy that has nothing but contempt for innocent life, the civilian rises to the occasion to face him down. While British civilians are masculinized as well in this editorial, there is nothing to suggest that the traits – honor, pride, and the fear of nothing but defeat – exhibited by those fighting the enemy alongside soldiers could not be those of women and even children as well as of non-combatant men.

---

[72] "Zeppelins and Psychology," *Times*, 10 Sept. 1915.

Some newspapers also provided firsthand accounts that showed women exhibiting such qualities. While describing the experience of "being zepped" for readers of the *Pall Mall Gazette*, Mrs. Rentoal Esler observed that if panic was "contagious ... serenity is also contagious." On a visit to the East Coast, Mrs. Esler encountered the effects of a zeppelin raid and could report that "not one occupant of the house was conscious of the smallest emotion of fear." She did note, however, that "a good many visitors to the neighborhood left by an early train next day." Still, when required to take shelter in the cellar in the middle of the night, she found that between her warring emotions of fear and common sense, common sense prevailed.[73]

A more personal (and private) account by a young nurse revealed a more complicated set of emotional responses. On 10 September, Maggie Turner described her ordeal at Great Ormond Street Hospital in a letter home:

> Never in my life will I forget last night.... I fell asleep in a few moments only to wake up to hear the most *awful* noise.... [I] felt the *whole* of my room shake, things falling down all over the place, screams from nurses flying down the stairs and passages, saying quickly 'Nurses the Zeppelins are here!' All lights were turned out at once from the main & we were in utter darkness.... I didn't feel a bit frightened at the time & shouted out to the Nurses as we flew downstairs not to cry out. Some, at least most, of the Nurses were down in the basement, but I flew up to my ward & found the night nurse & Doctor carrying in screaming children from the balcony. The gas & the smell of the bombs exploding was awful, one after the other – the noise & darkness was too terrible. We shut all the windows down in the ward ... & the children were so good when we were with them.... Several of us slept together as we were all so shaken with fright. Nearly every window in Great Ormond St. is smashed to bits, & there was a huge fire in one of the houses.... We could see the Zeppelins dropping bombs....
>
> The sky was one blaze from the fire at the back of the hospital. All the Nurses really behaved in a splendid way, only a few lost their heads & nearly fainted. I feel sure they will be here again tonight, & am dreading it, but would not leave for anything.... Dont get nervous about me as I am as safe here as anywhere & would not leave if I was asked to.[74]

Not surprisingly, the letter conveys a multitude of reactions – fear, defiance, pride, and excitement. Turner wanted to record an unforgettable

---

[73] "On Being Zepped," *Pall Mall Gazette*, 10 Sept. 1915.

[74] IWM, Department of Documents, Papers of J H Merivale (P471), Maggie Turner, Letter to Hetty Turner (mother), 10 Sept. 1915, copied over and included in B. Merivale Diary, 17 Sept. 1915. Emphasis in original.

night and to reassure her mother that she survived the ordeal relatively unscathed. The assertion that she was "as safe here as anywhere" is particularly suggestive, accepting in essence that no place was *entirely* safe. In any event, Turner found it better to comfort children and bear witness to destruction; in this case, even a woman found it better to take action rather than sit passively and wait to be bombed.

Another public account stressed the "folly and futility" of these raids by insisting that nothing of any military character whatsoever, including morale, was affected by the bombs. Instead, it listed the damage as including such actions as reducing "the carefully kept living rooms of a small family to a mass of soot and dust and plaster and broken glass. In what conceivable respect did it contribute to the progress of the war?" Nor was the war effort helped in any way by an attack such as the one that destroyed a small block of houses turned into flats inhabited by "a widow, her daughter aged 18 ... a family with three children, two of them girls, a working man and his wife with five children, four of them girls" and that killed most of them.[75] Even those at the "front" expressed their concern; "British soldiers, nurses and others in France" felt real sympathy with Londoners because of the recent raids: "They thought far more of our dangers in London than of their own. 'We can dodge shells in dug-outs and so on,' they said, 'but in London it must be terrible.' " The implication here is that civilians were facing even worse conditions than those on the traditional battleground, a seemingly outrageous suggestion for those who insisted that nothing could be worse than the horrors of the Western Front.[76]

The diaries of two London hospital workers reflected the matter-of-fact nature with which some were able to face the raids. George Williams dutifully noted in his diary the reports of the number of people killed along the coast in early September; like the media, he highlighted the damage done to particular groups: of the 56 casualties "19 being children (5 killed & 10 wounded) and 21 women." And he described going to see the damage, with one house "still smouldering" in Gresham St., and viewing such a large hole at the corner of Broad and Liverpool Streets "that you could see the drain pipes."[77] According to Winifred Tower, volunteering at Londonderry House Hospital in London during the September and October raids, the first raid "lasted about 10 minutes and then all

[75] "The Zeppelin Raids: An Official Report," *Times*, 18 Sept. 1915. The note above this article states that this was a description "drawn up by an impartial observer at the request of the Home Secretary and ... authorized for publication."

[76] "The Army's View of Air Raids," *Times*, 24 Sept. 1915.

[77] IWM, Department of Documents, Papers of G H Williams (99/71/2), G[eorge] H[oward] Williams, Diary, 7 and 9 Sept. 1915.

was quiet again. We saw the shells bursting from our windows but didn't see the Zep herself; many people did as she was already lit up by the searchlights and looked like an enormous silver fish.... The next morning I went to the hospital where all kinds of yarns and rumours were busy." Most of the rumors concerned false reports that the zeppelin had been shot down. Tower's diary entry for 13 October 1915 is more detailed, describing how she "hung out of the window and distinctly heard the machine flying from the south-west in an easterly direction." She could see shells bursting – "some right over the house as it seemed" – but they made little noise. Her own experience was limited, but she reported the larger scale of the attack thoroughly: "a lot of casualties taken to Charing Cross Hospital.... [T]he loss of life was heavier than ever before. About 100 casualties were taken to the hospitals of which ... 22 died. There were said to be one or two cases of gas-poisoning and the wounded did not do very well, many becoming septic. People began to get very excited about the Zeps and to blame the Government for not providing better protection against them, and there were meetings held to suggest air reprisals."[78] Here, anxiety is displaced outward onto others who get "excited" and "blame the Government;" her own tone is interested but detached.

In mid-October, the *Daily Herald* offered public praise for this sort of calm behavior, especially by women, in the following poem:

> You heard last night?
> Yes, I heard!
> Had you fear?
> No fear!
> And the women?
> No!
> Wonderful, the nerve of the women.
>
> We sat down below, guns blazing, blazing;
> Some stood in their doorways, saw the shrapnel bursting;
> One a mere girl
> Found her place in her book to finish her tale.
> Wonderful, wonderful nerve of the women![79]

The same edition of this paper also carried an article by Margaret McMillan, who acknowledged the zeppelins as perhaps breaking the

[78] IWM, Department of Documents, Papers of W L B Tower (P472), Diary of W[inifred] L. B. Tower.
[79] C. H. G., "Zeppelins – Baptism of Fire," *Daily Herald*, 16 Oct. 1915.

stoic calm of the women "but only for an hour or two. Next day the women went about their tasks as usual and the children were gay again till dusk."[80] Thus, on the one hand, the ability of women (and in some cases children) to carry on is what one might expect, but, on the other hand, it is "wonderful" – something to be remarked upon. Blazing guns and the noise of bombs are disturbing, but even mere girls can show no fear.

The reaction of London's children, widely viewed as one of the most vulnerable segments of the population, received detailed attention in the media in the fall of 1915. The *Daily Mail* celebrated the heroic behavior of a nurse in a London hospital caring for children, actions "which would lessen the glee of the baby-killers if it were known in Berlin." When a zeppelin raid awakened children under her care, the sister declared it "a Guy Fawkes night" and distributed chocolate as "the chorus of 'The Fifth of November' rose higher and higher.... [F]ar from causing panic, one small section of the community at any rate found the Zeppelin raid enjoyable." Yet the article concluded by noting that the "dead bodies of five children" were taken to another hospital during the same raid.[81]

In September 1915, Dr. C. W. Kimmins presented some of his research on the effects of the war on children to the Psychological Section of the British Association. Kimmins conducted a study of their reactions by asking 1,511 boys and 1,570 girls attending London schools to write "as much as they could about the war in fifteen minutes," without giving them any time to prepare. He came away from the investigation noting that girls of ten had a "bellicose attitude," while those of eleven were depressed, and only at twelve had they resumed "normal interests." In contrast, boys "become more warlike at eleven, and though a period of depression follows upon this, it is much less marked than in the case of girls."[82]

In a later talk given to the Child Study Society at the Royal Sanitary Institute on 9 December and reported in the *Times*, Kimmins offered more of his research, including an analysis of 945 essays written by London schoolchildren in the immediate aftermath of their direct experience of the September and October raids. He again described the essays as having been written "without preparation ... from 10 to 14 days after the

---

[80] Margaret McMillan, "Citizens of Tomorrow," *Daily Herald*, 16 Oct. 1915. McMillan was a notable feminist and Labour activist who focused on child welfare and education, and the article went on to describe the wartime suffering of children from poverty rather than war itself.

[81] "Babies' Raid Joy," *Daily Mail*, 14 Sept. 1915.

[82] "Children's War Essays," *Pall Mall Gazette*, 10 Sept. 1915.

raids."[83] Kimmins stressed the difference that maturity made, noting that for eight-year-olds, the "noise of the firing bulked very largely" and that fear began to be expressed by girls as young as nine, although not by boys until age ten. By eleven years of age, both boys and girls showed no signs of fear and this attitude continued into their early teens. Indeed, children of both sexes expressed criticism of the raiders: "[G]irls of 13 gave a general verdict that the raids would do good because they would show the people what war really was." The following example was used to illustrate the older girls' lack of fear and burgeoning bellicosity: "Afterwards (said another) I knew what our brave soldiers and sailors have had to go through day after day. This kind of thing makes one realise what war is; and yet dropping bombs on harmless people is not war. That night I felt bitter towards the Germans. I felt I could fly to Germany and do the same thing to them." Kimmins then noted how many of the girls seemed to take a "mothering attitude towards those more helpless," providing the anecdote of a girl who rescued her teddy bear to take to the cellar, but also concluding that the "children who suffered most were girls of about 12, who were really frightened but would not show it."

Interspersed with such broad conclusions about reactions to raids based on age and gender came excerpts from the essays themselves. There are indications in these selections of stoicism and of other coping mechanisms. One girl wrote, "I was a bit frightened when the bomb burst, but we have only to die once." Another girl reflected, "I could have seen the Zeppelins, but I thought, 'If I do I shall always see them when I look up into the sky,' so I would not look at them." Kimmins commented that many respondents mentioned the behavior of their mothers: "A picture over mother's bed fell on her head and on the baby. The baby went unconscious, and my mother shook her, and then she was alright," or "My mother rushed up into my room and carried me bodily down into the kitchen." In contrast, Kimmins found it "particularly striking" that 95 percent of the essays made no mention of fathers, and in many cases the references to fathers, and to "men, generally, apart from policemen, soldiers, and firemen were … uncomplimentary." He quoted an essay that described a father being "frightened during the raid…. [H]e ran into a beer shop and got under the counter and stayed there until it was all over." Another child wrote, "A man came into the publichouse and said, 'Give me half a pint. If I am going to die I will die drunk.'" The experiences

---

[83] "Air Raids as Seen by Children," *Times*, 10 Dec. 1915. Here Kimmins was given his full title, chief inspector of schools for the London County Council.

FIGURE 2.2. Damage caused by a zeppelin raid on Croydon on the night of 13–14 October 1915. Home Office photograph. Reproduced by permission of the Imperial War Museum.

recounted by these children reveal a range of emotions, suggesting that heroism was exhibited by women and children, while ordinary civilian men were conspicuous by their absence or misbehavior. As was the case with the June letter written by Dorothy Perkins, the words of children highlighted the ability of these quintessential civilians to reject the panic-stricken terror that presaged the full-blown collapse of morale that the air raid was meant to unleash.

Meanwhile, in more official responses, the renewal of raids in October led to proposals to stop evening theater performances, calls for greater protection of London's monuments, and a visit by the king and queen to Charing Cross Hospital to comfort about twenty-five injured. It also prompted a long account of the "futile murders of civilians" in the *Times*, which emphasized that of the 127 casualties caused by the 13 October attacks, only 2 were soldiers. As for the "moral effect," "the raid occurred at an hour when practically no one except children were in bed.... [P]laces of entertainment were full and the masses of the population were about their ordinary evening's pleasure or business.... [T]he population of London ... remained cool and free from panic."[84]

After air raids beset civilians along the British coast in early 1915, more sustained attacks on London followed. Whether or not the varied inhabitants of the metropolis could avoid panic and respond with fortitude was a question that the media eagerly engaged. The answer, across gender and age boundaries, was seemingly affirmative. However, one source of frustration for the entire population was how slowly government agencies seemed to react and how little seemed to be done to protect those at home. The evolution of responses to air raids by the British government reflected how truly shocking and unsettling this new form of warfare was despite prewar predictions. The criticism that efforts to respond seemed so piecemeal suggested the improvisational quality of dealing with the civilian rather than military aspects of air raids.

RESPONDING TO THE RAIDS

Towards the end of 1915, it had become clear in government debates over official responses to the raids that no one had a clear idea of how best to serve an embattled civilian population. Initially, there was not even a consensus that public warnings should be issued at the approach of enemy aircraft; indeed, public announcements after early raids suggested that "to avoid the creation of panic ... it is most unlikely that any warning will be given by the authorities."[85] Thus, in addition to figuring out how to inform the population of impending raids, government officials had to determine a policy regarding the provision of public shelters and the dissemination of information to inhabitants about what measures could be taken individually to safeguard lives and property.

---

[84] "London Under Zeppelins," *Times*, 18 Oct. 1915. The term "moral effect" appears regularly during and after the First World War to describe what we might understand as "morale," but had broader implications in terms of thinking about air power strategically. Two early studies of air power refer to it as actions taken for the "purpose of breaking down the enemy's will to resist." See J. M. Spaight, *Air Power and War Rights* (London, 1924) and M. W. Royse, *Aerial Bombardment and the International Regulation of Warfare* (New York, 1928).

[85] "Enemy Air Raids," *Times*, 10 June 1915.

By mid-1915, instructions about how to take precautions against aerial attacks were appearing in major newspapers. The *Times* offered recommendations for private citizens about preparing their homes for the fires that followed in the aftermath of incendiary bombs, for "no one would willingly risk his or her life or the lives of their children, not to mention the serious damage that might be done to property simply by neglect." It described a new type of inexpensive device, "antizep" hand grenades – "so absolutely harmless that even a little child can play with them" – which could be kept in every room of the home and then easily thrown into a raging fire to extinguish it.[86] About a fortnight later, another article on precautions for Londoners instructed them on the obvious, to wit: avoid going outside, leave any bomb alone, and ensure that water, sand, and an approved chemical fire extinguisher were readily at hand.[87]

Shortly following the zeppelin raids on London in early September 1915, the *Times* reprinted the instructions issued by the commissioner of the Metropolitan Police, namely that the civil population should take cover, avoid streets, and move to a cellar if possible. By early October, official policy had begun to take shape in the form of new lighting restrictions, especially for the capital.[88] Independent charitable agencies also began to take it upon themselves to offer advice and "practical hints for air-raids." In October, directives to the Jewish population of London from the Society for the Distribution of Jewish Literature sought to reassure its constituency by combining advice such as having a plan as to where to take shelter with more didactic instructions to "seek shelter quietly, calmly and without showing fear ... [which] is contagious and quickly spreads and thereby causes panic." It repeated these strictures several times: "Try your utmost to conquer your fear and keep a stout heart. Refrain from shrieking, crying, or talking overmuch, all of which only add to the confusion." The pamphlet closed with a line from the psalms, "The Lord is with me and I will not fear."[89]

---

[86] "Zeppelin Raid Dangers," *Times*, 5 June 1915. The identical advice can be found in other papers; see "Zeppelin Raid Dangers," *Pall Mall Gazette*, 9 June 1915.

[87] "Advice on Air Raids," *Times*, 18 June 1915.

[88] See instructions from Sir Edward Henry, commissioner of Metropolitan Police, advising residents to take shelter and to have water and sand ready in case of fire, "Danger of Air Raids," *Times*, 20 Sept. 1915; on lighting restrictions, see "London in the Dark," *Times*, 2 Oct. 1915.

[89] "A Message from the Society for the Distribution of Jewish Literature," Whitechapel, c. 22 Oct. 1915, enclosed in TNA HO 45/ 11192.

The question of air raid warnings was debated more publicly during October 1915. Discussing the issuing of warnings in the House of Commons, William Anderson laid out the dilemma as follows:

> It is pretty clear that the approach of Zeppelins ... is known to the authorities. I think it is quite safe to say that warnings are given ... to certain offices ... and the question arises as to whether it would be wise or unwise to extend these warnings to the public generally. It may be said that this in itself would lead to something in the nature of a scare or panic, but, so far as I have observed – and I have been within a very short distance of where bombs were actually falling – the people seemed to take the matter with a great deal of detached interest.... [I]f warnings were given, I think the streets would very quickly be cleared of people.... It is certain that children would be taken out of the streets if warning were given in time. [90]

Anderson wanted the government to discuss this in a non-political way in order to determine how best to save lives during the raids.

Home Secretary Sir John Simon responded by, in essence, defending the government's policy of not issuing public warnings. He did not advocate the continued absence of warnings for the alleged reason that civilians would succumb to fear, for he deliberately noted that "my anxiety ... is not that London will become panic-stricken. Nothing is more remarkable, nothing is more worthy of praise than the consistent coolness with which the population of the Metropolis has taken the visits of these airy strangers when they happen to drop in."[91] Rather, Simon was concerned that the House and the public realize that the authorities might know that zeppelins were nearby but not that they were going to attack. It was crucial that publicity not give any aid to "these invaders" in identifying where they had succeeded in bombing. A loud audible warning might thus serve to guide a zeppelin attack. The second problem emerged from the very "coolness and courage, and ... contempt with which the Londoner regards these dastardly outrages"; a Londoner might therefore be more likely to go outside to look at the zeppelin if warned it were coming than to seek shelter, and this would do little to protect his or her life. While casualties might result from bombs dropping on places where the public gathered at night such as theaters or cinemas, Simon suggested that "on the whole it is better not to attempt

---

[90] William Anderson, *Parliamentary Debates – Commons*, 21 Oct. 1915, vol. 74, cols. 2118–2119.

[91] It is interesting to note the domesticating of the image of the zeppelin itself here – "airy strangers" and "dropping in."

to warn people of the suggested approach of Zeppelins. The public must therefore understand that if they feel, as some of them very naturally do, that this leaves them in more than one sense in the dark, they really must take their own risk if they choose to go to places where a number of people are assembled together at night." He assumed that civilians would calculate such a risk "reasonably and fairly" and recognize that government policy had not been to conceal the truth but arose from a "practical decision." He concluded:

> [T]he number of false alarms that have been given have produced a very great deal of consternation and disappointment, and the total result ... is extremely doubtful from the point of view of perfect public security and safety. The truth is that in this and other matters, since we are at war, and since our enemy chooses to adopt these devices, we have got to show him that it is not an idle boast, but that it is a genuine fact that Englishmen, men and women, Londoners no less than others, are prepared to face even the tragic incidents of war with courage, calmness and resolution.... [T]hese horrible attacks ... we here at home have got to bear.

At this point, the government had concluded that warnings could have little positive effect, and the main task for civilians was to remain calm and remember that their endurance, as was the case with soldiers, was necessary for victory.[92]

The issue about how civilians might or should respond individually to the raids infiltrated literature as well. In mid-August 1915, advertisements appeared in a number of papers, including the *Daily Chronicle*, calling attention to a forthcoming short story by Rudyard Kipling. Under the banner headline "The Air Raid," the copy read as follows:

> If you were in your garden and a German aviator came hurtling through the tree-tops, landing stunned and speechless almost at your feet –
>
> And if you had just seen the murderous work of a bomb dropped from a German Zeppelin and killing a sweet little English girl –
>
> And a fine upstanding lad whom you loved devotedly, passionately had just been killed in his aeroplane –
>
> If all these thing happened to *you*, came in a quick, torrential rush, brought you face to face with a series of ghastly facts – would you have acted as *Mary Postgate* did?[93]

[92] Sir John Simon, *Parliamentary Debates – Commons*, 21 Oct. 1915, vol. 74, cols. 2119–2224.
[93] "The Air Raid," Advertisement, *Daily Chronicle*, 19 Aug. 1915.

Readers of Kipling's odd and ambiguous short story might have been forgiven for wondering at the disjuncture between the story as advertised and the unsettling tale of "Mary Postgate," a spinster who refuses to aid a fallen pilot in her garden. And literary critics seem to have overlooked the immediate context of the story – the ongoing debates over how British civilians were to respond to being under fire – by focusing instead on its sexual, gender, and xenophobic overtones.[94]

The issues of reprisal and retaliation – whether against Germans living in Britain or in their own country – and the questions of international law and morality permeated wartime media. As we have seen, some advocated internment for all Germans in Britain, others massive aerial reprisals; still others thought that refusing to retaliate in any forum other than the traditional battleground was wrong – let the bombs that killed English baby girls spur enlistment in the military instead of encouraging "us" to become like "them."

"Mary Postgate" offers thus one of the most gruesome, early responses to aerial attacks on Britain. Kipling's story begins with forty-four-year-old Mary Postgate living in her quiet village and working as lady's companion for Miss Fowler. Miss Postgate has recently had to face the death of her mistress's nephew, who had joined the Royal Flying Corps and been killed in a crash. In the aftermath of learning of Wynn Fowler's demise, Mary Postgate witnesses the death of a small girl, whom she had known since her infancy, from what she takes to be an aerial bomb. Later that same afternoon, while burning the unwanted remnants of young Fowler's possessions in her garden, she finds herself facing a downed and badly injured pilot, who asks for help in broken English (actually a combination of French and mispronounced English). She responds by refusing to save him and thus ensuring his death, telling him (in German) that she "has seen the dead child."

Those who denounced the barbarity of German raiders – for killing little Elsie Leggett or Edna Gerritt (the girl in this story, whose name evokes the real-life victim) – may have endorsed the sentiments of the character of Mary Postgate.[95] In the context of the tale, however,

---

[94] See the discussion in Peter E. Firchow, "Kipling's 'Mary Postgate': The Barbarians and the Critics," *Études anglaises* 29:1 (Jan.–Mar. 1976), 27–39, reprinted in *Critical Essays on Rudyard Kipling*, ed. Harold Orel (Boston, 1989), 168–181. See also Trudi Tate, *Modernism, History and the First World War* (Manchester, 1998), 32–40, and, for a discussion of the story as the articulation of bereavement, William B. Dillingham, *Rudyard Kipling: Hell and Heroism* (Basingstoke, 2005), 141–147.

[95] The similarity of names was surely not coincidental.

Postgate's blossoming after causing the pilot's death is unsettling. She embodies neither the calm fortitude called for by the government nor the heroism of someone who defeats the enemy honorably. This makes the widely available advertisements for the story even more puzzling, for they suggest that readers will thrill to Mary's wartime encounter with the enemy, grieve over her lost love, and applaud her actions, instead of being disturbed by the sense that they are being asked to identify with a blood-thirsty, potentially mentally deranged woman.[96] In their presentation of this one short tale, Kipling and his publisher chillingly captured a crucial aspect of the militarization of civilian life in response to air war.

If the government was not ready at this stage to sound warnings, its critics raised the issue of whether it was then in a position to retaliate in kind, to seek collective vengeance as Mary Postgate had done on an individual level. One of the most vocal opponents of government inaction as early as 1915 was a member of Parliament, William Joynson-Hicks, who spoke at a public meeting on 21 October and demanded that stern measures be taken because "the cold-blooded murders of civilians could be met only by force."[97] Yet as far as public reaction was concerned, Joynson-Hicks noted in further parliamentary debates in November of that year, "the Zeppelin incursions into London have merely a moral effect. There is no military effect ... at all events very little, except, per-haps, in frightening the population."[98] This was an admission of a sort.

The return of zeppelin raids in the early months of 1916 prompted messages of defiance and renewed rejection of the idea that those under fire were afraid or unhinged. An article in the *Spectator* began by stat-ing that the "result of the raid ... was on the whole very satisfactory." Admitting this to be a surprising statement, the author supported the claim by noting that the raid did little damage and failed to achieve its singular aim of "subduing of London by terror."[99] On the eve of the first January raid, Viola Bawtree noted matter-of-factly that the current mild temperatures were "just the weather for another raid over London" and

[96] It is possible that the entire episode is a hallucination (no one else witnesses the events in the garden), that the pilot may be French (an ally rather than an enemy), that the bombs did not fall on the village, and that the girl's death was due to the collapse of a building. Mary's feelings about Wynn, who is shown to have treated her rather horribly, are also ambiguous.

[97] "Air Raids and Reprisals: Public Meeting to Demand Protection," *Times*, 22 Oct. 1915.

[98] William Joynson-Hicks, *Parliamentary Debates – Commons*, 11 Nov. 1915, vol. 74, cols. 1356–1357.

[99] "The Zeppelin Raid," *Spectator*, 5 Feb. 1916. Media coverage also noted the renewed airship raids on Paris in January; see "Second Raid on Paris," *Times*, 1 Feb. 1916.

then wrote of her nervousness at being alone in the house, "expecting a bomb to burst somewhere near any minute," when the raid occurred the following day.[100]

Newspapers once again provided accounts as detailed as they possibly could be of the types of damage and number of casualties, without mentioning any names of the victims or of the locales where they had been hit. Under the heading "Stories of the Raid: Wanton Slaughter of Civilians," the *Times* highlighted the fact that of the 160 dead or wounded, twenty women and six children had been killed, and both a church and a chapel badly damaged. Numbers were not enough to convey the horror of "how unsuspecting civilians – men, women, and children – were surprised by the aircraft and wantonly killed or savagely injured." The stories about this raid included one that described a child, whose arm had been severed by a bomb that hit his back garden, crying out to his mother, "They have killed my daddy, and look what they've done to me." Just below this account came the following: "A married woman nursing her baby was buried up to the neck, only her face being visible to rescuers. She was badly crushed, but alive, … the child, when rescued, was dead." In addition, in the Midlands, a woman missionary was killed, "Bible in hand," as was an entire family who had been "sitting round the fire."[101] A few days after the raid, the *Daily Mail* recorded the "strange freaks of fate" that occurred during the raid, listing in addition to the death of the woman missionary and nursing infant the fact that two sisters of a "well-known government official" were struck on the head, one being fatally injured and the other surviving.[102]

Women, nursing mothers, babies, sisters, families: these were the victims of the air raid. The media presented these attacks as war upon civilians without scruple or military value. The *Daily Mail* also noted that the geographic area of the raid was larger "than on any previous occasion" and, in announcing the total death toll from all raids to date, wrote that "the women-and-baby-killers have now Killed 253 and Injured 488."[103] The *Daily Mail* hammered home this idea with a headline that declared "Baby-Killers Beg for Help" when reports of a raider having been downed appeared in the immediate aftermath.[104]

[100] IWM, Department of Documents, Papers of V Bawtree (91/5/1),Viola Bawtree, Diary, 30 and 31 Jan. 1916.
[101] "Stories of the Raid: Wanton Slaughter of Civilians," *Times*, 3 Feb. 1916.
[102] "Air Raid Details," *Daily Mail*, 3 Feb. 1916.
[103] "220 Bombs on 6 Counties," *Daily Mail*, 2 Feb. 1916.
[104] "Zeppelin in the North Sea," *Daily Mail*, 4 Feb. 1916. The paper went on to praise the English trawler that discovered the wreck for *not* rescuing the zeppelin's crew: "The Hun Baby-Killer Cannot Be Trusted."

Coverage of the inquests following this winter raid in Leicestershire and Staffordshire provided more details about the dead. In the former county, a soldier "returned on Tuesday to find his home in ruins and his wife, aged 44, his boy, aged 18, and his daughter, aged 16, lying dead." In Staffordshire, the dead included two men more than fifty years of age, three elderly women, one young woman, and seven children. Here, the coroner's jury returned a verdict of "Willful Murder against the German Emperor and the Crown Prince," and the coroner declared that despite differences of opinion over reprisals, "it might be that it would be impossible to conclude the war without them."[105]

Given how much the press coverage focused on the loss of innocent lives and condemned German aviators as "baby killers," letters to the editor reflected the ongoing debate about reprisals. In the *Times*, Lord Roseberry denounced the nation's "passive and excessive patience" with the Germans and urged Britain to bring war "directly to their hearts and homes."[106] A response the next day from a senior field marshal rejected the advocacy of reprisals as wasteful and displaying an ignorance of military tactics, trusting, moreover, that "our fighting Services will never sink to such deeds of infamy."[107] Others weighed in on either side of the debate for the next week, one insisting that the "'women and children' part of the business is perfectly irrelevant," as the real issue was the British incapacity to enact reprisals.[108] Letter writers to the *Daily Mail* were, on the whole, more supportive of reprisals. One declared that "if the fact of our killing, say twenty German babies would be the means of saving the lives of say, 100 English babies, through our reprisals putting a stop to these raids, would not this so-called 'sinking to a base level' be justified and advisable?"[109] Others demanded to know "what the women have to say about" seeing "their children slaughtered in their beds while the men of England stand about talking of the 'English code of honour.'"[110] Alternatives to reprisals were also put forward. One letter writer

[105] "Air Raid Inquests," *Daily Mail*, 4 Feb. 1916.
[106] Roseberry, Letter to the editor, *Times*, 4 Feb. 1916.
[107] Evelyn Wood, Letter to the editor, *Times*, 5 Feb. 1916.
[108] H. W., Letter to the editor, *Times*, 7 Feb. 1916. See other letters on this date.
[109] F. L. Alexander, Letter to the editor, *Daily Mail*, 3 Feb. 1916. Other letters adopted a more sarcastic tone. James B. Miskin of York wrote that "the people really must be made to understand that the killing or maiming of a few civilians (provided always that they are not Cabinet Ministers) and the destruction of property are of no military importance whatever. Then why make a fuss about it?" See Miskin, Letter to the editor, *Daily Mail*, 7 Feb. 1916.
[110] H. De Vere Stacpoole, Letter to the editor, *Daily Mail*, 10 Feb. 1916.

proposed that camps for interned aliens be built close to manufacturing districts and that "wooden platforms should be erected over shipbuilding yards, munition workshops" with huts placed upon them "in which interned Germans of note or importance should be lodged." Another suggested that for every civilian killed in a raid, "a thousand Germans [should be] raked up and deported" and German money held in England should then be used to compensate victims.[111]

Not surprisingly, the left-wing *Daily Herald*'s front page offered a slightly different perspective, calling the recent zeppelin raids part of "the ghastly game of militarism ... [whereby] any and every means ingenuity can compass will be utilised for destruction." It praised the work of those who were speaking out against reprisals, which "can never be right; they are simply indiscriminate and horrible."[112] Others agreed, arguing that there was no reason to believe reprisals would be effective. Instead, citizens needed to ask themselves, "Have these attacks [air raids] had any effect in our own case other than to strengthen our resolve and to stimulate us to fresh exertions? ... Of all the many mistakes that Germany has made none has been more striking than her complete miscalculation in this respect." Given that "we have throughout this war protested in the name of law and humanity against the brutal disregard for noncombatants that Germany has shown," Britain's "good name" and "sense of decency" were at stake in any decision to engage in reprisals.[113]

Nonetheless, others continued to issue a public cry for reprisals. Writing in the *Daily Mail*, Lovat Fraser claimed that the mood after the Midlands raid was one of fury rather than fear: "The country is bitterly angry because the Zeppelins were able to enter this once inviolate land with the utmost ease and apparently without the slightest opposition.... We are a pugnacious nation, and we do not like to take such an attack lying down." Fraser continued that the advice given by most of the press and government, "to take no notice," was insulting "to the oldest democracy in the world." After invoking Milton in describing the national spirit, Fraser claimed that in retaliating, given the contrasting German character, "there will be no need to bomb their babies in order to make them squirm."[114]

---

[111] Andrew Thomson, Letter to the editor, *Daily Mail*, 10 Feb. 1916, and G. Woolley, Letter to the editor, *Daily Mail*, 3 Feb. 1916.
[112] "Zeppelins and Reprisals," *Daily Herald*, 5 Feb. 1916.
[113] W. P. Herringham, Letter to the editor, *Times*, 15 Feb. 1916
[114] Lovat Fraser, "Why Don't We Hit Back?" *Daily Mail*, 7 Feb. 1916.

This emphasis on the cowardly nature of German attackers appeared in other articles that same week. A piece on "Papa Zeppelin" began by stating that somewhere in Germany there lives a joyful, old gentlemen who "never walks with a jauntier step, never strokes his white whiskers with a happier gesture, than when news is brought him that he has done to death a fresh batch of women and children." The piece by "an Englishman" continues, "In the wicked and useless demolition of women and children he has had few rivals since the beginning of time. As a baby-killer he stands apart upon an eminence of specialism." What particularly marks the zeppelin – "the ripest fruit yet plucked from the tree of German 'culture' " – is its ability to inflict death "without exposing the Huns … to any risk at all. To strike those who cannot strike back is in truth an achievement worthy of the men who butchered Belgium.… [T]hey claim for their victims the helpless and unarmed-poor civilians, innocent women and children – and thus illustrate the solemn doctrine of terror." The indignation of the author culminates in his condemnation of all Germany for celebrating such dishonorable and vicious deeds: "Is it not meet that the infants of Germany should rejoice that in England infants of like age and size with themselves were lying dead and mutilated? Thus only shall the little Huns grow to the full stature of their cult."[115] This rhetoric created a stark contrast between those who inflict such death from the air and the victims of such attacks, the "helpless," the "poor," the "unarmed," and, above all, the "innocent." Yet in a sign of the stakes of this new type of warfare, the blame is laid upon Teutonic "kultur" and all German inhabitants – even the infants of the enemy have become guilty.

The need to keep this idea – disgust for Germany – alive after the war appeared in a proposal by William Fenn in a letter to the editor of the *Daily Mail*. Worrying that defective memories would lead Britons "to forget the Zeppelin murders of innocent people" after the war was over, Fenn proposed "that in each place where murders have been committed by the Huns the local authority shall cause to be erected a suitable memorial, giving the date of the outrage and the names of the victims, and let the record end with 'Lest we forget.' " He insisted that such shrines would be "useful places to show traveling Huns who want jobs or try to sell goods" after the war.[116]

---

[115] "Papa Zeppelin," *Daily Mail*, 5 Feb. 1916.
[116] William Fenn, Letter to the editor, *Daily Mail*, 1 Feb. 1916.

In a letter to the editor of the *Times*, T. B. Napier offered another way of understanding the growing equivalence of combatants and non-combatants and the potential unifying effect of *all* being under fire:

> As to lives, what matters it, if a few hundred civilians amongst us, even women and children, are killed by the German fiends if their death is an item in the stupendous effort which alone can bring victory to Britain and its Allies? Ought we not to be thankful to be allowed to bear without complaint this risk, small as it is? Ought we not to demand that no care for our safety, or the safety of our dear ones, shall make the Government turn by a hair's breadth ... from ... bringing the foe to his knees?[117]

Facing shared danger became something that all citizens, regardless of their status, could now offer to the wartime state.

A more poignant evocation of a shared sense of danger in response to the early 1916 air raids can be found in Vera Brittain's diary entry for 31 January through 1 February. Shortly after the death of her fiancé, Roland Leighton, and her return to hospital work as a V.A.D.,[118] she recorded:

> There was very much of a Zeppelin scare to-night. The Hospital was in utter darkness, passages black, lamps out, blinds down. I stood at the window of my ward, feeling strangely indifferent to anything that might happen. Since He [Leighton] had given up all safety I was glad to be in London, which is not safe. But nothing happened.[119]

Brittain referred to the damage inflicted by air raids and the reaction to them in other passages, but what is worth noting in this instance is her assertion that London's lack of safety made her risk akin to that of the soldier she loved.

The reappearance of raids prompted some new, clandestine government initiatives. In February, the British Fire Prevention Committee issued a set of confidential guidelines ("air raid precautions") for theaters and other places of public entertainment and places of public worship. The committee suggested that if people were not under direct attack, "every endeavour should be made to ignore the raid" and continue the performance or service. At the bottom of the suggestions came the reminder, "[T]he plan of action must not be published or posted up"; in keeping

---

[117] T. B. Napier, Letter to the editor, *Times*, 8 Feb. 1916. See letters on this date, and on 10 and 15 Feb. 1916 as well.

[118] Voluntary Aid Detachment, the medical (primarily nursing) service.

[119] Vera Brittain, *Chronicle of Youth: War Diary, 1913–1917* (1982, rpt. New York, 1981), 313.

with government policy, no detailed public instructions or warnings were to be issued.[120]

Another and more deadly coastal raid in mid-February displayed the limitations of such a policy. This raid was followed both by renewed calls for warnings and by several coastal raids in March and April, which brought the total number of inhabitants killed from the air to 255, with 534 injured.[121] These raids also led to renewed advertisements for "air risk insurance."[122] In addition, a secret government circular explained that the raid over Hull on 5–6 March was not only a "deliberate and callous" act, but one that showed the Germans taking advantage of weather that offered "the best opportunity of bombing a defenceless city... killing and maiming defenceless non-combatants, women and children as well as men."[123]

In the media, the appearance of zeppelins over eight counties in early March prompted more human interest stories of mothers, children, and the elderly at risk. A special correspondent for the *Daily Mail* reported on a "pilgrimage of mothers" seeking shelter in Yorkshire after the first bombs fell:

> [There were] many women, mostly in their night attire, some with shawls or tablecloths thrown over their shoulders, and all or nearly all carrying children. Barefooted little toddlers ran along by their side, their eyes wide with wonder, but fearing neither the bitter cold nor the strange adventure so long as mammy was with them.
>
> 'Save our children!' was the cry which went up out of the midst of this moving poignant pilgrimage; and presently kindly folk managed to check the exodus and shepherd shivering mothers and children into a sanctuary more hospitable than the open air on this bitter March night.

These were the lucky ones; elsewhere "a poor woman and her four young children" were killed "in the complete wreck of their little house"; "one poor old pensioner of ninety, lying bedridden in one of the almshouses was killed"; and "three maiden sisters living together in a tiny house in the east end of town died in the ruins of their collapsed and

---

[120] See confidential memos addressed to "Places of Public Worship" and "Theatres and Other Places of Public Entertainment," c. Feb. 1916, TNA HO 45/ 11193.

[121] See "Another Daylight Raid," *Daily Mail*, 10 Feb. 1916, and the report in the *Times*, 1 Apr. 1916.

[122] See advertisement for the "Union Jack Policy" issued by the Gresham Fire and Insurance Society, *Daily Mail*, 6 Mar. 1916.

[123] Home Forces General Headquarters, Report, 5–6 March 1916, *Air Raid Secret Circulars*, 1914–1916, Collection of IWM.

shattered home." Others survived only by chance, as "there were targets to satisfy the lust of the bloodthirstiest Hun ever out for slaughter and devastation."[124]

Eyewitnesses suggested that often the first indication of a raid was the sight or sound of the aircraft or, sometimes, the damage it left behind. Lydia Peile of Margate described an attack in March that began with "an awfully loud explosion, quite close, followed quickly by another – Bombs of course, & we wondered if the next one would come on the house." Only after the raid did she learn that a bomb had landed on a house across the street; she "quickly heard that a little baby had been killed. It was hateful seeing the ambulances arrive, but the other people were only suffering from shock.... I only hope we shall never have such a close experience of bombs again." Yet only three weeks later, she was recounting in her diary that "we have had another air raid, but this time it was more exciting than alarming."[125] As Viola Bawtree recorded in her diary in April, "There was another raid.... [W]e stood outside and scanned the horizons.... At last, over to the north east, we saw the shrapnel go up.... Some of them had cleared the trap door, ready to go to the cellar in case the Zeppelins came over us. But I don't think any of us would really have gone down. If you must be killed, best not to choose being buried alive." She was delighted to learn that a zeppelin had been brought down.[126] If these personal accounts reveal that there

---

[124] "Zeppelins over Eight Counties," *Daily Mail*, 7 March 1916.

[125] IWM, Department of Documents, Papers of L Peile (94/2/1), Lydia Peile, Diary, 1 and 19 Mar. 1916.

[126] IWM, Department of Documents, Papers of V Bawtree (91/5/1), Viola Bawtree, Diary, 1 and 11 Apr. 1916. At times, those writing from abroad could suggest that what Britain witnessed was exciting as well as heart-wrenching or terrifying. Dorothy Higgins, writing home to her mother from Rouen in April 1916, noted: "I hope that the Zepps haven't worried you at all. [T]hey *have* had a happy week-end in poor old England." She applauded that one had been brought down, but "it is not enough." Two weeks later, she was similarly annoyed and yet thrilled: "Thank goodness those devils didn't get you. But 200 yards is much too near to be pleasant. How I wish I'd been at home: I'd have given anything to see all this to-do. It is too absolutely thrilling. What on earth did 2 Zepps think they were going to do with poor little Alford." See IWM, Department of Documents, Papers of D E Higgins (86/73/1), Dorothy E Higgins Letter to Mother, 4 and 20 Apr. 1916. An account of air raids in France by an ambulance driver, twenty-two-year-old [Caroline] Muriel De Wend, appears in a letter to her mother: "Of course I can't tell you much about it, but I don't think any of us had any idea what an air raid really was, before this last week..... the girls are behaving top hole. But the din of the whistling shells & bombs is indescribable." Parts of her letter are then censored, but not her conclusion, where she professes no sympathy for any German pilot shot down for his own "disgustingly brutal country's method of warfare. This isn't a very cheerful letter I'm afraid, but its been H—. really!" See IWM, Department of Documents, Papers of M C de Wend (02/3/1).

were varied reactions to air war, they all indicated an awareness of the altered status of civilians as a result.

These spring raids contributed to debates over shifting to an organized system of public warnings that played out through 1916 among various government officials at both the national and local levels. A report for the home secretary in March 1916 assessing the desirability of warnings found that chief constables in areas affected by raids were "strongly against giving public warnings." This report asserted that, if there were no raid, the warning would only do harm, and if there were a raid, "the risk of loss of life is much increased because crowds assemble in the open to watch for the Zepps; factories, theatres, cinemas, etc. are emptied into the streets at the critical moment, and large numbers collect at railway stations and tramway termini on their way home."[127] There was also a fear that false alarms would disrupt work and thus hinder the war effort, increasing the value to the enemy of the attack.

Yet the raids of the spring of 1916 prompted renewed talk of issuing audible warnings. A May 1916 memorandum on the suggested use of such signals in greater Birmingham indicated a clear split between workers and employers. Not only did the factory workers want to be informed of an impending raid "by the extinction of lights," but "the men want to know that their families at home will have notice, otherwise they may be disinclined to work night shifts." Meanwhile, the employers were "almost unanimous *against* sound signals" because they would make it more difficult to control their workers. They were especially concerned about factories with a majority female workforce, where "any tendency to panic might have very serious results."[128] Whether or not women workers were actually more likely to panic or whether male concern about their families under attack could be managed, the key issue was whether warnings would themselves provoke the least desirable outcomes: fear and the disruption of war work.

In public efforts to combat such fears, stoicism was mixed with humor to reinforce the calm heroism of ordinary, particularly female, civilians in response to the air raids. Following the early winter raids of February 1916, the *Daily Mail* printed the following anecdote from a rural grocer's shop as having been "vouched for by a correspondent." On the morning after the raid, the shop assistant asked "Mrs. Jones" if she heard the zeppelins last night, to which the "Old Lady" replied: "Naw

---

127 "Public Warnings of Air Raids," [16 Mar. 1916], TNA HO 45/11194.
128 "Use of Sound Signals for Air Raid Warnings in Birmingham and the Black Country," 9 May 1916, TNA HO 45/11195.

I didna ... but they tell me there was one at the next town for a long while, *an'* it called at Brown's shop for some petrol. They got some cheek, these 'ere Germans hav'!"[129] As the preeminent British humor magazine *Punch* noted in August 1916, among the war's other changes were "maids who announce Zeppelins as if they were ordinary visitors." It also printed cartoons about aerial attacks; in one, a "Mistress (coming to maid's room as the Zepps approach)" cries, "'Jane! Jane! Won't you come downstairs with the rest of us?'" to which the "Little Maid" replies, " 'Oh, thank you Mum, but I can see beautiful from here, Mum.' "[130] Far from inducing the terror and demoralization that Germany aimed for, such images both made fun of the raiders and implied that the air raids simply aroused interest. This stood in stark contrast to German cartoons that depicted "panic in Trafalgar Square" resulting from the mere appearance of zeppelins much earlier in the war.[131]

Still, if scenes of visible large-scale panic remained more imaginary than real, private accounts reflected concern with renewed attacks in the late summer and autumn. In early September, Jeanne Berman described in her diary the return of zeppelin raids to Grimsby:

> Last night there was a Zeppelin raid. We heard the engines quite distinctly & for a considerable time, at least so it seemed.... We heard shooting here, & the noise of falling bombs. Minnie in a terrible state.... We stayed up till all danger was over. I felt sleepy & tired out when I got to bed. Some must have suffered in the night. Not pleasant now the dark nights are coming, so Zepps beginning to be active again. Heavens knows how things will end. [& my own prospects not bright, miserable in fact].

Two days later, she expressed her relief that no one was killed and that some of the rumored destruction had proved false. Still, she "should like to have seen the burning Zeppelin descending from the sky when it fell in Hertfordshire, must have been a grand fearsome spectacle, terrible deaths for the poor wretches inside, but they came to deal death out to others, so it was but just that they got it themselves."[132]

The "annihilation of the first Zeppelin to fall on British soil" in early September, an event that was visible from most of London, caused mixed

---

[129] "Woman's Zeppelin Adventures," *Daily Mail*, 5 Feb. 1916.
[130] *Mr. Punch's History of the Great War* (London, 1919), pp. 107–108, 185.
[131] Cartoon, "The Arrival of the Zeppelins," from *Simplicissimus* (Munich), Jan. 1915, reproduced in *Je Sais Tout*, 1915.
[132] IWM, Department of Documents, Papers of H Miller (02/38/1), Jeanne Berman, Diary, 3 and 5 Sept. 1916.

emotions.[133] Muriel Dayrell-Browning described it as "the sight of my Life! ... [As it went down] the flames tore up into the sky.... The glare lit up all London and was rose red. Those deaths must be the most dramatic in the world history ... watched by 8 million of their enemies." Yet she also hoped that the "air men" will be buried with full military honors and called them "brave," an interesting reversal of typical coverage that denounced the raiders as barbaric cowards.[134] More publicly, the *Times* weighed in with an editorial that praised the pilot who brought the zeppelin down while noting that "the flying men of the two peoples have a mutual respect for one another" and thus that members of that branch of the services should determine how the funeral of the crew should be ordered.[135] Still, the tragic vulnerability of victims remained a dominant theme in media coverage under headings such as "Man and Wife Killed," "Death on the Doorstep," or "Casualties in a Suburb."[136] The raids had one further concrete effect: on 1 November, the *Times* reported that theaters, concert and music halls, and other places of "public assembly" would receive telephone warnings of future raids as early as possible, as would tramway authorities; rail and omnibus services would continue uninterrupted "for the public safety and convenience."[137]

The bravery of "ordinary" British civilians was underscored as well in newspaper coverage of air raids in the autumn of 1916. A female journalist reflected:

> In visiting the scenes of the disasters caused by German bombs, in listening to the vivid stories of those who escaped with slight injuries or those who by miracle were absolutely unhurt in the midst of devastation, one waits in vain for descriptions of the hysterical woman, the woman who shrieked with fear or the woman who fainted. There are no such descriptions because there were no such women.
>
> The most extraordinary feature of each of the recent raids has been the calm with which they were faced by the inmates of those little cottages which were destroyed or just escaped destruction by a happy chance.
>
> And in most of these suburban homes there were only women and children.[138]

---

[133] "After the Zeppelin Raid," *Times*, 6 Sept. 1916.

[134] IWM, Department of Documents, Papers of M Dayrell-Browning (92/49/1), Muriel Dayrell-Browning, Letter to Mother, 4 Sept. 1916.

[135] "After the Zeppelin Raid."

[136] See coverage in the *Times*, 25 Sept. 1916.

[137] "Air Raid Warnings in London," *Times*, 1 Nov. 1916.

[138] Marion Ryan, "The Women's Splendid Courage in the Raided Areas: How They Met Frightfulness from the Sky Alone and Unprotected," *Weekly Dispatch*, 1 Oct. 1916.

Despite many previous public messages to the contrary, that women could be cool and collected under attack continued seemingly to upset expectations.

That non-combatants undergoing raids could be perceived as experiencing stresses normally associated with combat is suggested by the fact that they could be affected by war-induced nervous ailments. From Hull, where she was teaching French, Dorothy L. Sayers wrote a letter to a close friend in which she described a bald patch on her head that her doctor ascribed to a "nervous disease, resulting from mental strain or shock.... Eventually put down to shock of Zeppelin raids."[139] By 1916, the *Lancet* had acknowledged that civilians could also suffer from "war neuroses."[140] The cases associated with such injuries would intensify with the more damaging raids of the war's last years. Yet two years into the First World War, contemporaries acknowledged the alterations that air raids had inflicted on civilian life and well-being.

CONCLUSION

In the middle of 1915, Evelyn Shaw wrote a short story for the *Daily Herald*, "The Bomb in Laburnum Villas," describing the consequences of a suspected Zeppelin raid on outer London. The residents of the quiet suburban street hurry from their beds with a "mixture of delicious terror and gratified desire" rather than panic, and the inhabitants include one young woman, Miranda Brown. When the special constables hurry those gathered in the streets into the nearest dwellings, Miranda is separated from her family and finds herself in a house with "strangers," among them a man in a respirator, whose face is thus invisible. As the folks taking shelter begin to talk, the man in the gas mask asks Miranda if she is afraid, to which she replies, "One isn't afraid of real things." The man replies that he has found most people are afraid of "real things – things that matter – like truth, and being born, and dying." Miranda insists that "women aren't," but the man retorts that he knows one woman who is, that the man who loves her, a doctor, wants her to be his equal and "gave up going to the front because he thought it mattered more to stay here

---

[139] Dorothy L. Sayers, Letter to Muriel Jaeger, 5 Aug. 1916, reprinted in *The Letters of Dorothy L. Sayers, 1899–1936: The Making of a Detective Novelist*, ed. Barbara Reynolds (New York, 1996), 125.

[140] "War Shock in the Civilian," *Lancet*, 4 Mar. 1916. Also cited in Trudi Tate, "HD's War Neurotics," in *Women's Fiction and the Great War*, ed. Suzanne Raitt and Trudi Tate (Oxford, 1997), 242.

and save babies," and instead of being able to offer her this, he must pretend to offer her nothing but a home and clothes and an income. At this reply, Miranda recognizing the voice, decides to speak the truth, for "at any moment a bomb from above might destroy her," and replies: "She wants all the real things he has to give. She wants to stand in with him and fight to save the babies; she wants him to be the father of her babies, too. She wants all that, but she can't say so – a woman can't – unless there's a chance of a bomb falling on her every minute." As the false raid ends, the "light of the lamp shone on the faces of a man and a woman who had just spoken the truth to one another."[141]

There are a number of ways in which this fictional tale reveals something genuinely new about life under the bombs. The prospect of death at any moment, as in more conventional war stories, provides an occasion for truth telling and the facing of "real things." It offers opportunities for heroism, real emotions, and the saving of lives, literally and figuratively, and it offers these things to men and women, combatants and noncombatants alike.

By the end of 1916, everyone – men and women, young and old – had to adjust to the new reality of aerial warfare. In light of this, the state itself demonstrated a degree of uncertainty over which tactics to implement, ranging from warnings to reprisals. Coverage in the media emphasized the victimization of women and children to underscore the barbarity of the enemy and the vulnerability of civilians in this new kind of war. Yet news accounts and some personal testimony suggest that many civilians coped surprisingly well. Stoicism and good morale were qualities that could be exhibited as much at home in England as on the traditional battlefield in France, and they needed to be promoted if the nation were to survive. The extent to which this new sense of shared determination to face down air raids continued during the war's last years will be taken up in the next chapter.

[141] Evelyn Shaw, "The Bomb in Laburnum Villas," *Daily Herald*, 26 June 1915.

3

Redefining the Battle Zone

Responding to Intensified Aerial Warfare, 1917–1918

INTRODUCTION

In 1917 the airplane, especially a new type of German plane known as the Gotha, became the main vehicle for delivering renewed devastation upon the inhabitants of Great Britain. By the middle of 1917, secret government accounts of air raids had concluded that "the development of the aeroplane as a raiding instrument has grown far more serious." As we will see, the more serious nature of the attacks led to expanded action by the state as it tried to determine how best to protect British homes and lives. In addition, 1917 was a year of war weariness in Britain and, to even greater effect, elsewhere. As a result, some of the more informal morale-boosting organizations and propaganda efforts at the local level came under the auspices of the National War Aims Committee (NWAC), whose explicit aim was "to keep before our nation both the causes which have led to this world war and the vital importance to human life and liberty of continuing the struggle until the evil forces which originated this terrible conflict are destroyed for ever." NWAC activities included organizing and sponsoring speakers to deliver this message. A sign of the new meaning attached to the home under fire can be seen in an October 1917 letter to the NWAC calling for speakers such as "a special constable who has been under fire in an air-raid," someone who could recite "*actual* war experiences."[1] Thus, we see the beginnings of a cultural shift recognizing

---

[1] Minutes and Reports, 1917–1918, and A. Wallis Myes, Letter to Thomas Cox (NWAC), 12 Oct. 1917, TNA T 102/16. Emphasis added. For more on British morale in 1917, see Adrian Gregory, *The Last Great War: British Society and the First World War* (Cambridge, 2008).

that air raids were genuine experiences of war akin to what soldiers faced on the front lines.

Although the year began quietly, the "actual war experiences" of civilians under fire increased dramatically over the course of 1917. There were no aerial attacks on Britain from November 1916 until March 1917, and the smattering of attacks in Essex, Kent, Norfolk, Suffolk, and London in March, April, and early May of that year did only minimal harm. Damage intensified, however, with the commencement of airplane raids on 26 May in Kent and Folkestone, which killed seventeen men, thirty-four women, and twenty-six children and injured twenty-eight men, fifty-one women, and fifteen children.[2] This heightened death toll from the most lethal raid thus far in the war prompted the following response in the *Times*:

> There are three main conclusions to be drawn from the well-planned and disastrous air attack which took place on the English coast.... The first conclusion is that it is mere folly to dismiss a visitation like Friday's as a casual act of 'frightfulness' or a flight of 'baby-killers.' It is true that the casualties were largely among women and children ... but the failure of the German airmen in this respect was no more than an inevitable accident....
>
> The second conclusion ... is that the aeroplane, not the Zeppelin, is the really formidable instrument of invasion.... The third conclusion ... is that the only means of coping effectively with this prospect is by an aggressive aeroplane policy of our own.... In the air ... the overwhelming advantage is always with the attack.

The *Times* also condemned the policy of secrecy – which led to the wildest rumors – when it was clear that "everyone" in Germany knew the location of the attack. What was noticeable in addition about this commentary was the abdication of any attempt to defend the "home front." Women and children would be vulnerable, but denouncing Germany for this was futile. The only response could be counter-aggression – a theme that would now resonate throughout the history of air power.[3]

[2] See the reprinted "Air and Sea Raids on Great Britain: Official Return of Casualties," *Times*, 13 Jan. 1919, and "Record of Bombardments," vols. 1 and 2, TNA HO 45/10783.

[3] Fifteen years before Stanley Baldwin's oft-quoted line that "the bomber will always get through," this statement reveals the core understanding of how air war would be waged: aggressively in the hope of a knockout blow against the enemy, because nothing could be done to prevent aerial attacks entirely. For a narrative of the rise of air power, see Stephen Budiansky, *Air Power: The Men, Machines, and Ideas That Revolutionized War, from Kitty Hawk to Gulf War II* (New York, 2004); see also Tami Davis Biddle, *Rhetoric and Reality in Air Warfare: The Evolution of British and American Ideas about Strategic*

What was also new about this late May raid was that it occurred during daylight. The *Weekly Dispatch* was among the other newspapers deeply critical of the official and immediate press coverage, stating that it knew where and when the raid had occurred "but we are not allowed to tell you" and that for all of the Press Bureau's claims that it took place on "Friday night," "the fact remains that it took place in broad daylight" just before 6:30 P.M. Like the *Times*, it criticized the government's policy of secrecy about place; stating frankly that every German pilot knew the shape of the southeast coast. Still, its coverage could state only that a "South-East Town" had had its business district virtually destroyed in an "intensely violent" bombardment that left "human bodies and horse carcasses" in the main street. It reported that "one fireman, who took the fire alarm call, afterwards learned that his wife, his mother, and his children were all buried in débris."[4]

In a sermon delivered at a memorial service for those who had died in Folkestone, the archbishop of Canterbury described those in this part of Britain as having the "solemn privilege of being the bit of England nearest the Enemy ... and we mean to be worthy of it." He continued:

> Of course we want security and every reasonable precaution we can get for those who are not combatants. But war involves peril, and we are prepared to face peril bravely and quietly.... This war ... has dwarfed even the darkest expectations as to its scale, its prolongation, its horrors, and the manner in which our foes have waged it.... We have had a terrible reminder of the fearfulness of war at first hand in the horror of the blood-stained streets of Folkestone, where our own men, women, and children were killed.

He added that "we are passing through ... experiences in human life that none of us even expected to see." The news account of the primate's address to an overflowing crowd of mourners highlighted the poignancy of some of these experiences by singling out the following bereaved individuals: "a motor mechanic who lost his wife and two children ... the manager of a local grocery store whose wife and only daughter were killed. The aged grandmother of two children who were killed outside a shop just after she had gone inside ... the family of a girl who was blown to pieces." Despite the nature of these losses and the deaths of women

---

Bombing, 1914–1945 (Princeton, NJ, 2002); Robert A. Pape, *Bombing to Win: Air Power and Coercion in War* (Ithaca, NY, 1996); and Yuki Tanaka and Marilyn B. Young (eds.), *Bombing Civilians: A Twentieth-Century History* (New York, 2009).

[4] See "Invasion by Air," *Weekly Dispatch*, 27 May 1917.

and children, the article concluded by noting how "the look of fortitude on the face of people who had been left utterly alone by the deaths of their dearest was wonderful to behold."[5]

Interspersed with accounts of sorrow and stoicism came renewed calls for vengeance and demonstrations of hostility to foreigners. Local officials and the population in general spoke of needing to address the "dangerous situation" that coastal towns faced because of the presence of "enemy aliens." A mass meeting in Folkestone was in the offing, with the clear aim of lobbying for the removal of such people from coastal districts. The martyrdom evoked by the "blood-stained" streets called attention to the new dangers of aerial warfare and the ways in which it evoked emotions that were perhaps more deeply rooted, such as the desire to find scapegoats among a local yet "enemy" population.[6] The alleged dangers posed by "aliens" emerged even more forcefully when daylight raids came to London.

The deadliest raid of the war occurred during the daylight hours of 13 June 1917 when Gothas attacked via Essex and did extensive damage to London's East End. As one of the first news accounts stated:

> The raid on London yesterday morning ... was the most audacious, and it may yet prove the most murderous.... [Y]esterday the bombs came out of an almost cloudless noonday sky, and no searchlights were needed to detect the machines from which they were loosed. Save for this, the raid was but a repetition of the exploits of the Zeppelin. It killed and maimed with the same wanton, undiscriminating ferocity. It slew women and children as well as men. It wrecked buildings of no greater military value than a warehouse here, a tobacconist's shop there, and a school not far away. It made London quiver, not with fear, but with sorrow and anger.[7]

The damage to a London County Council school in Poplar caused the most "sorrow and outrage" as it struck the infants' classroom and none of the victims were older than six years of age.

It also prompted local Labour MP Will Crooks, who arrived quickly at the scene of the devastated school, to praise the behavior of the school personnel, the students, and the neighborhood families:

> Although injured, the two infants' teachers helped to tend their charges, and Mr. Crooks spoke with pride of the gallantry of these young women.

---

[5] "In Memory of Raid Victims," *Weekly Dispatch*, 3 June 1917.
[6] See final paragraph of "In Memory of Raid Victims."
[7] "Story of the Raid," *Times*, 14 June 1917.

He could say of the other scholars no less than they behaved like little
heroes.... Mothers and fathers, of course, came running to the school
from the neighboring streets. There was no panic, and little hysteria. Still,
it was a scene of emotion and nervous tension that few are called upon
to go through. A woman wept here on finding her child safe. A woman
wept there on seeing her baby dead. 'But,' said Mr. Crooks, with pride in
the pluck and patriotism of his native East-end, 'I did not hear anyone in
the crowd, man, woman, or child ask when peace was coming.'[8]

The raids were thus immediately extolled as underscoring the bravery of
Britons of all ages and genders, and as exposing their heroism despite the
horrendous personal losses.

At the inquest following the raid, the coroner, the borough mayor,
and, once again, Will Crooks used the occasion to express sympathy for
the victims and to condemn the attackers. The courthouse – situated in
"a poor and populous part of London" – was "filled with relatives of the
dead, dressed in deep mourning." These relatives had to listen as one father
described identifying his five-year-old son, whose head was missing, "by a
particular button which his mother sewed on to the wristband of his shirt
on the previous evening." The coroner emphasized civilian trauma at the
inquest: "In all countries [at war] there is a considerable amount of trouble which women and children have to suffer. Often they have to suffer
the worst. But we have never had anything of this kind before." Crooks
insisted that the courage shown by the teachers was beyond compare:
"No bravery displayed on the battlefield could be greater." Perhaps even
more revealing of the altered nature of this form of warfare, the mayor
went on to offer his praise of the lost children, comparing them to fallen
soldiers and sailors: "These boys and girls have died as truly for their
country and for everything worth dying for as any of our men at the front
or on the high seas."[9]

This deadly raid, and particularly the age of the victims, led to perhaps the most direct statements to date equating the civilian and military
experience of this war. If little boys and girls could "die for their country,"
there were no limits to the patriotic sacrifices that the nation could
demand and no group that could not claim a new wartime civil identity
based on their response to shared sacrifice. At the same time, the expres-
sions of shock, horror, anger, and grief suggest that no one was ready
to accept that such young children should die in war at school or home.

[8] "Bomb on East End School," *Times*, 14 June 1917.
[9] "Child Victims of the Enemy," *Times*, 16 June 1917.

REACTIONS AND REPRISALS

The aftermath of the 13 June raid on the East End also prompted a renewed and heated debate about reprisals. The *Weekly Dispatch* reported that the "East End demands reprisals"; it quoted the mayor of Bethnal Green as stating that "to meet such an enemy we should adopt some of the inhuman methods that he has."[10] A series of passionate letters to the *Times* considered whether war waged against civilians was ever acceptable. A writer signing him- or herself "Retribution Not Revenge" demanded an answer to the question of "how much longer the Government intend to adopt the policy of 'turning the other cheek to the smiter' and thus encourage the Hun to continue his dastardly outrages on defenceless women and children? By his absolute disregard of all the rules for the conduct of civilized warfare he has repeatedly placed himself beyond the pale and forfeited all right to consideration as a human being." By so changing the rules of war, the "Hun" deserved whatever treatment Britain chose to mete out.[11]

Two powerful letters to the *Times* from women, each of whom asserted the status of "bereaved" mother, showed how grief and a claim to sacrifice could lead to diametrically opposed perspectives on retaliatory bombing. The first writer signed herself "bereaved," declaring herself to be the mother of a son killed in an air fight in France. For her, the distinction between civilians and combatants was gone and all must now share the risks and sacrifices:

> This is a war of nation against nation – no longer only army against army – and therefore the civilian population should not make any outcry that would induce the authorities to play into the German hands by withdrawing our best machines and best airmen from the front to defend us here.... We must all take our risks, which are, after all, not one-thousandth part of what our soldiers face every day. It is rather absurd to hear the cry about 'innocent' people being bombed. Our Army is innocent too.

This mother would gladly retaliate if it were strategically feasible. Her call for vengeance reinvigorated the sense of fighting a merciless, barbaric enemy.[12]

[10] "East End Demands Reprisals," *Weekly Dispatch*, 17 June 1917.
[11] "Retribution Not Revenge," Letter to the editor, *Times*, 16 June 1917.
[12] "Bereaved," Letter to the editor, *Times*, 16 June 1917.

The other grieving mother used her status to argue against reprisals, suggesting that her sacrifice gave her a special right to comment on war policy:

> I have given two sons to the war (my only two) and they will never come back to me. I gave them willingly, and I have no regrets. I gave them to help free the world from tyranny and barbaric savagery, and I believe that by giving up their young lives they have 'done their bit' towards that end. But should I live to see Englishmen sent to murder in cold blood German women and children and harmless civilians, then indeed I should begin to ask, 'Have my sons died in vain?' I believe that my feeling is generally shared by those who have suffered personally in the war as I have suffered.[13]

Other, less emotive letters concurred that reprisals would not deter "the German babes and young children who would fall victims to reprisals," as they would not reach the "real authors of these crimes – the Kaiser and his myrmidons."[14]

A sense of outraged helplessness resonated in the media and among politicians. There were public appeals to Parliament for both reprisals and the "more stringent internment of enemy aliens."[15] Among the responses from the political leadership was a proposal to allow the Committee for the Prevention and Relief of Distress to disperse funds to victims of air raids, reflecting the desire to do something to ameliorate the effects of these attacks.[16]

Private views expressed a mix of emotions but also revealed the extent to which details of the raid, despite press censorship, were fairly well known. Rifleman Maurice Gower wrote to his sister Flo from the Isle of Sheppey describing a raid that struck while he was in a "picture palace," where nobody became excited as "they told the women that it was only practice to keep them calm until a number of women and children were brought in from the streets in a fainting condition which caused some uneasyness."[17] Writing shortly after these raids to her son serving in the armed forces (but based in Britain), Elizabeth Fernside described the aftermath: "The damage is considerable all round.... Two trains were hit at Liverpool St. and a *school* demolished at London wall. I believe

---

[13] "A Mother," Letter to the editor, *Times*, 18 June 1917.
[14] Bradford Leslie, Letter to the editor, *Times*, 18 June 1917.
[15] "Air Reprisals Petition," *Times*, 23 June 1917.
[16] See discussion of this proposal in Commons, 28 June 1917, in TNA HO 45/11198.
[17] IWM, Department of Documents, Papers of M F Gower (88/25/2), Maurice Gower, Letter to Flo [Gower], 8 June 1917.

that accounts for most of the casualties, as they are chiefly children."
She added that her daughter "Edie's nerves are a bit shaken.... I tell her
she will have *some* experiences to tell her grandchildren. She says she
would prefer to be without the experience."[18] Other civilians, such as
Edie Bennett writing to her husband, Edwin, who was serving in the
army, expressed anxiety more directly: "I don't seem to have the heart
to get things ready the day raids have taken all the go out of me. I feel to
nervous to go out shopping even now & Grace wants me to go & see her
next week one day & Im afraid to go dear."[19]

The June raids also led to renewed discussion of what to do to warn
the civilian population of an air raid's approach. Responding to a query
from Warwick Brookes (the MP representing Tower Hamlets in London's
East End), Home Secretary Sir George Cave stated that while it had not
previously been government policy to give warnings of aerial attack, a
shift in strategy was now under consideration, especially the idea of finding a mechanism via the Board of Education to ensure that warnings were
issued to schools.[20] The popular mood seemed now more inclined toward
the issuing of public warnings. Additionally, in a piece published on 24
June, the *Weekly Dispatch* surveyed a variety of public figures about
how they would respond if warned of an air raid. Politicians such as MP
Ronald McNeill and Sir George Greenwood replied that they would certainly seek cover and "stop indoors," and they both supported the idea of
issuing warnings. So too did Maude Royden, a suffragist, described in the
paper as "the Woman Preacher," who referred to the tragic, recent raids,
saying that "the women of Poplar demand that they shall be warned in
case of impending air raids!" In contrast, several other women such as
Baroness Percy de Worms feared that "warnings would do more harm
than good. They would keep people in a state of apprehension," and
Mrs. Belloc Lowndes, the novelist, concurred, "I fear that the effect on
the nerves would be very bad." For some, children became the overarching reason for issuing warnings. The wife of Admiral Da Costa echoed
Royden's reference to the Poplar school disaster, saying that she would
"sacrifice a great deal to prevent the recurrence of the school disaster in
the East End." Lady Huntington suggested that schools be warned and

[18] IWM, Department of Documents, Papers of E Fernside (92/49/1), Elizabeth Fernside,
Letter to Fred Fernside, 14 June 1917. Emphasis in the original.

[19] IWM, Department of Docuents, Papers of E S Bennett (96/3/1), Edie Bennett, Letter to
Edwin S Bennett, 27 June 1917. As was the case in previous chapters, quotations from
the letters and diaries have been left uncorrected and unmodified.

[20] Sir George Cave, *Parliamentary Debates – Commons*, 18 June 1917, vol. 94, col. 1415.

children provided with "special bomb-proof shelters," while the "rest of us" accept that we "cannot altogether expect to escape acts of war now the air is invadable territory."[21]

June's daylight raid further prompted leading officials from metropolitan London to meet with the home secretary and urge a new system of public warnings.[22] In private, not all local leaders agreed. The mayor of Islington, George Elliott, wrote to the Home Office on 26 June that "one has only to remember the unfortunate and prejudicial effect upon health, especially in the case of delicate women, that the general warnings would undoubtedly create ... for one to realise that much evil would probably result by needlessly causing disturbance."[23] Elliott was echoing the sentiments of several officials within the government, such as Sir Edward Henry, who still believed that public warnings would adversely affect the ability of police to take action and would encourage "women," for instance, "to leave work and make off home," creating further problems of congestion on public transport and dislocation of factory work.[24] A thick file in the records of the Home Office reveals that many ordinary citizens, both men and women, were weighing in as to the best type of warning or whether a warning was desirable at all.[25]

There remained a consistent concern for the detrimental effects on women, in particular, of air raid warnings. Many in public and private assumed that women were more likely to panic, some women themselves fretted about "nerves," and as the testimony of Edie Bennett suggests, raids could and did have an deleterious effect on ordinary women (as they surely did on men). On the other hand, when, after a short lull, airplane raids returned to London on 7 July with deadly effect, media coverage again insisted on the fact that the raid "caused no panic; the people in the bombed area behaved extremely well, and the comparatively low casualty list can in a great measure be attributed to the coolness and

---

[21] "'What I Should Do If I Were Warned About an Air Raid,'" *Weekly Dispatch*, 24 June 1917. Maude Royden's postwar anti-militarist and feminist activity was significant; see Johanna Alberti, *Beyond Suffrage: Feminists in War and Peace, 1914–1928* (Basingstoke, 1989), and Jill Liddinton, *The Long Road to Greenham: Feminism and Anti-Militarism in Britain since 1820* (London, 1989).

[22] See "Air Raid Warning," *Times*, 22 June 1917, and reports of teachers in the metropolitan district also asking for special warnings and assistance for schools in *Times*, 23 June 1917.

[23] George Elliott, Mayor of Islington, Letter to Sir George Cave [Home Secretary], 26 June 1917, TNA HO 45/11197.

[24] Sir Edward Henry quoted in memorandum, "Public Warning at Approach of Hostile Aircraft by Day," 11 June 1917, TNA HO 45/11197.

[25] See letters c. 1917 in TNA HO 45/11197.

wisdom shown in taking cover." The most vivid emotion was disappointment and anger at German "impudence."[26] Women were also capable of calm and resolute heroism. The worry that they might be more afraid than men and more likely to panic was contradicted, at least in a number of public accounts, by their actions.

A soldier on leave, serving as a special correspondent for the *Times*, provided a gripping firsthand account of the 7 July raid: "To come to London from the Western front on a hard-earned holiday of 10 days and find oneself still in the battle zone is a strange experience. It is an experience that befell many officers and other ranks on leave in London on Saturday morning."[27] This soldier described his wonderment at seeing so many German planes sweep over the city despite their sinister task, and as a result, he ducked into a district railway station, "just as I would have done in the subsidiary line in front of the Messines Ridge." The station did not seem safe enough, so he went into a train, where "the ticket girl must have thought me anything but a brave soldier. But even a soldier does not want to get killed on holiday in London." When he left the station, he found everyone looking up – "again the scene reminded me of the battle front in Flanders," and eventually, after surveying some of the damage, his thoughts turned to reprisals. He claimed that most soldiers want to finish the job in the field and "not kill helpless women and children," but the experience of the raid on London had made him rethink this. He urged civilians to refuse to be terrorized and instead to be all the more determined to resist ending the war "prematurely." Finally, he called upon non-combatants to take cover, something that soldiers could not always do, "but there is no earthly reason why civilians in a city" should subject themselves to unnecessary risk.[28] This soldier returned from battle to find battle waging at home, and he urged his fellow Britons both to be cautious and to hold on.

Once again, the *Times* weighed in with an editorial, warning on 9 July that the latest raid "has produced much anger in the public mind, and the Government must be prepared to face widespread indignation." It stated categorically that the complaints of Londoners "do not arise from fear, and the universal testimony is that the population as a whole remained singularly calm. The instinctive feeling of the people of London rather seems to be that such attacks are a humiliation." It then urged the

[26] "Air Raid on London," *Times*, 9 July 1917.
[27] "Germans' Biggest Air Exploit: London on the Battle Front, *Times*, 9 July 1917.
[28] "Germans' Biggest Air Exploit."

FIGURE 3.1. Soldiers and civilians clear rubble from a building hit during an airplane raid on London, 7 July 1917. Home Office photograph. Reproduced by permission of the Imperial War Museum.

creation of a standardized means of warning London of an approaching attack, a better air defense, and a recognition of the new reality of strategic air bombing as a means of waging war.[29]

Another flurry of letters to the editors of various newspapers after this raid also raised the question of adequate defense and of how to regard civilian casualties. A letter signed "Watchman" said that the government must hold firm in not altering procedures to defend London if this would leave troops vulnerable in France: "It is stated to-day that 37 persons were killed and 141 wounded in this latest raid. I would ask my fellow-townsmen to consider seriously how much better this is than if the 20 aeroplanes which raided London on Saturday last, had been employed

---

[29] "The Bombing of London," *Times*, 9 July 1917.

behind our lines ... and had killed and wounded an equal, or even a much smaller, number of soldiers. It may be a very shocking and disgusting thing deliberately to kill civilians; but lives of civilians are much less valuable in time of war than those of soldiers." It concluded by urging the government not to waste "precious" resources on defending London – "[a]fter all our soldiers in France are bombed and shelled most days in the week: surely London can stand being bombed now and again."[30]

A letter the following day objected to this core argument, the writer pointing out that the "loss of 37 killed and 141 wounded among our ranks in France causes infinitely less effect than that of as many unarmed and unprotected citizens in the capital of the Empire... the ultimate aim of the enemy. London is now on the battlefront and undefended."[31] It was thus crucial for military reasons to defend the capital, since its fall could lead to the end of the war. Other writers argued ever more forcefully that it was also crucial that Britain retaliate in kind.[32]

After this second set of daylight raids in early July 1917, some ordinary civilians communicated their own perspective on air raids and their capacity to hold on. Elizabeth Fernside, for instance, could still joke as she asked her soldier-son if he knew of a safe place for the family: "We have had enough of London and it is evidently *safer* where you are.... This time I saw all the fun and strange to say, did not feel the least frightened. It was too exciting." She compared the fleet of planes to "a swarm of pigeons" and added, "(Putney looks as if the suffragettes had been at their pranks. Our guns have played havoc with the windows)."[33] Despite this sense of excitement and even dismissal, later that summer she wrote of her desire to find new employment away from the city due to her seventeen-year-old daughter's "nervous strain" caused by the raids. She continued: "We are anxious for her to leave the City for she gets in such a nervous state when the Huns visit us. The night before last (Tuesday) she came into our bed when the bombs began to fall. Most of the people got up & went into the streets. Thats how they take cover!"[34]

[30] Watchman, Letter to the editor, *Times*, 9 July 1917.

[31] A. J. C., Letter to the editor, *Times*, 10 July 1917. These letters cite the latest casualties, which would eventually rise to 55 dead and 190 wounded; see the Official Return of Casualties printed as "Air and Sea Raids on Great Britain," *Times*, 13 Jan. 1919, and "Record of Bombardments," vols. 1 and 2, TNA HO 45/10783.

[32] See Dum Spiro Spero and Charles Bright, Letters to the editor, *Times*, 10 July 1917.

[33] IWM, Department of Documents, Papers of E Fernside (92/49/1), Elizabeth Fernside, Letter to Fred Fernside, 9 July 1917. Emphasis in the original.

[34] IWM, Department of Documents, Papers of E Fernside (92/49/1), Elizabeth Fernside, Letter to Fred Fernside, 6 Sept. 1917. She also reports the news that not a single pane of glass in Charing Cross Hospital (filled with soldiers) was left intact after the raid.

While Fernside was worn down by repeated raids, other women writing to their men in uniform were deeply upset from the start. Edie Bennett began a letter to her husband Edwin, known as Welsh, on 7 July as follows:

> I am not writing much as I feel so terribly shaken up, but thank God we are all safe
>
> no doubt you will read all about it before you get this.... Well darling such a sight I've never seen & hope not to again talk about a swarm of birds wasn't in it
>
> they were all over us in less than 10 min. & no warning was given whatever & I never thought Ruby & I would be alive now
>
> I wished you good bye dearest with dear little Ruby clenched in my arms with Winnie & mum was at work
>
> Oh Welsh this life is shocking & the damage done is outrageous....
>
> I thought to myself while it was on I shall die alone after all but still God was good to me & spared us both.

Bennett signed the letter from your "Unhappy Wife & Baby."[35]

A few days letter, she had not recovered:

> God knows how long we shall be on this earth, if only I could see you once more before we are parted for ever yes for ever. Im sure, dear little Ruby & I will be taken from you in one of these terrible raids which are getting worse every time & we are absolutely undefended as you have read
>
> Oh darling this life is getting too terrible for words & ones nerves cannot stand much more. When I shut my eyes can see those huge things like great blackbirds right over us ... coming all directions to London....
>
> So dearest you can see we had a warm time & they promise us another & God help us next time for we are absolutely beaten & no warning whatever. Baby & I stood in the passage clenched tightly together expecting the last of our lives. So should anything happen any time your address is stuck on the Wall so someone is sure to wire you & every hour we do not know but what will be our last.... I assure you I am quite prepared & ready to meet our Supreme Father when he calls dear Ruby & I so dont think I have any fear, but should like once more to see you. Oh this wicked war will it ever end.[36]

---

[35] IWM, Department of Documents, Papers of E S Bennett Collection (96/3/1), Edie Bennett to Edwin S. Bennett, 7 July 1917.

[36] IWM, Department of Documents, Papers of E S Bennett Collection (96/3/1), Edie Bennett to Edwin S. Bennett, 9 July 1917.

A short while later, she was trying to reassure her husband that there was no point in trying to find a safer place to go, "as they seem to be making for places that never knew anything befor." She complains of "feeling so queer I suppose its the raids" and that "life seems just one misery night & day & for ever in fear, but there I suppose we must try & keep smileing for your dear sake."[37] Edie Bennett had absorbed the message that she ought to remain calm, cheerful, and resolute for the sake of her soldier-husband, but the letters convey all too well the terror she felt huddling with her baby beneath the bombs.

Later that month, the *Lancet* discussed civilian responses to raids in an essay entitled "Air Raid Psychology." It drew a distinction between the reactions of individuals and those of crowds, but asserted that fear or excitement were entirely natural:

> When, therefore, without warning, a bomb drops from the blue in a crowded thoroughfare to dash for the nearest shelter is as instinctive an act as for the puppy to hunt the first rabbit that crosses its path. Further, what is strange also excites the instinct of curiosity, which, once aroused, may come into conflict with the other instinct.

Such an explanation of individual reactions drew an explicit connection between the two fronts, suggesting that for specific persons in the bombed areas of the homeland, their "state of nervous fear is not far removed from the 'shell shock' of the firing line." But as for crowds, the *Lancet* claimed that "above all, what has often been regarded as a fundamentally important factor, that of race, is seen *par excellence* in the response of the crowd to stimuli of the character that we have become familiar with since the outbreak of the war.... [W]e believe in the traditional British phlegm, and we think it no exaggeration to assert that our public, as a whole is calm and its conduct exemplary." It predicted that this "racial" trait would serve Britain well in trials of air raids yet to come.[38]

Such pronouncements of widespread "British phlegm" did little to halt the public outrage that followed the daylight London raid, and this

---

[37] IWM, Department of Documents, Papers of E S Bennett Collection (96/3/1), Edie Bennett to Edwin S. Bennett, 12 July 1917.

[38] "Air Raid Psychology," *Lancet*, 14 July 1917. I have also found at least one infanticide case in the London Central Criminal Court that was blamed on "air raid shock." See Coroner's Depositions, 26 Dec, 1917, in TNA CRIM 1 171/1, and a more detailed discussion of this in Susan R. Grayzel, *Women's Identities at War: Gender, Motherhood, and Politics in Britain and France during the First World War* (Chapel Hill, NC, 1999), ch. 1.

outcry prompted the prime minister to call a special, secret session of the Commons to discuss air defense. Before the session began, members of Parliament raised the issue of public warnings, with Sir Frederick Banbury promoting a warning system and Sir William Pearce pointing to "his own experience in a working-class district" to argue against such warnings for fear that they would cause agitation and interrupt business, especially in cases where the raids did not then materialize.[39] The *Times* urged the government to issue warnings, to "yield to a demand which is now widespread and almost overwhelming," as it emphasized the lack of disruption caused by Saturday's attack and the lack of "panic and disorder" that ensued.[40] An interim system to deliver warnings was announced by the commissioner of the Metropolitan Police, Sir Edward Henry in mid-July; at the news of an impending air raid, police constables would proceed into the streets carrying signs that read, "Police Notice Take Cover." This was clearly a short-term solution, for by the end of July 1917, the government announced that clear, audible public warnings would be given.

The new use of public warnings received fairly extensive publicity, and inhabitants of the "home front" continued almost universally to be portrayed as reacting calmly to the new warnings, even when they proved to be false alarms. The *Manchester Guardian* stated that "people behaved very well, and there was not much panic, although naturally the crushing of women into insufficient shelter created much excitement."[41] The *Daily Telegraph* concurred that people reacted easily and speedily in both the East End and West End.[42] Other accounts distinguished the "correct" behavior of some groups, such as men and native Britons, over others, namely women and foreigners: "[T]he alarm among women and children in some districts was considerable.... There was considerable alarm among the friendly foreigner population of the East End. They rushed from the side streets of Whitechapel, Spitalfields, and Aldgate in droves to seek cover."[43]

---

[39] Accounts and quote taken from "Commons and Air Raid," *Times*, 10 July 1917. For more details, see also "The Air Raids," *Times*, 10 July 1917.

[40] "Parliament and the Air Raid"

[41] *Manchester Guardian*, 17 July 1917, press cutting in TNA HO 45/11197.

[42] "Air Raid Warning," *Daily Telegraph*, 16 July 1917, press cutting in TNA HO 45/11197.

[43] "False Warning, *Daily Mail*, 16 July 1917, press cutting in TNA HO 45/11197. Accounts of tests of sirens and smoke bombs in the *Times* on 18 and 19 July 1917, respectively, suggest that the government was still experimenting with the best method of public notification.

The state was clearly trying to manage public reaction to air raids and the large-scale loss of life in the June and July attacks. On 16 July, the Local Government Board announced that it was granting immediate relief to victims of air raids equivalent to military separation allowances. It provided a certain amount for each adult (sixteen shillings for each of the first two adult victims) and children (seven shillings for the first child, five for the next two children, and three for any additional children). The measure also authorized additional maintenance in cases where a "bread-winner has been killed or rendered physically unfit for work," funds toward the replacement of "essential articles of furniture" for poorer families, and payment toward funeral expenses of up to nine pounds per case.[44] In addition to financial aid designed to prevent resentment and hardship resulting from the raids' casualties, the government gave notice of two sound signals, one that would indicate that citizens should "take cover" and the other an "all clear."[45]

Yet the issuing of public warnings met with reactions that contradicted the media accounts. A letter from Frank Karstake of Hampstead to the home secretary, Sir George Cave, on 24 July 1917 described his reaction to hearing the audible warning of a raid that never materialized:

> I was shaking all over; not from fright but from nervousness at the thought that here was another Air Raid and that at any moment a bomb might destroy our house, together with my wife and family.... We are not the kind of people who lose our heads and fly in the face of Regulations; so we did what we were told to do, viz. remained under cover.

He continued by recording the panic of others at the warning and noted that "I think the real thing bad enough without being frightened by a simulation of it in advance, thus unstringing our nerves and making us unfit to stand the real Raid. And the newspapers are assuring us that the population took it 'calmly!' ... [I] am not excitable, but I *am* nervous, and if the Government wish to kill all the nervous inhabitants of London they are going the right way about it by giving bomb 'warnings.'"[46] Karstake's reaction may be an unusual one, but it raises an interesting and privately voiced objection to what by 1917 was an emerging consensus about appropriate public responses to air raids. If any members of the public were susceptible to panic, it had been assumed that these would be

---

[44] "Air Raid Grants," *Times*, 16 July 1917.
[45] "Air Raid Warnings," *Times*, 27 July 1917.
[46] Frank Karstake, Letter to Sir George Cave, Home Secretary, 24 July 1917, in TNA HO 45/11197.

women (or women and children) or some foreign element abiding in the
East End, not "nervous" men such as Karstake living in leafy, suburban
Hampstead.

Some men responded not only with worry, but also with indignation
to attacks at home. Jim Sams, a member of the armed forces writing on
16 July to his family in Hackney, recorded hearing that:

> you have been haveing a hot time in London with air raids. We heard you
> had one last Sat week and what they had done a lot of damage … and
> that they drop some near St Pauls, but did not know for sure, so you can
> bet I was get worry untill i had a letter from Mabel which I got the same
> time as yours, she told me what they passed over her place she said they
> loke like a swarm of birds in the sky.… I think it is about time some-
> thing was done to try and put a stop to them getting over.[47]

When he wrote home less than a month later, he expressed his frustration
more clearly: "i don't wonder but you haveing no nerves left, it get on my
nerves to think that the men are giveing there lives to protect the women
and children. while them at home do nothing to stop them d—d things
from coming over, it's very nice to read that after 3 years war we have not
enough aircraft to defend them, it make me sick to think of it."[48] Not only
were civilians frustrated by the state's impotence in light of aerial attacks,
but so too were men in arms.

The next set of summertime raids fell on the coast, in Essex, Suffolk,
Kent, and Dover. Not until 4 and 5 September did bombing raids hit
London again in a so-called moonlight raid, which inflicted only "slight
damage."[49] Other attacks occurred in quick succession from 24 September
until 2 October. The *Times* felt obliged to remind its readers that people
should take shelter and "not risk life or limb to gratify their curiosity." It
noted the increased use of Tube (or underground) stations as shelters and
that "we believe steps are about to be taken to regulate their use during
raids."[50] Accounts of the damage suggested that "Londoners were fairly
calm during the attack, though it would be ridiculous to say they were
unperturbed."[51] The last of these successive raids caused some damage,
but not enough to halt a performance of "Tristan and Isolde" in Drury

---

[47] IWM, Department of Documents, Papers of J Sams (02/55/1), Jim Sams, Letter to parents, 16 July 1917. As indicated earlier, spelling and grammar has been left uncorrected.
[48] IWM, Department of Documents, Papers of J Sams (02/55/1), Jim Sams, Letter to parents, 5–6 Aug. 1917.
[49] "The Moonlight Air Raid," 6 Sept. 1817, and "London Damage Slight," *Times*, 6 July 1917.
[50] "The Air Raids," *Times*, 26 Sept. 1917.
[51] "Another Air Raid," *Times*, 26 Sept. 1917

Lane.[52] Pleas to Londoners to stay calm emanated from the pulpit as well, as the bishop of London offered his "thoughts during an air raid," urging his listeners "to show the fortitude and courage which our fathers, sons, brothers, and friends show under far greater dangers every day and night."[53]

Behind the scenes, the government was busily making plans to deal with both old and new problems emerging from these London raids. First, it decided to extend the system of warnings in place for daytime raids to nighttime raids, and then it came up with a more organized plan for using some eighty-six underground stations as shelters, requiring that staff members at each station open it when a warning was given and that lighting be provided for those taking shelter.[54] It also addressed the issue of "air raid refugees," dealing with reports (and complaints) from neighboring districts of London about how to cope with "the arrival of large numbers of persons who are desirous of residing, or at least sleeping out of London during the prevalence of Air Raids."[55]

Firsthand accounts of this set of raids contained a variety of responses, but several women stressed their desire to be stoic and accept that these attacks were now the realities of wartime life, even for civilians. Writing to her father from London on 25 September, Celia Croft described "a tremendous raid last night, at least it seemed tremendous because they came so much nearer to me personally than they have ever done before." When another raid struck a few days later, she again wrote, "We have just been having the dickens of a time, but though the noise was pretty bad it was not so terrific as last night."[56] Lilah Morrison-Bell, the wife of a prisoner of war and the mother of a young girl, described being caught up in the raid near King's Cross station in London with her daughter: "It really was rather awful, though I never felt the least frightened, only very excited and interested, but I was afraid all the time for the effects of it on

[52] "Wagner in an Air Raid," *Times*, 2 Oct. 1917.

[53] "Thoughts During a Raid," *Times*, 1 Oct. 1917. Here is an instance where civilians' potential equivalance to soldiers is denied rather than stressed.

[54] See memorandum, "Tubes as Shelters," 9 Nov. 1917, TNA HO 45/ 11198. A number of files in this dossier deal with warning systems in the fall of 1917; see especially the Cabinet memorandum of 26 Oct. 1917. An article publicizing the warnings at night can be found in "Raid Warnings at Night," *Times*, 29 Oct. 1917.

[55] See correspondence from Walton-Upon-Thames Urban District Council and Home Office, 2 Oct. 1917 (source of quote), 18 Oct. 1917, and 3 November 1917, TNA HO 45/ 11198.

[56] IWM, Department of Documents, Papers of C G Knollys (94/10/1), Celia Croft Knollys, Letter to father [Mr. Croft], 25 and 30 Sept. 1917.

her, & then too one felt so sorry for all the poor people around who were
in *terror*. It is rubbish to say London isn't in a panic, but I suppose by the
end of this winter they will no longer be, as we shall all be so used to it!"
Despite reporting women who fainted beside her and other traumas of
the raid, she closed her letter by stating that "when one thinks that night
of horror is what the people at the front go through *hourly*, it makes one
feel ashamed to make any fuss."[57]

Some soldiers were inclined to agree with her. South African Lieutenant
Brian Wade was lying wounded in a London hospital during the
September–October raids and wrote home to his mother about them:

> The air raids have lent a bit of excitement each evening I've been here....
> One can hear the drone of the Hun engines quite distinctly during lulls
> in the firing. They dropped some bombs about a mile away; we could
> hear them gradually getting closer & closer – quite exciting. The civil-
> ians seem to be properly scared at having death so near them, but I've
> no sympathy for them (except the women & children) as the aver-
> age middle class Londoner has been getting fat on the war & letting
> other people shed their blood for him.... [A] taste of shell-fire will do
> them good.[58]

Here, a soldier expressed his approval of the bombing of middle-class
civilian men (although not women and children); he was glad that adult
male civilians were experiencing the horrors of war and thus finally and
justly sharing what the soldiers faced.

Others serving in the military continued to be increasingly upset by the
idea of civilians being under fire, especially their families. Jim Sams wrote
again to his family after these raids that he was "glad to hear that you are
all quite safe after the raids." He heard from his sister Mabel "what you
have had a very warm time of it," and continued:

---

[57] IWM, Department of Documents, Papers of Clive Morrison-Bell (91/12/1), Mrs. [Lilah]
Morrison-Bell, Letter to mother, 3 Oct. 1917. Emphasis in original.
[58] IWM, Department of Documents, Letters of F B Wade (98/34/1), [Frederick] Brian Wade,
Letter to mother, 1 Oct. 1917. He added that one of his visitors "Mr Ford is awfully
nervous & should not be as he had a jolly good cellar under his house." Some immediate postwar accounts of the war were similarly scathing about civilians and air raids.
In Philip Gibb's 1919 (revised 1929) *Realities of War*, he sums up the English soldiers'
view as follows: "The soldier listened to excited tales of air-raids. A bomb had fallen in
the next street. The windows had been broken. Many people had been killed in a house
somewhere in Hackney. It was frightful.... The soldier on leave saw crowds of people
taking shelter in underground railways, working-men among them, sturdy lads, panic-
stricken. But for his own wife and children, he had an evil sense of satisfaction in these
sights. It would do them good. They would know what war meant – just a little.... An
air-raid? Lord God, did they know what a German barrage was like?" (339).

[T]hey have upset her nerves and haveing two little ones to look after, do not make them any better, and i don't wonder at it. for it is enough to make anybody feel bad. My pal had a letter from his brother he was on leave from the front and he was in London while the raids was on, he said what he was d—d glad to get back here again, so i can guess what it was like.... sometimes i think we are being sold in regards to air raids, for ... it is allways the poor people that cop it, for you never hear of any of the big people getting knock over by them. it makes me mad to think that after three years of war, we are just as far advanced agains stoping them as we was when we first started. its very nice for the men out here to know that they have give up everything to come out here to guard there wifes and little ones, and that they are slowly being done to death by them German Dogs, and that they can come and go just when they like.[59]

Sams expressed both class resentment and the frustration of men in uniform being unable to stop the enemy from attacking their families and homes. His rage comes palpably through his letters, revealing something very unlike the calm with which Britons were meant to face the raids.

Stoic representations of civilians, particularly those of women, continued to be part of the stock images of post-raid journalism. An article in the *Spectator* on air raids noted that the people of London were able to accept the small risk posed by the raids "quietly as a point of pride and honour."[60] Another discussion of "Air Raid Psychology" in the *Lancet* stated confidently that based on the responses to the recent attacks it was clear that "growing bravery ... has become a feature of our psychology."[61] As a *Punch* cartoon of October 1917 indicated, such bravery could produce other "reasonable" responses to air power. It showed a "Stout lady (discussing the best thing to do in an air-raid): 'Well, I always runs about meself. You see, as my 'usband sez, an' very reasonable too, a movin' target is more difficult to 'it." While it makes fun of this working-class woman's naïveté, the caricature also suggests that fundamentally Britons of all sexes and classes would not be intimidated by air raids. However, the underlying issue also remains that neither could they defend themselves. If the best advice is to keep moving, then there is no real protection.

---

[59] IWM, Department of Documents, Papers of J Sams (02/55/1), Jim Sams, Letter to parents, mid-October [undated] 1917. Sams noted in a letter of 23 October that one of his letters to his brother Tom had been returned to him because it contained "some remarks that should not be there, i expect it is about the air raids."

[60] "Topics of the Day," *Spectator*, 6 Oct. 1917.

[61] "Air-Raid Psychology and Air-Raid Perils," *Lancet*, 6 Oct. 1917. This essay is also discussed in Lee Kennett, *The First Air War, 1914–1918* (New York, 1991), 62.

The actual movement of the civilian population, particularly that of the poorer classes, during these nighttime raids caused some concern for the government. It issued instructions to the press at the end of September: "The natural fear of the consequences of air raids has been greatly increased by the statements recently published in some newspapers describing the crowding of the underground railways and kindred matters and a very urgent appeal is made to the Press to refrain from publishing anything which might add to ... the feeling of apprehension which is already prevalent specially amongst the poorest and most ignorant classes of the people of London."[62] The government applauded the work of newly created volunteer Air Raid Committees, "whose duty it is on the occasion of air raids to warn the residents and, so far as possible, ensure their taking cover under circumstances of personal convenience and public advantage.... In some of the poorer districts, they even provide cocoa for the old and very young.... They are doing most useful work ... guaranteeing that on the occasion of any future air raids the utmost efforts will be locally forthcoming to ensure order, tranquility and public safety." The voluntary (rather than state-sponsored) nature of these practical responses to air raids also indicates how unprepared the government was to respond adequately to this new warfare.[63]

Behind the scenes, the government was investigating the death of ten-week-old Lillian Alice Trower, who died the night of 2–3 October during an air raid. According to her mother, the child was nursed sometime during the night of the attack and found dead and cold at 6 A.M. A post-mortem revealed "acute inflammation of the whole of the lungs ... caused by some irritant gas, which caused death by suffocation." An inquest found that her death was "caused by irritant gases caused by bombs dropped from enemy aircraft at Shoreditch during the night of 1 October 1917." The possibility of a shift in bombing that included chemical weapons caused further inquiry. However, prolonged investigation by New Scotland Yard concluded that "many houses were hit and gas mains damaged, and it is not impossible that the child may have been thus affected." Thus, while the baby could still be considered a casualty of war, she was not the victim, as initially feared, of aerially delivered gas or of chemical warfare.[64]

---

[62] Memorandum to the Press, 28 Sept. 1917, TNA HO 45/11198.
[63] Memorandum to Sir George Cave, 29 Nov. 1917, TNA HO 45/11198.
[64] See file on "Air Raid Casualty," inquest, 4 Oct. 1917, and New Scotland Yard Report, 3 Nov. 1917, TNA HO 45/10883.

Still, the continuation of regular air raids produced other deadly consequences; a raid on London in early November 1917 killed a father and his
twelve-year-old son while injuring his wife and daughters and prompted
renewed outrage.[65] Ethel Bilbrough was quick to condemn the enemy:
"The cowardly wickedness of such raids is almost incredible; to think of
defenceless innocent women and children, and old men and boys being
ruthlessly murdered and mutilated by these devils in the air is unspeakably
horrible. But as someone said the other day, 'There are no civilians now,
we are all soldiers.' Still, soldiers have the power to *hit back*, but what
chance have poor frightened folk in their beds?"[66] Again, this suggests
an awareness that while the "home front" was now a war zone, those at
home had no way to take action, which made it seemingly worse.

An additional aspect of the trauma and impact of raids that witnesses
discussed was their aural effect. By 1917 the sounds of air raids were
readily distinguished, as Virginia Woolf noted in her diary on 20 October:
"We heard two soft distant but unmistakable shocks about 9.30; then a
third which shook the window, then silence. It turns out that a Zeppelin
came over, hovered unseen for an hour or two & left."[67] In her diary entry
for 6 December of the same year, Woolf records taking shelter from an air
raid at 5 A.M., being struck by the noise, and how "having trained one's
ear to listen one can't get them not to for a time."[68] Woolf was describing
an attack by twenty-five planes. The final attack of 1917 on London and
Essex involved fewer planes but did more damage. Its victims included
"Elsie Bates, a nurse, home on leave from France suffering from shell-
shock, who was struck on the head by a splinter of a bomb" and killed.[69]

Other, more public accounts of the behavior of women celebrated a
female heroism that came not from indifference to danger but from stoicism in its face. Here, for example, is a report on the destruction in
London in December 1917:

> In a poor district five bombs dropped within 200 yards, two of them ...
> [on] a philanthropic organisation's shelter and work premises.... Some
> 1300 people were sheltering....

[65] Details about the victims are given in "Victims of Air Raid," *Times*, 3 Nov. 1917.
[66] IWM, Department of Documents, Papers of E M Bilbrough (90/10/1), Ethel Bilbrough,
Diary, 4 Nov. 1917. Emphasis in original.
[67] Virginia Woolf, *The Diary of Virginia Woolf*, vol. 1: *1915–1919*, ed. Anne Olivier Bell
(New York, 1977), 63.
[68] Woolf, *The Diary of Virginia Woolf*, 85.
[69] See "Morning Raid on London," *Times*, 7 Dec. 1917; "The Attack on London," *Times*,
20 Dec. 1917; and "Air Raid Inquests," *Times*, 24 Dec. 1917.

> The man in charge said ... 'One young lady was a real brick.... She
> bandaged about 40 people ... [and] pacified the women and children
> although the guns were still going.'[70]

While such a description might not differ if a nurse or indeed a soldier
were being shelled overseas, the fact that such actions occurred in working-class London altered the perception of those who faced them. A letter
written to Lieutenant William Hooper from his wife in Croydon reassured him that she and their children had weathered the raids: "I did not
write last Evening as there was an air raid & some commotion. The kid-
dies had not got to bed. The gun fire started at 6–45 and kept going till
9–30 but we are all quite o.k."[71]

A war in which wives could tell their distant soldier-husbands about
gunfire while putting the children to bed was one in which the borders
between the fronts had dramatically shifted. The reactions of civilians in
public and private to the more devastating raids of 1917 reveal a growing consensus not only about what the correct response should be – stoic,
cheerful acceptance, lack of panic – but also who could express it. The
limits to such a new civil identity can be found in efforts to distinguish
which groups did not have what it took to do their bit.

THE BRAVERY OF "OUR OWN PEOPLE"

A particularly nationalistic overtone to depictions of civilian behavior
permeated discussions of air raids by the winter of 1918. In response
to a written question in Parliament on 1 February 1918, Sir George
Cave insisted that the "regrettable loss of life" due to panic "among
some aliens in the East End" was no reason to change the nature of
warnings.[72] Implied was the idea that panic at this point was something
exhibited only by specific groups. A further articulation of a belief in
the limited nature of stoicism and bravery emerged in a rather detailed
and celebratory account of London under attack, *Records of the Raids*,

---

[70] See *South London Press*, 21 Dec. 1917. See also "Women Raid Helpers," *Leeds Mercury*,
 15 Dec. 1917, on proposals to train women to look after women and children taking
 refuge during air raids.
[71] IWM, Department of Documents, Papers of W Hooper (Misc. 687), Letter of
 Mrs. William Hooper ["kid"] to "my darling hubby" William Hooper, 19 Dec. 1917.
 The letter concludes with her heart overflowing with gratitude to him and his brave pals
 fighting so those at home may have a "good xmas."
[72] Sir George Cave, *Parliamentary Debates – Commons*, 1 Feb. 1918, vol. 101, cols. 1943–1944.

a pamphlet published by the Church of England in early 1918.[73] This began with a preface dated 8 February 1918, by Francis Lloyd, lieutenant-general overseeing London, extolling the virtues exhibited by those experiencing the raids: "so much courage and so much of the best qualities ... shown by those who can do nothing but sit and suffer and hope to escape" (3).

The document itself singles out for praise the peculiarly stoic characteristics of working-class Londoners – "East-enders have a name for good spirits and ready wit, and they are living up to their reputation" – again emphasizing the bravery of ordinary working-class women and children. In one anecdote, a widowed mother returns to her home in the midst of an ongoing bombardment and finds that "her eldest child, a little girl of seven-and-a-half, had got her four little brothers and sisters out of bed at the beginning of the air raid, had dressed them, brought them downstairs, gathered them all under the kitchen table, had lit a candle, and was reading to them out of the Bible" (21). This calm competence seems especially striking because – after numerous anecdotes detailing the amazing ease with which the raids are faced by other children, including one young girl who sits all night in the ruins with a tiny baby – the pamphlet concludes with a discussion of the contrasting behavior of the "foreign folk."[74] In this recounting of air raids, the stoicism of the "East-enders" became even more apparent when compared with their "alien" co-residents, the Jews, whose "fearfulness is shown particularly in air-raids," a sign of their "Eastern temperament" that "makes them far more subject to alarm than our own people."[75]

This sets out the boundary against which the national (and natural) virtues invoked earlier were set. Such an idea was hardly new, as we have seen in earlier public commentary that asked for reprisals precisely because it was clear that raids would have an effect on any and all Germans due to the visible fear shown by "aliens in the Underground

---

[73] Henry Luke Paget, Bishop of Stepney, *Records of the Raids* (London, 1918). Further references will appear parenthetically in the text.

[74] Paget, *Records of the Raids*, pp. 6, 41, 44. See also the discussion in Chapter 2 of efforts to reassure the Jewish population sent out in 1915.

[75] There is a very brief discussion of anti-Semitism during the First World War, largely with reference to conscription debates, in Anthony Julius, *Trials of the Diaspora: A History of Anti-Semitism in England* (Oxford, 2010); and a more substantive one in Adrian Gregory, *The Last Great War* (Cambridge, 2008), and in David Caesarini, "An Embattled Minority: The Jews in Britain during the First World War," in *The Politics of Marginality: Race, the Radical Right and Minorities in Twentieth Century Britain*, ed. Tony Kushner and Kenneth Lunn (London, 1990).

railway" during raids (in contrast to the behavior of native Britons).[76] Rumors of the behavior of the immigrant and Jewish populations during the January raids even reached soldiers. Jim Sams wrote to his sister and her husband on 17 February that:

> i am very please to hear what you are all quite safe after haveing the bing boys over two nights running and from what i have heard and read you must have had a very warm time on the monday night.... i also read about a lot of Jews in the East End getting kill[ed], fighting to get into a shelter and the number of young fellows there was in it to that should be in the army, you know i do not wish to see any fellow in the army, but the likes of them i do, well from what i can see of it you are just as safe if you stay in your own place ... you take a risk of getting hit while you are making for the shelters, as you say it's the innocent people who suffer, it was allways the same and allways will be, but i will say no more about it in case i go to far.[77]

Such sentiments could foster resentment against certain groups, and this could become dangerous for the unity required to continue the war effort.

The winter raids after so many years of war seemed especially hard to take, even for "true" Britons. Ethel Bilbrough's diary finds her trying to knit her way through the raid of 28 January, but to no avail. When she retired "raid-racked" early in the morning, she lay awake "thinking of all the horrors those fiendish Gotha's had accomplished in their hellish night's work. The papers said 58 were killed and about 200 injured, but they keep things back." She concluded by focusing on a particular aspect of raids that others like Woolf had emphasized, the lingering effects of the sounds of the attack: "Apart from any personal fear during these hateful raids, one cannot help feeling *sick* with apprehension as to what is going on ... *some*where all the while one listens to the incessant booming of the guns.... And for nights afterwards the sound seems to recur, and it eats into one's brain in the still hours of the night; however much one may fight against it."[78]

One public portrayal of the winter raids of 1918 tried to adopt a more comic tone. Journalist Max Pemberton entitled a piece about one of the night raids "Tube-ee or Not Tube-ee" and proceeded to inform his

---

[76] Henry Morris, Letter to the editor, *Times*, 3 Oct. 1917.

[77] IWM, Department of Documents, Papers of J Sams (02/55/1), Jim Sams, Letter to Maud and Alf, 17 Feb. 1918.

[78] IWM, Department of Documents, IWM, Papers of E M Bilbrough (90/10/1), Ethel Bilbrough, Diary, 28 Jan. 1918. She adds that "a powerful imagination is a tiresome thing to have!" as if this alone accounts for why the raids haunt and disturb her.

readers that every Tube station in which the inhabitants of London take shelter has a particular quality to it. For "London is a thousand miles from being scared by any air raid nowadays, but it is very proper that nervous and delicate women should be encouraged to put themselves in a place of safety if they can." Yet if shelters were for delicate women, the bravery of other women was also made evident by the raids. As a policeman informs him, he will know when it is a bad raid only when the bus girls "leave their buses" and take shelter. The scene underground is "picturesque enough.... Tired women sleep upon the stones but they smile at you when they wake. The children are in all attitudes." It was a peaceful "concourse of all nationalities, old and young, rich and poor," waiting for the raid (and perhaps the war) to end.[79]

The raids of late January did some damage, but all was relatively quiet both before and after a series of attacks on 7–8 March. It was during this set of raids that Lena Guilbert Ford, the author of the lyrics to the immensely popular song "Keep the Homes Fires Burning" and her son Walter were killed in London. Despite two bombs falling on her home, which then collapsed, Mrs. Ford's eighty-six-year-old mother was saved by the family's maid, Annie Coxall. Whatever irony or poignancy was entailed by the author of the song celebrating the quiet stoicism of the home front through an image of home fires burning dying from a direct hit by a bomb – another kind of home fire burning – the death of Lena Ford raised further legal questions. The attorney of her former husband, Walter Ford, from whom she was divorced, shocked the inquest by demanding to know whether Ford's estranged wife or his son had died first; for if his son had died first, he would then inherit Mrs. Ford's estate.[80]

After a lull, the return of aerial attackers produced one of the most damaging raids of the war on 19–20 May, accounting for 192 dead or injured in London.[81] Even these circumstances could be faced with calm by some inhabitants, but not by everyone. Writing to her air mechanic husband, Dora Stanton began, "It is midnight and a nasty air raid has been in progress since eleven but the children are sleeping peacefully."[82] It was after these raids, in June 1918, that Virginia Woolf recorded her

[79] Max Pemberton, "Tube-ee or Not Tube-ee," [*Daily Sketch?*], 24 Feb. 1918, enclosed in IWM, Department of Documents, Papers of Burford-Hancock (92/22/1), diary of Lady Burford-Hancock.

[80] See coverage in "Mrs. Ford's Estate Raises Knotty Point," *New York Times*, 13 Mar. 1918.

[81] "The Whitsun Air Raid," *Times*, 21 May 1918.

[82] IWM, Department of Documents, Papers of A C Stanton, Dora Stanton, Letter, to Arthur Stanton, 18 May 1918.

feelings of revulsion at the idea that women could be engaged in aerial attacks: "L[eonard] was told the other day that the raids are carried out by women. Women's bodies were found in the wrecked aeroplanes. They are smaller & lighter, & thus leave more room for bombs. Perhaps it is sentimental, but the thought seems to me to add a particular touch of horror."[83] If women could come equally under fire, it only made sense that rumors might circulate that they would equally become full combatants of the new air war – speculation that was in the end false.

The horror invoked by air raids did not diminish with repetition for everyone. A mother of five living in Essex, Annie Purbrook, described air raids in her diary as follows: "Glorious moonlight nights will ever be associated in my mind with these terrible experiences. No sooner has the moon fairly risen ... than our ears are disturbed by the sounds of bombs or guns.... [T]o-night it seems to be all round, gun-fire, shell-fire, little spurts of flame, search lights, bombs dropping, shells screeching. It is devilish, damnable. But language is altogether inadequate to express the wickedness of it all."[84] Such a combination of sights and sounds are reminiscent of battle; they are in fact the sounds of a battle waged at home, one that had made, in Purbrook's words, "one place ... as safe as another for all one can know."[85]

By 1918 the air raids of the war had started to become mythologized in various wartime cultural media. In his 1918 novel, *The Pretty Lady*, Arnold Bennett recorded first the standard, accepted line that civilians under fire greeted the arrival of aerial warfare with "calm" and "stoicism." As Bennett explains, "It was the autumn of 1915.... Zeppelins had raided London and all present ... were aware, from positive comments in the newspapers, that whereas German moral was crumbling, all Londoners, including themselves, had behaved with the most marvelous stoic calm in the ordeal of the Zeppelins."[86] This was wartime heroism incarnate and, apparently, universally possible.

Later in the novel, however, the protagonist experiences a raid directly and does not respond to it with such equanimity:

> A spasm of horrible fright shot through him. He thought, in awe and stupefaction:
> 'A bomb!'

[83] Woolf, *The Diary of Virginia Woolf*, 153.
[84] IWM, Department of Documents, Papers of A Purbrook (97/3/1), Annie Purbrook, Diary typescript, 1918, pp. 15–16,.
[85] Purbrook, Diary typescript, 14.
[86] Arnold Bennett, *The Pretty Lady* (London, 1918), 159–160.

He thought about death and maiming and blood. The relations between him and those everyday males aloft in the sky seemed to be appallingly close. After the explosion perfect silence – no screams, no noise of crumbling – perfect silence, and yet the explosion seemed still to dominate the air! Ears ached and sang. Something must be done. All theories of safety had been smashed to atoms in the explosion....

The earth swayed up and down. The sound alone of the immeasurable cataclysm annihilated the universe. The sound and the concussion transcended what had been conceivable....

He remembered that he had had a stick; he had it no longer. He turned back and, taking from his pocket the electric torch which had lately come into fashion, he examined the road for his stick. The sole object of interest which the torch revealed was a child's severed arm, with a fragment of brown frock on it and a tinsel ring on one of the fingers of the dirty little hand. The blood from the other end had stained the ground.[87]

And here is another, potent way in which the air raid hit home, through apocalyptic images of "annihilated" worlds and the visceral maiming of the innocent – a little girl's severed arm with "tinsel ring" still attached lying in a London street. There is nothing heroic about the incident or the man's reaction. If there is any stoicism, it is only retroactive.

CONCLUSION

The extent to which air raids, despite provoking a range of individual responses, had been domesticated and normalized in daily life by the war's end can be seen in the following account of Armistice Day from the perspective of an eighteen-year-old student. Olive Wells noted: "At 11 o'clock A.M. the guns were fired, the church-bells were rung, the sirens were blown – we did not think of air raids as we would have done any other day."[88] Air raids had become part of the lived experience of this war, as civilians – especially women and children – had been attacked at great distances from the conventional battle zones. As a result, contemporary reactions to the raids revealed the development of a consensus on appropriate "heroic" behavior expected now of women as well as men, and of subjects of all ages. This public image of the exhibition of a stoic virtue that crossed lines of age, class, and gender, if not ethnic (or even national and racial) ones, became commonplace by the last years of the

[87] Bennett, *Pretty Lady*, 230–232.
[88] IWM, Department of Documents, Papers of O Wells (91/5/1), Olive Wells, Diary, 11 Nov. 1918.

war. Fear and anxiety minimized by humor, quiet acceptance, and, ultimately, civilian bravery appeared in both public and private accounts
of the First World War's air raids. So too did denunciations of German
deviance and barbarism in attacking innocent people and places. Old
assumptions about "civilized" war died hard, but it was clear by the war's
end that there was no such thing as an "open" city or a truly protected
status for non-combatants.

It was also the case that the government's responses had to be improvised and that they were largely regarded as ineffective. Yet one of the legacies of the First World War was its bequeathing to the state the new task
of the defending its citizens *at home*. Part of that task would be public,
but the war had further shown that private heroism mattered during the
raids as much as the ability of trained special constables or medical personnel to aid and comfort the civilian population. Official warnings, the
provision of shelters, grants of financial aid, and public sympathy helped
the raids' victims, but there was no getting around the fact that civilians
at home were no longer safe and that the state could never completely
defend the homeland from attack.

War had changed utterly. Under aerial attack, British soldiers at leave
in London could find themselves still in the battle zone. And in the same
city, young mothers could clutch their babies tightly in their arms while
bombs exploded around their homes, wondering if their lives would end.
There was no going back; the trick was how to proceed. What became
especially important for the post-1918 world was not only the "myth"
of a nearly universal stoic heroism, but also the breakdown of the divide
between combatant and non-combatant and thus the mixing up of the
gendered spaces of home front and front line. In the war's aftermath,
the air raid became a central component of interwar efforts that through
memoirs and fiction tried to shape a cultural understanding of this new
reality, and a feature of secret government planning that sought to use
the lessons of the home under fire to prepare the entire population for
the wars to come.

4

Writing and Rewriting Modern Warfare

Memory, Representation, and the Legacy
of the Air Raid in Interwar Britain

INTRODUCTION

In the foreword to the 1928 revision of her 1922 novel *Theodore Savage*, now entitled *Lest Ye Die*, feminist Cicely Hamilton reflected back on its origins during the early summer of 1918. In particular, she emphasized that her cautionary tale came about precisely because she had experienced air raids in northern France during World War I:

> I remember thinking ... that here was [a] phenomenon unknown to the wars whereof history tells us. In the old wars men sheltered behind walls and found safety in numbers[.] But in our wars, the wars of the air and the laboratory, the wall, like enough, is a trap that you fly from to the open, and there is danger, not safety in numbers – the crowd is a target to the Terror that strikes from above. All the country, nightly, was alive with men and women who, in obedience to the principles of the new warfare, had fled from the neighborhood of the target – the town – and scattered in small groups that they might be ignored and invisible.... [W]hat we saw was but a promise of terror to come.[1]

Hamilton went on to reflect that such "terror from the air" inherent in future wars would "transform the citizen into a nomad, useless and starving." Scattered into the countryside by the destruction of their homes and livelihoods, modern men and women would return to a Hobbesian state

---

[1] Cicely Hamilton, *Lest Ye Die: A Story from the Past or of the Future* (New York, 1928), ix. Almost the same wording appears in her autobiography (see Cicely Hamilton, *Life Errant* [London, 1935], 148–149), although here it is recounted as what she remembers rather than as a prelude to her novel. Further references appear parenthetically in the text.

of nature. All hope of a modern democratic citizenship – of belonging to a state that could allow for more equitable relationships between the sexes – would erode. And no one would be safe.

This chapter traces the paradigm shift in public discourse that accompanied this growing realization that because of the air raid, warfare itself had fundamentally changed.[2] In the years following the First World War, the published writings of those exposed to aerial bombardment in the raids of that conflict ushered in a new understanding of what future wars might bring. Yet unlike many examples of wartime media, such post-lapsarian works did not seek to assign blame to one nation by, for example, highlighting the particular evils of German aggression or militarism. Instead these works asserted that more general human as well as political failings were responsible for potential aerial devastation. The experience of having lived through air raids intensified the reaction of both citizens and, as we will see in later chapters, their government to potential warfare. It could prompt individuals such as Cicely Hamilton to observe in the interwar period that life had changed for her – and for all others – on a "red wicked night" when she realized that "at the beginning of air power ... we saw ... a foreshadowing of full-grown achievement" (ix).

By exploring both how participants, especially women and non-combatants, recounted their experiences of air raids in postwar memoirs and fiction and how others imagined the prospect of the next aerial and/or chemical war, this chapter engages with a variety of interwar cultural artifacts. The discussion that follows pays particular attention to how feminist and female authors drew on their encounters with air raids to contribute to public discussions about war and gender in light of modern warfare. As early as 1922, Cicely Hamilton transposed her witnessing of air raids into her dystopian *Theodore Savage*, which warned of the horrors of the next conflict and their consequences for relationships between

---

[2] Other studies have traced the impact of the rise of the airplane, aviation, and air-mindedness on the interwar era more generally, see Robert Wohl, *The Spectacle of Flight: Aviation and the Western Imagination, 1920–1950* (New Haven, CT, 2005); for Britain, Uri Bialer, *The Shadow of the Bomber: The Fear of Air Attack and British Politics, 1932–39* (London, 1980); Tami Davis Biddle, *Rhetoric and Reality in Air Warfare: The Evolution of British and American Ideas about Strategic Bombing, 1914–1945* (Princeton, NJ, 2002); David Edgerton, *England and the Aeroplane: An Essay on a Militant and Technological Nation* (Manchester, 1991); and Barry D. Powers, *Strategy without Slide-Rule: British Air Strategy, 1914–1939* (London, 1976). For other examples, see Peter Fritzsche, *A Nation of Fliers: German Aviation and the Popular Imagination* (Cambridge, MA, 1992).

men and women. Later in the interwar period, some writers drew upon the threat of future aerial warfare as way to insist that women now had an experience of wartime risk and danger that was equivalent to that of male soldiers and thus a new relationship with the state. Other writers took up the issue of how the next war raised the stakes for gender equality, human progress, and the survival of modern life itself.

RELIVING THE AIR WAR

While usually far less well known than the autobiographies and other works by soldier-authors, civilian texts also offered often acute perspectives on the First World War in its aftermath. Many such postwar memoirs include discussions of aerial attacks as a key element of wartime life, one that provoked feelings of danger, fear, and excitement. While few memoirists focus solely on air raids, for many the experience of aerial warfare forms a crucial aspect of the wartime narrative. Particularly for the women whose memoirs will be discussed in this chapter, having felt, heard, and witnessed aerial attacks made it possible for them to claim the *authentic* participation that being under more conventional fire lent to soldier narratives. In other words, the air raid and one's reaction to being attacked became a central element of the civilian "wartime" experience, separating it from what had gone before and came after. Not surprisingly, reactions to the raids varied, yet most postwar depictions emphasized that whatever fear or terror the raids engendered could be overcome. Often, writers depicted the raids as having a cumulative effect, but women made a point of showing that heroism, even of a shaky variety, could be expressed regardless of gender or class. They also made clear that the raids were literally shocking.

For those in the capital city, the appearance of weapons designed to combat air power offered proof that the entirety of the nation was now "at war." In her 1923 autobiography, Elizabeth Butler recounted how war had changed London as early as the end of 1914: "Wherever I looked now there was some new sight of absorbing interest, telling me we were at war ... 'pom-pom' guns began to appear, pointing skywards from their platforms in the parks, awaiting 'Taubes' or 'Zepps.'"[3] The transformation of the city was echoed by the transformation of individual civilians. In a memoir published just a year later, Australian Winifred James, who

---

[3] Elizabeth Butler, *An Autobiography* (London, 1923), 328.

returned to London from Panama suffering from malaria, describes her
encounter with her first air raid in 1915:

> Last night an air raid which didn't come off. We got word of it when it
> was about eight miles from Fleet Street. Every one gathered in the smok-
> ing room at the club; no one seemed to mind very much except the Irish
> servants who came flapping down the back stairs in their nightgowns
> and curl-pins, squealing to the saints. I wasn't too heroic; but thank
> God it was only a physical disability, a sort of blow on the heart that
> flattened it out, a shock to a muscle and not to a feeling. A kindly soul
> with an observant eye got some brandy quietly, and no one was any the
> wiser, for I only sat a little stiller than I had been sitting, which was due
> to a form of dying.[4]

As we have seen in previous chapters, certain groups – in this case one distinguished by both class and ethnicity, namely Irish servants – are offered
as examples of *others* behaving badly. That an Australian woman would
make this comparison to assert her more stoic English Britishness despite
acknowledging her fears is striking. She may bemoan her lack of heroism,
but at least she is able to keep it from becoming visible. The emotional
cost is clear: she experiences "a form of dying" but does so quietly and
manages to carry on.

Ethel Richardson's memoir related the effect of air raids in a different
context, explaining how aerial warfare's attacks on civilians could spur
a distinct embracing of the call to arms for British men. The wife and
mother of three men serving in the military overseas, Richardson offered
her perspective on the war at home. As Richardson recalled the June
1915 zeppelin raids, she noted how they speeded up recruitment: "It was
remarkable to note the instant effect which one taking place in a town
had upon the number of men enlisting for active service. Ocular demonstration of war brought home the fact better than any number of posters and newspaper appeals. It was as though danger threatening wives,
children and old people, left no choice but to 'accept the shilling.' "[5] This
notion of a lack of choice is worth highlighting, suggesting as it does
the power of "ocular demonstration" of war's destruction of particularly
"vulnerable" victims for an audience far removed from the traditional
battlefields.

---

[4] Winifred James, *Out of the Shadows* (London, 1924), 92.
[5] Ethel Richardson, *Remembrance Wakes* (London, 1934), 58. This work also received a
very favorable, if short, review in the *Times Literary Supplement* (henceforth *TLS*) under
the category of "military" works; see *TLS*, 22 Mar. 1934.

Like those writing at the time, postwar memoirists also distinguished between raids by "Zepps" and the later, more destructive Gotha attacks. In her 1935 account of her hospital war work, aristocratic Monica Salmond provided this glimpse of the daylight raids of 1917:

> A fleet of aeroplanes came over this time, flying low.... The bombs were dropped in clusters, close together. The noise was shattering and terrific. The peculiar thumping, the dullness of the thuds, is still in my ears now. We were working in the out-patients' department of the hospital, which was on the level of the basement, so we could not see anything. It was just a bombardment of noise and conjecture, and some bombs fell very near.... I had never fussed about air raids before, but this one shook me very much. I could not forget it, and I began to dread future raids, and to think about them too much.[6]

Initially appropriately "calm" ("I never fussed") in the face of the attacks, Salmond ultimately succumbed to her feelings of anxiety in the face of this more relentless assault. Its lingering effects are shown in her prose – the noise "is still in my ears now," and she "could not forget" the attack. It is not clear why this raid, during which she was theoretically safe below ground and could only hear its effects, was so traumatic. Such anxiety was certainly not unique to her.

Alice Head, working as a journalist in 1917, recalled how "air-raids shattered our nerves." She described the particular anxiety provoked by the arrival of daylight raids: "The first day light air-raid happened one Saturday morning in Tavistock St.... I heard sudden shouting and looked out of the window to see several aeroplanes slowly sailing over Covent Garden, and then there was an explosion. I didn't wait to see more but shouted to the staff to get downstairs.... We fled to the basement and remained there for half an hour in a state of shivering excitement. The damage done on this occasion was not very great, but the fact that we now were liable to be bombed in the day-time was very upsetting."[7]

For others, *where* they experienced the raid was crucial for how they coped. Gladys Stern went so far as to describe her "favourite" raid as occurring outside of London, noting that this was actually a series of raids that coincided with the full moon of September 1917, when she

---

[6] Monica Salmond, *Bright Armour: Memories of Four Years of War* (London, 1935), 226. The lengthy review of this work in the *TLS* not only notes the significance of her background – starting the war as Miss Monica Grenfell, Lord Desborough's daughter – but concludes by stating that her book "is a contribution to the history of women's effort in the War." See *TLS*, 12 Sept. 1935.

[7] Alice M. Head, *It Could Never Have Happened* (London, 1939), 52–53.

was visiting Leigh-on-Sea. Her memories emphasized the raids' effects on
the senses – "[f]rom the window, we could see them following the silver
sash of the river" – especially the sounds, first of screeching sirens, then
the hum and whirr of the zeppelins: "[W]e were not frightened, probably because we were seeing nothing ghastly, nor hearing any agony that
could start the imagination. If there were such a thing as sound pure and
simple, this was it."[8] The raids near the sea were, according to Stern, not
only "not at all bad," especially compared with London raids; they were
also "romantic" and "exciting." She continued, "All air raids were fantastic affairs; an inconsecutive jumble of nightmare, funny adventures and
fiction."[9] The worst raid "had the quality of real horror about it, because
I was in the streets and forced to take cover in the Underground," which
made her feel claustrophobic and "definitely under ground." As it had
been for Salmond, for Stern seeing the raid was far less frightening than
being tucked somewhere presumably safer out of sight.

Stern also described herself as being "abashed" by the reactions "of
the bunch of old ladies to be found in nearly every London boarding-
house." Although Stern herself had decided "to conduct myself with coolness and reticence and presence of mind, it had never occurred to me
that the bunch of old ladies could display not only the same ostensible
lack of fear; but the same amount of coolness, reticence and presence of
mind." She noted how they folded up their knitting and debated taking
cover in the cellars or going up to bed. "One very frail and white-haired
lady asked a little anxiously: 'But is it *safe* to go to bed?' and blushed
when her friend, a wag, replied: 'Well, my dear, that depends, doesn't
it?' And the others chuckled and shipped her for her naughtiness and
her conquests." Such apparent lightheartedness and staples of wartime
domestic life (knitting and joking) prompted Stern to ask, "[W]as this,
here in front of me manifesting itself, the much advertised backbone of
England?" What Stern remembered was how her "young arrogance" was
tempered by realizing that even old women could exhibit sangfroid in the
face of London raids.

Being in London when raids took place deeply affected those who had
also spent time near more conventional battle zones. In writing of her life
during the war in one of the best-known postwar memoirs, *Testament of
Youth* (1933), Vera Brittain reflected on how differently air raids felt later
in the war, when she was "safely" at home with her parents before going

---

[8] G. B. [Gladys] Stern, *Monogram* (London, 1936), 268–270.
[9] Stern, *Monogram*, 271–272.

back to serve in France. The daylight raid of 13 June 1917 struck her as confirming that war "was everywhere now" and "I perceived danger to be infinitely preferable when I went after it, instead of waiting for it to come after me."[10] Brittain described a "sinister group of giant mosquitoes sweeping in close formation over London" and recounted listening "glumly to the shrapnel raining down like a thunder-shower upon the trees in the park – those quiet trees which on the night of my return from Malta had made death and horror seem so unbelievably remote" (365). She continued that witnessing broken glass and dead horses in "terrifyingly quiet" streets made her think such things "less inappropriate when they happened in France, though no doubt the French thought otherwise" (366). Death and horror, however "inappropriate," have, as she vividly evokes it, come "home."

Mabel Rudkin's memoir of Dover's experiences of the war combined civilian responses of both fear and resignation to the raids of the First World War, with her own reflections on the postwar world. After a series of raids in the late summer of 1917, the residents of Dover literally took to the hills and hid out in caves. As the newly married wife of a clergyman assigned to the region, Rudkin recalled that this was prompted by one night when

> forty bombs fell around Dover, the fatalities among the civilian population numbered seven, of whom one or two died from shock. The latter was not a surprising outcome of this terrifying visitation.[11]

In response to this attack and other following attempts, the inhabitants of Dover – "[a] long procession of women, youngsters, and aged men ... advancing from all directions" (166) – begin to take to caves, where an "excellent order ... characteristic of the nation" was maintained. Rudkin noted too how the local population had adapted, one woman creating an " 'air-raid frock,' an ingenious invention with many pockets ... [for] money, cheque book, emergency rations, and a flask of brandy" (173). Others quietly make what she called "pilgrimages to the caves until the Armistice was signed," the term "pilgrimage" suggests something extraordinary, spiritual, and even peaceful (173). Yet Rudkin clearly remained

---

[10] Vera Brittain, *Testament of Youth* (1933; rpt. London, 1977), 365. Further references appear parenthetically in the text. Vera Brittain became a lifelong pacifist as well as feminist campaigner after the First World War.

[11] Mabel S. Rudkin, *Inside Dover, 1914–1918: A Woman's Impressions* (London, 1933), 161. Further references appear parenthetically in the text.

worried about the implications of this new warfare and closed this chapter by asking, "Will those dreary passages [in the cliffs] ever shelter another vast company, still more terror-stricken?" (174).

For Margaret Mackworth, better known as Viscountess Rhonnda, other kinds of wartime trauma reinforced the effects of air raids. Mackworth survived the sinking of the *Lusitania*. For eighteen months after her rescue, she noted that she was left with "an unreasoning fear of air raids. I used to try to keep out of London on full-moon nights (that was during the early days of the war when the Zepps used to come, and needed full moons ...) but it was a bit difficult." She claimed that this lasting effect on her nerves gave her some insight into soldiers' experience of war: "If four hours' danger and exposure could do all that to me, what must one feel like after months in the trenches? I still cannot understand how any of our soldiers remained sane."[12] Despite settling down to raids by 1918, she reported that she could never achieve the "sang froid" exhibited by her mother: "I felt my heart turn over inside me when the bangs began." Moreover, her reaction to raids had a political resonance; during one raid, "we went down to the flat of the woman below. It seemed safer than ours, which was next but one to the top of the building. But she was a pacifist, and proceeded to discuss pacifism. Pacifism during an air raid seems curiously inappropriate, so we never went again" (269–271). If speaking out against war during a raid seemed "inappropriate" to Lady Rhonnda, it did not stop others who opposed the war from recalling the raids' effects as further solidifying their anti-war convictions.

Other women who shared the pacifist sentiments of Lady Rhonnda's neighbor, such as Emmeline Pethick-Lawrence, detailed how their homes in the countryside became places of escape from the war-torn city. Emmeline Pethick-Lawrence, a suffrage activist who opposed the war, recalled how "our home in Surrey became at the week-end a welcome refuge from the war-haunted London streets." She also reflected on the unseen damage of the raids by describing the experiences of her sister, who "was called out repeatedly at night when the air raids were on, to deal with the emergency, and help in removing the patients in the Women's Hospital in the Euston Road to safety. Both her physical strength and her compassionate heart were overtaxed. She broke down suddenly, became delirious, and her spirit left her like a flame."[13] Dr. Pethick was thus portrayed as another of the war's air raid casualties.

---

[12] Lady Rhonnda, *This Was My World* (London, 1933), 262–263. Further references appear parenthetically in the text.
[13] Emmeline Pethick-Lawrence, *My Part in a Changing World* (London, 1938), 320–321.

In her 1935 autobiography, feminist and anti-militarist activist Helena Swanwick described her reaction to the air raids of the First World War:

> I experienced a considerable number of air raids, and I felt no fear except once... [when after injuring her eye] I heard in the street the scouts' cries: 'Air raid! Air raid! Take cover!' I became afraid, horribly afraid. For the only time I was afraid of an air-raid. It seemed that I was afraid because I was shivering for I had started shivering long before I was afraid.[14]

More so than many other writers, Swanwick translated this sense of fear into an appreciation of what subsequent wars could bring. In constructing a plea for disarmament at the end of her memoir, Swanwick related that "if our children are condemned to be burnt or asphyxiated in torments by the bombing planes of some 'enemy', it will be no alleviation in that hour of agony, to think that his children, too, are being burnt or asphyxiated or flying hither and thither in the horror of universal panic" (500). Swanwick made the leap from the civilian experience of the First World War to the anticipated horrors of wholesale war against civilians.[15]

Another prominent anti-war and feminist campaigner, E. Sylvia Pankhurst, put forth her own striking version of air raids in her account of the war years, *The Home Front: A Mirror to Life in England during the First World War*. Taking as one of its central themes the suffering of women and children at home as being akin to the suffering of soldiers in the battle zones, Pankhurst devoted an entire chapter, "First Air Raid," to depicting one that she experienced in the East End of London. She was quick to point out the raid's frightening characteristics and the emotions that it awakened in her:

> [H]uge reports smote the ear, shattering, deafening, and the roar of falling masonry....The awful grinding still pulsated above.... Again that terrific burst of noise; those awful bangs, the roar of the falling buildings, the rattle of shrapnel on the roof close above....The thought of the bombs crashing down on the densely populated city was appalling – yet for our household I had no least shade of apprehension – and for myself Life had no great claim. I was only a member of the salvage corps, saving and succouring as I might amid this wreckage.[16]

---

[14] Helena Swanwick, *I Have Been Young* (London, 1935), 177.
[15] Her more theoretical responses will be taken up in more detail in Chapter 7.
[16] E. Sylvia Pankhurst, *The Home Front: A Mirror to Life in England during the First World War* (London, 1932; rpt. 1987), 191. Further references appear parenthetically in the text.

Pankhurst's emotive reaction put the abstract cost – the appalling nature of an attack on a densely inhabited region – ahead of her own risk.

Pankhurst also commented on what followed from the raid by juxtaposing an image of children digging in the road for shrapnel with the simple statements "Anti-German rioting broke out again. Panic ran rampant" (192). Fear brought out attacks on innocent German-speaking inhabitants, which Pankhurst condemned after vividly depicting a woman beaten unconscious, by stating, "poor Patriotism, What foolish cruelties are committed in thy name!" (195). She also criticized the morbid curiosity that the raids provoked and the influx of tourists to the East End seeking to observe the damage. Pankhurst insisted that the ordinary sights that these "West End folk" witnessed – "miserable dwellings, ... hopeless unhappy beings ... half-clad, neglected little children" – were sadder "even than the havoc wrought by German bombs." She further described in detail the pathos of the raids: "[C]rowds mostly made up of women gathered before each ruined home. One, where a child had been killed, was still inhabited.... The people who lived there were scarcely able to force a way to their own door.... A chorus of wailing stirred amongst the women: 'Oh, my God! Look at the home! Oh, my God!' " (193–194). As a summation of the impact of the First World War's air raids, this is both succinct and potent.

Elsewhere in her text, Pankhurst insisted upon the lingering effects of raids, particularly when they became more frequent. She mentioned the zeppelin raids as having produced the following effects: "the dread roar of falling buildings. The angry glare of conflagration rose from the devastated scene where the bombs had fallen" (265). Pankhurst's book did not describe events beyond 1916, so it did not address later deadly raids on the East End. However, she attributed various changes – such as the giving of warnings and the shift in strategy – to public outcry. Most strikingly, she used the terminology of the war years themselves, referring to the "terror-stricken populace" and observing that "terror grew," causing panic, and that some people were killed "by the press of others crowding behind them" seeking shelter (265). This was consistent with those civilians who wrote about the war in the interwar period and rejected the carefully cultivated stoicism and the kind of civil identity that new forms of warfare seemingly required if civilian morale were to be maintained.

By the early 1930s, experts in other fields, such as sexologists, were trying to assess the legacy of the war, including the impact of the kind of war that it was. Thus did Magnus Hirschfield in his chapter on "atrocities" in *The Sexual History of the World War* emphasize that the allegations of sexual violence – the extreme form of atrocity propaganda – were entirely false. Instead, Hirschfield asserted, the true atrocities were not sexual but technological; in the First World War, chemical weapons were used only against soldiers, "which will certainly not be the case in the next war for the ultimate consequence will be the gassing of whole populations of cities." He continued by noting that in "great cities like Paris, London and Karlsruhle ... the ancient distinction between combatant and civil population was completely destroyed ... [by] a new type of warfare where such a distinction is wiped out." Actual atrocities past and present lay in "the ghastly murderous inventions of technology."[17]

Postwar civilian memoirists and commentators were consistent in asserting that air raids had changed the nature of warfare. In particular, in several non-combatant autobiographies, aerial warfare demonstrated that the distinction between combatants and non-combatants had ceased to be as meaningful as it might have been before the onset of air raids. Women, the elderly, and children found themselves under attack, and most of the writers discussed here were willing to concede that air raids made them afraid but also that they were able to find various coping strategies. In light of what had *already* been experienced, the fear of what future war might bring animated a range of interwar literary responses.

AERIAL WARFARE REPRESENTED
AND THE NEXT WAR IMAGINED

During the interwar period, the wartime transformation of the role of civilians, and especially of women and children, served as the basis for a variety of fictional works. What follows reflects on some of the most vivid examples of this interwar literature, mainly popular fiction but not exclusively so. A variety of novelists either used the air raids of the First World War as a pivotal feature in representing the experience of that war or contemplated what horrors might come from the interlinking of science and mass death, especially from the air. In so doing, they helped to imagine and in some ways to prepare the population for what future war could bring.

One of the first such works to convey the bleak sense of a world destroyed by aerial warfare was Cicely Hamilton's *Theodore Savage* (1922). When Hamilton's postwar evocation of a world utterly destroyed by air power found an American publisher and, along with some

---

[17] Magnus Hirschfield, *The Sexual History of the World War* (New York, 1934), vol. 3, 304.

revisions, a new title, *Lest Ye Die*, in 1928, she remarked in her foreword
that she hoped readers have "ceased to turn … from books dealing with
war and its issues."[18] Hamilton wanted her audience to pay attention to
the political implications, to the new stakes of war, particularly for non-
combatants. As H. G. Wells had done before the First World War, she
conjured up a world where a golden age of scientific success cannot reign
in human emotions and leads to utter, universal devastation. The novel
then recounts the story of the dissolution of a society, much like that of
"modern" England/Europe, from aerial bombardment involving chemical weapons. In this sense, Hamilton expressed a common post-World
War I fear, one that conflated two new forms of warfare witnessed during
that war – aerial and chemical – into a horrifying union.

　　Lest Ye Die traces the life of an English civil servant, named Theodore
Savage, who begins the book as a well-satisfied product of modern civilization, an urbane (and urban) man. As he contemplates whether to
pursue marriage, an obscure crisis in the Balkans that has provoked the
"League" begins to stir into a war. Suddenly the country is mobilized,
and Savage is recalled from his vacation and put to work at a northern
food control center to ensure the equitable distribution of goods. At first,
England escapes the actual fighting, experiencing only pre-emptive ration-
ing and wild rumors. Then air war descends, and "Disaster" begins:

> The skyline to the south and southwest was reddened with a glow that
> flickered and wavered spasmodically … there were flashes – the bursting
> of explosive of starshells.…
>
> With the morning came news and – more plentifully – rumor; also, the
> wind having dropped, a persistent thunder from the south … an attack
> in force, since the invaders did not find it needful to desist with the pass-
> ing of darkness. Rumor, in the absence of official intelligence, invented
> an enveloping air-fleet which should cut them of from their base; and
> meanwhile the thunder continued. (74–76)

Soon all road and rail stops, post to and from London disappears, and
the refugees appear: "a horde of human rats driven out of their holes by
terror, by fire and gas.… A wave of vagrant destitution rushed suddenly
and blindly northward – anywhere away from the ruin of explosive, the
flames and death by suffocation; while authority strove vainly to control
and direct the torrent of overpowering misery" (77–78). After a few days

---

[18] Hamilton, *Lest Ye Die*. I will discuss this version as her more definitive statement rather
than compare the two renditions.

of this disorderly panic, whatever state had existed begins to break down; looting, rioting, and a brute struggle for survival ensue.

In some cases, terrified inhabitants desert towns and cities before the enemy can obliterate them. Engines give "no warning" and "the first announcement of danger was the bursting of gas-shell and high explosive, or the sudden vivid pallor of the poison fire as it ran before the wind and swept along dry fields and hedgerows. Where it swept it left not only long tracts of burned crop and black skeleton trees, but, often enough, the charred bodies of the homeless whom its rush had outpaced and overtaken" (88). Only when York is destroyed does Theodore look "his last on the towers of the Minster, magnificent against a sea of flame. Death, inhumanity, had ceased to move him greatly; but turned away his head from the death of high human achievement" (89). The ties that bound the nation together, government and media, cease to function. Finally, Savage himself faces an enemy air attack that destroys the small garrison he has been defending, and he finds himself part of the vagrant throng.

The fall from "civilization" follows swiftly: "He lived thenceforth as men have always lived when terror drives them this way and that.... He hunted and scraped for food like a homeless dog.... His life was summed up in two words, starvation and fear" (109). Slowly, Savage realizes that the war has come to an end, or at least played itself out in his corner of England, as days pass without alarm, clouds of smoke, or the flare of bombs. What is left is only "the daily, personal and barbaric form of war, wherein every man's hand was raised against his neighbor and enemy" (125). By a combination of embracing the newly brutalized state of the world, craftiness, and sheer luck, the aptly named Savage manages to survive. He almost literally picks up a female companion, Ada, and sets about learning how to "know the earth as primitive man ... knew it-as the source of life, the storehouse of uncertain food, the teacher of cunning and an infinite and dogged patience" (141). When he ventures into vacant communities to scavenge, he finds only evidence of the war's destruction – skeletons of children and women clutching for each other, of sudden death from "a cloud of gas rolling down the street before the wind" (149). Eventually, he and Ada join a small community of survivors of the "Ruin."

In the book's final section, Hamilton offered a detailed and harrowing depiction of the remade world, of a compact for mutual aid among largely mistrustful men, of "primitive" relations between men and women, and of the constant threat of external dangers. Most tellingly, it is a world that has renounced "civilization" – science, mechanics, and engineering have been deemed "devil's knowledge" and forsworn.

It is, to say the least, a grim vision and a sobering, cautionary read – not least for its evocation of a world where whatever equality that might have occurred between the sexes has also fallen away. The return to the power of brute force means that progress in such relations will collapse when total war destroys government, order, and a cosmopolitan culture that values the mind over the body. That Hamilton insisted on the origins of this nightmare emerging when she experienced an air raid reveals how transformative this event was to those seeking not only peace and disarmament, but also the securing of feminist values – of the equality of men and women as emblematic of the best aspirations of modern society – in the postwar world. Reaction to Hamilton's postwar work, especially to the 1928 *Lest Ye Die*, was quite mixed. A short review in the *Spectator* described it as "forcible and earnest" but "it fails to convince."[19] The *Times Literary Supplement* called it "fantastic propaganda ... supremely against the next war... [set] in an England where towns have disappeared.... The idea is interesting enough, but [the book] captures neither our reason nor our imagination."[20]

When Vera Brittain, another witness to the First World War's devastation both in Britain and abroad, began to fictionalize her war experiences, aerial attacks provided a key backdrop for the transformation of the protagonist of one of her novels, published a few years after her influential autobiography. *Honourable Estate* (1936) was a self-described "novel of transition," and one of its main goals was to illustrate the changing nature of women's lives from the late nineteenth through the early twentieth century.[21] Brittain's stand-in, Ruth Allendyne, also participates in the war as a V.A.D. prompted to serve by her beloved brother's death. While overseas and learning the truth about her brother's end, she falls in love with an American officer, Eugene Meury, her brother's friend.

One of the crucial scenes between Eugene and Ruth that clarifies both their feelings and the altered nature of war itself occurs during an air raid while both are on leave in London. The backdrop of war literally brought home forces them into close physical and emotional intimacy. Further, the aerial attack makes Ruth aware of the nature of courage in facing

---

[19] "Fiction," *Spectator*, 14 July 1928.
[20] "New Books and Reprints," *TLS*, 23 Aug. 1928.
[21] Vera Brittain, *Honourable Estate* (London, 1936). Further references appear parenthetically in the text.

combat and of her ability to do so. Almost as soon as they embrace and admit their feelings for one another, "the dull thud of a distant gun reverberated through the night, carrying to London the sinister warning of an air-raid.... [T]hey listened, grown suddenly taut in each other's arms.... [A] brilliant fountain of star-shells from the batteries on the outskirts of London announced the approach of the raiders.... [F]alling bombs began to mingle hideously with the clamour and clatter of the anti-aircraft bombardment" (368). As the ground beneath them rocks violently, Ruth senses "a convulsive shudder pass through the man beside her," although he persists in sounding calm and cheerful.

> She knew, then, the cost of his heroism; she realised, from the quiver of his flesh communicated to hers, the long story of raids and attacks and bombardments in which his indomitable spirit had conquered the shrinking panic of his body.... This is superb courage that I am witnessing, she thought; the conquest over nerves tortured by a thousand indescribable experiences that I can't even imagine (369).

As a plane circles directly overhead and unleashes its arsenal, Eugene pulls Ruth into a ditch where they are barely concealed as a "terrific explosion ... rocked the earth ... as though the ground itself has burst asunder" (369). Despite this, Ruth remains calm; "[e]ven in that moment of mortal terror, his nearness and the compelling power of his physical virility entered her blood.... At least, she thought, if we die, we die together.... Don't let me show my fear or do anything to make him ashamed of me!" (369). Far from showing her fear, the raid's end finds Eugene properly awed: "'Gosh, you've got some courage!'" – to which Ruth responds, " 'It doesn't cost me anything to have courage, as you call it.'... She felt half-drunk with ... the matchless exhilaration of danger survived, of fear overcome, of love found equal to a sudden demand" (369).

One could read the exploding shells in this moment of sexual tension as expressing the suppressed. The moment is also significant for its role reversal. If air war, as other feminists would argue, no longer allowed for masculine chivalry, then perhaps it allowed women a kind of equivalent heroism. The brave soldier clings to the woman he loves in a ditch because they are both under fire, but they both rise to the occasion – together they accept a "masculine" notion of bravery that equates the display of fear with weakness, as "feminine." Both exhibit heroism through stoicism. In another way, air war feminized everyone except the fighter pilot; the rest were, as Hamilton put it in her wartime novel, *William: An Englishman*, reduced to "scuttling into holes like beetles," showing bravery through how they *reacted* but not by taking action.

When Eugene must return to the firing line, Ruth insists on their becoming lovers and, after his death, flings herself into the work of reconstruction in postwar Russia. Here she re-encounters the novel's male protagonist, Denis Rutherston, who convinces her to return to Britain and embark on a career of left-wing political activism. Once again, a crucial scene between a couple is set against the hum of airplanes. After a year's careful friendship, Denis proposes to Ruth, who feels obligated to confess her lack of virginity. Discussing their views on sexual morality – Ruth's opinion that "the really immoral people are the ones who punish and ostracise without understanding a thing about the person they condemn" (472), Denis replies, "If people want something to detest and spit on, why don't they go for modern war and those who make it" (473). Suddenly an "aeroplane, like a giant dragon-fly, hummed again overhead, a timely reminder of the race already begun between the inexorable advance of science and the tardy growth of human wisdom" (473).

Brittain's point here was akin to Hamilton's in *Lest Ye Die*. Both emphasized the disjuncture between what new forms of warfare (the products of modern science) and old patterns of human behavior (aggression and the urge for domination – defined in these works as more masculine than feminine traits) had brought about and potentially might bring about with even more destructive energy in the future. Although Brittain's novel showed how such a calamity might be avoided as it records Allendyne's gaining of a public, political voice as a triumph for women, both she and Hamilton tested the parameters of what might emerge in a postwar world where war itself has been transformed and the experience of war has in turn altered forever the lives of men and women, the state and the home.

Like other witnesses to the destructiveness of air power during the First World War and other writers committed to depicting inner psychic change across time, Virginia Woolf explored aerial warfare and its impact in a number of her interwar novels.[22] In one of the most vivid representations, she set almost the entirety of the chapter "1917" in her 1937 novel *The Years* against the backdrop of an air raid. Not only did she use the searchlight piercing the sky to convey the fraught emotional state

---

[22] For an important discussion of Virginia Woolf and the imagery of air power focusing largely on *Between the Acts* (1941), see Gillian Beer, "The Island and the Aeroplane: The Case of Virginia Woolf," in *Nation and Narration*, ed. Homi K. Bhabha (London, 1990). For a thoughtful analysis of the legacy of air power for interwar literature, see Paul K. Saint-Amour, "Air War Prophecy and Interwar Modernism," *Comparative Literature Studies* 42:2 (2005), 130–161.

of her characters, but she also suggested that this is what the distancing effect of being a civilian in war is like – trying to find something in the darkness, something to bring meaning. In "1917" the wail of sirens erupts in the midst of conversation, but clearly those already dining in the London basement know that this is a raid, and if they curse the "damned Germans," they also know how to carry on (288). Asked point blank if she minds the raids, as "people differ so much," Eleanor, one of the protagonists, responds, "Not at all.... The chances of being hit oneself are so small" (289). The reassurance offered by contemporary newspapers and the government was thus repeated here. As a crescendo of booming echoes intensifies until they are right overhead and "a violent crack of sound" rends the air, the sense of danger passes. The diners below ground try to resume eating and drinking but are acutely aware, as one of them puts it, of spending "the evening sitting in a coal cellar while other people try to kill each other above my head" (295). The chances of being hit are small, but the awareness that their non-combatant status cannot protect them against war-induced death remains.

Unlike many of the other works discussed here, Woolf's writings and their relationship to the wars through which she lived received a rich critical analysis. In her study of Woolf and the First World War, Karen Levenback points out that while Woolf was completing *The Years*, she was remembering the noise and impact of the raids and the responses they evoked as well as the civilian experience of waiting for death.[23] In a similar vein, Nancy Bazin and Jane Lauter comment that *The Years* mirrors Woolf's perception that the very continuation of civilization was now threatened.[24] While such a perception in the mid-1930s undoubtedly came from more than the legacy (and return) of the air raid, it remained a common thread in other interwar literature.

A number of less elite 1930s fictional depictions of aerial warfare used the First World War's raids as jumping-off points for their own warnings about the dangers of the wars – of the air and the laboratory – to come. Some presented irredeemably bleak versions of the future, presenting the kind of cautionary tale that Hamilton did in the 1920s. Still other authors offered a form of hope that movements and leaders could emerge who would yet save the future from the new threats that air power wrought.

[23] Karen Levenback, *Virginia Woolf and the Great War* (Syracuse, NY, 1999), 123–125.
[24] Nancy Topping Bazin and Jane Hamovit Lauter, "Virginia Woolf's Keen Sensitivity to War: Its Roots and Its Impact on Her Novels," in *Virginia Woolf and War: Fiction, Reality, and Myth*, ed. Mark Hussey (Syracuse, NY, 1991), 23. See also the discussion of Woolf's *Mrs. Dalloway* in Saint-Amour, "Air War Prophecy," 140–149.

Historian Martin Ceadel nearly thirty years ago characterized the mass of such interwar novels as "appalling and dreadful in both the original and modern senses of the word," but concluded that "it was only in the interwar period that the genre developed its particular obsession with the bomber and gas attack" and that these texts thus modeled larger concern "with the threat of air war to society as it then stood."[25]

The plot of *The Gas War of 1940* (1931) by "Miles" (the pseudonym of Stephen Southwold) highlighted the dangers of new weaponry that was not even under the control of those in power. The novel, which purports to be the reminiscences of Raymond Denning, the "first dictator of Britain," is addressed to his son. Despite his absolute power, this father can protect his infant from the destruction of civilization only by sending him into orbit above a now unsafe earth. Meanwhile, the novel spares no punches in illustrating the force of bombs that rain destruction down across the globe and of gases that cause London schoolchildren to scream and "run round and round in frantic circles, until deadlier gases halted them and flung them over to lie, twisting and jerking convulsive limbs, tearing at the floor, biting through lips and tongues, until death at last suffered them." What is left when the war is over, as seen by the dictator from the sky, is described in the following hyperbolic prose: "a wilderness of desolation, a waste of ruins, a place of disaster, a shambles where despair had waited in slow agony for death."[26] The novel concludes with the death of the dictator, but not before he has made a plea for peace and for stopping "the perfection of instruments of destruction." In a rather dry review, the *Times Literary Supplement* commented that "the slaughter is not so impressive as it ought to be"; it did not provoke enough horror. Still other interwar novels would attempt to remedy this lack.

Given the centrality of threatened women and children to narratives of the First World War's raids, the particular role of women in relationship to the next war became the subject of three 1930s novels: Maboth Moseley's *The War upon Women* (1934), George Cornwallis-West's *The Woman Who Stopped War* (1935), and Eric Linklater's *The Impregnable*

---

[25] Martin Ceadel, "Popular Fiction and the Next War, 1918–39," in *Class Culture and Social Change: A New View of the 1930s*, ed. Frank Gloversmith (Brighton, 1980), 161, 182.

[26] "Miles," *The Gas War of 1940* (London, 1931), 249–250, 274, 300. Information about the author is briefly discussed in Ceadel, "Popular Fiction," 171, and the novel is also addressed in I. F. Clarke, *Voices Prophesying War*, 2d ed. (Oxford 1992), 159.

Women (1938).[27] These works range from trying to suggest the full barbarity of this war against civilians, as in the first of these books, to a kind of updated Lysistrata, a world where women combine together to force their men to abandon war itself, as in the last.

The War upon Women belongs not only to the anxious next-war novels of the 1930s, but also to the long tradition of atrocity literature, and it contain the rape and sexual violence against innocent women that were hallmarks of that genre during the First World War.[28] Maboth Moseley tried to underscore the universality of her work by providing us with the setting as "the present ... anywhere in the world" and dividing her work simply into three sections: bombardment, invasion, and counter-attack. The characters themselves hardly matter, but the dictator who unleashes war is a parody of a narcissist, a superstitious man terrified of losing power. The young couple who will be torn apart by war are similarly stock figures, although Sandy believes what her fiancé, Derek, has told her: "In the next war all women will be involved" (62). Yet just as Sandy is breaking off her engagement over Derek's pacifist principles – now that war seems upon them – aerial bombardment begins. The second part of the book opens with the trapped English civilians, regrettably overseas when the war begins, taking shelter in the cellar of their rented villa. Once they emerge from its safety, they must face the invaders. Derek is killed trying to come to Sandy's aid, and the dictator's son rapes Sandy, whom she in turn shoots and kills. The book's final section ends with the flames and noise of a counter-attack, but the horrors of war invoked by this novel are both new and old. If modern war, as Sandy realizes, "was not confined to men, but extended to women and children, to princes and politicians, to staff officers and conscientious objectors," then the sooner those waging war had a taste of its results, the sooner they would reject warfare altogether (281). However implausible the plot, Moseley

---

[27] Maboth Moseley, *The War Upon Women* (London, 1934); G. Cornwallis-West, *The Woman Who Stopped War* (London, 1935); and Eric Linklater, *The Impregnable Women* (London, 1938). References to these novels in the discussion that follows will be made parenthetically in the text.

[28] Moseley, *War Upon Women*. A discussion of atrocity literature can be found in Susan R. Grayzel, *Women's Identities at War: Gender, Motherhood, and Politics in Britain and France during the First World War* (Chapel Hil, NC, 1999), ch. 2, and Nicoletta F. Gullace, *The Blood of Our Sons: Men, Women, and the Renegotiation of British Citizenship During the Great War* (New York, 2002). The *TLS* review summarized the plot, including the outrage suffered by the heroine and the inability of her pacifist fiancé to protect her, see *TLS*, 1 Mar. 1934. Moseley's plot echoes aspects of Cicely Hamilton's *William: An Englishman* (London, 1918).

reinforced an instrumental shift – war now involves *everyone* and *every-place* – that accompanied new forms of warfare unleashed in 1914.[29]

The Woman Who Stopped the War similarly addresses both the new and old forms of suffering that war inflicted on women. The innovative aspect is once again that women are not spared direct bombardment via aerial warfare, and the more traditional aspect is, of course, the fact that they must cope with the deaths of their loved ones serving in the military. This novel uses the raids of the First World War as both foreshadowing and counterpoint; it commences with a young couple, Mary Kaye, who is lovely in a "typically English" way, and John Sarn, celebrating their marriage in the dining room of the Savoy Hotel before he heads off to fight (12). During the course of their evening, Mary's looks attract the attention of the arms manufacturer (and war profiteer) Enthoven, whom John denounces as a bounder, when suddenly an air raid begins. It is Mary's first experience of such attacks, and she expresses her pride in how well people are responding, although she can't help observing to her husband, "It's awful to think that people are being killed quite close to us while we sit here" (15). As the raid continues, some of their fellow diners can no longer contain their agitation; a women cries out that she "must get to the children," while her husband tries to reassure that they will be safe as usual in the cellar. As the all clear sounds, John compliments Mary's resolve: "You've been marvelous ... you haven't turned a hair," while she only wants to leave, as "despite herself her nerves were on edge" (17). Danger has threatened this wartime couple at home in London, and they have remained outwardly resolute, but the threat is far from gone and the first part of the novel ends with the War Office's announcement of John's death.

The scene then shifts to 1922. Mary, now a young war widow, is determined to support herself, her sister-in-law, and her brother, who is chronically ill from having been gassed during the war, and becomes a model. Outwardly, Mary has become more beautiful in her grief but also more committed to life as an active citizen. When her brother comments that "the League of Nations isn't a very exhilarating subject for young women," Mary fervently rejects this idea: "It ought to be the most exhilarating thing in the world if only they [women] realized that it was formed to resist war, to outlaw it, to make war impossible" (31).

---

[29] Ceadel comments that this work toys "with the argument that women could prevent war by refusing to have children," but this is such a minor point that it hardly shapes the anti-war message of the novel, which is that war damages non-combatants as much as soldiers. See Ceadel, "Popular Fiction," 178.

She recognizes, however, that the only way to do this is to mobilize the power of women, to channel "the massed opinion of the women of the civilised world" (32).

This prompts Mary to dream of a new kind of political organization, one that would employ women's new political and economic role:

> Since the last war, which threw women into the pell-mell of public life whether they wanted it or not, there's hardly a branch of public service that doesn't depend largely on them for its maintenance. If they went on strike ... what would happen? You couldn't send a telegram or use a telephone.... [T]he running of the great majority of businesses would be paralysed with no typists or book-keeper or cashiers; thousands of factories would be at a standstill. (33)

And men could not replace the women who went on strike at the threat of war because they would all be needed as soldiers. After this epiphany, Mary embarks on her new mission, to create a "Save the Race League," "because after all it's the whole race that's going to suffer in the next war" (34). Her League would inform women of the threat that war posed directly to them and their loved ones in order to mobilize them to "strike" against its occurrence. There is a disturbing eugenic undertone to both the organization's name and Mary's subsequently expressed belief that the purpose of her organization is in part to prevent the loss of "the best and bravest" who are killed in war "to the detriment of their race" (48).

However, Mary also seeks to persuade women to work for peace as she endeavors to create an international women's movement against war by highlighting how the next war will be different:

> there will be no bereaved wives and mothers, because there won't be any wives and mothers left.... They – and the children – will all be gassed or blown to bits just the same as the husbands and fathers.... The men in the front line trenches will be safer than the women and children who are waiting for them at home. (50)

The main obstacle Mary faces remains how to fund such a movement of women when women have few resources. Then Mary has a second, quite cold-blooded epiphany: she will seek out the attentions of a wealthy man in order to pay for the Save the Race League. In due course, she sets out to "persuade Sir Edward Enthoven to pay Mary Sarn for – services rendered" and use the money to fund the women's league (86).

One way that she will balance being the rich arms manufacturer's mistress with her devotion to a league that aims to undo his business is to make the organization secret, "a sort of freemasonry among women"

(137). Much of the novel then traces the relationship between Mary and Enthoven as, unbeknownst to her lover, Mary and her cohorts create the Save the Race League. Even after having a son with Enthoven, Mary continues to deceive him as to what she is doing with the funds he gives her, although this is complicated by the growing emotional attachment she feels for him. Readers are also privy to Enthoven's company's insidious development of a new gas, "mosogene," more deadly than anything yet developed and against which gas masks are of no use.

The book's final section finds Europe on the verge of war while Mary's League has grown in size and importance. When England prepares for war, the League goes into action and the women all go on strike. Phone messages and telegrams can't go through, and factories come to a halt: "The idea conceived in the brain of one young girl ... [has] upset the designs of the most astute politicians in Europe" (273). Even Enthoven panics and comes to regret his actions and profits when he thinks that his son and Mary will fall victim to an enemy gas attack using mosogene (276–277). Instead, at the end of the novel, implausibly (or as implausibly as anything else in the plot) Mary delivers the news that the women of the world have prevented war and confesses her love for Enthoven. Despite her seemingly questionable moral choices (deception, sex and motherhood outside of marriage), the author depicted Mary's sacrifices as being for humanity itself and capable of turning even hardened war profiteers into loving family men. The underlying message reveals the power of women acting as both women and citizens.[30]

In Cornwalis-West's *The Woman Who Stopped the War*, an international general strike of women's labor halts the violence; the withholding from men of sex in exchange for peace is dismissed as unnecessary. Yet in the last of these interwar novels to focus on women, Linklater's *Impregnable Women*, the potential for women to stop war by this particular kind of strike, one led by the Lady Lysistrata (there is nothing subtle in this text), unfolds. First, Linklater felt compelled to describe in great detail the devastation unleashed by aerial warfare, beginning with an attack on London out of the blue on a Sunday morning. This is a world

---

[30] Ceadel's brief discussion of this novel suggests that this melodrama "took its cue from the liberated role of the post-war woman," but this may be overstated. Its heroine echoes both the scheming women of Victorian gothic melodramas (à la Wilkie Collins) and the tragic war widow; she is certainly not liberated sexually – her affair is entirely dispassionate and even distasteful to her at the outset. What is new is her postwar political and civic role, one that a woman like Mary could fully embrace as worker and citizen. See Ceadel, "Popular Fiction," 178.

that has been expecting war, however, "and the value of the air-raid drills, which for several years everyone in London had been obliged to attend, was sufficiently demonstrated. The first panic quickly subsided, and grief had less chance of utterance when those who had most cause for sorrow were given familiar work to do" (38). Still, gas masks and drills cannot prevent the inhabitants from realizing that despite a general lack of panic and relatively few human casualties, they have witnessed the destruction of their capital city, with its centers of government, business, banking, religion, and law all lying in ruins. And even this, "the annihilation of London," was "only the beginning" of what was to follow.

What does follow, as we have seen in works by Wells, Hamilton and others, is the general assumption of universal war, with destruction from the air and on the ground. Here, in a new twist, people also take up arms and destroy their own air forces: burning and breaking bombers and trampling pilots underfoot (51). Chaos then reigns across Europe, but the airplane has been destroyed even as war by other means continues without end. Midway through the novel, Lady Lysistrata decides that "if poor and wretched women could breed soldiers, then women could bring soldiers to their knees" (135).

Gathering a hundred women together, this modern Lysistrata appeals to their desire to keep the men they love alive – "it is our happiness that is being thrown away on every battle-field" – and unite to stop war. Interestingly, the withholding of sexual relations with their men is implied rather than stated, but the women agree that precisely because they are not "ruled only by their appetites," then they can take this action. As Lysistrata puts it (apparently persuasively), "For a little while give up the joy of love, and you will make love safe forever.... You must be strong.... Make yourselves as lovely and attractive as you can.... Be glamorous, alluring irresistible. And then, then draw back and make your denial! Then be strong and refuse your love till the war's over and peace has come again" (157). The women initiate their movement by seizing control of the castle and center of government (now in Edinburgh), and a "love siege" begins. Cleverly, Lady Lysistrata has extended the purview of the women's strike to include "domestic as well as connubial service" and generally encourages her followers to do nothing to bring men comfort (213). As the siege continues, an army of women marches into Edinburgh to come to its aid, and in the end, the "Love Strike" spreads to the enemy. The result: the war "ended in a passion of fear and remorse, and the soldiers hurried home to beg forgiveness" (338). And what of the striking and victorious women? They decide to enter politics.

Reflecting a generally critical response to the novel, the *Times Literary Supplement* commented that while the war and bombardment itself was "described with the proper degree of gravity ... not for a moment does one believe" the rest of it. Moreover, "it is in doubtful taste to try to capitalize on common fears in this way and ... this Aristophanic comedy has a distressing artifice.[31] Making the next-war novel and the work of women against war more comedic than tragic does seem jarring in a work of the late 1930s. But the men in the novel appear to be as ridiculous as the women, and the underlying assumption that the next war might last a fairly long time despite the innovation of air power delivers another message about its potentially devastating effects. It could destroy London, and this would still not mean the end of war.

A more somber mood pervaded a novel published only a year later than Linklater's, indeed appearing in print only a few months before the start of the Second World War (although written, as the preface tells us, in 1938). Neville Shute's *What Happened to the Corbetts* was thus one of the last interwar novels to predict the next war, with a tone far more realistic than the last three novels examined here. It plunges a typical Southampton family, decisively middle class and complacent, into the horrors of aerial warfare and the chaos that ensues. What remains arresting about this novel is its very lack of implausibility – there is no movement to stop the war by women or anyone else. Instead, as Nevil Shute explained: "Although I have written fiction, I have written what to me are very real forecasts of what may be coming to us. I wanted to make them real to you, and so I have laid them in real places."[32] Thus, instead of chemical warfare, Shute depicted bombing raids that are deadly less because of the spectacular damage that they cause than because of their disruption of all aspects of everyday life.

In *What Happened to the Corbetts*, the side effects of the initial attacks – the lack of electricity, gas, petrol, water, and food – cause the crisis to worsen. Contaminated water supplies lead to an outbreak of cholera, and soon other contagious diseases like typhoid ravage the population. In short, very quickly, the ordinary "civilised" life of the highly domesticated family crumbles and turns into a struggle for survival. When Peter Corbett debates enlisting, his doctor friend tells him that he

---

[31] [R. D. Charques,] "Novels of the Week," *TLS*, 9 July 1938.

[32] Nevil Shute, *What Happened to the Corbetts* (London, 1939; rpt. 1961). Moreover, the British publisher, William Heinemann Limited, distributed a thousand free copies to Air Raids Precautions workers on the date of its publication in April 1939. See the preface to the novel as reprinted in 1961.

has a higher responsibility: "You've got three strong and healthy children. The country's going to need them presently. Your job is to keep them safe through this, and that's the only job you want to think about. If you get Joan and your three kids through this in safety you'll have done your stuff.... Get them away ... anywhere they'll be safe from the bombs and from disease ... get them out of this" (67). This Peter learns is what a "man's job" under these conditions has become. The family takes refuge on their boat but find that their biggest challenge comes down to finding milk to feed the baby. In desperation, Joan and Peter Corbett steal enough tins of milk to survive what they hope will be a sea voyage to a place of safety.

At the novel's end, they reach Brest, where Joan and the children will take a ship to Canada, while Peter returns to join the navy. The novel ends with war still going on and the family now separated. Yet Peter is reassured by a Frenchman that England will win this war:

> All the world comes to the aid of England, because of the bombing.... Only a nation of no understanding who did not know the world psychology, would make such mistakes. In your Empire, every Dominion has declared war, all are hastening to fight. Without the bombing, M'sieur, it would not have been so.... It had to come. Once in the history of the world this had to be tried, this blind bombing of the towns. But ... it has lost the war for them. (228–229)

In the ambiguous message of the novel's conclusion, the bombing has brought unity of purpose, a determination to fight, and global support for Britain, but it has also destroyed, perhaps forever, the quiet English world of this typical family.

In the 1930s, audiences could also visually witness the fictional evocation of a Britain subject to aerial and chemical attack when the film version of H. G. Wells's 1933 *The Shape of Things to Come* was released as *Things to Come* in 1936.[33] Providing more narrative structure than the novel, the film tells the story of "Everytown," which looks startlingly like London, beginning in 1940. Whether or not the filmmakers were aware of the Christmas raid of December 1914, they chose to set the opening scene during Christmastime 1940. While revelers pack the streets of Everytown and neon lights entice them to the cinema or a pantomime, ominous words appear on posters: "World on the Brink of War" or "War Scare Latest News," a foreshadowing of the threat of war very reminiscent

---

[33] H. G. Wells, *The Shape of Things to Come* (New York, 1933) and *Things to Come* (1936), dir. W. Cameron Menzies.

of *The War in the Air*. The scene then shifts to a family celebrating
Christmas; the children play with tanks and helmets, while the men discuss whether the rumors of war should be taken seriously. Suddenly, the
sky is alight, guns sound, and the household receives word of an order of
general mobilization. The camera fades out and then back in to the main
square of Everytown; loudspeakers mounted on a truck proclaim that air
raids are coming and everyone should "go home." Meanwhile, the film
returns to the cozy domestic interior of the family just seen celebrating
Christmas, but now the focus is on two parents looking at their sleeping
children as the mother asks her husband if he "is sorry we had them," to
which he replies simply, "Life must carry on."[34]

Shortly thereafter, the camera fades in on the city center, and the sound
track reveals crowds being told to take cover and put on gas masks. An
air raid commences, but the audience sees little except shells, smoke,
chaos, falling buildings, and an eerie white dust that reveals itself to be
gas. With the city a mess of ruin and flames, the camera focuses on the
face of a dead child in the rubble. One of the male figures that we have
seen celebrating Christmas gives his gas mask to a little girl as he lies
dying. Abruptly, we shift to scenes of more typical battlefields: tanks, a
sky full of planes, the drone of airplanes. Years flash by on-screen – 1945,
1955, 1960; in the background, we are shown barbed wire, soldiers, and
desolation, and told of the breakdown of social order, of the spread of a
disease with no cure. We watch innocent victims of the illness shot dead
to prevent them from infecting others, and gradually we arrive in the
primitive, modern world of 1970, where brute force has seemingly tri-
umphed in a world still waging war.

Unlike Hamilton's vision of a post-air and chemical war apocalypse,
Things to Come offers one vision of how the return to barbarism may
be overcome. The solution lies in empowering scientists and engineers.
The 1970 Everytown is rescued by a lone pilot, who represents "law
and sanity," and a government that eradicates war by placing humanity under the rule of United Airmen; no one and no state can have air
power. The United Airmen drop the "gas of peace" upon the inhabitants
and the scene switches to a twenty-first-century utopia, the Everytown
of the future, built upon a century of progress. Instead of a world that
denounces science and civilization as the source of destruction as in *Lest
Ye Die*, *Things to Come* suggests that ignorance and trying to tie science to war are the problem, not these things in and of themselves. The

[34] *Things to Come* (London Films 1936).

Everytown of 2036 is a white, clean, technological marvel, where humanity survives and prospers.

Critics immediately saw the parallels between the Wells of 1908 and 1936. Writing in the *Spectator*, Graham Greene declared that "no one but the author of *War in the Air* could have created so vividly, with such horribly convincing detail, the surprise air raid with which the great war of 1940 opens." However, he added that the film "steadily deteriorates" after this point.[35] Others tried to situate the film's importance as lying not in the thing itself but in its context, having "some special significance at this time of threatening war clouds over Europe."[36] Indeed, as another reviewer stressed, "Mr. Wells gives us 1940 for the great war, and if it is anti-war propaganda to show us the intrusion of the bomber into the peaceful jollifications of a London Christmas, this could scarcely be better done. If he is right about the next war – and it is difficult at the moment to see how he can fail to be – few, if any, of us to-day will live to see the shape of things to come; we shall only hear them coming." Still others noted the timing of the film. As the review in the *London Mercury* made plain, "Many people surrounded just now with fears of actual war, may not much care to buy seats in order to watch the wiping out of civilization with air-bombs on the screen."[37] The film was both expensive to make and, for reasons that the preceding review implies, far from a popular success. This suggests one reason that films in the next-war genre did not proliferate. Nonetheless, the power of this film to show what war might do, its images of the dead child and the child in the gas mask, echo some of the real-life developments of this era, as we will see in the chapters ahead.

CONCLUSION

The inhabitants of the postwar world knew with certainty that war would now rain down upon civilians; terror would come. Thus, one key legacy of the First World War was that it demonstrated that no one and no place could be made completely safe during the next war. This changed the postwar landscape in both predictable and unexpected ways. First, postwar non-combatant memoirs, while offering a variety of responses to

---

[35] G. Greene, "The Cinema," *Spectator*, 28 Feb. 1936.
[36] J. P. Cunningham, "The Play and the Screen," *Commonweal*, 10 Apr. 1936. A few others described the overall effect as "boring"; see J. Agate, "The Cinema," *Tatler*, 4 Mar. 1936, and M. Forrest, "Cinema," *Saturday Review*, 29 Aug. 1936 .
[37] "A London Diary," *New Statesman & Nation*, 29 Feb. 1936. Charles Davy, "Films," *London Mercury*, April 1936.

these first raids, underscored how much they shaped claims to have been "in the war," how much they showed that civilians at home were deeply aware of the human costs of war, especially to themselves. In postwar fiction, the previous war's air raids highlighted the equivalence of the fronts and provided the foundation for anxious visions of what the next war would be like – a war of massive civilian death wrought from the sky.

Against these public depictions of air raids, the British government set to work to try to mediate and mitigate the effects of the air war it assumed would arrive. The cultural work laid by interwar representations of air war helped both scare and prepare the population to accept the measures that the state was also planning behind the scenes. For those within the British government figuring out what would become official Air Raids Precautions, the question of what to do with civilians, their character, their potential for quiet heroism, and the lessons of the First World War also resonated. We will take up the imaginative work of the secret government planning committees in the next chapter.

5

Inventing Civil Defense

Imagining and Planning for the War to Come

INTRODUCTION

If civilians under fire could come to embody a new kind of heroic civil identity, it might, however, seem unlikely that a teenage girl would be capable of this. Yet here is the story of Violet Buckthorne on the night of 8 September 1915 as recounted in Arthur Mee's postwar *Hero Book*:

> Violet Buckthorne was thirteen when the Zeppelins came to London and dropped a bomb through the roof of her home. Her parents were out; only she and granny were at home, with baby in the cot upstairs. When the bomb fell, Violet, instead of rushing in panic to the street, thought of the baby, and darted upstairs. But as she descended all the stairs were rocking, and several had given way and disappeared.
>
> How Violet got down she does not know, but she did get down, and she brought the baby with her and went out into the darkened street. She knelt down on the pavement and prayed with all her brave heart, and then she ran fast to the nearest hospital. They took the baby in. "But what about you?" they said. Violet thought she was all right, but the doctors thought differently. They found her streaming with blood, and from her ear, they took a piece of glass.[1]

[1] Arthur Mee, *Arthur Mee's Hero Book* (London, 1921), 221. This anecdote, entitled "Zeppelin Night" in the book, appeared in the chapter "The Heroism of Everyday: Ordinary Folk." The book was designed for children – Arthur Mee was the editor of the *Children's Newspaper* – with stories of the heroism of girls and women scattered throughout the volume, but the placement of Violet Buckthorne's tale is worth highlighting, since there is an entire chapter devoted to "heroes of the war," which excludes any mention of girls or women. This story was also quoted in Albert Henry Ross, *War on Great Cities* (London, 1937), 76, where a footnote records that "Violet Buckthorne's name was inscribed upon the Illuminated Roll of Heroes by the Carnegie Trust in October 1916. She was also awarded a Gold Watch and an Educational Grant of £30."

This description of such an ordinary yet exemplary girl reinforced the notion of both the air raid's horror – its attack on babies (on women and children) – and its simultaneous production of undisputed heroism among the presumably weak, again such as women and girls. In a postwar world where wartime heroism belonged – once more – to military men, these documents reminded readers of some of the forgotten hero(ines) of the war.

Another concrete measure of the immediate impact of the air raids of the First World War can be found in the memorials to those who fell victim to air raids during this war. These monuments went up as early as November 1918. On 2 November of that year, a memorial was dedicated in Camberwell Cemetery "in honour of the above," who died from "bombs dropped by raiders in the Great War." A list of twenty-one names, more than a third of them female victims, then appears on the roll of honor. Citizens of Camberwell also erected a memorial in honor of Calmington Road air raid casualties, which noted that the honor roll marked the spot where twelve of them including two children had died. A memorial in the Brockley Cemetery lists the names of seventeen Deptford residents killed in two raids, one on 7 September 1915 and the other 24 August 1916. Other monuments were erected in Dallington Cemetery, Northampton, in memory of Mrs. Eliza Gammons and her twin daughters, Gladys and Lily (aged thirteen) killed on 19 October 1917 when their house was struck by "an Incendiary Bomb during a German Air-Raid." And in June 1919, a little less than two years after the deadly attack in Poplar, a memorial to the "18 children who were killed by a bomb dropped from a German aeroplane" was unveiled at the Poplar Recreation Ground on East India Dock Road. A list of the dead children killed in July 1917 and their ages was placed at the base of the monument, while a statue of an angel rose above the names. If one looked for them, war memorials for the civilian casualties could be found scattered throughout the postwar nation.[2]

Such public memories and memorials implicitly called for government action to make these sacrifices, like those of more conventional war dead, worthwhile. They suggest that, at least initially, the legacy of the First World War's air raids lingered in the public arena, thus reinforcing

[2] For information about these war memorials, see IWM, National Inventory for War Memorials Database. All quotes are from the monuments themselves. More information and a photograph of the Poplar memorial can be found in Andrew Hyde, *The First Blitz: The German Bomber Campaign Against Britain in the First World War* (Barnsley, 2002), 155–156.

government action that began early in the interwar period. This chapter examines the ways in which the emergent public discourse around the air raid was also echoed in the first decade or so of government planning for the protection of civilians in the next war. It argues that the practices in which the state engaged were as much cultural as practical, as revealed perhaps most overtly in the suggestion of a Committee of Imperial Defence sub-committee member that the government ask H. G. Wells for help in figuring out exactly what the next war's scenario might involve in order to be prepared for it.

At the same time that the horrors of the next war played out in the cultural landscape, as we saw in the preceding chapter, the Committee of Imperial Defence's Sub-Committee on Air Raids Precautions (ARP), created in 1924, was similarly drawing lessons from the air raids of World War I to imagine the next war and lay the groundwork for what would become civil defense.[3] A close analysis of the ARP committee's secret proceedings reveals how much the foundation of ARP was based on interpretations of the raids of the First World War and the extent to which these plans belonged as much to the realm of the imagination as to that of calculated policy.

THE LESSONS OF THE FIRST WORLD WAR IN GOVERNMENT PLANNING FOR THE NEXT WAR

The arrival of aerial warfare raised the question for the government of how to protect the civil population, especially women and children. State preparations for the air raids of the future proceeded regardless of international agreements such as the modified Hague Conventions of 1922–23 that prohibited "aerial bombardment for the purpose of terrorizing the civilian population, of destroying or damaging private property not of military character, or of injuring non-combatants."[4] Government planning also took little note of the growing literature influenced after 1921 by Italian theorist Guilio Douhet's advocacy of air power as *the* way to win the next war.[5]

---

[3] For more on the institution of the Cabinet's Committee of Imperial Defence and its functions after the First World War, see John Ehrman, *Cabinet Government and War, 1890–1940* (Cambridge, 1958).

[4] Article 22, Draft Rules of Aerial Warfare from Hague Convention of 1923, as cited in M. W. Royse, *Aerial Bombardment and the International Regulation of Warfare* (New York, 1928), 212.

[5] Guilio Douhet, *Il Dominio dell'Aria* [The Command of the Air] (Rome, 1921). The first English translation of Douhet's work was published as *The Command of the Air*, trans.

State agents involved in thinking about how to prepare civilians for air war assumed that this *would* come. Their goal was thus to ensure not only the civilian population's survival of potentially deadly air attacks, but also the maintenance of something the state came to consider almost as crucial: daily life and thus morale. Such concerns shaped the top-secret planning for the next war. From 1924 until 1935, the government sought to keep virtually all aspects of preparing civilians for aerial warfare hidden. Yet the anxieties raised at the start of this process and the personnel of those in the know remained strikingly consistent, despite changes in domestic political leadership (and agendas) and in world conditions.

The first meeting of the Committee of Imperial Defence's (CID) Sub-Committee on Air Raids Precautions, chaired by Sir John Anderson, took place on 15 May 1924.[6] It came up with the following list of items for the committee to consider: warnings, prevention of damage, maintenance of vital services, repair of damage, movement of the seat of government, and the legislative and departmental powers and responsibilities that all of the foregoing would entail. The sub-committee then elaborated what fell

---

Dino Ferarri (New York, 1942). For works discussing Douhet's influence on British thinking, see Tami Davis Biddle, *Rhetoric and Reality in Air Warfare* (Princeton, NJ, 2002), ch. 2; more generally see Stephen Budiansky, *Air Power: The Men, Machines, and Ideas That Revolutionized War, from Kitty Hawk to Gulf War II* (New York, 2004), 136–139; Robert Wohl, *The Spectacle of Flight: Aviation and the Western Imagination, 1920–1950* (New Haven, CT, 2005), 213–216; Paul K. Saint-Amour, "Air War Prophecy and Interwar Modernism, " *Comparative Literature Studies* 41:2 (2005), 130 – 161; and Yuki Tanaka and Marilyn B.Young (eds.), *Bombing Civilians: A Twentieth-Century History* (New York, 2009). See also the writings of an even earlier theorist than Douhet, Pierre Lacroix, *Le Domaine Aérien et la Guerre: Essai sur les hostilités et la neutralité aériennes dans le conflit de 1914–1918* (Toulouse, 1919), and of the leading interwar British proponent of air power as the way to win future wars, Basil H. Liddell-Hart, *Paris: or the Future of War* (London, 1925). For an interesting reflection on French preparations for future war, see Roxanne Panchasi, *Future Tense: The Culture of Anticipation in France between the Wars* (Ithaca, NY, 2009), ch. 3.

[6] Sir John Anderson started his civil service career in the Colonial Office, assumed a variety of roles during the First World War, worked in Ireland from 1920 to 1922 at the height of the Troubles, and became permanent under-secretary at the Home Office for a decade, during which time he chaired the ARP sub-committee. He won election to Parliament as an independent MP holding the Scottish Universities seat in 1938 and proceeded to play an active role in shaping civil defense. From serving as lord privy seal prior to the outbreak of the Second World War, he became the first wartime home secretary and minister of home security, before being replaced by Herbert Morrison in September 1940. All biographical information here is from G. C. Peden, "Anderson, John, first Viscount Waverly (1882–1958)," *Oxford Dictionary of National Biography* (Oxford, 2004; online ed., 2008). He became one of the most visible government officials, if not the most visible official, associated with ARP and civil defense.

under each category. For instance, vital services would include not only the food and water supply, but also traffic control, post and telegraph services, and lighting and power. There were three areas for further consideration as far as the "prevention of damage" was concerned. One was increasing the difficulty of attack; this might involve lighting restrictions such as blackouts and the creation of other impediments to navigation or targeting. Another area was evading the purpose of an attack; the main object of this endeavor focused on plans to evacuate the "non-essential" members of the population from potential targets, especially London. The third arena was the development of some means of "protecting the population." Within this area, discussions would include arrangements about shelters, civilian respirators (i.e., gas masks) in case of chemical weapons, and other measures that householders, business owners, and local authorities could adopt to minimize the effects of aerial bombardment.[7]

From the moment that the CID's Sub-Committee on Air Raids Precautions (ARP) began to meet, it highlighted the necessity of psychological and cultural means of defense as much as practical measures. As Sir John Anderson commented in June 1924: "The most suitable means of mitigating the evils that might be apprehended from air attack in the future ... must be anticipated in the early stages of the struggle. The civil population would be better able to support these, since at this early stage it would be the *glamour* and not the *horrors* of war which would exercise the greater influence on men's minds."[8] This commitment to masking the dangers most inherent in the next war was echoed in decisions to "secure writers who would be able to impart the necessary information in regard to the implications of attack from the air in the future without causing undue panic."[9]

By focusing on preparations to allow all civilians to carry out their daily activities, the state sought to domesticate air raid precautions. However, their ultimate success or failure depended on the willingness of these same ordinary citizens to respond "correctly" to these provisions. Thus, when the CID ARP Sub-Committee convened in 1924, those involved in the serious planning for the next war envisioned that civilians had to be taught the following: "They must realize they are living within the zones of active operations, and therefore must expect to suffer casualties, [and]

---

[7] CID Sub-Committee on ARP, Minutes, 15 May 1924, the National Archives (TNA), Cabinet (CAB) 46/1.

[8] Sir John Anderson, quoted in CID Sub-Committee on ARP, "Appendix" to minutes, 23 June 1924, TNA CAB 46/1.

[9] CID Sub-Committee on ARP, Minutes, 13 Oct. 1924, TNA CAB 46/1.

that the enemy people is being subjected to similar but harsher treatment
than they themselves are called upon to support; and that victory will fall
to the nation with the greater powers of endurance."[10]

There was now no question that civilians at home would die in future
wars. Nor, unlike the situation during the First World War, when reprisals
were fiercely debated in both public and private, was there any question
of Britain's attacking civilians in return.[11] The greater suffering of "enemy
people" was here conceded as bolstering morale at home and encouraging the "endurance" crucial for victory. The preservation of civilian
morale through the construction of practical measures, propaganda, and
the sustaining of a new kind of civil identity available across class, gender, and ethnic lines – one presumed to have been forged in the last war
and that must now be invoked again – were all key components of ARP
planning.

Among other tasks, the Sub-Committee on ARP tried to make use of
examples from the First World War to determine when and if "panic" had
occurred and what had mediated it. To this end, it commissioned a study
entitled the "Effects of Aerial Attack on the United Kingdom during the
Great War"; a final report with that title was delivered on 18 June 1924.
Here the planners sought to determine the effects on productivity as well
as on morale of aerial bombardment during the last war. It soon became
clear that it was hard to disassociate the two, nor could any group, including men, be relied upon simply to carry on during such attacks.

The study compiled detailed information from manufacturers. For
instance, steelworkers, as the representative of a Sheffield firm reported,
exhibited a higher degree of tardiness, refusal to work overtime, and
absenteeism after a raid; "these raids have naturally a very bad effect on
the men." The Birmingham Metal and Munitions factory noted that output decreased after the February 1916 raids, and the Birmingham Small
Arms Company observed that warnings alone caused work to cease for

[10] Maurice Hankey, quoted in ARP no. 8, Appendix to minutes of 2 July 1924, TNA CAB
46/3. Maurice Hankey served as secretary for the Committee of Imperial Defence and
clerk of the Privy Council, and was an active advocate of Britain's need to prepare for
war in the interwar period. See John F. Naylor, "Hankey, Maurice Pascal Alers, first
Baron Hankey (1877–1963)," *Oxford Dictionary of National Biography* (Oxford, 2004;
online ed., 2008).
[11] A report from the Air Staff to the CID Sub-Committee on ARP in June 1924 made the
following point as a "lesson" learned from the preceding war, that the best defense lay in
the "prosecution of a vigorous offensive.... [T]he only possible solution was to make the
enemy suffer more harm than he was able to inflict." See Appendix, Report of Chief of
Air Staff, CID Sub-Committee on ARP, 23 June 1924, TNA CAB 46/1.

"an average of some six hours," reducing production by 7 percent. One major firm, Vickers, reported that "the moral effect of bomb raids was very high. Even in the case when no actual attack was made in the neighbourhood, the noise, possibly only of own guns firing, had a very adverse effect on somewhat overworked workmen." In addition to a drop-off in productivity, "it was noticeable that on the days following the raids the workpeople made more mistakes in precision work than usual; the quality was inferior and the proportion of rejected work was high."[12] Not surprisingly, raids thus affected the productivity and possibly the morale of male workers.

One interesting comment from the Atlas works in Sheffield sheds some light on the opposite side effect of the air raid. It noted that work ceased on many occasions because of warnings and that in one raid, where the works took a direct hit "involving a certain amount of loss of life among employees," this had "a serious moral effect on workers." However, in management's opinion, the deadly raid "did more good than harm as it brought home to them the fact that we were really at war, and they realised that their own efforts would play no small part in bringing hostilities to a successful conclusion." This was something the government wanted to foster, the transmutation of fear into the desire to do something to help end the war. Crucially this was an action that both women and men could undertake.

A large part of the report discussed the vital munitions industry, noting that "the frequent air raids which took place over Woolwich from the autumn of 1915 onwards raised the question again of the suitability of the site as a national arsenal ... production being seriously affected on many occasions." It recorded declines in production at other important munitions works due to aerial attacks, such as the National Projectile Factory in the Hackney Marshes in October and December 1917, and at factories in Rainham as well as Birmingham.

Wartime clothing manufacturers had even more to say about the behavior of specific types of workers. H. M. Selby, the managing director of Schneiders and Son (described as one of the largest clothing manufacturers in England) recounted that "the effect of the raids on production was most serious. The general result of a single raid or even of a warning was that the factories ceased work for twenty-four hours, as the workers could not be induced to return that day." Since workers continued to

---

[12] All cited in ARP no. 7, "Effects of Aerial Attack on the United Kingdom during the Great War," Extracts from CID Paper no. 106-A, 18 June 1924, TNA CAB 46/3.

receive wages if work stopped because of a raid, he was of the opinion that "many took advantage of this fact." The "type" of workers also affected their response. Thus Selby noted that "90 per cent of the employees were women, easily frightened and liable to panic," while "the other 10 per cent were alien Jews, who were even more liable to panic than the women."

A Mr. Jacobs of Lottery and Co. similarly disparaged Jewish workers. He "attributed a large part of the panics which invariably accompanied air raids to the fact that they employed so many aliens of Jewish extraction.... [W]hen raids were fairly frequent the output dropped by 50 per cent for weeks at a time" or ceased entirely for a time immediately after a raid. This section of the report concluded:

> Manufacturers were most emphatic as to the results which would follow continuous air raids; they said that production would cease entirely not only in their own trade, but in any trade which was situated in the East End of London. They attributed this to the enormous preponderance of Jewish aliens, about whom they spoke in no measured terms. It might be added that the gentlemen interviewed appeared only to be separated from the class they so vigorously denounced by the narrow margin of wealth.

On the one hand, good morale in these accounts was constrained by gender, as women textile workers were blamed for being "easily frightened" and liable to "panic." On the other hand, even "worse" than women from the perspective of their employers – often of the same ethnic identity as the report so snidely noted – were "alien" Jews, especially of the working class. As was the case during the war itself, since they were considered so markedly less robust, less stoic, and implicitly less manly than their fellow co-residents, allegedly true Britons, the presence of "alien" Jews compromised the morale and thus productivity of an entire industry.

Such coded anti-Semitic biases can be found in the report's more general conclusion. The findings stressed, for instance, that as far as London was concerned "the worst period [in terms of civilian morale] was during the autumn and winter of 1917, when aeroplane raids had become of frequent occurrence. The inhabitants of the East End, a large proportion of whom were aliens used to flock into the Underground stations of the Tube Railway almost every evening and camped there with their families for the night."[13] This emphasis on the problematic behavior of aliens was

---

[13] All above quotes from "Effects of Aerial Attack."

again nothing new; it had been a factor in assessments of behavior at the time, as we saw in preceding chapters.

In contrast, a case study of how presumed normal Britons could respond emerges in an interview with the town clerk of Margate. This coastal community witnessed raids during the First World War, but the town clerk was quick to stress that "it was not by the moral effect on the population that the town suffered most." As a seaside town, the community was "entirely dependent for its support on visitors," and once German raiders began to attack in early 1916, such "visitors were afraid to spend holidays there." As a result, "trade came to a standstill" after the summer of 1916, depriving many of their livelihoods and reducing the overall population from thirty thousand to sixteen thousand by the middle of 1917. Those remaining in Margate faced acute financial distress, alleviated only by charity from a variety of funds. In the clerk's view, in a "future war which lasted any length of time, apart altogether from any damage which might be done to Margate by actual bombs, the majority of the inhabitants would be financially ruined."[14] The committee therefore had to consider the extent to which the economic consequences of the raids could be as devastating as their psychological ones, depending on the type of population involved.

In light of the report, the committee meetings in June 1924 focused on the question of London. Sir John Anderson suggested, for example, that no decision about relocating the seat of government could take place until the committee had "some estimate of what the population of London would stand in regard to bombardment." Gibbon, the assistant secretary of the Ministry for Health, then commented that "actual casualties were not the criterion but rather the fact that London was the nerve centre of the whole country and ... could not be moved elsewhere at short notice." As far as warnings were concerned, the committee took note of evidence that factory workers of either sex and in any industry might fail to show up in the event of air raid warnings. Thus, in the 23 June meeting Anderson proposed distinguishing between towns "like London or Birmingham" that might suffer on a larger scale and required warnings and those towns "over which raiders will pass but not attack." He suggested calling the latter "raids" and the former "attacks" and developing strategies accordingly.[15]

---

[14] Interview with Town Clerk, Margate, dated 8 Mar. 1922 and cited in "Effects of Aerial Attack."

[15] Anderson and Gibbon, CID Sub-Committee on ARP, Minutes, 2 June 1924, and Anderson in CID Sub-Committee on ARP, Minutes, 23 June 1924, TNA CAB 46/1.

In the early years of the CID Sub-Committee on ARP, which became a standing committee at the end of 1925, practical problems such as how to shelter and feed a population under constant bombardment often raised "moral" ones. There was general agreement that the "moral effect" of aerial bombardment was and would remain "out of all proportion to the material effect which it can achieve."[16] A 1924 ARP memo by Maurice Hankey suggested that the knowledge of what war now entailed should be publicized very carefully, since members of the committee themselves were only now coming to realize

> the full implications of the new conditions ... the fact that consider-
> able damage to life and property must be accepted as inevitable ... that
> victory will rest with that country whose people will endure bombard-
> ment the longer and with the greater stoicism.... [T]he public has no
> realisation of what is in store in the event of another war on a large
> scale.... [T]he full realisation would come as so great a shock that panic
> would ensue.

In order to avoid such panic, publicity at the start of the next war would have to inform civilians that they "must consider themselves to be in much the same position as the inhabitants of a besieged city," and government measures would have to secure their confidence.[17] As Anderson later reiterated, "If the moral factor was removed there might be no food problem to solve." In other words, if the population could be kept from panicking, logistical matters like food distribution could perhaps be easily managed.[18]

The first draft report of the committee, issued in November 1924, emphasized that the initial estimates of damages that could be sustained in the next war were so overwhelming that any measures taken to respond must seem inadequate. Such estimates were based on the assumption that France would be the enemy, not because of any likely motive but because it was the nation most able – given the technology of the time – to launch damaging aerial attacks. Among the conclusions, for instance, was the fact that "we do not see that it is possible to secure immunity for our Capital. The measures which we suggest, therefore, must only

[16] ARP no. 4, CID Sub-Committee on ARP, 6 May 1924, TNA CAB 46/3.
[17] Hankey, quoted in ARP no. 8, "Education of the General Public to a Realisation of the Significance of Air Attack," Appendix to minutes of 2 July 1924, TNA CAB 46/3.
[18] Anderson, CID Sub-Committee on ARP, Minutes, 15 Feb. 1926, TNA CAB 46/2. A fic-
tional illustration of this in *What Happened to the Corbetts* was discussed in the preceding chapter.

be regarded as palliatives." Such measures included educating the public about the menace in advance and keeping in touch with public opinion, for "it has been borne in on us that in the next war it may well be that the nation whose people can endure aerial bombardment the longer and with the greater stoicism will ultimately prove victorious." It went on to note that despite debates about the efficacy of a warning system and lighting restrictions in the last war, both measures had to be implemented. So, too, did special provisions to cope with a potential gas attack.[19]

During debates about how to best safeguard civilians, the notion of a separate organization to provide emergency and other services soon came to the forefront. By April 1926, Anderson was comfortable dismissing the idea of drawing upon precedents, arguing instead that "[a]ir attack in the future involved entirely new factors; the distinction between combatants and non-combatants would largely disappear"; as such, there would have to be "some form of general staff capable of organizing the civil population." Such an entity would have to be prepared well in advance.[20] This confirmed the altered state of affairs. No longer would distinguishing between combatants and non-combatants be possible; war would fall on everyone.

Given this profound transformation, how were civilians to be organized? One suggestion was to use the military as a model and establish "some control analogous to Martial Law." However, Anderson was adamant that the new set of problems that would arise in an air war would require new solutions: "It was not possible to turn the whole of the South of England into a battle area, it was not possible to impose Martial Law on the head city of the country." Several other committee members concurred, agreeing among other things that the War Office would have enough to do in the event of war without taking on the responsibility of managing the civil population.[21]

Yet among the ideas aired in these early meetings of the ARP Sub-Committee – but not implemented even in theory – were ones that considered the civilian population as effectively militarized, even if not under direct military control. For instance, a proposal was made to assume that all now shared a new kind of universal civil identity, that of a voluntary warrior: "[B]y placing everyone in the position of an enlisted soldier a different temper of mind would be secured." Among other things, if

[19] ARP no. 20, "Draft Report," CID Sub-Committee on ARP, 5 Nov. 1924, TNA CAB 46/3.
[20] Anderson, CID Sub-Committee on ARP, Minutes, 25 Apr. 1926, TNA CAB 46/2.
[21] Col. P. G. Stock, Anderson, Col H. D. G. Crerar, and Hankey, CID Sub-Committee on ARP, Minutes, 25 Apr. 1926, TNA CAB 46/2.

individuals then "bolted" from the metropolis during an aerial attack, they could be considered "deserters." There are two aspects of this idea worth highlighting: first, that this would prompt appropriate (calm) action among those fearful of being punished as "deserters" and, second, that treating everyone as an "enlisted soldier" would enhance state control over each and every inhabitant. In short order, others rejected the idea, insisting that such coercive measures would not necessarily work to keep the civilian population in London.[22] As Anderson pointed out, "If dragooning of the populace" became necessary, if "discipline was essential with sanctions if necessary including powers of life and death," then some sort of quasi-military organization might be needed but could prove extremely difficult to implement.[23]

What seems more significant even than the fact that coercion was rejected on practical rather than philosophical grounds is the developing idea that even if everyone were not to be given the status of "soldier" – even if all could not be subjected to military constraints or military justice – all could be taught to emulate certain traits expected of men in uniform, notably calm, stoic courage under fire. These virtues made endurance of direct warfare possible. Anderson was convinced, for example, that explanations of risk and patriotic appeals would enable people (regardless of gender, class, or age) to "very quickly adopt themselves to the new conditions" of London under aerial attack.[24]

Ideas about treating "the whole population as combatants" – as potential men at arms – also emerged in discussions about compensation for injuries sustained during air raids.[25] This was based in part on estimates made in June 1926 of the number of casualties that would occur in London, assuming 24,000 killed and 46,000 wounded in the first month, with the rate slackening off thereafter and producing in six months approximately 70,000 dead and 135,000 injured.[26] One way to ensure an adequate volunteer labor force would be to provide for dependents by assuming that the needed labor would be male and those in need of protection would be the dependents of male heads of households. As Anderson explicitly suggested, "Men would be willing to run risk for the sake of their country but would be quite unwilling to put their dependents in jeopardy.... [Yet]

[22] See discussion in CID Sub-Committee on ARP, Minutes, 1 Feb. 1926, TNA CAB 46/2.
[23] Anderson, CID Sub-Committee on ARP, Minutes, 25 Apr. 1926, TNA CAB 46/2.
[24] Anderson, CID Sub-Committee on ARP, Minutes, 31 May 1926, TNA CAB 46/2.
[25] CID Sub-Committee on ARP, Minutes, 14 June 1926, TNA CAB 46/2.
[26] Estimate of Casualties, CID Sub-Committee on ARP, Minutes, 14 June 1926, TNA CAB 46/2. Again these are based on damage from the French air force.

if the war was a popular one and ... adequate provision made for the wives and families of the volunteers in the event of death or disablement, sufficient volunteers would be forthcoming to keep ... [essential] activities going."[27] Even so, others on the committee speculated that volunteer labor might not be enough. E. W. H. Millar, assistant secretary of the treasury, made the point that it might not be possible to secure adequate numbers to serve without resorting to direct compensation or establishing something that would have the "appeal" or even compulsion of serving as a soldier in the ranks.[28] Anderson then argued strongly against compulsion on the grounds that "[i]t would be impossible for a country, which did not adopt conscription for the combatant Services to enforce compulsion for industrial services."[29] The question then boiled down to whether payment for injuries from air raids would be treated as a form of "Workmen's Compensation" or "War Pensions."

As will be discussed more fully later, compensation was further linked to debates about the conscription of civilian labor, the idea that a scheme to provide material support in a case of "death or dismemberment" could be tied to making it a "punishable offense" to relinquish work "of national importance."[30] This issue would be taken up at the start of the next decade, but in the meantime, planners went ahead with trying to determine how to organize civilians into a force that could manage their own protection and whether this must come under civil or military control.

An internal memo issued by the ARP Sub-Committee in 1926 emphasized the issue of how to inform the public of the necessity of preparing for the next war. "The process of education," it stated, "should be slow and gradual, so as to eliminate as far as possible the chance of creating undue alarm."[31] How could this alarm be avoided if, as sub-committee debates later in the 1920s asserted, "the Civil population could no longer hope to remain secure behind the fighting line.... On the contrary, they would be almost certain to find themselves ... the object of direct and special attack." The new war would thus "become a real test of the fibre of the British nation."[32] In this sense, the nation came to serve as a totalizing category of identity; in other instances, some sub-groups – based on gender, class, ethnicity, or age – remained the object of specific policies.

---

[27] Anderson, CID Sub-Committee on ARP, Minutes, 14 June 1926, TNA CAB 46/2.
[28] E. W. H. Millar, CID Sub-Committee on ARP, Minutes, 14 June 1926, TNA CAB 46/2.
[29] Anderson, CID Sub-Committee on ARP, Minutes, 14 June 1926, TNA CAB 46/2.
[30] CID Sub-Committee on ARP, Minutes, 26 Nov. 1927, TNA CAB 46/2.
[31] CID ARP memorandum, 1 Jan. 1926, TNA CAB 46/4.
[32] Anderson, CID Sub-Committee on ARP, Minutes, 23 July 1929, TNA CAB 46/6.

For much of the interwar period, the committee focused on what concrete measures to adopt, debating such things as the provision of warnings, shelters (both public and private), gas masks, financial compensation, the establishment of voluntary medical and emergency services, and evacuations. When it came to this final idea, as early as 1927, the ARP Sub-Committee had discussed removing specific members of the population from London, ideally all "not engaged in essential work for the ... prosecution of the war, such as the infirm, the sick, women and children."[33] Women thus presented one important category of persons singled out by ARP planners. On the one hand, these officials assumed that they might fall into a grouping – a rather large one – of civilians who would need to be removed from danger. On the other hand, their labor and their newly acquired full civic identity as voting citizens (on the same terms as adult men after 1928) might mean calling upon or even coercing their service, even if civil defense had also been construed as another form of male service to the country.

No matter what tasks might be required of civilian, and possibly female, civil defense volunteers and workers, the protection of all left at "home" remained a central aspect of ARP planning. From the very start, the protection of the civil population was a paramount government aim that might require the movement of civilians away from danger, into shelters, and potentially into a mobilized civil defense force. Questions concerning these aspects of safeguarding civilians were widespread and closely tied to such challenges as evacuation and relocating the seat or at least aspects of the national government. In theory, all of those deemed "bouches inutiles" (useless mouths) should be removed from danger – but this still left unresolved subsidiary issues such as how far removed and to where. London, of necessity, posed a special problem, as it presented the largest, likeliest target and the nerve center of the British Empire. Thus, debates about how to protect the nation often coalesced into discussions of how to attempt to safeguard the capital. In the end, by deciding to promote a variety of methods to relocate, mobilize, and shelter the civil population, the state helped transform the meaning of the "home front." Indeed, by envisioning the creation of family-based as well as public air raid refuges, civil defense helped turn the gendered space of the hearth into something all must now expect to be under attack.

One clearly stated goal of ARP planning was to allow "normal" life, and especially the labor necessary to ensure the nation's survival, to

[33] ARP no. 76, [Dec.?] 1929, TNA CAB 46/5.

continue despite aerial bombardment. By mid-1926, planners were relying on estimates of massive casualties in the first month, which would then taper off as the war continued. How startling or fantastical these estimates – of 70,000 killed and 135,000 wounded in the first six months of the conflict – appeared to committee members varied. Some noted that given London's ordinary population of 7 million, they were not high and, moreover, that many of the most vulnerable members of the city's population would already have left.[34] Of those remaining, the task at hand would be to prevent "people from learning by bitter experience the dangers to which they might be exposed" in early attacks while reminding them that it would remain "a patriotic duty for people to go to work."[35] Several committee members had faith that the population would adapt, but only if given opportunities to avoid confronting the damage that the first massive attacks might produce.[36]

Furthermore, Sir John Anderson emphasized that volunteer male labor to keep London, and by extension the nation, "going" would be forthcoming so long as "the war was a popular one and that adequate provision was made for the wives and families of the volunteers." At the same time, Anderson articulated a crucial feature of such service that was emerging in these debates, that it was a government task "to make it quite clear that those who continued to serve in their civilian capacity, although they were not actually serving the *State*, were, nevertheless, serving their *country*."[37] Anderson, on the one hand, thus implied a gendered divide that would continue to exist during the next total war between active, male military labor and the more passive safeguarding of "wives and families" (women and children). On the other, he asserted the need for a rhetorical appeal to a kind of transcendent civil identity that called upon all civilians to serve the country, even if this was not the same thing as serving the "state," that is, not the equivalent of military service. Every activity that contributed to the survival of the community – the country – became redefined as essential service.

Thus, CID ARP Sub-committee debates about maintaining the functioning of the community under aerial attack emphasized the need for

---

[34] Estimates of Casualties, CID Sub-Committee on ARP, Minutes, 14 June 1926, TNA CAB 46/2.
[35] Anderson, CID Sub-Committee on ARP, Minutes 31 May 1926, TNA CAB 46/2.
[36] Gibbon, Hankey, and Anderson, CID Sub-Committee on ARP, Minutes, 31 May 1926, TNA CAB 46/2.
[37] Anderson, CID Sub-Committee on ARP, Minutes, 14 June 1926, TNA CAB 46/2. Emphasis added.

morale ("allaying panic"), and questions about the ultimate role of the
civil population were intimately connected with those about shelters,
evacuation, transport, and the distribution of vital supplies.[38] By June
1928, various sub-committees of the original ARP committee had begun
to work out particular issues, including that of staffing the extensive net-
work of services that civil defense might require. Anderson summarized
the findings succinctly:

> [V]arious aspects of the protection of the civil population were all closely
> related to one another and failure in any one particular might well lead
> to failure of the whole scheme.... [T]he advent of aerial warfare had
> produced the necessity of creating a fourth Fighting Department to
> organize the civil population. It was not possible to create this fourth
> Fighting Department in peace time. It might in the future come into
> existence as the result of a war in which the air arm played a predom-
> inant part.[39]

Such a conclusion underlay the effort that emerged in the late 1920s
to create a central organization for ARP, one in which ARP personnel
would know "that they were engaged on work of the highest national
importance."[40]

   This aim decisively shaped debates over how to treat what one member of the ARP Sub-Committee called "bouches inutiles" and can be seen
when the question of compensation for personal injury caused by aerial
bombardment came under more careful consideration of the ARP Sub-
Committee in the late 1920s (and again in 1930).[41] Two related issues,
about compulsion and the duration of such service in a kind of "mobile
reserve," became subsumed under the question of compensating those
willing to carry out their duties despite the risk of death or dismemberment. Some committee members felt that coercion would be necessary –
that in order for ARP to work, "all persons engaged on national work
would be guilty of a punishable offence if they relinquished this work." If
"patriotism" were not enough, compulsion might be necessary.[42] Others
felt that the entire idea of ARP had to be based on the assumption "that
the mass of the people would continue to try to do their work," and
Anderson concurred that "if the right sort of appeal were made to the

[38] CID Sub-Committee on ARP, Minutes, 27 June 1927, TNA CAB 46/2.
[39] Anderson, CID Sub-Committee on ARP, Minutes, 4 June 1928, TNA CAB 46/2.
[40] CID Sub-Committee on ARP, Minutes, 23 July 1928, TNA CAB 46/2.
[41] Anderson, CID Sub-Committee on ARP, Minutes, 17 Nov. 1930, TNA CAB 46/7.
[42] See Hipwood, Anderson, and Gibbon, CID Sub-Committee on ARP, Minutes, 26 Nov.
    1928, TNA CAB 46/2. Quotes are from Gibbon and Hankey.

population and the situation properly explained to them, there would be an adequate response."[43]

By 1930, ARP committee members had dismissed the idea of evacuating London in its entirety, and instead focused on how to maintain "morale" and "order." One proposed that "if the population required to remain were given to understand that they were regarded in *just the same way* as the fighting soldier, it would raise their morale and they would be prepared to stick it out.... [I]f they were prepared to carry on, they would get a pension; but that if they cleared out nothing would be done for them."[44] Sir John Anderson once again insisted that "the problem was mainly one of morale and in order to maintain morale it would be necessary to announce the Government's intentions regarding their pensions scheme at the very outset of the war." He further pointed out that the main task of the government was to encourage workers to stay and that "no scheme of compensation was going to be sufficiently attractive to induce people to remain in London."

Without going into details, Anderson noted that "there would undoubtedly be a tendency on the part of *certain sections* of the population to drift out of London," and the trick was to ensure that such an exodus did not descend into "panic."[45] This prompted a debate over compensation between idlers and workers, with proponents of limiting compensation arguing that "this class of person" (i.e., those deliberately not contributing to the war effort) would have "the onus of producing a case why they should receive compensation."[46] As one member of the committee summarized, the question came down to whether "the motto was to be 'Business as usual' or whether London was to be treated as a beleaguered fortress."[47]

All of this suggests lines along which the civilian population might be divided: between those lacking the moral fiber that undergirded appropriate and expected behavior and those who maintained morale and order. These positive qualities had to be universally encouraged; neither age nor gender nor class could be allowed to excuse lapses in civil defense

---

[43] Pratt and Anderson, CID Sub-Committee on ARP, Minutes, 26 Nov. 1928, TNA CAB 46/2.

[44] Sir Charles Hipwood, CID Sub-Committee on ARP, Minutes, 17 Nov. 1930, TNA CAB 46/7.

[45] Anderson, CID Sub-Committee on ARP, Minutes, 17 Nov. 1930, TNA CAB 46/7. Emphasis added.

[46] Hipwood, CID Sub-Committee on ARP, Minutes, 17 Nov. 1930, TNA CAB 46/7.

[47] G. C. Upcott, CID Sub-Committee on ARP, Minutes, 17 Nov. 1930, TNA CAB 46/7.

or civilian morale. Those planning ARP understood that something fundamental had changed with the arrival of air power; all civilians would need to see themselves as a kind of soldier or at least to assume a military-like obedience and commitment to the state.

THE HOUSEHOLD AT WAR: EARLY PLANNING
FOR EVACUATIONS AND SHELTERS

The question of what to do about women in the home, about mothers and their children, raised the issue of removing some of them – notably those residing in likely targets such as London – to places deemed safer. In March 1931, a special sub-committee convened under the auspices of Sir Charles Hipwood to discuss plans for evacuation. The first meeting of this evacuation sub-committee began with the "very big question" of whether and how public morale could be maintained if such an evacuation should take place.[48] Unless the government decided to abandon London, it had to develop plans to preserve "the physical life and sanity" of the metropolis, to call upon those needed to do this to fulfill their "moral obligation to the State." Such an undertaking meant treating "people working in London as though they were in the front line" – a realization the entire committee had reluctantly reached. However, the groundwork to get people to accept this status had to be laid well in advance.[49] This, said Major Tomlin of the Metropolitan Police, was particularly difficult because "war was quite unthinkable in these days."[50]

In summarizing their goals, committee members also reflected upon lessons from the last war, concluding that "it would be quite reasonable to expect the population generally to act sensibly if they understood what was required of them: experience in the late war tended to show that, with certain exceptions, the population had not been disposed to panic." Once again the "exceptions" were left implicit but this also suggested there was a standard for behavior against which those unable to adopt

---

[48] Evacuation Sub-Committee of CID Sub-Committee on ARP, Minutes, 6 Mar. 1931, TNA CAB 46/22.

[49] Evacuation Sub-Committee of CID Sub-Committee on ARP, Minutes 6 Mar. 1931, TNA CAB 46/22.

[50] Evacuation Sub-Committee of CID Sub-Committee on ARP, Minutes, 6 Mar. 1931, TNA CAB 46/22. In testament to the belief that such war was "unthinkable," the committee still used the 1924 report (ARP no. 5) that based calculations of damage on the power of the French air force as the starting point for assessing the extent of the problem. See report included among other documents for use of the sub-committee in TNA CAB 46/23.

this new civil identity would be measured. The committee considered that even if a future war were worse than World War I, "there was no reason to suppose that this stoical attitude might not be maintained," especially if prepared by propaganda before war began. It acknowledged that the circumstances under which attacks occurred could make a difference. On the one hand, "the season of the year and the actual time of day or night" would affect the reaction to raids. On the other, whether the raids were sporadic or continuous would also have an impact, even among the normally stoic, as "continuous bombing is likely to produce a very marked nervous reaction on the population."[51]

The most anticipated exception to this appropriate stoicism lay with the "foreign element" in the London population, who "will provide a special problem ... in view of their liability to panic under the conditions envisaged."[52] Even as the evacuation sub-committee tried to gather more information and prepare for the "worst picture," for "reducing life to a very primitive scale," the majority of the population should be "able to stick it out" with preparation and support.[53] As was the case during the First World War, "foreign" often became synonymous with "Jewish" as naming a group deemed unlikely to stick it out. As Major Tomlin reported to his fellow committee members, a police superintendent from Whitechapel "told him that the Jewish population, directly, or even before the actual air raid warning was received had all flocked out of their homes leaving them just as they were and had made for shelters, of which sufficient had been provided in this area to accommodate 100,000 people.... No attempt had been made to control the movements of these people except that they had been made to stay inside some building or other." When he asked the same police officer what the "effect would be of continuous bombing for a whole day on this type of the population," he was told "they would be driven almost mad with fright." The English section of the population, by contrast, had "taken comparatively small notice" and would presumably be able to proceed without panicking.[54]

---

[51] Appendix, "Brief Summary of Important Points from the Discussion," Evacuation Sub-Committee of CID Sub-Committee on ARP, Minutes, 6 Mar. 1931, TNA CAB 46/22.

[52] Appendix, "Brief Summary of Important Points from the Discussion," Evacuation Sub-Committee of CID Sub-Committee on ARP, 6 and 13 Mar. 1931, TNA CAB 46/22.

[53] Hipwood, Evacuation Sub-Committee of CID Sub-Committee on ARP, Minutes, 13 Mar. 1931, TNA CAB 46/22.

[54] Tomlin, Evacuation Sub-Committee of CID Sub-Committee on ARP, Minutes, 13 Mar. 1931, TNA CAB 46/22.

If the entire population of London did not bolt, plans had to be prepared
to orchestrate an orderly evacuation, assuming that this would be more
desirable than encouraging the population to stay put. Hipwood advocated telling "the people of London at once that they were all regarded as
being mobilized and had got to obey orders," that they had to trust their
government when it decided "to ask them to stay," even knowing they
would face "casualties and privations."[55] Tomlin suggested ascertaining
more precisely how "the population itself would feel." It is fascinating
to note his suggestion that in order to determine if people could "carry
on normally under the continuous rain of bombs predicted," the government might co-opt "somebody like Mr. H. G. Wells ... to help fill in the
picture."[56] Perhaps only a writer of science fiction could envisage what
might befall London. And as we saw in the preceding chapter, Wells was
not the only author haunted by the devastation that might emerge in the
next war who might help officials visualize what was to come.

In addition, the committee decided to solicit information about potential problems associated with the evacuation of a town or city from those
who witnessed such actions during the First World War in other nations.
On 11 March 1931, J. L. Edmonds of the Historical Section of the CID
wrote to the sub-committee's secretary, E. J. Hodsoll, offering his perspective on evacuations conducted in Belgium and France during the last
war. While pointing out that while air raids caused some evacuations,
Edmonds noted that inhabitants were largely left to fend for themselves.
He also emphasized that some locales, such as Dunkirk, were not evacuated and "life went on as usual in spite of almost daily bombardments and
air-raids." Edmonds further reported that a colleague with knowledge of
French plans for evacuation claimed that "it was impossible to organize
arrangements, all that can be done is to try and lessen the disorder."[57]

Despite this less than encouraging perspective and regardless of the
challenge of imagining the conditions that might befall London, the evacuation committee proceeded to consider how to do the "impossible." For
instance, Hart (representing the Ministry of Transport) suggested that the
government could manage a civil population under aerial attack if it were
able to "give everyone concerned with essential services the idea that they
were to all intents and purposes 'national soldiers' engaged on national

[55] Hipwood, Evacuation Sub-Committee of CID Sub-Committee on ARP, Minutes, 20 Mar.
   1931, TNA CAB 46/22.
[56] Tomlin, Evacuation Sub-Committee of CID Sub-Committee on ARP, Minutes, 20 Mar.
   1931, TNA CAB 46/22.
[57] Letter, J. L. Edmonds, to [E. J.] Hodsoll, 11 Mar. 1931, TNA CAB 46/23.

works." By putting these workers under a kind of military discipline, the government could make them "realise that they were helping their country to defeat the enemy." In other words, civilian workers regardless of gender or physical location would have to accept that they were on the front line. Moreover, inhabitants of areas like London had to agree to some form of control over their movements in and out of the metropolis in order to ensure that the transportation infrastructure necessary for the smooth operations of the state would be available. All of these suggestions occurred before the sub-committee had even determined that evacuation would be a desirable response to future air war. Whatever the ultimate policy, members concurred that if evacuation were to be ordered, the general interest of the community had to take precedence over any individual need.[58]

After one additional meeting, the sub-committee issued a report to summarize its findings on 17 April 1931. The very start of the report underscored the importance of character and attitude, for it was only "on the assumption that public *moral[e]* is maintained" that the committee was able to discuss plans at all.[59] Working with estimates that within the first six days of an aerial war launched against London, casualties would amount to 18,750, of which 6,375 would be dead, it predicted that such an attack would also cripple transportation services, deeply affect gas, petrol, and electric supplies, probably not disrupt water supplies if vital water mains survived, and allow for some maintenance of food and coal, depending on the state of the docks and distribution networks. The report also presupposed that a substantial portion of the population and area of London would be relatively unscathed. Given these findings, the report suggested that the plight of the city would be "difficult enough" but "not desperate," especially if the civilian population had been prepared to face some of these adverse new circumstances. Maintaining morale and maintaining order were seen once again as inextricably tied together.

This issue, however, was once more linked with the *type* of population. The entire question of orchestrating an evacuation hinged on "how anyone [could] ... hope to persuade the population of say, Bethnal Green to remain at home when their ordinary work is at a standstill and when no

---

[58] Hart and summation of points, Evacuation Sub-Committee of CID Sub-Committee on ARP, Minutes, 20 Mar. 1931, TNA CAB 46/22. For the issue of general vs. individual need, see Evacuation Sub-Committee of CID Sub-Committee on ARP, Minutes, 27 Mar. 1931, TNA CAB 46/22.

[59] Evacuation Sub-Committee Report, 17 Apr. 1931, TNA CAB 46/23. Emphasis in the original.

real protection can be given them." Would such a constituency be willing to "wait to be killed in their ramshackle houses? Will their sense of duty, even if reinforced by all the moral and physical power which the State is able to bring to bear, be sufficient to prevent them breaking blindly and desperately for the open?" The report conceded that the answer to such questions was unknown, but if the impulse to go to ground was not stopped, the enemy "will have succeeded in his main purpose of disorganizing the capital and putting it out of action." Adequate preparation and a clear system of organization for an exodus might help to alleviate this, but "it must be so constituted as to command the confidence of the citizens in respect of its policy and power."[60]

By expressing so overtly the fear that a certain segment of the city would not easily come under control, the report fully implicates the civil population in the successful outcome of the war. It stresses long-held fears – Bethnal Green does not seem an incidental example, containing implications of class (poor and working) and status (alien, Jewish, foreign) – about those who might fail to embrace the new kind of civil identity that aerial war called forth. In terms of specifying the members of the population to be evacuated, the list began with "women and children and helpless persons," followed by "people whose homes have been destroyed" and "people living in particularly dangerous areas" as top priorities. Whatever scheme the government adopted, the sub-committee was clear that "if the movement [of the populace out of London] is not controlled there must be disaster."[61] By lumping women, children, and the "helpless" together, the report clearly differentiated between the groups deemed vulnerable because of some "natural" condition (i.e. age, gender, physical capacity) and those deemed vulnerable because of the actions of the war itself (i.e coming from damaged or dangerous locales).

The sub-committee was then reconstituted to tackle the details of a plan to avoid a disaster. At a meeting of this new committee (with virtually the same participants as its predecessor) in October 1932, members decided that London should be divided into an inner zone, where evacuation would be encouraged for the majority of the population; a middle area, where evacuation would be optional; and an outer suburban zone, where inhabitants would be encouraged instead to stay put. Furthermore, it seemed desirable to promote evacuation in several stages: a voluntary

---

[60] All quotes in this paragraph are from Evacuation Sub-Committee Report, 17 Apr. 1931, TNA CAB 46/23.
[61] Evacuation Sub-Committee Report, 17 Apr. 1931, TNA CAB 46/23.

period before the actual outbreak of hostilities, when the exodus could be orderly and managed; a "controlled" period "representing the time in which it might be decided to institute the official evacuation plans"; and a bombing period, when attacks were taking place. The committee conceded that the last two periods might well coincide, and the trick lay in handling the flow of the population. In addition, certain areas deemed less likely to be targets of aerial attacks would need to take in refugees. These locations should be within a "reasonable distance of the Metropolis," particularly since in "point of view of the maintenance of morale," workers required to stay in the city would want to see their families as often as possible.[62] Again, the issue of morale was paramount.

Along these lines, a revised report from this committee in late 1932 put forward the idea not only of evacuating entire families but also of creating a mechanism whereby male workers would commute daily to London. This suggestion fit in with the larger proposal that evacuation must be "voluntary" rather than "compulsory." Using force to compel people to leave their homes if they put up resistance could prove impractical. Above all, a voluntary scheme also required an informational campaign designed to reassure the larger population of the necessity of government measures; no plans for evacuation could work without this larger civilian acquiescence. In order to encourage the "helpless" to leave the inner zone of London, appeals would be made to the entire family rather than encouraging women to leave their husbands behind. Thus, at this stage, no special arrangements were planned solely to evacuate "women and children, on the grounds that it is doubtful if it would be possible to effect an arbitrary separation in time of war."[63]

Relatively little progress was made in formulating a detailed evacuation plan until later in the 1930s. Nonetheless, all such plans acknowledged that, as will be seen in the case of shelters or gas masks, evacuation could try to protect the civil population, including women and children, but it could not assure them that any place would be safe. It was how they then responded to their endangerment that could determine the course of the future, because they were now deemed as crucial to the war's outcome as soldiers.

From the very start of this process, the protection of the civil population was a paramount government aim that might require the movement

---

[62] Evacuation Sub-Committee of CID Sub-Committee on ARP, Minutes, 26 Oct. 1932, TNA CAB 46/22.
[63] See Report of Evacuation Sub-Committee, [undated, post-Oct. 1932], TNA CAB 46/23.

of civilians away from danger, into shelters, or even into a mobilized civil defense force. Questions concerning these aspects of safeguarding civilians were widespread and closely tied to such issues as evacuation and relocating the seat or at least aspects of the national government. Even if citizens considered non-essential could be removed from danger, this still left unresolved subsidiary issues about how many, how far removed, and to where. London, of necessity, posed a special problem, as it presented the largest, likeliest target and the nerve center of the British Empire. As we have seen, debates about how to protect the nation often coalesced into discussions of how to attempt to safeguard the capital. In the end, by deciding to promote a variety of methods to relocate, mobilize, and shelter the civil population, the government invention of civil defense helped transform the meaning of the "home front."

It also became clear to planners that some proportion of the population, even in central London, was going stay put despite the inevitable aerial bombardment of the next war. Thus, the ARP Sub-Committee had to find some mechanism by which the population could be protected from the worst damage such attacks might inflict. The entire issue of how to shelter civilians or to protect them from poison gas in their homes or in public spaces transformed into military ones became the focus of debate as ARP evolved.

Discussions about sheltering the civil population developed among members of the ARP Sub-Committee beginning in March 1926. It was here that Sir Frank Baines, director of works at the Office of Works, noted that at present "there was not one single spot with absolute protection" in all of London that could allow essential government work to continue uninterrupted. Baines advocated that the building of such an initial shelter take place immediately and that other types of responses might include using Tube stations as public shelters. When Gibbon (representing the Ministry of Health) observed that "the provision of shelters as refuges was contrary to the whole scheme which the Committee had in mind" because "to provide shelters might very well lead to the lowering of the morale of the population and to serious interruption of London activities," Baines responded that providing shelters would help to maintain morale. Baines then reiterated his support for the idea of utilizing the Tube, in part because if stations became overcrowded, people could be taken by trains to the outskirts of the city.[64]

---

[64] Sir Frank Baines and Gibbon, CID Sub-Committee on ARP, Minutes, 15 Mar. 1926, TNA CAB 46/1.

At a subsequent meeting that same month, Baines stated the conundrum faced by the planners. They had to provide some sort of shelter, and yet they could never have "shelters for all, on account of the difficulty and cost involved." Nonetheless, there was a "danger" in providing only a limited number of shelters "invaded possibly by large numbers of panic stricken people, unless some means of exit from these shelters was also provided to eliminate the risk of people being left in the streets exposed to gas and high-explosive bombs." The problem of shelters was also defined primarily as an urban one, especially in London; even in the city's outskirts, inhabitants could escape by walking into the country.[65]

Baines was adamant that the government would find it nearly impossible to persuade the civil population of London to "remain in their homes and keep quiet" after enemy bombardment commenced. If this were the case, then no matter the cost, "it was well worth while to provide shelters" so the prosecution of the war could continue unhampered by panic. Based on his own experience in the last war, Baines argued that panic "did generally not take place before the actual fall of the bombs." Dixon then pointed out that conditions in the future would be very different from those of the last war; "in a future war with a continental power ... it was anticipated for example that more or less continuous attacks by aircraft would be made on the principal seat of Government in London." This would effectively shut down commerce and necessitate the removal of collections from museums and galleries, and "the most valuable historical records from the Record Office." In the final stages of the discussion, the committee agreed to estimate the cost and feasibility of providing shelter for perhaps two-thirds of the population remaining in London in addition to looking for "places of safety" to store artistic and historical treasures.[66]

Further complicating these deliberations were the contradictory aspects of rendering the population safe from both conventional bombs and chemical shells. Protection from the former seemed best done in underground shelters, while these same conditions could prove fatal in a gas attack, since the circulation of air above ground would help to disperse the dangerous agents. While the distribution of gas masks would serve as a backup measure to gas-proof shelters (even if they failed),

[65] Baines, CID Sub-Committee on ARP, Minutes, 29 Mar. 1926, TNA CAB 46/1.
[66] Baines and Dixon, CID Sub-Committee on ARP, Minutes, 29 Mar. 1926, TNA CAB 46/1. Some committee members, such as Maurice Hankey, were certain that the cost of providing underground (presumably safer) shelters was "impossible for any government to sanction in time of peace."

figuring out how to have families construct a gas-proof refuge or room in their homes was also central to ARP plans. The committee calculated that if a room could be made safe for twelve hours, this would allow time for the gas to dissipate. Members of the committee were also concerned that educated persons might be willing to wait out a chemical attack for twelve hours but that "the ordinary man in the street" was more likely to become alarmed.[67] Additionally, the issue of sheltering the population was closely linked to plans to direct civilians away from the most dangerous areas. In all these scenarios, "education" linked to class and the promotion of an ideal civil (stoic) identity remained of paramount significance.

More serious discussion of the use of Tube stations and tunnels as shelters took place in 1929, when Frank Pick, the managing director of the Underground, was first invited to consult with the committee.[68] Pick was determined that Tube stations not be used. Once again precedent influenced opinions, as Pick noted that when Tube stations were used as shelters during the First World War, they were left "in a perfectly disgusting state." In addition to the sanitation problems and difficulties with the dangerous overcrowding of stations, any proposal to employ Tube stations "as bomb-proof shelters in time of war would appear to be very expensive and difficult."[69]

As was the case with other ARP provisions, as news of what other nations were doing filtered into the sub-committee, members began to question how Britain measured up. In 1931 Sir Maurice Hankey asked about provisions for what he called " 'bolt holes,' places where people could go during air attack rather on the lines of those used in the last war." Planning for such measures had now been assumed primarily by the Office of Works, and while Sir John Anderson pointed out that the committee was waiting to hear about "suitable places" for shelters, the use of the underground railways of London was still under consideration.[70]

Later that year and into the next, the CID committee again took up the issue of making shelters safe against both gas and high-explosive bombs.

---

[67] See discussion in CID Sub-Committee on ARP, Minutes, 28 Mar. 1927, TNA CAB 46/2.
[68] For more on Pick, see Michael Saler, *The Avant-Garde in Interwar England: Medieval Modernism and the London Underground* (Oxford, 1999).
[69] Frank Pick, CID Sub-Committee on ARP, Minutes, 27 May 1929, TNA CAB 46/7.
[70] Sir Maurice Hankey and Sir John Anderson, CID Sub-Committee on ARP, Minutes, 22 June 1931, TNA CAB 46/8.

The Office of Works, to which the principal designs had been left, had focused on the latter rather than the former. Such discussions still assumed that this was advice about transforming a "private" home, debating, for instance, how to reconcile contradictory advice about the safest place to take cover. Committee members recognized that "in places like the East End," some form of "public shelters" might have to be provided, even if "it might be impossible to provide protection for the masses."[71] The reluctance to provide large-scale public shelters would continue until the very late 1930s. The primary unit left to face the air raid remained the household, a sign of the new status of, and reliance upon, ordinary civilians at home in a future war.

CONCLUSION

Government planners through the 1920s and into the 1930s underscored a vital lesson from the First World War – the need to understand and thus shape behavior and morale, especially among certain categories of civilians. They affirmed the wartime realization that a new kind of civil identity was required to face the traumas that modern war would inflict on civilians of all ages and both genders in their homes and neighborhoods. London became a central focus of concern given its strategic, demographic, political, and cultural significance, but even with reports on what the metropolis had experienced during the war, planners' minds boggled at what the future might bring. Hence, one member wanting "someone like Mr. H. G. Wells" to help the ARP Sub-Committee fully visualize the sorts of devastation that could occur. Charged by their government with developing plans to face the nearly unthinkable, planners struggled to determine how to prepare non-combatants – even those "naturally" set apart from warfare by age or gender – to become, as they now were, integral to war itself.

If the home was now an acknowledged target, not everyone responded with the calm fortitude that new notions of civil identity insisted upon. For

---

[71] Major Galwey and Anderson, CID Sub-Committee on ARP, Minutes, 16 Nov. 1931, TNA CAB 46/8. For instance, in February 1932, the committee debated the possibility of providing shelters, either below or above ground near London's docks, concluding this was not feasible. See Minutes, 15 Feb. 1932, TNA CAB 46/8. The committee also took up the question, posed in a letter, of using underground garages as both gas- and high-explosive-proof shelters in March, only to conclude that this was not an option, as London lacked any such spaces. See Minutes, 14 Mar. 1932, TNA CAB 46/8.

several groups, notably anti-militarists, pacifists, and especially feminist pacifists, the scenario for which the government had started to plan was totally unacceptable. For them, the only option was to do everything possible to ensure that the next war with its destruction from the air – and perhaps by the unleashing of a rain of deadly toxins – would never come. We will take up their struggles in the next chapters.

6

Trying to Prevent the War to Come

Efforts to Remove the Threat of Air Raids

INTRODUCTION

In May 1929, the Women's International League for Peace and Freedom sponsored a conference in Frankfurt on "modern methods of warfare and the protection of civil populations." The organizers quickly published the findings of the conference, which contained papers on aerial attacks with chemical weapons, the nature of poison gas, and the transformation of modern war. While the overall objective of the proceedings was to enhance pleas for disarmament, individual participants did so by calling attention to the stakes of future wars and to the idea that such wars would expose civilians, particularly women, to new dangers. According to one of the participants:

> The new and decisive factor of the next war will be the danger to social life now that the air fleet can use its weapons for *mass attack on the civil population.* "It is to be feared," says the Gas Committee of the League of Nations in its Report for 1924, "that the less conscientious of military leaders will make no distinction between the use of poison-gas against the troops on the battlefield and the use of these gases against the centres which provide these troops with weapons." The factory girl who makes a projectile is as important as the soldier who uses it. The transformation of warfare turns the whole of the enemy's country into a field of battle.[1]

---

[1] Captain Brunskog, "The Transformation of Warfare," in *Chemical Warfare: An Abridged Report of Papers Read at an International Conference at Frankfurt am Main* (London, 1930), 26. Emphasis in the original. The French version of the proceedings appeared under the original title of the conference; see *Les méthodes modernes de guerre et la protection des populations civiles* (Paris, 1930).

The author continued by noting that this "tendency" was already apparent in the First World War, although other conference speakers emphasized that "the worst of the past gives little idea of what would be the horrible reality of a future war," one where "the civil population ... will be massacred by gas bombs from thousands of aeroplanes, and peace will only be concluded over the dead bodies of the enemy nation. In comparison even Dante's hell pales into insignificance."[2] One such response to these possibilities, on behalf of newly and fully enfranchised women, was to embrace the civic responsibility to prevent such horrors from occurring.[3]

As we have seen, the imagined confluence of several new forms of war – aerial and chemical – called for serious consideration of the consequences of the next war. Officials responded with detailed – and sometimes contentious – planning, but voices outside the government seized the opportunity provided by the existence of this terrifying new technology to call for a variety of actions. As studies have shown, pacifism, or more broadly anti-militarism, had gained adherents in response to the deadly waste of the First World War, and as was noted in previous chapters, those who had experienced air raids themselves often felt a particular horror at the civilian death tolls and loss of innocent life that these produced.[4] Along with strict pacifists urging the abolition of war came those who focused on more particular measures. Some concentrated on garnering support for the League of Nations as an instrument to mediate international conflict and promote disarmament, including placing restrictions on the nature and kind of weaponry that future wars could entail. Others put their energies into broader anti-militarist and social justice campaigns.[5]

---

[2] Getrud Woker, "The Effects of Chemical Warfare," in *Chemical Warfare*, 45.

[3] While most British women over thirty received the vote in the Representation of the People Act of 1918, it was only in 1928 that women could vote on the same terms as men, i.e., at age twenty-one. See Nicoletta F. Gullace, *The Blood of Our Sons: Men, Women, and the Renegotiation of British Citizenship During the Great War* (New York, 2002), for more on the 1918 legislation.

[4] Nor was pacifism purely a postwar phenomenon; see the discussion of pacifism and militarism prior to 1914 in James Sheehan, *Where Have All the Soldiers Gone? The Transformation of Modern Europe* (Boston, 2008), 22–41, and his analysis of post-1914 pacifism (105–106), especially his assertion that "pacifism was no longer an eccentric opinion" (105) after the collective horrors of the First World War.

[5] See overviews on pacifism in Britain such as Martin Ceadel, *Pacifism in Britain, 1914–1945: The Defining of a Faith* (Oxford, 1980); Martin Ceadel, "The Peace Movement between the Wars: Problems of Definition," in *Campaigns for Peace: British Peace Movements in the Twentieth Century*, ed. Richard Taylor and Nigel Young (Manchester, 1987); and the recent analysis of anti-war activism as a measure of fatalism in the "age of anxiety" in Richard Overy, *The Twilight Years: The Paradox of Britain Between the Wars*

That the home was now a potential battleground motivated feminist peace campaigners in particular. While examining efforts to curtail the dangers of war, this chapter and the next repeatedly find themselves engaged with the efforts of feminist pacifists in theory and practice. Organizations such as the Women's International League (itself a creature of the war from its founding 1915 conference) saw women qua women as having a special, even unique, role to play in reminding the public of the dangers posed to women and children by a future war.[6] Feminist anti-militarists could speak as sisters, in solidarity with women as victims of war; as mothers, who risked losing the lives of all of their children if war should come; and as outsiders in their states, immune theoretically to appeals to patriotism, militarism, and nationalism. Many of the proposals and arguments made by women against war were far from new, and women had played an active role in campaigns for more general disarmament since the nineteenth century.[7] However, the use of new technologies of war exemplified by the air raid had intensified the sense of home life in danger and thus became a crucial target of their interwar efforts.

After chronicling some of the calls for the prevention of war in general and of aerial warfare in particular that began early in the 1920s, this chapter investigates the growing realization that aerial warfare had changed the nature of war itself through the eyes of those who tried to utilize this insight to end either war or its particular modern guise. It examines, therefore, how such efforts culminated in specific calls for

---

(New York, 2009), 175–264. None of these focuses especially on feminist pacifists, as do studies such as Johanna Alberti, *Beyond Suffrage: Feminists in War and Peace, 1914–1928* (Basingstoke, 1989); Gertrude Bussey and Margaret Tims, *Pioneers for Peace: Women's International League for Peace and Freedom* (London, 1965; rpt. 1980); Jill Liddington, *The Long Road to Greenham: Feminism and Anti-Militarism in Britain since 1820* (London, 1989); and Leila Rupp, *Worlds of Women: The Making of an International Women's Movement* (Princeton, NJ, 1997). For attempts to curtail chemical weapons, see Edward M. Spiers, "Gas Disarmament in the 1920s: Hopes Confounded," *Journal of Strategic Studies* 29:2 (2006), 281–300.

[6] The Women's International League later became known as the Women's International League for Peace and Freedom (WILPF). Its British Section continued to call itself the Women's International League, or WIL, throughout this period. Thus these terms will be used. The history of WILPF during the period is summarized in Bussey and Tims, *Pioneers for Peace*.

[7] See Liddington, *The Long Road*, for an overview of such activities in Britain. In the First World War's immediate aftermath, appeals for disarmament began to appear in the *Women's International League Monthly News Sheet* (the newsletter of the British Section of the Women's International League) from October 1921 onward. See *Women's International League Monthly News Sheet*, vols. 7 and 8 (1921–1922).

measures related to aerial disarmament addressed by the failed League of Nations Geneva Disarmament Conference of 1932–1934.

"THE MOST DANGEROUS OF ALL PLACES": THE HOME UNDER FIRE

> The military planes that cross my sky in squadrons many times a day and night never allow me to forget their purpose…. When I talk with the little brown-eyed or fair-haired children that hang about my garden and want to know the why of everything, I am glad they have never asked me, 'Why do those aeroplanes fly over like that?' For I could not bring myself to tell them that they are practising so that they may be able to drop bombs on little children in other countries. I am haunted by visions of what I might see in this little lane alone during 'the next war' of which people talk so lightly….
>
> [I]f a war occurred, it would be primarily the destruction of populations without discrimination, by enemy air men. Not much 'chivalry' about that! … 'Woman's place is the home'? They threaten to make that the most dangerous of all places.[8]

Thus did feminist and pacifist activist Helena Swanwick reflect in her 1935 autobiography on the war of the future, based on her own memories of the air raids of the First World War and the technology of war that had developed in the interim. Along with some of the other civilian writers discussed in Chapter 4, Swanwick channeled her experiences into activism.

In interwar Britain, such feminists, among others who recognized the threat to civilians posed by modern warfare, realized that the next war would bring women and the home into the direct line of fire to an even greater extent than the war just concluded. This acknowledgment was dual-edged, however, as it both recognized that the air raid had closed the borders separating war and home fronts and yet aimed to avert the next war by suggesting that the particular horrors of having *women and children* under fire signified by this collapse should prompt action to prevent

---

[8] Helena Swanwick, *I Have Been Young* (London, 1935), 500–501. In addition to her leadership in feminist campaigns, Swanwick spent the interwar period campaigning for disarmament through several organizations, including the League of Nations Union, the Union of Democratic Control, and the WIL. For more biographical information, see José Harris, "Swanwick [née Sickert], Helena Maria Lucy (1864–1939)," in the *Oxford Dictionary of National Biography* (Oxford, 2004). Other studies of feminist anti-war activity that discuss Swanwick include Alberti, *Beyond Suffrage*, and Beryl Haslam, *From Suffrage to Internationalism: The Political Evolution of Three British Feminists, 1908–1939* (New York, 1999).

such a catastrophe from ever occurring. Not only did the war of the future threaten to make the home "the most dangerous of all places," according to Swanwick, but it also threatened to destroy all vestiges of the modern world, transforming even domestic spaces into public targets.

Helena Swanwick played a crucial role in articulating a feminist critique of air war, highlighting not only the threats that it posed to women and their particular sphere of influence, but also the ways in which it called into question the notion of male claims to valorous conduct during war. A pilot dropping bombs on children in a quiet street could not maintain that he did so bravely or with honor. Swanwick, as we will see later, consistently offered a critique of war and of air power, and she sought public forums in which to do so. She was the first leader of the British Section of the Women's International League from the moment of its inception during the First World War, and she was also a fervent supporter of, and the only female British delegate (albeit a substitute one) to, the League of Nations.

Her work for disarmament could be both explicitly and implicitly feminist. When the League began to consider disarmament and the arbitration of international disputes as early as 1924, Swanwick gave a speech in which she stressed:

> At last we are told that arbitration is going to take the place of war; at last we are told that security is going to come to us, and I hope that that security will be of a very different order from that which women have been promised by men all down the ages. Do not you think that Hector told Andromache that he was protecting her? Do not we remember that throughout all the World War and the years that have followed it the cry of Asytyanax has run in our ears all the world over: 'Remember that when you turn your arms against each other, my brothers, the first victim is the child.'

Men promised women that they would protect them, but women continually suffered "the very worst that women can suffer in the loss of their dear ones." Even more remarkably, according to Swanwick, despite such bitter losses women, unlike men, maintained the ability to plead for "reconciliation" and not "revenge."[9]

Similar ideas were also aired at a meeting sponsored by the International Council of Women held in Wembley, also in 1924, on the role of women

---

[9] Helena Swanwick, "Speech to General Assembly of the League of Nations," reprinted in *Women's International League Monthly News Sheet*, 14:1 (Nov. 1924). See also WIL press cuttings, BLPES.

in "the prevention of the causes of war." As the preface to the conference's report put it, women must "realise the power with which they are endowed but do not use":

> It is they [women] who create the atmosphere which either leads to antagonisms between the nations and the consequent poverty of all, or on the other hand, to mutual understanding, happiness, peace, and prosperity.
>
> What we need is the willingness to do that sort of work for the world that in a simple state of society the ordinary Mother did for the Tribe to which she belonged.[10]

This appeal relied upon the power of motherhood, which had been a vibrant part of women's anti-war rhetoric before, during, and after the First World War, as a way to define the place of women in opposition to war.[11] It also emphasized the power that women possessed purely behind the scenes to shape warfare or undo it. Moreover, this postwar text also explicitly spoke of the danger that lay "not with the growth of existing armaments, but in the invention of new ones," especially "poisonous gases by which whole civilian populations can be killed within a few hours, dying in agony."[12] In the face of such dangers, the race was now "between education and catastrophe," with women serving as model, and necessary, educators. Here, too, the lessons of the First World War are once again made manifest: women must act in the world because they and their children are now directly at risk. Appealing to women, this document asks them not to make any pledges that would foreclose giving "aid to their own country if the madness of War overtakes it," but "to endeavour to save their country and their homes from the horror of such madness." They can save the spheres of both state and home that are now "mixed up."[13]

Such calls for campaigns specifically to address new and terrifying forms of warfare were not solely the province of female activists, but the effect of these measures on women and children remained a key element of interwar pacifist arguments. Notable political leaders, especially on the left, continued to issue calls for disarmament. In July 1923, the House of

---

[10] International Council of Women [ICW], "Explanatory Preface to the Report of a Memorable Conference Held at Wembley, May 1924, on 'The Prevention of the Causes of War,'" 5–6.
[11] For more on this, see Susan R. Grayzel, *Women's Identities at War: Gender, Motherhood, and Politics in Britain and France during the First World War* (Chapel Hill, NC, 1999), ch. 5.
[12] ICW, "Explanatory Preface," 5.
[13] ICW, "Explanatory Preface," 7.

Commons witnessed a vigorous debate over a resolution proposed by Labour's Ramsay MacDonald that the House denounce increased government spending on naval and air forces, call for such funds to be used to ameliorate pressing social issues, and ask the government to convene an international disarmament conference. MacDonald spoke out against the increasing expenditure on arms, including those for air forces, by quoting the wartime martyred nurse Edith Cavell: "Patriotism ... is not enough." Further, he maintained that distinctions between offensive and defensive uses for weapons had become meaningless, because "[t]he real fact is that we are sitting here to-day still under the dark gloom of war" partly as a result of competition over air power. MacDonald also made clear why the stakes for disarmament were so high given what was now known about warfare:

> When one nation declares war against another nation, it is not the soldiers, the armies that fight each other, but the women are fought, the civilian population are fought, the children are fought, the old people are fought. There is not a single person breathing within the boundaries of the State that is not fought.
>
> The next war will be worse than ever.... [T]here will be the air raids, with poison gases, which will simply devastate whole towns and whole countrysides.

Such rhetoric recognizes that warfare has changed; the solution on the left is to do everything possible to prevent its horrors from being enacted.[14] It is important here to highlight the category that heads the list of those now "fought" under the new terms of war: women. That this category of subjects should be under fire is still raised as being somehow shocking, despite the experiences of the First World War. Moreover, this appeal made what became a common assumption of the interwar, that air war against civilians would involve chemical weapons.

Some members of Parliament who responded immediately to this measure justified the continuing funding of air power as necessary "to protect us against air attack by the strongest air force within striking distance."[15] Sir Samuel Hoare, then secretary of state for air, defended government calls for further funding of air defenses by stating that most members of

---

[14] Ramsay MacDonald, Military Expenditure and Disarmament, *Parliamentary Debates – Commons*, 23 July 1923; quote about Cavell from col. 76; other quote from vol. 164, col. 82.

[15] Hugh O'Neill [member for Antrim], quoting Official Report on Air Power, 26 June 1923, *Parliamentary Debates – Commons*, 23 July 1923, vol. 164, col. 92.

Parliament had come to see this as a "regrettable necessity," having made
the important realization that "[w]e have ceased to be an island."[16] On
the other hand, parliamentary supporters of disarmament, such as Arthur
Posonby, spoke of how the aerial war of the future would not consist of
"little raids," as had been the case during the First World War, but "raids
of annihilation" – perhaps with chemical weapons – destined to re-create
"no man's land" in the zones under attack.

Using a gendered example once again as *the* emblem to suggest how
the conduct of war had changed, Posonby added that "it should be borne
in mind that the women and children are not going to be the last, but
they will be the first to be affected by this form of attack." There is no
protection for the innocent mother and child, who should be the last,
unthinkable target of attack. Moreover, there will be no time to respond
gradually, because the bombing of civil spaces and populations will be
immediate, "and by the time the next war comes we cannot foresee what
diabolical engines of destruction are going to be constructed to devastate
humanity and all the possessions of mankind." According to Posonby, it
was the "heartfelt craving" of humanity that those who knew the horrors
of the past war and the dangers of future war would help to contain "this
hideous menace of destruction."[17]

Even more emphatically, Frank Rose, a member from Aberdeen,
denounced the entire existence and costs of the Air Ministry. In his call
for limits on arms, he argued:

> Do they wonder why a few hundred thousand pounds is not available
> for child welfare[?] They do not understand the elements of economy.
> You do not need to fatten babies when later they are to be killed with
> bombs. Thin babies are quite as good as fat babies to be hit by bombs....
> You do not want a Ministry of Air unless it is to kill babes, and if you
> want to kill them, well go on with this policy![18]

[16] Sir Samuel Hoare, *Parliamentary Debates – Commons*, 23 July 1923, vol. 164, col. 120.
Hoare also emphasized that moral disarmament must accompany and perhaps even pre-
cede actual general disarmament; see col. 124. It was this assertion, a direct result of the
emergence of aerial warfare, that energized both proponents of ramping up Britain's
own air power and those calling for disarmament. The wider cultural implications and
explorations of this idea were taken up in earlier chapters.

[17] Arthur Posonby, *Parliamentary Debates – Commons*, 23 July 1923, vol. 164, cols. 109–
110; 112. Other speakers spoke in favor of international resolutions to stop the use of
chemical weapons; see col. 115.

[18] Frank Rose [member for North Aberdeen], *Parliamentary Debates – Commons*, 23 July
1923, vol. 164, col. 132. Edmund Morel echoed this argument when he asserted that the
suffering working people of Britain would begin to ask themselves, " 'Why ... should we
go on sweltering and toiling and sweating under these conditions when all these millions

The horrors of aerial warfare once again come down to an attack on innocence personified by the helpless infants injured twofold: by the lack of funding for their welfare because it has been spent for military purposes and by the raids themselves.[19]

The response of the Conservative government was that the subtext of the entire discussion revealed that something fundamental had changed during the First World War. In his address to the House during this debate, Stanley Baldwin asserted:

> There is not a man in this House who does not remember the first air raids and the first use of poison gas, and the cry that went up from this country. We know how, before the War ended, we were all using both those means of imposing our will upon our enemy.... But there was left behind an uncomfortable feeling in the hearts of the millions of men throughout Europe that ... we had all of us slipped down in our views of what constituted civilisation.[20]

Thus, progress on disarmament must be made, but only in an appropriate manner with the League of Nations, and not Britain alone, taking the lead. In the end, MacDonald's measure was soundly defeated.

The issues raised during this debate, however, would resonate outside Parliament throughout the 1920s. Notably, the League of Nations itself provided one of the early significant postwar attempts to restrict new kinds of warfare, the Geneva Protocol. This began by defining a war of "aggression" as "an international crime."[21] It implicitly acknowledged the new reality that non-combatants would be victims of war by noting – in Article 15 – that reparations could be demanded of an aggressor state "for all losses suffered by individuals, whether civilians or combatants."[22] The foundation was also laid during this decade for further work to mitigate some of these effects and to promote disarmament through this international body.

are being spent for the next war, of which our children will be the predestined victims?'" See col. 143.

[19] Labour MP Thorne, arguing that nothing would stop war except getting rid of the means to wage it, singled out the role of "women," who drew on their experience of the last war "to demand that the world shall not be cursed by war again." *Parliamentary Debates – Commons*, 23 July 1923, vol. 164, col. 163.

[20] Stanley Baldwin, *Parliamentary Debates – Commons*, 23 July 1923, vol. 164, col. 177. It is worth noting that this is well before he made his most famous remarks on air power, that "the bomber will always get through," delivered on 10 November 1932 and discussed later in the chapter.

[21] *Synopsis of the Geneva Protocol for the Pacific Settlement of International Disputes* (New York, 1924), 4.

[22] *Synopsis of the Geneva Protocol*, 28.

Outside of official circles, peace campaigners sought to keep alive the issue of disarmament by highlighting the costs of continuing to fund arms in general and air power in particular. Throughout the 1920s, the Women's International League attempted to raise public awareness of the dangers inherent in a future war – the war of the air and the laboratory. As a subsidiary body of an international organization, the Women's International League for Peace and Freedom (WILPF), the British Women's International League (WIL) worked both in common with broader goals set by the larger entity and on issues of particular relevance to Britain, sometimes in conjunction with other interwar pacifist groups. In the mid-1920s, it helped arrange protests calling for "no more war" and in favor of immediate land, sea, and air disarmament.[23] The WIL was also eager to inform its members about developments in the regulation of the international arms trade put forward by the League of Nations in 1925.[24]

A year later, it decided to participate in a more ambitious public project. In February 1926, under the slogan "Law Not War," a variety of women's groups came together to organize a peace pilgrimage for the coming summer, whereby "pilgrims" would take a variety of routes leading to London for a mass demonstration. As Katherine (K. D.) Courtney, one of the leaders, put it, "The psychological moment had come for women to express their views about such things as arbitration and disarmament."[25] Taking the idea from the 1913 campaign for women's suffrage, the entire spectacle was designed to showcase women's stake in preventing future war, pushing Britain's government to support measures for international arbitration and disarmament. WIL took an active role in the forthcoming pilgrimage, but it also relied upon the support of, and worked with, the Women's Cooperative Guild and the League of Nations Union. The timing of the eventual pilgrimage was compromised by the General Strike; nonetheless, on June 19 thousands gathered in London's Hyde Park to hear voices calling for disarmament and peace.[26]

A wide range of public responses accompanied the agreements on arms limitations and peace that developed during the first interwar

---

[23] See "No More War and Disarmament Demonstrations," *Women's International League Monthly New Sheet*, May 1923.

[24] "The Arms Conference, 1925," *Women's International League Monthly News Sheet*, June 1925.

[25] "Peacemaker's Pilgrimage," *Women's International League Monthly News Sheet*, Feb. 1926.

[26] See the discussion of the 1926 Peace Pilgrimage and of some small-scale pilgrimages that followed in 1927 in Liddington, *The Long Road*, 144–146.

decade. International laws governing the future use of air power drafted in 1923 had prohibited bombing for the purposes of "terrorizing the civilian population" and rendered such attacks legitimate only if used against a "military objective."[27] Further, the Geneva Protocol of 1924 banned poison gases; this was expanded to include biological weapons in 1925. Other international agreements, notably the Treaties of Locarno and the 1928 Kellogg–Briand Pact, had contributed to a sense of potentially sweeping changes that could emerge from a full-scale disarmament conference. First, Locarno and ultimately the Kellogg–Briand agreement bound signatory parties to renounce war as a means of solving international conflicts; these measures had clear limits at the time, notably that the Kellogg–Briand pact had no mechanism to enforce the agreement. Steps had also been taken in the late 1920s and early 1930s to curtail naval power.[28] As far as air power was concerned, preliminary proposals for a Geneva conference on disarmament not only stressed a reduction in armed air forces, but also called for no preparations "in time of peace for the installation of warlike armaments" on civil aircraft.[29] It was air disarmament, rather than disarmament in the abstract, that came to occupy government and unofficial voices in the years leading up to the long-anticipated (and long-delayed) Geneva Conference that began in 1932.[30]

For several years prior to 1932, calls for the government to promote disarmament continued to issue forth from Labour Party leaders like Ramsay MacDonald on a regular basis when his party was out of power from November 1924 until June of 1929. To give one example, in November 1927, MacDonald berated the Conservative government in the House of Commons for its slow progress in working for disarmament and arbitration in international politics. He argued:

> [I]f we are to give peace to Europe, we have to attack the psychology of the people. In the beginning, and as a start, peace is a purely psychological

---

[27] See the discussion of these rules in Tami Davis Biddle, "Air Power," in *The Laws of War: Constraints on Warfare in the Western World*, ed. Michael Howard, George J. Andreopoulos, and Mark R. Shulman (New Haven, CT, 1994), 148.

[28] For a contemporary British synopsis of these measures, see Stephen Heald, "Memorandum on the Progress of Disarmament, 1919–1932" (London, 1932). An overview of these measures can be found in the introductory section of Phillip S. Meilinger, "Clipping the Bomber's Wings: The Geneva Disarmament Conference and the Royal Air Force, 1932–1934," *War in History* 6:3 (1999), 306–307.

[29] Heald, "Memorandum," 46.

[30] See a summation of some of these debates in Uri Bialer, *The Shadow of the Bomber: The Fear of Air Attack and British Politics, 1932–1939* (London, 1980), ch. 1. For British pacifist activity around these issues, see Ceadel, "The Peace Movement between the Wars," 77.

> problem, and we found ... there is no objection to disarmament, that
> there is no objection to arbitration, there is no objection to any gesture
> for peace ... to any declaration in favour of peace.

What had to be overcome was a popular lack of understanding of collective security and the government's belief that it could either support the British Empire or the League of Nations, but not both.[31]

One of the organizations dedicated to changing the psychology of the civil population and urging their support for disarmament was the League of Nations Union. On the tenth anniversary of the end of the war, it published a short pamphlet, "A Machine Gunner Looks at the League," that offered not only vivid details about the horrors personally witnessed during the First World War, but also appeals to specific constituent bodies to support the League's efforts to promote disarmament and peace. The gunner J. Wickham Murray, for instance, rhetorically asked women if they wanted to sit in "a room darkened against aircraft" waiting for news of their loved ones fighting far off – evoking the experiences of some civilians during that war. He concluded by urging direct participation in the political process by both men and women, especially those of the middle class: "I know how dignified you are. I know you hate taking actions that make you lose that dignity by appearing odd. Let me tell you it is very difficult to be dignified when enemy aircraft smash up the nice little house you so luckily secured with the small deposit and the large mortgage." By reminding his audience not only of the suffering of soldiers, but of the suffering and destruction that would be felt by those at home, Murray urged his readers to join the League and become active, even if it meant appearing "odd" – agitated, not stoic but engaged.[32]

By the end of the 1920s, an array of responses in leading journals also highlighted the differing perspectives on disarmament. In 1929 an article in the *New Statesman* pointed to the "signs of a growing and more interested public opinion, alive to the stupidity and waste of war," noting that even better than a reduction in armaments would be "a fifty per cent. increase of rational pacifists."[33] Writing in the *Nation & Athenaeum* in December 1930, Georg Bernhard argued for the necessity of international authority as the "one effective method of control." Anything else

---

[31] Ramsay MacDonald, Orders of the Day: Motion on International Peace and Disarmament, *Parliamentary Debates – Commons*, 24 Nov. 1927, quote from vol. 210, cols. 2096–2097; further discussion in cols. 2098–2101.

[32] League of Nations Union, "A Machine Gunner Looks at the League," (London, 1928).

[33] "Arms and the Man," *New Statesman*, 28 Sept. 1929.

was "at best" a half-measure, leaving individual states to evade easily provisions designed to curtail their military prowess.[34]

The 1931 appearance of a four-hundred-page tome on the "character of a new war" based upon an inquiry by the Inter-Parliamentary Union suggested a growing international consensus on the dangers that the world faced in the next war. *What Would Be the Character of New War?* included contributions from leading international scholars and strategies on everything from the military to the potential demographic, economic, legal, and psychological effects of another modern and all-encompassing war. It deliberately sought to influence the forthcoming Geneva Disarmament Conference, stating that "if useful work is to be done the Conference must be backed by enlightened public opinion."[35] The remainder of the volume set out to enlighten the public, paying particular attention to how warfare had changed. Military experts stated dispassionately that "in a future war, belligerents will employ every conceivable means" of waging war. Thus, "the effect upon the whole nation will be immeasurably greater than was the case in the World War. Everyone and everything will be involved in the war."[36] Dr. Gertrud Woker of Switzerland, a speaker at the 1929 WILPF conference, wrote of the prospect of chemical warfare, asserting that "in the event of another war ... it is safe to reckon on an even more extensive and terrible gas warfare than that which was developed from 1914 to 1918."[37] The cumulative effect of the volume was to support efforts to "prevent war, not to humanise it," for no restrictions on the nature of warfare itself would prove feasible.[38]

By the time the League of Nations was preparing seriously to take on the issues of disarmament at the start of the 1930s, the WIL was advocating the "definite and drastic measures of disarmament on land, sea and air ... the abolition of air warfare ... [and the] international control of civil aviation."[39] As 1931 proceeded, the WIL solicited signatures on

[34] Georg Bernhard, "The Crux of the Disarmament Question," *Nation & Athenaeum*, 27 Dec. 1930. There was also support from the religious establishment on the question of disarmament as seen in the Report of the Lambeth Conference in 1930, which is explained in Rev. E. A. Burroughs, "The Lambeth Series: The Christian Church and War," (1931, US rpt. Milwaukee, WI, 1931).

[35] P. Munich, "Preface," *What Would Be the Character of a New War?* (London, 1931), x.

[36] Lieut-General Von Metzsch, "The New Tendencies of Development in Warfare," in *What Would Be the Character of a New War?* 30–32.

[37] Getrud Woker, "Chemical and Bacteriological Warfare," in *What Would Be the Character of a New War?* 357.

[38] *What Would Be the Character of a New War?* 411.

[39] General Resolution of the International Executive Committee of the Women's International League, Jan. 1931, attached to British Section-WIL, Minutes, 19 Jan. 1931, WILPF 1/7, BLPES.

petitions urging disarmament and a true reduction in the size of "the armies, navies and air forces of the world."

Members of other women's organizations such as the Women's Co-operative Guild (WCG) also expressed a renewed commitment to disarmament at the start of the 1930s. In a WCG pamphlet, "Disarmament and Security," Lilian Harris noted that the postwar world now had "bitter experience of the fact that armaments can never give security" and directed attention to the threats posed by aerial warfare. Outlining the differences between civil and military aviation, Harris continued by urging the abolition of "all war air forces" and the further prohibition of "research for new and more deadly weapons," such as those involving chemicals or poison gas.[40]

The League of Nations Union also directly participated in efforts to educate and sway the public on the issue of international and aerial disarmament. It issued a series of short pronouncements, often two- to four-page leaflets, using words and pictures to appeal to the British population to support the reduction and limitation on armament. One such leaflet, entitled "An Airman Tells You," drawing on the expertise of Brigadier-General P. R. C. Groves (described as "Director of Air Operations for British Forces in 1918"), declared that in the first phase of the next war gas bombs dropped on cities like Paris and London "might entail the loss of millions of lives in a few hours." No remedy could be devised for this. If the words in this short document evoked aerial chemical war, the obverse of the text offered a stark reminder of the First World War. In the center appeared a photograph of the bombed-out ruins of a house; beside it came the lines "A House in Streatham in the Great War ... YOUR HOME NEXT TIME."[41] Support for disarmament via the League thus entailed relying on both the stark depiction of what air war had done in the last war (ruined houses) and what it would do in the next: destroy "your home" in addition to murdering millions. Such appeals had an impact.

Along with other groups such as the National Committee for the Prevention of War, women's peace organizations such as the WIL had spent time gathering signatures to show popular support for disarmament on the eve of the Geneva Conference. By July 1931, more than a million people had signed a petition urging the government to take action on immediate disarmament. Even closer to the start of the Disarmament Conference in early January 1932, the number was close to 2 million.[42]

[40] Lilian Harris, "Disarmament and Security" (London, [c. 1931]).
[41] League of Nations Union, "An Airman Tells You" (London, [c. 1931]).
[42] See British Section-WIL, Minutes, 14 July 1931 and 12 Jan. 1932, WILPF 1/7 and 1/8, BLPES.

While this can correctly be read as yet another indication of popular support for anti-militarist and pacifist measures, it also must be seen as responding to specific threats posed by modern methods of war, such as the air raid with its attacks on civilians and homes that the state could not prevent.

With such a widespread buildup both in the media and through demonstrable public opinion, the work of the Disarmament Conference when it began to meet in 1932 garnered national attention and the support of leading politicians. In addition, the knowledge that all fronts could potentially come under fire informed the words of the British foreign minister, Sir John Simon. At the opening of the 1932 World Disarmament Conference, he famously stated:

> For of all the horrible features which warfare presents, there is nothing which so fills the imagination with forebodings of the future ... nothing ... which is so repulsive to all who are actually engaged in the profession of arms, as the promiscuous character of the destruction which modern war threatens.... [T]here is no calling however peaceful, no home however distant and humble, no innocence of life, no weakness of sex, no immaturity of age which is not in peril of the consequence if the most modern methods of warfare cannot be curbed or abandoned[43]

Simon then urged delegates to outlaw aerial bombardment along with chemical warfare as the most pernicious of the technological innovations of the First World War.

A few days after the Conference opened, a dramatic demonstration of popular support for such ideas occurred in Geneva. On 6 February 1932, representatives of more than fifteen women's international organizations, as well as members of religious groups and peace societies, trade unionists, workers, and students addressed the Conference's delegates. Part of the women's international effort was to present the petitions collected in individual states by groups such as WIL and articulate the specific nature of the women's appeal for disarmament:

> Behind each of these eight million names stands ... a human being oppressed by a great fear – the fear of the destruction of our civilisation.... It is not for ourselves alone that we plead, but for the generations

---

[43] Sir John Simon, British Foreign Minister, Speech at Geneva Disarmament Conference Opening Session, Feb. 1932, quoted in H. Montgomery Hyde and G. R. Falkiner Nuttall, *Air Defence and the Civil Population* (London, 1937), 41. For an overview of Britain's official and, at times, contradictory aims at the conference, see Carolyn J. Kitching, *Britain and the Geneva Disarmament Conference: A Study in International History* (Basingstoke, 2003).

to come. To us women, as mothers, the thought of what another great war would mean for our children is the strongest incentive impelling us to spend ourselves in the endeavour to make their lives secure from such a disastrous fate.[44]

This familiar language of a call for peace and disarmament based on women's maternal role shows the long continuity of such emotionally charged appeals. Yet there also appears a relatively new concern about what novel methods of war would mean for all children.

Delegates representing various nations spent the early sessions of the Conference putting forward their own specific plans and publicizing them fairly widely. As the WIL newsletter, the *Monthly News Sheet*, made clear in April, it wholeheartedly endorsed French proposals – collectively know as the Tardieu Plan – that called for a League of Nations air force and the outlawing of aerial bombardment. Its advocacy for the Disarmament Conference included affirming that "the internationalisation of civil aviation is a proposition which we can all support."[45] Britain's particular status as an island-nation made support for the prevention of aerial warfare of greater public concern than other kinds of disarmament.[46] However, the support of the government splintered when it was asked to do more than outlaw bombers or attacks on the civil population from the air. It opposed the Tardieu Plan and was reluctant to allow the international control of civil aviation or the establishment of an air force under the control of the League of Nations.[47]

Developments at Geneva were especially closely followed in the antimilitarist press and among pacifist organizations. Thus the National Peace Council's representative to the Conference, Arnold Foster, wrote special reports, offering up-to-the-minute accounts of the Conference's early stages, including addresses made to the delegates by and on behalf of women. When the Conference opened, Foster, for example, quoted Sir John Simon's speech with approval and noted that other delegations spoke in favor of devising effective measures "to protect civilian populations against bombing from the air."[48]

[44] Mary A. Dingman, President of the Disarmament Committee of the Women's Oganizations, quoted in *Vox Populi* (Geneva, 1932), 17. Another account of this session is found in "Towards Disarmament: Campaign Notes Published by the National Peace Council," 13 Feb. 1932.

[45] *Women's International League Monthly News Sheet*, 23:4 (Apr. 1932).

[46] Bialer, *Shadow*, 20–21.

[47] Bialer, *Shadow*, 27.

[48] Arnold Foster, *The Disarmament Conference*; see issues no. 1, 10 Feb. 1932; no. 2, 12 Feb. 1932; and no. 3, 16 Feb. 1932. Quote is from no. 3.

By the end of the month, Foster reported on competing proposals to abolish naval and military aircraft and to place civil aviation under international control. The French delegation continued to advocate the Tardieu Plan, the internationalization of civil aviation, but Germany's representatives, among others, stood firmly opposed. When summarizing the various proposals in March, Foster noted the divergences along national lines, with Germany, Sweden, and Spain calling for the abolition of military aviation; others, such as Switzerland, Italy, Austria, and Belgium, urging the abolition of bombing aircraft; France arguing for the League to control civil aviation; and Germany and Russia calling for a prohibition on arming civil aircraft.[49]

After several months of debate, the Air Commission Sub-Committee of the Conference had agreed upon a set of draft rules. As far as material was concerned, civil aviation must be constructed purely for "civil purposes," and arming civil aircraft or constructing them in such a way as to facilitate their being turned to military purposes should be strictly prohibited. In terms of personnel, contracting parties were to agree not to train those engaged in civil aviation so as to prepare them for military aviation. France's representative made note of its particular objections to these principles, reiterating that "no rules can fulfil the purpose in view – namely 'to prevent the employment of civil aviation for military purposes.' " Therefore, "in order to be certain that States will not develop their civil aviation for military purposes, it is necessary to delegate to an international organisation, not a mere right of inspection … but *a right of decision and supervision over* public air transport."[50]

In the autumn of 1932, a debate in the House of Commons on international affairs revealed some of the conflicting views on air power and efforts at disarmament, a debate that was also wrapped up with the actions of the Japanese against China. Here both Labour and Conservative members of Parliament spoke of their support for disarmament.[51] In particular, Clement Atlee spoke in support of the internationalization of civil

[49] Foster "Review of Disarmament Conference," *The Disarmament Conference*, no. 9, 22 Mar. 1932.

[50] "Position of the Sub-Committee's Work After the Meeting on July 18th, 1932," in "Minutes of the Air Commission," *Records of the Conference for the Reduction and Limitation of Armaments*, series D, vol. 3 (Geneva, 1936), 313–314. Emphasis in the original. For reactions to the work of the conference at this point, see "War in the Air," *New Statesman and Nation*, 19 Nov. 1932.

[51] See Samuel Vyvyan Adams, *Parliamentary Debates – Commons*, 10 Nov. 1932, vol. 270, cols. 594–595; see also Mary Pickford, col. 587; Sir Austen Chamberlain, col. 556; Sir Arthur Steel-Maitland, cols. 572–573; and Frederick Cocks, col. 571.

aviation, and George Lansbury not only supported this idea as one that would preserve peace, but also advocated "total disarmament."[52]

These debates were also the occasion for one of the most famous statements uttered during the interwar period by a British politician, namely the words of future prime minister Stanley Baldwin. Baldwin began his remarks by noting the most fundamental difference introduced by the First World War:

> Up to the time of the last war, civilians were exempt from the worst perils of war. They suffered sometimes from hunger, sometimes from the loss of sons and relatives serving in the Army, but now, in addition, they suffer from the fear, not only of being killed themselves, but, what is perhaps worse for a man, the fear of seeing his wife and children killed from the air.[53]

That this had occurred during the war animated many postwar discussions of air power. Baldwin then uttered what quickly became a catchphrase: "I think it is well also for the man in the street to realise that there is no power on earth that can protect him from being bombed. Whatever people may tell him, the bomber will always get through."[54] In this speech, Baldwin was not heedlessly advocating any particular policy of rearmament or disarmament; he was offering information, namely that Britain, like other states, had begun to prepare for this possibility, and urging that action proceed slowly and thoughtfully. As he reminded the House, "Aerial warfare is still in its infancy, and its potentialities are incalculable and inconceivable."[55] As such, he argued that any prohibition against bombing civilians was doomed to fail "so long as any bombing exists at all."[56] The challenge for all remained how then to proceed.

Meanwhile, the British delegation to the Disarmament Conference continued publicly to support the discussion of aerial disarmament. The Executive Committee of the WIL sent a letter to the British delegation in February 1933 welcoming its "proposal for further consideration of the possibility of the entire abolition of military and naval aircraft combined with the effective control of civil aviation" and stating its belief

---

[52] George Lansbury, *Parliamentary Debates – Commons*, 10 Nov. 1932, vol. 270, cols. 628–630.

[53] Stanley Baldwin, *Parliamentary Debates – Commons*, 10 Nov. 1932, vol. 270, cols. 631–632. It is worth noting that the emphasis on the shock air power produces here is gendered; it is that *men* can no longer protect female dependents.

[54] Baldwin, *Parliamentary Debates – Commons*, 10 Nov. 1932, vol. 270, col. 232.

[55] Baldwin, *Parliamentary Debates – Commons*, 10 Nov. 1932, vol. 270, col. 633.

[56] Baldwin, *Parliamentary Debates – Commons*, 10 Nov. 1932, vol. 270, col. 634.

"that public opinion will support the Government if it will press strongly for the measure."[57] Even as the Conference's prospects deteriorated, the WIL continued to urge delegates to work for resolution: "The present difficult situation confronting the Disarmament Conference makes it all the more necessary that it should not adjourn but should press on" and support the reaching of an agreement on the abolition of naval and military aircraft.[58]

Britain's Royal Air Force (RAF) opposed any such measures. Britain had a relatively small air force, and leading members of the RAF felt that Britain's safety hinged on its ability both to defend its territory and to counter-attack. In addition, supporters of the RAF and of its inter-war role in helping control imperial territories, particularly in the Middle East and northern India, insisted that restrictions on the use of air power exclude these territories. A succinct defense of imperial air control can be seen in a 1930 letter to the editor of the *Times* by Henry Dobbs, the high commissioner for Iraq from 1923 to 1929. In his letter, Dobbs defended "Air Control" as providing an inexpensive and humanitarian way of exercising authority; it offered a "cheap and rapid pervasion of the whole tract by a show of irresistible force, which can stifle disorder at its birth and prevent its spread." Dobbs continued to describe the "civilizing effect of the Royal Air Force" in areas such as Iraq, where officers "themselves constantly visit tribal encampments and villages, take doctors to leading men who are ill ... and pervade the whole country with their cheerful and helpful presence."[59] Given such a belief in the efficacy of air control, it is hardly surprising that the government strongly resisted efforts to subject this to international oversight. Thus, in the Conference's later stages, the British government proposed prohibitions on aerial bombardment, "except for police purposes in certain outlying areas."[60] This was a proposal greeted with skepticism by everyone else, including the British women active in the WIL, who agreed to draft a letter to the prime minister, Ramsay MacDonald, the minister for air, Lord Londonderry,

---

[57] See Letter, drafted by Dr. Hilda Clark, in British Section-WIL, Minutes, 14 Feb. 1933, WILPF 1/9, BLPES.

[58] British Section-WIL, Minutes, 9 May 1933, WILPF 1/9, BLPES.

[59] H[enry] Dobbs, Letter to the editor, *Times*, 8 May 1930. For more on Dobbs, see David Omissi, *Air Power and Colonial Control: The Royal Air Force, 1919–1939* (Manchester, 1990), 31–37.

[60] Quoted in Meilinger, "Clipping the Bomber's Wings," 323. Meilinger offers a thorough account of British politics and the issue of aerial disarmament at the Geneva Conference in this article.

and the foreign secretary, Sir John Simon, "on the subject of bombing from the air in outlying areas."[61]

That the Conference tried to adopt disarmament measures prohibiting the use of the two most frightening modern tools of war – air power and chemical weapons – became a moot point after March 1933, when the Nazi seizure of power after the Reichstag fire led to Germany's resistance to any disarmament agreements. After Germany formally withdrew in November 1933, it was clear that the Conference was doomed to fail, although it limped along until June 1934.[62] Despite efforts to resurrect some mechanism to promote disarmament, the threat of air power would remain unchecked for the rest of the decade.

FIGHTING AGAINST AERIAL WARFARE AFTER GENEVA

The lost opportunity of the Geneva Conference resonated bitterly with disarmament's supporters. Within a few years, feminist activist Sylvia Pankhurst commemorated not the actual victims of aerial warfare, but those who opposed it. She solicited and raised funds in 1936 to erect a small "Anti-Air War Memorial" in Woodford Wells, Essex. Literally placed in a backyard, the monument depicts an aerial torpedo (a stone bomb), and its inscription reads:

> To those who in 1932 upheld the right to use bombing planes
> This monument is raised as a protest against war in the air.[63]

When the monument was unveiled on 21 June 1936, it was meant to offer a warning about the dangers of future war that could now literally hit home. It was also taken as a commentary on contemporary politics, and the first stone bomb was stolen, although quickly replaced.[64]

Throughout the mid-1930s, British feminist pacifists continued to work on the means to avert the next war and mitigate some of its more destructive elements. Moreover, despite the clear failure of the Geneva

---

[61] British Section-WILPF, Minutes, 9 May 1933, WILPF 1/9, BLPES.

[62] Meilinger, "Clipping the Bomber's Wings," notes that Japan was also in the process of leaving the League and the conference over the censorship of its behavior in China, especially its attacks on Shanghai.

[63] See the dossier on the "Anti-Air War Memorial," Woodford Wells, Essex, IWM National Inventory of War Memorials, especially the article announcing its unveiling and containing a drawing of the memorial in *New Times and Ethiopia News*, 5 May 1936.

[64] For more on the monument and particularly its sculptor, Eric Benfield, see Patrick Wright, "The Stone Bomb," *Open Democracy* (www.opendemocracy.net), 7 Apr. 2003.

Make a note of this date and keep it clear:

SUNDAY, 21st JUNE, 1936
3 p.m.
UNVEILING OF THE FIRST
ANTI-AERIAL WARFARE PROTEST
MONUMENT
WOODFORD WELLS, ESSEX.
(on the way to Epping Forest).

FIGURE 6.1. Drawing for the 1936 "Anti-Air War Memorial" in Woodford Wells, Essex, appearing in *New Times and Ethiopia News*, 5 May 1936. Reproduced by courtesy of the Imperial War Museum.

Conference – and the WIL chronicled its many vicissitudes in its *Monthly New Sheet* – when the government began to hint at its exploration of measures to combat chemical warfare, such as the development of civilian gas masks, pacifist critics condemned any such maneuvers to "protect" non-combatants. The assumption that any aerial attacks against civilians could involve poison gas only solidified the calls of air war opponents for disarmament and the peaceful resolution of international conflict. They vigorously denounced anything that seemed based on the idea that one could prepare for chemical warfare. WIL activist Mary Sheepshanks articulated this perspective at a WIL council meeting in late 1933, when she first became aware of efforts to offer protection in the event of gas attacks. Here she shared a letter that she had written with the rest of the organization's leaders, one in which she objected to "the fallaciousness of so-called protection against poison gas and the danger of promoting both panic and military spirit by the proposed gas mask drill."[65] Sheepshanks was particularly agitated by the fact that women were being called upon to organize and facilitate such efforts.

In November 1934, another representative of the WIL wrote a letter of protest to various authorities, including the Red Cross (copied to the prime minister), regarding recent press accounts of a staged gas attack in Camberwell. The letter noted that some children "as young as six years of age" had been subjected to a "harmless, although very realistic gas attack" and that

> such an experience must have a harmful effect on all children.... Their minds are likely to be dominated by fear of an experience which our present Government is striving to avoid, so that we hope it may never be the lot of these children to have to put such training into practice. Any psychologist could give you instances of the whole lives of people being ruined by experiences in childhood far less calculated to rouse terror than the one to which I am referring.[66]

For those opposed to the idea of normalizing chemical attacks, such protective measures themselves were harmful.

One demonstration of the continued concern of women with these larger issues can be found in the proliferation of writings by Helena Swanwick, already intimately involved in internationalist (and pacifist) activities. In the middle to late 1930s, she wrote a series of books and pamphlets on foreign policy and international affairs that articulated not only a general position on the contemporary political scene, but also, as she had done during the First World War, a particular vision of the relationship of women to war, especially to new technologies of war, such as air power. These titles included, in 1934 alone, "New Wars for Old" (on the creation of an international police force under the control of the League), "Pooled Security: What Does It Mean?" (a reply to critics of "New Wars for Old"), and "Frankenstein and His Monster."

---

[65] Letter cited in British Section-WIL, Minutes, 12 Dec. 1933, WILPF 1/9, BLPES.
[66] Letter, B. M. Baker, British Section of the Women's International League for Peace and Freedom, to Mrs. L. Roberts, Hon. Sec. Camberwell Branch of the British Red Cross [cc. Prime Minister], 23 Nov. 1934, TNA CAB 16/1578.

Swanwick's arguments about aerial warfare culminated in this third pamphlet, whose full title read, "Frankenstein and His Monster: Aviation for World Service." Her work pulled few punches, beginning by stating unequivocally that "there is no defence at all" against aerial attack. The only hope "is to be found in the possibility that, if State A were certain that its mass-murder of the population of State B would result in the mass-murder of its own population, this certainly might act as a deterrent." Yet Swanwick immediately added that this "hope is a faint one." The next war – the aerial war – will thus be widely different from previous wars, "a monstrous orgy of reprisal on civilian populations." An engagement of the entire population "as never before, would immeasurably increase the disaster of any large-scale war" in Europe. Humanity is akin to Frankenstein and the science of aviation the monster it has unleashed upon the world.[67]

Swanwick encouraged her reader to look skeptically at the government's claims to provide civil defense. In what may seem a prescient statement – until one considers that word of Britain's own ARP planning had slowly begun to emerge – Swanwick suggested that it was "impossible to believe" that countries like Germany and Poland that were currently "organising distribution of gas-masks, holding of gas-drills, construction of gas-proof shelters, can have any belief at all in the efficacy of such measures in face of a serious assault" (4). She found it intolerable to imagine a world in which infants might have to live in gas masks for days at a time, one where ordinary life had to continue in bomb-proof shelters. Thus, a deeper purpose must lie in government planning that can serve as no real buffer against the horrors of this future war: "[T]hey want to work their peoples up to a state of 'nerves' which will make them uncritically obedient to any alarmist summons" (4).

Swanwick's words in 1934 echoed those of the many who had advocated the abolition of military aviation and the internationalization of civil air power before the Geneva Disarmament Conference. For example, Swanwick proposed that "the menace from the air is so fraught with the possibilities of complete destruction of organised societies that all responsible governments must desire its withdrawal" (8). As we saw in Chapter 4, the complete disintegration of modern life as a result of deadly air power formed a vividly realized core of interwar works like *Lest Ye Die* and *Things to Come*. Now Swanwick tried to make a similar point more prosaically, by arguing that when humanity was faced with

---

[67] H[elena] M. Swanwick, "Frankenstein and His Monster: Aviation for World Service" (London, 1934), 3. Further references are made parenthetically in the text.

annihilation, international control over aviation offered the only reasonable, practical hope. It is clear in the evidence marshaled by Swanwick that the higher priority must be the abolition of military air power: humanity must demand "the complete absence from the world of all military aviation, with its evil tradition that it is permissible (whether for so-called national or international purposes) to rain down promiscuous death from the air" (10). The difficulties of achieving this, for Swanwick, were mainly "moral," although she acknowledged that the internationalization of civilian aviation involved more practical challenges. That said, she also stressed that air traffic between countries was already subject to international control; therefore, she envisioned an international body to license all aviators and all aircraft (10–13).

More particularly, Swanwick called for the work of reaching a negotiated solution to the problem of air power to begin immediately. One could not expect governments to live up to promises about forgoing weapons when they might feel compelled to use them in a time of crisis. The solution was to make "in peace time, all sorts of arrangements which would increase the difficulties of making war at all" (15). Support for such measures would come with the growing realization that the days when non-combatants could be excluded from danger by the rules of war were gone forever, prompted in part by the accession of women to the vote. The other pressing task was to remove "once for all, the idea of aviation from the idea of destruction" and instead retain its positive role (22).

In this brief pamphlet, published and distributed by the WIL, Swanwick drew on the prospect of total annihilation to make her points, but she recognized pragmatically that "the national sentiment is as yet stronger than the international" (22). In that case, using the laws governing air traffic as her model, Swanwick urged the pursuit of a less rigid and "more gradually developing policy of international cooperation" (22). The stakes for her were too high to permit any alternative.[68]

Persistently throughout the middle to late 1930s, when the government unveiled ARP measures, the WIL (among other organizations) was

[68] Nor was Swanwick alone in continuing to advocate the need for internationalism, specifically in terms of the future use of air power. Of the fifteen short essays in Storm Jameson's 1934 *Challenge to Death*, two pieces by Philip Noel Baker focused on the use of an air force in a future conflict. The first denounced investment in a "national" air force as offering no defense; the other put forth an argument similar to Swanwick's in favor of an international air police. See Philip Noel Baker, "A National Air Force No Defence" and "The International Air Police Force," in *Challenge to Death*, ed. Storm Jameson (London, 1935). See the discussion of the text and the larger anti-militarist movement behind it in Overy, *The Twilight Years*, ch. 6.

quick to condemn them. Pacifist and anti-militarist groups responded vigorously to news about government proposals concerning ARP and anti-gas measures. In May 1935, the Executive Committee of the WIL drafted a memo that condemned these efforts:

> Such preparation is bound to contribute to the creation of a war mentality, which in itself is a contributory factor in causing war.... Where children are obliged to share in such preparations it is highly probable that such an experience will have a harmful effect on them....
>
> Preparation of the people for gas attack is further to be deplored, because it is based on the assumption that obligations not to resort to war but which all the Governments concerned are bound, are not going to be kept. We believe this to be bad psychologically.[69]

The WIL's specific response to the initial ARP circular of July 1935, the first widely publicized announcement of ARP plans (about which we will hear more in Chapter 8), was to "urge the Government to recognise that the only measure of effective defence of the people from Air attack is the abolition of War Aircraft by all countries." It continued by challenging government proposals in quite specific detail, noting that its own close reading of the circular revealed that "very little protection can be given to most of the population"; thus, "there is danger that people will be led to rely on precautions that are entirely illusory." As a result, a large number of those who supported WIL and like-minded organizations "will find themselves unable to co-operate in any way with such services and propaganda." This suggests one new path of resistance to efforts to mobilize civilians in a new type of war.[70]

In August 1935, the WIL publicized work being done to demonstrate that "no such measures can either protect our own children or justify us in reprisals against the children of a nation whose Air Force might attack us." Instead, it urged continued action to abolish national air forces and install an international system of control over civil aviation as had other internationalist organizations such as the League of Nations Union.[71] It pointed out that the Women's Peace Crusade had prepared a mock window

---

[69] "Anti-Gas Drill and Air Disarmament," Statement by the Executive Committee of the British Section of the Women's International League, 14 May 1935, WILPF 1/11, BLPES.

[70] "Statement on the Air Raid Precaution Circular," Executive Committee of the British Section of the WIL, 30 July 1935. WILPF 1/11, BLPES.

[71] C. A. Innes, "A.B.C. of Air Disarmament: An Account of the Efforts Made to Abolish Military and Naval Aircraft," (London, 1935). This leaflet reflected on both the potential for resurrecting some of the draft proposals raised at the Geneva Conference and the new visibility given to ARP, which in its view offered no security.

display on this issue, designed as a "practical way of reaching people who never go to meetings" in order to encourage them to look at photographs, accept leaflets, or possibly enroll as Air Disarmament workers.[72]

When the Executive Committee of the British Section of the WIL learned of official plans for "the supply of gas masks to the whole population," it deputized member Kathleen Innes to write a letter to the press pointing out that the only defense against poison gas was "abolition."[73] In 1936 the Peace Pledge Union recommended that pacifists refuse to participate in any gas drills, and it issued a pamphlet emphasizing what awaited a population unwilling to renounce war. Citing a variety of experts who foretold the inevitability of future war being air war, it stressed that: "To kill civilians from the air is not to put them quietly to sleep."[74] Rather, death by chemicals unleashed from the air would be slow and painful.

A similar point was raised by Captain Philip Mumford's 1936 *Humanity, Air Power and War*, which asserted that a future air war might well destroy civilization. The solution, akin to that proposed by Swanwick, was that "all air power must be removed beyond the reach of nationalism."[75] Mumford made explicit what was at stake if this failed: "The coming of the aeroplane has diverted the whole force of the fury of war from the battleground to the home and nursery." Home life and the lives of infants weighed in the balance. Given these altered circumstances – a Europe "which is finding it necessary to organize its entire civil population against gas attacks from the air" – it was now the duty of every citizen to be informed and involved in calling for measures to combat this threat.[76] Mumford emphasized that "the ordinary civilian, his wife, children and home, his public library, hospital, water supply and drainage system, in fact the whole of his normal life have now been swept wholesale into this new war game in which he can have no defence or protection."[77] As a result, he must realize the necessity of fighting against

[72] See "Air Disarmament Campaign" and "An Air Disarmament Shop," *Women's International League Monthly News Sheet*, 27: 8 (Aug. 1935).

[73] Executive Committee of the British Section of the WIL, Minutes, 10 Dec. 1935, WILPF 1/11, BLPES.

[74] See "Three Recommendations for Members of the Peace Pledge Union" and "The Peace Pledge: Are You Prepared to Support or Sanction Another War?" (Peace Pledge Union, [c. 18 Dec. 1936; date mark in copy in British Library]).

[75] Philip S. Mumford, *Humanity, Air Power and War* (London, 1936), 13.

[76] Mumford, *Humanity*, 16.

[77] Mumford, Humanity, 45–46. A number of related works appeared in the middle to late 1930s starting with J. M. Spaight, *Air Power and the Cities* (London, 1930); L. E. O. Charlton, *War over England* (London, 1936); Albert Henry Ross, *War on Great Cities: A Study of the Facts* (London, 1937), and others. A number of key thinkers on air power in

placing air power in the hands of national governments. The only possible safety would lie in transferring control over aviation in all its forms to an international body. Otherwise, all the trappings of modern daily life would be lost.

Other works on air power that appeared in the late 1930s had somewhat more modest goals. For instance, the Cambridge Scientists' Anti-War Group (CSAWG) offered a pointed critique of ARP measures in a climate subtly altered by the Spanish Civil War (as will be discussed in the next chapter). In its 1937 *The Protection of the Public from Aerial Attack*, the CSAWG described the proposed government plan as inadequate. Taking on the conflation of aerial and chemical weapons, the group systematically demonstrated the limits of any individual or home-based protection. More particularly, it questioned why the fear of panic was the "dominant note of all speeches of Air Raids Precautions officials" and suggested that the government's real aim was to prevent the uncontrolled alarm that would cause a population to support peace. For the CSAWG, the true purpose of ARP was thus the "acquiescence of the people," not their protection.[78]

The established scientific community also weighed in on the debate over ARP. In 1937 the scientific journal *Nature* published an editorial on "the civil population and air attack," which summarized various aspects of the public debates launched by the Air Raids Precautions circulars. As far as the proposed gas masks were concerned, the editors brought up criticisms of their practical effectiveness even while noting that the confidence having such a mask might engender "may help to sustain morale and diminish casualties by avoiding or diminishing panic." On the other hand, "the fact should not be overlooked that air raid drill and practice with gas masks" may have the opposite effect, producing "hysteria and nervous strain that may more than outweigh all the advantage gained against panic." Conceding that opponents who argued that any such preparations helped to foster a "war mentality," the editorial urged that the public be informed that "most scientific workers are agreed" that

the interwar era are discussed in Tami Davis Biddle, *Rhetoric and Reality in Air Warfare: The Evolution of British and American Ideas about Strategic Bombing, 1914–1945* (Princeton, NJ, 2002), ch. 2.

[78] Cambridge Scientists Anti-War Group, *The Protection of the Public from Aerial Attack* (London, 1937), 37–38. This report itself prompted the publication of works that criticized the group's findings; see James Kendall, *Breathe Freely: The Truth about Poison Gas* (London, 1938). Kendall acknowledges building his arguments on the provocative work of J. B. S. Haldane, *Callinicus: A Defence of Chemical Warfare* (London, 1925).

"there is no possible protection of the civilian population from air attack other than the abolition of bombing from the air."[79] Events elsewhere soon overwhelmed such proposals.

CONCLUSION

As we have now seen, a variety of voices reflected on the enormous destructive potential of air power in interwar Britain, and many determined to prevent the imagined horrors of the next war from coming true. Several important constituent bodies of the nation – including key segments of women, trades unionists, and members of the state itself – worked fervently for disarmament and to challenge efforts to accept aerial and perhaps even chemical attacks as somehow inevitable in a future war. Feminist pacifists in particular took to heart the dangers posed to women and children in their homes. Organizations such as the Women's International League consistently suggested that given such possibilities, the only defense against the air raid was its abolition, that to prepare for modern war was to ensure its arrival.

The government was aware that because of the new reality of air power, Britain could no longer rely for its security on being an island nation. Thus, it had to balance the need to protect the state and its civil population with managing the popular anxieties voiced by feminists, pacifists, and others. The interwar period had two major turning points as far as the issue of air disarmament was concerned. The first was the Geneva Disarmament Conference, which raised hopes and then dashed them. The second was the Spanish Civil War, which offered a vivid and visceral reminder of the wider and more deadly air war to come, as we will explore in the next chapter.

[79] "The Civil Population and Air Attack," *Nature*, 6 Mar. 1937.

7

Facing the Future of Air Power

Air Raids Abroad and Reactions at Home

On the eve of the publication of his account of fighting for the Republican cause in Spain, George Orwell reviewed Arthur Koestler's *Spanish Testament* in February 1938.[1] Orwell praised Koestler's acknowledgment of his own lack of "objectivity" regarding what had happened in Spain, and went on:

> You cannot be objective about an aerial torpedo. And the horror we feel of these things has led to this conclusion: if someone drops a bomb on your mother, go and drop two bombs on his mother. The only apparent alternatives are to smash dwelling houses to powder, blow out human entrails and burn holes in children with lumps of thermite, or to be enslaved by people who are more ready to do these things than you are yourself; as yet no one has suggested a practicable way out.[2]

The bombing of "your mother" – the quintessential civilian and the emblem of the home – renders "objectivity" impossible. This, as we have seen before, was a moment when the full horror of this new form of war hit home.

It is interesting that Orwell makes this point after his experiences in Spain. Only a few years earlier, in 1936, Orwell had published a novel, *Keep the Aspidistra Flying*, in which the protagonist, Gordon (a struggling poet alienated by modern life), keeps imagining the airplanes descending upon and destroying London. In this earlier context, aerial war is not a

[1] *Homage to Catalonia*, which came out in March 1938.
[2] George Orwell, Review of *Spanish Testament* by Arthur Koestler, *Time and Tide*, 5 Feb. 1938, in *The Collected Essays, Journalism and Letters of George Orwell*, vol. 1, ed. Sonia Orwell and Ian Argus (New York, 1968), 296.

horror committed against mothers and children, but a kind of revenge on an already barren modern world:

> Our civilisation is dying. It *must* be dying. But it isn't going to die in its bed. Presently the aeroplanes are coming. Zoom – whizz – crash! The whole western world going up in a roar of high explosives.
>
> Gordon squinted up at the leaden sky. Those aeroplanes are coming. In imagination he saw them coming now; squadron after squadron, innumerable, darkening the sky like clouds of gnats. With his tongue not quite against his teeth he made a buzzing, blue-bottle-on-the-window-pane sound to represent the humming of the aeroplanes. It was a sound which, at that moment, he ardently desired to hear.[3]

Gordon's desire "to see our money-civilisation blown to hell by bombs" is repeatedly described as passionately felt; but witnessing air war in Spain could change its meaning for Orwell.[4]

Through an analysis of British reactions to aerial attacks in reality in addition to theory or prediction, this chapter explores the deepening response to air raids after the collapse of efforts at disarmament in the early 1930s. It begins with a brief examination of reactions to imperial air power, as wielded by Britain, Italy, and Japan. It then demonstrates the crucial turning point provided by the return of air raids to *European* soil during the Spanish Civil War. It concludes by engaging with how the role of gender shaped the way such conflicts came to be understood, focusing on several critiques of air war generally and the conflict in Spain in particular, culminating in writings by feminist pacifist Helena Swanwick and in Virginia Woolf's 1938 *Three Guineas*.

RESPONDING TO IMPERIAL AIR POWER

Before air raids returned to Europe in the middle years of the 1930s and rendered the objectivity that Orwell criticized a moot point, air power had already been used to deadly effect by Britain itself in colonial struggles in the Middle East and parts of India, by Japan in China, and by Italy against Ethiopia. All of these conflicts provoked responses from a variety of public voices in Britain that saw implicit lessons in the conflicts abroad for future wars at home. Throughout much of the interwar period, as we saw in earlier chapters, reactions to aerial warfare were based on the

---

[3] George Orwell, *Keep the Aspidistra Flying* (1936; rpt. Harmondsworth, 1975), 21. My thanks to Joe Ward for pointing out this passage.
[4] Orwell, *Keep the Aspidistra*, 84.

memory of what had occurred and fearful speculation as to what might come. Such responses intensified as reports of the increasingly lethal use of air power in foreign settings during the interwar period circulated in the public domain.

Victory in the First World War had placed new territories in the Middle East under British control, but such control was soon tested. In order to maintain Britain's new mandates, especially in Iraq, the fledging RAF resorted to bombing, and its attacks had high civilian casualties. In fact, to a great extent, the existence of Britain's air force was justified by the significant role it played in policing the empire. As David Omissi points out, the use of bombers "extended the reach of the imperial state into marginal areas," despite the hostility that such raids created.[5] We have just seen how long this policy lingered in efforts to preserve the right to use aviation for "policing of outlying areas" in debates during the Geneva Disarmament Conference discussed in Chapter 6.

Yet from the outset, such attacks provoked a response not only in the media but also from opposition politicians. In April 1923, Labour MP George Lansbury pointedly asked the secretary of state for air how much damage had been inflicted in both India and Iraq during the past year's RAF raids, and how many members of the RAF had been injured or killed in such attacks. Sir Samuel Hoare replied by denying that any "punitive" attacks had been carried out against indigenous populations in India's frontier but admitting that approximately nine raids had taken place in Iraq and southern Kurdistan, resulting in the deaths of eight members of the RAF and injuries to an additional three. Hoare claimed to be unable to give particulars about the damage to the local population but stressed that all attacks were "only undertaken at the request of the civil authorities" in place of using regular forces. Lansbury then followed up by making clear his underlying point: asking first about retaliation and then whether "the time has arrived to stop this Hunnish and barbarous method of warfare against unarmed people."[6] The use of air power in these colonial settings was clearly deemed akin to German

---

[5] David E. Omissi, *Air Power and Colonial Control: The Royal Air Force, 1919–1939* (Manchester, 1990). Interwar imperial raids are also discussed briefly in Sven Lindqvist, *A History of Bombing*, trans. Linda Haverty Rugg (New York, 2001), 42–43, and more thoroughly in Yuki Tanaka, "British 'Humane Bombing' in Iraq during the Interwar Era," in *Bombing Civilians: A Twentieth-Century History*, ed. Yuki Tanaka and Marilyn B. Young (New York, 2009).
[6] Lansbury and Hoare, *Parliamentary Debates – Commons*, 12 Apr. 1923, vol. 162, cols 1300–1301.

atrocities – hence the use of "Hunnish" – during the Great War. At stake was the moral issue of using such arms against a population unable to protect itself.

As recent work by Priya Satia has shown, those in favor of using air power for the purposes of imperial policing unabashedly affirmed that "terror was the scheme's underlying principle."[7] The demoralizing effect of raids in helping to control indigenous populations was seen as one of its core purposes, and officials considered air power less costly and inhumane than more conventional methods of waging war, especially in the Middle East, as we saw in Henry Dobb's 1930 letter discussed in Chapter 6. More strikingly, British officials excused the damage done to women and children in these raids by suggesting that their lives counted for little in the local culture. Satia quotes the British commander as stating that "[sheikhs] ... do not seem to resent ... that women and children are accidentally killed by bombs."[8] The presumably indirect casualties produced by these "peacetime" raids are thus suggested to be of a different caliber than calculated attacks on European or British civilians.

However, distinctions of this sort were not accepted by all British citizens. The Women's International League, for instance, had been quick to condemn British imperial air power when used against civilians. Before the Geneva Disarmament Conference disbanded, the WIL's Executive Committee was asking Mary Sheepshanks in August 1933 to draft a letter "expressing the deep regret of the W.I.L. that bombing [of northwest frontier tribes in India] should be resorted to, especially in view of the attempts being made by the Disarmament Conference to secure the abolition of bombing from the air." A few months later, the WIL made the point that any condemnation of Fascist war measures was compromised by the use of such tactics as air bombing by colonial powers, including Britain.[9] It also protested the fact that the annual RAF Air Display in Hendon featured a mock attack on "Native Tribesmen" and mounted a public campaign against this.[10]

Groups such as the WIL also vigorously condemned the Italian campaign in Abyssinia.[11] New fears of gas attacks emerged in response to

[7] Priya Satia, "The Defense of Inhumanity: Air Control and the British Idea of Arabia," *American Historical Review* 111:1 (2003), 18.
[8] Quoted in Satia, "Defense of Inhumanity," 22.
[9] See British Section-WIL, Minutes, 1 Aug. 1933 and 9 Oct. 1933, WILPF 1/9, BLPES.
[10] See British Section-WILPF, Minutes, 16 June and 14 July 1936, WILPF 1/12, BLPES.
[11] See British Section-WIL, Minutes, 4 June 1935, 3 Sept. 1935, 14 Jan. 1936, WILPF 1/11 and 1/12, BLPES.

reports of Italy's use of chemical weapons in 1935. While a variety of voices, and not exclusively on the left, condemned these actions and urged the British government to address them, others applauded Britain's reluctance to intervene. Under the heading "Britain Must Keep Out of It," the *Daily Mail* suggested that calls for coercive measures against the Italian government were the work of a "noisy minority" of "international sentimentalists."[12] Yet other mainstream media portrayed the attacks in a deeply critical way.[13] A *Punch* cartoon of January 1936 mocked Italy, representing it as a knight spraying poison gas in the face of a cowering, spear-carrying African. Pictures in the *Illustrated London News* portrayed the extensive devastation suffered by the locales of Dessie and Daggah Bur in Abyssinia; photos depicted rows of casualties, destroyed homes, and bomb damage outside a hospital, with a clearly identifiable Red Cross flag.[14] A *Punch* cartoon in April, under the ironic caption "The Dawn of Progress," showed what is clearly meant to be a non-Western man stumbling through a fog labeled "poison gas," while a group of what appear to be women and children huddle behind him.[15]

Shortly after retreating from Ethiopia, the second in command of the British Ambulance Service, John MacFie, published an account of his work there that vividly described the horrors of aerial and chemical warfare. MacFie's *An Ethiopian Diary* began by insisting that he had to convince many in England upon his return not only that mustard gas had been used, but also that it had played a "decisive part" in Ethiopia's defeat. Aerial gas warfare was "terrifying and demoralising. I am not convinced that our own people would be immune from panic under similar circumstances." MacFie also viscerally depicted the effects of such attacks, describing a patient who "looked as if someone had tried to skin him, clumsily" and men and women "with blurred crimson apologies for eyes." After witnessing an air raid on his Red Cross hospital on 4 March 1936, MacFie explained that "none of us would wish to make a fuss about being bombed.... There was a war on! But our patients? That was the difference."[16]

There was more to this account than condemnation although, of course, MacFie denounced an enemy who would attack hospitals and

[12] "Britain Must Keep Out of It," *Daily Mail*, 8 July 1935.
[13] See, e.g., "Abyssinian Casualties from Poison Gas," *Times*, 16 Oct. 1935.
[14] "Air Raids on Abyssinia," *Illustrated London News*, 4 Jan. 1936.
[15] See *Punch*, 13 Jan. 1936 and 8 Apr. 1936.
[16] J. W. S. MacFie, *An Ethiopian Diary: A Record of the British Ambulance Service in Ethiopia* (London, 1936), xii, 77, 85.

unleash poison gas on civilians. MacFie offered his work as both testimony to the sufferings of Ethiopia and as warning:

> I could cover pages recounting horrors, but what would be the use? ...
> [N]one would comprehend. Ethiopia is very far away. Who would
> believe that one day it may be the villagers and townsfolk of England
> who may suffer like this; that a passing shadow over a playground
> may one day rain worse than death on scores of happy children? Your
> children!
>
> The people seemed stunned by the effects of "gas." It was something
> outside experience, a mysterious devilish thing.[17]

It had not been outside the experience of combatants in the First World War, but it was now no longer their unique province. And next time, MacFie warned, it might be felt in an English playground.

Brutal attacks on civilians, especially in this instance by an allegedly more civilized European power, inspired the core of the outrage expressed over the return of aerial warfare in the interwar period. The conflict in Ethiopia seemed to offer startling evidence of something new, feared, and predicted: the direct targeting of civilians by chemical weapons. Criticism of air power used against civilian populations by Italy and Britain itself only grew more vociferous when these populations came to include "white" civilians as air war returned to Europe in the Spanish Civil War.

ADDING TO THE VOCABULARY OF MASSACRE: THE AIR WAR IN SPAIN

Criticism of aerial attacks deepened when bombs returned to European soil in Spain. The civil war in Spain had begun in July 1936 when nationalist insurgents led by General Francisco Franco attempted to overthrow the democratically elected republican and Popular Front government. It provoked an immediate international response, although the loyalists' logical allies – the democratic regimes of Britain and France – refused to lend their official support. On the other hand, Mussolini and Hitler became active supporters of Franco and his followers. For those in Britain (and elsewhere) who had been campaigning to control or end aerial warfare or planning for its consequences, the Spanish Civil War offered a vivid reminder of the stakes of total war waged by air against civilians.[18]

---

[17] MacFie, *Ethiopian Diary*, 77–78.
[18] The classic narrative study of the Spanish Civil War remains Hugh Thomas, *The Spanish Civil War* (London, 1961). I have also made use of Ronald Fraser, *Blood of Spain: An*

During the war's first year, the locus of fighting and of air raids was the capital city of Madrid, and the focus of British media accounts was on the loss of security and the danger faced by civilians. "Bombs Kill 70 School Children," proclaimed the *Daily Herald* on 31 October 1936, detailing the damage done by overnight raids in and around Madrid. In order to convey to British readers the nature of these attacks, the paper described bombs falling "in the crowded Calle De Fuencarral – Madrid's Edgeware road" and "the Plaza Callao – counterpart here of Oxford circus" – in other words, the equivalent of shopping districts filled with ordinary folk. The paper was also quick to highlight the damage done to women and children. The tally of seventy dead came from a bomb falling in Getaffe, "a village as near to Madrid as Golders Green is to London." The paper continued its coverage with this image of the effects of a bomb that fell on a food queue: "[O]n the pavements lay the bodies of seven women, who had been waiting patiently to buy food for their families."[19] The victims of these raids were the innocent: women and the families they were trying to feed.

Madrid came under renewed attack from the forces of General Franco in early November, and the *Daily Herald* headline read, "Rebel bombers rain death on capital," describing it as "the most ruthless air raid that any modern city has known." The *Daily Mail* described "Air Raid Havoc," with hotels "packed with wounded.... [S]treets are strewn with dead and dying."[20] A few days later its headline read, "Madrid's Night of Terror," as "inky darkness prevails in the capital to-night. Families huddle in cellars and basements."[21] As had been the case during the war in Ethiopia, the *Illustrated London News* provided extensive photographs of the damage sustained in the capital, showing churches, streets, and houses in ruins.[22] Such attacks on ordinary homes and the families who inhabited them were precisely what British ARP planners had feared and predicted would accompany the next war.

The most intense reaction to aerial warfare in Spain came with the infamous and devastating attack on Guernica in April 1937. Guernica

Oral History of the Spanish Civil War (New York, 1979), and the best overview of Britain and the war, Tom Buchanan, *Britain and the Spanish Civil War* (Cambridge, 1997).

[19] "Bombs Kill 70 School Children" and "Women Killed in Food Queue," *Daily Herald*, 31 Oct. 1936.

[20] "Rebel Bombers Rain Death on Capital," *Daily Herald*, 9 Nov. 1936; "Air Raid Havoc," *Daily Mail*, 9 Nov. 1936.

[21] "Madrid's Night of Terror," *Daily Mail*, 11 Nov. 1936.

[22] "The Capital of Spain Undergoes an Ordeal ...," *Illustrated London News*, 12 Dec. 1936, and "Madrid Under Terror from the Skies," *Illustrated London News*, 26 Dec. 1936.

quickly came to symbolize the threat that air power posed to innocence. As an editorial in the *Daily Express* explained, although it took no sides in the war and urged "the British people to maintain neutrality":

> [T]here are some things that pass all bounds and cry for protest. The bombing of Guernica is one. The Basque people met in that place as devout Catholics to pray and give praise to God. They were not under arms.
>
> The insurgent air-raiders have added a new word to the vocabulary of massacre-GUERNICA.[23]

To explain further just what this "massacre" entailed, reporters for the paper became quite personal. *Daily Express* staff reporter Noel Monks began his account by stating that "I have seen many ghastly sights in Spain in the last six months, but none more terrible than the annihilation of the ancient Basque capital of Guernica by Franco's bombing planes." He went on to mention walking through the still-burning town to see hundreds of bodies lying amid debris, and of an aged priest killed while trying to save children from a burning building.[24] The *Manchester Guardian* echoed some of this outrage, calling the attack a "massacre from the air" that found the town "reduced to ruins."[25] The reporter for the *Star* described hearing "people screaming while bombs were crashing half a mile away. People in panic ran in all directions.... [F]leeing women and children were mown down with machine guns from low sweeping planes.... [H]undreds of men, women and children must have been roasted alive, torn to pieces by explosives and drilled with machine gun bullets."[26] Other reports described the ancient town center as having been "blotted out," and papers picking up early reports from Reuters, such as the *Evening News*, called it "the most appalling air raid in the history of modern warfare."[27] Most accounts emphasized the fires that could be seen burning for miles, the corpses lying

---

[23] "Opinion," *Daily Express*, 28 Apr. 1937. A detailed study of the international press coverage of Guernica can be found in Herbert Rutledge Southworth, *Guernica! Guernica! A Study of Journalism, Diplomacy, Propaganda, and History* (Berkeley, CA, 1977), and a reconstruction of the events of the attack based partly on oral interviews can be found in Gordon Thomas and Max Morgan Witts, *Guernica: The Crucible of World War II* (New York, 1977).

[24] "Priest Blesses City as Bombs Fall," *Daily Express*, 29 Apr. 1937.

[25] "Basque Town Wiped Out by Rebel Planes," *Manchester Guardian*, 28 Apr. 1937.

[26] "Hundreds Dead in Worst Air Raid Yet," *Star*, 27 Apr. 1937.

[27] "Basque Capital Blotted Out," *Evening News*, 27 Apr. 1937.

everywhere in the desolate city, the ruthlessness of the attack, and the pathos of the victims.[28]

As might be expected from the more partisan press, the *Daily Worker*'s coverage emphasized the unprovoked horror, as Fascist raiders "concentrated on machine-gunning women and children, bombing homes." Elizabeth Wilkinson, the *Daily Worker*'s reporter on the scene and a member of the Women's Committee Against War and Fascism, evoked a heartbreaking sense of ordinary loss by simply describing people amid the burning rubble "still searching for missing relatives, for wives, daughters, husbands, sweethearts and children."[29]

Other articles in the more mainstream press made clear the larger stakes. According to the *Daily Sketch*, "Modern warfare, in its most ghastly guise, has transformed the beautiful Basque countryside into a nightmare of horror.... For five hours rebel airplanes poured death and destruction on the panic-stricken populace." Such accounts emphasized particular types of victims, including "50 women and children [who] were trapped and burned alive" in a shelter.[30] Other reports underscored the non-combatant status of the victims: "Hundreds of civilians in the town for a Feast Day were killed in three and a half hours' continuous bombing by German airplanes." To add to the horror, after the entire town was in flames and the local convent hospital full of wounded, planes swooped to machine-gun those fleeing to the surrounding fields for safety.[31]

When Franco and his German allies issued denials that their airmen had destroyed Guernica and killed eight hundred civilians, British reporters were quick to offer their own eyewitness accounts of watching planes and being attacked themselves.[32] A few days after the destruction of the

---

[28] See "Basque Capital Blotted Out"; "Town Wiped Out by Rebels," *Evening Standard*, 27 Apr. 1937.

[29] "They Murdered Hundreds in Guernica" and "Planes Rained Bombs," *Daily Worker*, 28 Apr. 1937. Even the first headline with its suggestion of "crime" rather than an ordinary "act of war" stresses the emotive response. The language of "murder," "massacre," and "atrocity" permeates this coverage.

[30] "Town's Nightmare of 1,000 Fire Bombs," *Daily Sketch*, 28 Apr. 1937.

[31] "Town Wiped Out by Rebels"; the machine-gunning of fleeing victims is also recounted, among other places, in "Hundreds Dead in Worst Air Raid Yet," *Star*, 27 Apr. 1937; "Priest Blesses City as Bombs Fall"; and "Air Raid Wipes Out Basque Town," *Daily Mail*, 28 Apr. 1937.

[32] See "Bombed City of the Basques?" *Daily Express*, 29 Apr. 1937. See also the Reuter statement that Franco's denial "is adequately refuted by many thousands of survivors, including a number of priests" quoted in "New Allegations on Guernica," *Daily Telegraph*, 30 Apr. 1937.

city, reports emerged of the British Embassy at Hendaye conducting its own inquiry into Guernica, even as Franco's supporters claimed that "Red hordes" had deliberately set fire to the town.[33] A few days after the destruction of Guernica, members of Parliament also expressed deep-seated concern about these attacks. Foreign Secretary Anthony Eden reiterated that the British ambassador in Spain was looking into contradictory statements about the responsibility for the town's destruction but maintained the officially neutral stance that "the Government deeply deplore the bombardment of the civil population in Spain, wherever it may occur, or whoever may be responsible."[34] As evidence mounted that German planes had conducted the attacks, some used this for political ends; the *Daily Worker* called for an end to "non intervention" and for "arms for Spain!"[35]

A variety of British organizations also condemned the attack on Guernica. The Trades Union Congress (TUC) issued a joint statement with the Socialist Party's executive:

> The dreadful sufferings of the Spanish people have reached a climax of horror and shame in the criminal bombing of Guernica by German aeroplanes under the command of the rebel generals. British labour denounces this monstrous crime perpetuated upon the defenceless Basque city ... as an outrage upon humanity and a violation of the principles of civilisation.[36]

The National Conference of Labour Women issued its own statement, expressing horror "at the barbarous slaughter by rebel aircraft at Guernica" and calling upon the government to demand "an immediate

---

[33] "Burning of City" and "New Allegations on Guernica," *Daily Telegraph*, 30 Apr. 1937.

[34] Anthony Eden, *House of Commons*, 30 May 1937, quoted in "Eden's 'Urgent' Demand to Franco," *Evening Standard*, 30 Apr. 1937.

[35] "Guernica the Guilty," *Daily Worker*, 30 Apr. 1937. This account cites both Noel Monks from the *Daily Express* and also, authoritatively, the *Times*, whose reporter described finding unexploded German incendiary bombs in Guernica as well as spotting German planes. Coverage by George Lowther Steer, the unattributed *Times* reporter on the scene, proved quite controversial, especially the then-challenged assertion that he had clearly identified German aircraft. See Tom Buchanan, *The Impact of the Spanish Civil War on Britain: War, Loss and Memory* (Brighton, 2007), ch. 2, and Steer's own published account, George Lowther Steer, *Tree of Guernika* (London, 1938). Other discussions of the denial by Franco and responses to this in Spain can be found in "Nationalists Victory Near Bilbao," *Daily Telegraph*, 29 Apr. 1937, and "Rebels Deny Part in Spain Massacre," *Daily Mirror*, 29 Apr. 1937.

[36] Reprinted in "Trade Unions on 'Monstrous Crime,'" *Daily Telegraph*, 29 Apr. 1937, and in "Labour Indicts Murderers," *Daily Herald*, 29 Apr. 1937.

meeting of the League Council to deal with this atrocity."[37] An editorial in the *Daily Mirror* reprinted the TUC statement, suggesting "it's at least something that thousands of British workers have the courage to protest. Some day the fate of Guernica may be the fate of English cities. Remember!"[38] It was in light of such reminders of potentially similar attacks in Britain that Labour's condemnation of Guernica also saw in "the horror excited by this example of 'frightfulness'" the impetus for "instant action" – to wit, urging the government "to take the initiative through the League of Nations for an examination of the whole problem of the bombing in warfare of open towns and the indiscriminate slaughter of the non-combatant population."[39]

Writing at length in the WIL's *Monthly News Sheet*, Mary Sheepshanks commented that the attacks on Guernica had shown that "[n]o horror is too frightful to be perpetrated to-day" and that this locale's deliberate destruction was "but a rehearsal for London, Paris or what you will.... Such is modern war." Questioning how this point had been reached, she urged the renewal of efforts to curtail the use of air power. Among other things, "bitter regret must be felt at the previous failures of the Great Powers to utilise the Disarmament Conference to secure an agreement for the total abolition of military and naval aircraft and the internationalisation of civil aviation." Only limits on air power could ward off "totalitarian war" and promise a future for the human race.[40]

Guernica thus also provoked renewed calls for action, although not all writers or politicians were as clear as Sheepshanks about how to proceed or in agreement about what should be done. A letter to the editor of *Reynold's News* posed the question directly in terms of the protection of vulnerable civilians: "Is the world going to accept the butchery of women and children and the destruction of churches and hospitals in silence?"[41] An editorial in the *News of the World* pushed the consequences for Britain: "[T]he latest tale of destruction wrought by aeroplanes in the Spanish war has its moral for the British people," as "it has to be remembered ... that the bigger the town the easier the target, unless the defence

---

[37] "Horrified at Atrocity," *Daily Herald*, 29 Apr. 1937.
[38] "Humanity's Shame," *Daily Mirror*, 29 Apr. 1937. This suggests that the memories of the First World War's raids had already faded.
[39] "Labour Indicts Murderers," *Daily Herald*, 29 Apr. 1937. The use of the phrase "open towns" brings us back to the pre-1914 climate produced by the Hague Conventions.
[40] Mary Sheepshanks, "The Bombing of Guernica," in *Women's International League Monthly News Sheet*, 29:6 (June 1937).
[41] James Pearce, Letter to the editor, *Reynold's News*, 2 May 1937.

is adequate." Arguing for rearmament, the editorial concluded: "In the old days, there was time after the first shock on a more or less distant battlefield to muddle through. To-day the first battlefield ... would be found on our doorsteps."[42] War would come home, and the home must therefore be defended.

Montague Smith, writing in the *Daily Mail*, saw the attacks on Guernica as having a special relevance to a forthcoming parliamentary by-election in Wandsworth. He quoted approvingly the stance of Conservative candidate Roland Jennings, who stood for "rearmament to keep the peace, and for security against aggression." In remarks as he campaigned at the last minute, Jennings stated that he stood for a strong air force, "which will make it impossible for any aggressor to treat London as General Franco's aeroplanes have been able to treat the Red territories in Spain.... If the policy of my Communist and Socialist opponents had prevailed this country would be as much at the mercy of a foreign invader by air as the people of Guernica." The *Daily Mail* was happy to endorse this view, urging its readers to realize "that a strong Air Force is the only real defence" and thus to vote for Jennings.[43]

Meanwhile, the public debate over Guernica continued. An editorial in the *Star* began: "The Spanish war has touched a new low level of shame and brutality .... The attack on Guernica has no excuse, and every criminal characteristic.... [It] underlines once more the essential evil of the new weapon of war."[44] A few days later, the *Star*'s editorial called for an investigation into the war against civilians in Spain, claiming "the whole moral standard of Europe ... is involved in this squalid and unchivalrous perversion."[45]

Others proposed a new urgency in going after the "air menace" itself. A form appeared in *Reynold's News* within a week of the bombings offering its readers a chance both to register their outrage and to insist that their government take action. The motivation for the campaign was clearly put forward:

> For the first time in history an open town has been reduced to ruins without any military objective; men, women and children have been massacred – Devil's tribute to the cruelty of the bomb and the horror unleashed by modern war.[46]

[42] "Battle on the Doorstep!" *News of the World*, 2 May 1937.
[43] "Spain Lesson for Electors: Air Terror Shows Need of Defence," *Daily Mail*, 28 Apr. 1937.
[44] "What We Think," *Star*, 27 Apr. 1937.
[45] "What We Think," *Star*, 30 Apr. 1937.
[46] "Guernica," *Reynold's News*, 2 May 1937. The form also appeared in other papers.

It called upon citizens to press Parliament to act now, and at the bottom of the form it offered two statements, one of protest and one of action: "I/We Protest against the barbarous bombing of the civil population of Guernica. I/We Demand that the Government take action, through the League of Nations, (1) To outlaw immediately air attack on open towns; and (2) To prevent a repetition of the slaughter of civilians by air bombing and machine gunning." What is striking about this document is its emphasis on the ability to identify "open towns," to distinguish between "civilians" and "combatants," a line that as we have seen had been increasingly blurred and yet retained considerable cultural and political significance.

On behalf of the British government, Lord Plymouth, meeting with the Non-Intervention Committee in London, proposed that all sides in the Spanish conflict refrain from aerial bombardment.[47] In opposing this idea, unofficial sources in Italy referred to the ideas of the Hague Conventions, the difficulty of distinguishing between "open towns and military objectives."[48] Thus, some in Britain appeared to support one measure defeated in Geneva, the prohibition on military uses for aviation. The other side hearkened back to before the First World War, as if the idea of separating legitimate targets from illegitimate ones had not been fully challenged during that conflict.

The call for a new look at international law also appeared in public forums. A long essay in the *Daily Sketch* on the "Worst Air Crime" offered the following perspective on the "atrocity" that "the worst crime that the aeroplane has yet committed against humanity" represented. Comparing the bombing of Madrid and Guernica, the author stressed that what made Guernica worse was the lack of military objectives and the brutality of the destruction. The incident offered an opportunity not for taking sides but for reflection:

> I know no accepted code of law which lays down how far a combatant is entitled to wage war on civilians and women and children, or whether he is entitled to wage war on them at all. Is not that a great gap in our humanity for which all of us in a greater or lesser degree are to blame?

Guernica thus provided the opportunity to establish a code of law that would address these issues, a rule "which forbade air raids on open towns." The essay concluded: "Air raids on open towns serve so little

---

[47] The Non-Intervention Committee was the international organization wherein twenty-seven states, including Italy and Germany, agreed not to offer either side in the Spanish Civil War military supplies.

[48] "Air Bombing in Spain," *News of the World*, 9 May 1937.

military need that any Power really determined to abolish them, and to concentrate on this elementary service of humanity, could not fail to be successful. Let Great Britain be that Power."[49] Here was an attempt at solving the problem of aerial warfare, not through rearmament or abolition, but by restricting the possible uses of this weapon, something that had been tried – in vain – since before the First World War.

Guernica was also publicly linked to previous examples of interwar aerial bombing, notably by Fascist Italy in Ethiopia. A late April editorial in the *Daily Herald* made this explicit:

> [E]ven in war decency and humanity generally set some limits to what one side is prepared to do to its enemies and especially to the civilian population.
>
> That is why the whole of the humane world will be sick with disgust at the merciless bombardment of the Basque town of Guernica ... [of the] bestial murder by cowards of unarmed and defenceless people.
>
> The lesson of Guernica is the same as the lesson of Abyssinia. Fascism is a lust for power and supremacy whatever the cost....
>
> If the Abyssinians fight for their homes and country, they shall be tortured with poison gas. If the Basques fight for theirs, their towns will be razed and death will be rained upon their women and children.[50]

Echoes of the earliest responses to the air raids of the First World War as atrocities committed by cowards could be heard in this reflection. However, it also made evident just how far the stakes had grown since the end of the Great War.

The association of aerial bombs with barbarism, of their use being the act of the "uncivilized," was again made vividly clear in a political cartoon that appeared in the *Daily Herald* the next day. The image is of a heaven filled with children's bodies floating upward. On a cloud appear two "Abyssinian Cherubs" – stereotypically dark-skinned, wearing African clothing – addressing two "child victims of Guernica." The dead African children hail their Spanish counterparts: "'Golly, white children, am the white Christians civilising you, too!'"[51]

In a further critique of the use of air power in imperial settings, the WIL wrote to Anthony Eden in early May 1937 comparing the bombing in Guernica to Britain's own actions in India. First urging the government "to make every possible effort to avert a repetition of such actions under any circumstances," the letter continued by stating that "in this

---

[49] Candidus, "Worst Air Crime," *Daily Sketch*, 30 Apr. 1937.
[50] "Murder in Guernica," *Daily Herald*, 28 Apr. 1937.
[51] "Golly White Children," Political Cartoon in the *Daily Herald*, 29 Apr. 1937.

ABYSSINIAN CHERUBS (to child victims of Guernica): *"Golly, white children, am the white Christians civilising you, too!"*

FIGURE 7.1. "Golly, White Children." Cartoon by Will Dyson responding to aerial attacks in Ethiopia and Spain appearing in the *Daily Herald*, 29 April 1937.

connection we deplore more than ever the recent bombing raids on the North West Frontier of India which ... create a feeling of hypocrisy and shame in English men and women who protest on humanitarian grounds against such outrages in Spain."[52] The WIL also wrote directly to the secretary of state for India:

> We are well aware that the analogy of Spain is by no means exact in detail, that it will be claimed that punitive measures were rendered

[52] B[arbara] Duncan Harris, Chair, WIL Letter to Anthony Eden, Secretary of State for Foreign Affairs, 5 May 1937, WILPF 1/13, BLPES. The text of this letter indicates that it is sending an enclosed letter to the secretary of state for India and to the press.

necessary by the provocative action of fanatical leaders in Warziristan, and that before bombing operations take place warning is given so that non combatants can escape. At the same time my Committee feel that charges against us of hypocrisy by other nations are not altogether without reason when on the same day protests were made in the British press with regard to the bombing at Guernica, it was possible for such headlines to appear as "Trapped Tribesmen mown down by R. A. F. on Indian Frontier." ...

There is also in Great Britain a growing opinion which holds that the cause of world peace is seriously retarded by this kind of action on the part of the British Government.[53]

Such views, while coming from a select population of feminist pacifists, may not reflect popular opinion, but they display the consistency of the WIL's underlying belief that all states must abolish aerial bombardment for the sake of all humanity.

It was in light of the brutal demonstration of air power in Spain, which of course did not end with Guernica, that some works on aerial warfare appeared in late 1930s on the prospect of the next air war against Britain. Some of these works, as we saw in earlier discussions, made use of examples of the damage inflicted during the First World War, but after 1938, studies of air power acknowledged the new urgency provided by the devastation wrought from the air upon the civil population of Spain and, to a lesser extent, on populations in Asia.[54] The intensification of Japanese aerial attacks on China in 1938 also received some concerted press coverage. The *Times* reported on heavy raids on Nanchang and Hankow in March, on damaging raids around Canton in April, and on increased raids in Kwangsi and Canton in September 1938.[55] By the time many of these new studies appeared in Britain, there was ample evidence of the destructive nature of aerial warfare from both Asia and Europe.

The 1938 study *Air Defence of Britain* began with the raids of World War I as showing "the peculiar aptitude of the aerial bomb, later to

---

[53] B[arbara] Duncan Harris, Chair, WIL, Letter to Marquess of Netland, Secretary of State for India, 6 May 1937, WILPF 1/13, BLPES.

[54] There had been earlier influential studies such as James Spaight, *Air Power and the Cities* (London, 1930); L. E. O. Charlton, *War Over England* (London, 1936); Albert Henry Ross, *War on Great Cities* (London, 1937); and H. Montgomery Hyde and G. R. Falkiner Nuttall, *Air Defence and the Civil Population* (London, 1937), and the highly critical works of T. H. Wintringham, *Air Raid Warning* (London, 1934) and *The Coming World War* (London, 1935), but it is *after* 1937 that the example of Spain for Britain emerges most forcefully.

[55] "Fighting on the Yangtze: Heavy Japanese Air Raids," *Times*, 18 Mar. 1938, and "Japanese Air Raids Round Canton," *Times*, 2 Apr. 1938.

be evinced in Barcelona, for the massacre of innocents."[56] The authors continued by pointing out that with the evidence from Spain came the recognition that "[a] longish war may well reduce Western Europe to the condition portrayed in the early part of Mr. H. G. Wells's film, when we had gone back to quite an elementary form of life in the ruins of our civilization. We have no right to assume that the next war will be short.... We should therefore go back to the old principle of 'women and children first.'"[57] However, the writers also looked to other, more recent examples from abroad in asserting that "the first raid of the next war will be a completely bestial affair, mass murder to an extent which has been approached but not reached in China during the last few months."[58]

Attacks on Barcelona alone prompted a lengthy study by John Langdon-Davies, himself a direct observer of the Spanish Civil War, advocate of the republican side, and longtime enthusiast of Catalan culture.[59] His 1938 *Air Raid: The Technique of Silent Approach, High Explosive Panic* focused on the impact of aerial warfare on Spain and its lessons for Britain. According to Langdon-Davies, what happened in Barcelona had more direct relevance to Britain because it was more closely comparable to London than either Madrid or Guernica. The March 1938 raids on Barcelona demonstrated "what happens when an air fleet attacks a large population congregated in a city."[60] In terms of loss of life and injury, they did not measure up to the worst battles of the First World War. The purpose of such raids, however, was to erode morale and induce panic:

> The object of the manoeuvre was itself psychological. The aim was not casualties, but the creation of panic. The technique employed was designed to nullify existing Defence measures against panic. It succeeded ... [because all were] reduced to a state of impotent terror by the end of the period, and careful observers went so far as to suggest that had the techniques been used for another forty-eight hours there would have been a total paralysis of the life of the city and of the power to resist.[61]

[56] L. E. O. Charlton, G. T. Garratt, and Lt-Com. R. Fletcher, *Air Defence of Britain* (Harmondsworth, 1938), 10.

[57] Charlton et al., *Air Defence*, 156. This was an explicit reference to the 1936 film *Things to Come*, discussed in Chapter 4.

[58] Charlton et al., *Air Defence*.

[59] A discussion of Langdon-Davies's writings on Spain and the Spanish Civil War can be found in Buchanan, *The Impact of the Spanish Civil War*, 141–157.

[60] John Langdon-Davies, *Air Raid: The Technique of Silent Approach, High Explosive Panic* (London, 1938), 12.

[61] Langdon-Davies, *Air Raid*, 15. For a contemporary response to this work, see J. B. S. Haldane, "Can London Learn from Barcelona?" *New Statesman and Nation*, 9 July 1938.

The nation in its totality would thus be tested and so too would the power of the state to persuade its civilians that promised defense measures – including those set up precisely to avoid panic – would work in the face of air power.

In private, the British government had been collecting information about the damage inflicted by raids in both Asia and Europe. In August 1938, the Intelligence Branch of the ARP Department offered a report entitled "The Effects of Air Raids in Spain and China," summarizing the nature of the raids, the methods of attack and type of bombs employed, and finally, their effects. The report noted, for instance, that thermite bombs often had to be left to burn themselves out, and that while some of the Spanish air raids seemed to have specific military targets, others had "taken the form of indiscriminate bombing." In Spain, moreover, "a great many casualties have been caused to people in the streets by blast, splinters and falling A. A. [anti-aircraft] fragments," and in a ratio of "about 18 killed and 20 wounded per ton of bombs dropped."[62]

The commonsense conclusion that taking shelter protected the population during air raids was starkly underscored in this report but so too was the inadequacy of the provision of shelters, especially in the case of Barcelona. Taking shelter in cellars had led to people being buried beneath collapsing buildings, thus highlighting the need for underground shelters or for the dispersal of the civil population. In China, troops were saved when they left their barracks and took cover in the surrounding countryside in anticipation of a raid. A concentrated population that was not able to shelter itself adequately was at high risk, but apparently not for a collapse of morale. While comparing the amount of notice given in advance of an air raid between Chinese inland cities that had about twenty minutes of warning and Spanish coastal towns that had very little notice, it reported the following important consequence for Spain: "[T]he moral effect of bombing civilians, although great, seems, however, in Spain to have stimulated the hatred and endurance of the people." If morale was thus sustained by turning reactions from despair to anger, nonetheless "war conditions have forced the authorities in Spain, regardless of cost, to give the population a greater degree of protection against direct hits by the larger bombs than is at present contemplated in the plans of this or any other European country."

---

[62] Confidential Admiralty Monthly Intelligence Report, "Effects of Air Raids in Spain and China," 15 Aug. 1938, TNA CO 323/1592/66. All quotes in this paragraph and the one that follows are from this report.

One of the lessons that the British government thus learned from raids in China and Spain was that such attacks stimulated "endurance" and stoicism rather than despair or capitulation. This was something that it seemingly already knew, based on reactions to the aerial attacks of the First World War, and something that it wanted to cultivate among its own civilian population. However, the greater extent and longevity of interwar aerial attacks also prompted renewed and vigorous calls to challenge the use of air power itself. The enduring images of innocence under attack, of war waged against women and children and destructive of domestic life itself, spurred a powerful feminist response at the decade's end.

FEMINIST REFLECTIONS ON MODERN AERIAL WARFARE

In her well-known 1938 treatise on women and peace, *Three Guineas*, Virginia Woolf reflected on the visual power of photographs of air raids from the Spanish Civil War:

> They are not pleasant photographs to look upon... [of] dead children, ... the section of a house. A bomb has torn open the side; there is still a birdcage hanging in what was presumably the sitting room, but the rest of the house looks like nothing so much as a bunch of spillikins suspended in mid air.[63]

It is the domestic details – the birdcage that still hangs, as much as the dead children – that bring home the central difference of the air raid. Woolf made extensive notes on Louis Delaprée's *The Martyrdom of Madrid* while working on *Three Guineas*, as well as collecting press cuttings, including photographs of the damage to Madrid.[64] As was the case with many others, the visual evidence of this war, of damage to ordinary lives, prompted outrage. Woolf also associated the war with a deeply personal loss, that of her nephew Julian Bell, who died in Spain in July 1937. In a letter to her sister while writing the book, she wrote, "I am always wanting to argue it with Julian. In fact, I wrote it as an argument with him."[65]

---

[63] Virginia Woolf, *Three Guineas* (1938; rpt., Harmondsworth, 1982), 13–14. Further references are made parenthetically in the text.

[64] See the discussion of this in Patricia Laurence, "The Facts and Fugue of War: From *Three Guineas* to *Between the Acts*," in *Virginia Woolf and War: Fiction, Reality, and Myth*, ed. Mark Hussey (Syracuse, NY, 1991), 232–238.

[65] Virginia Woolf, Letter to Vanessa Bell, 17 Aug. 1937, in *The Letters of Virginia Woolf* Vol. 6: *1936–1941*, ed. Nigel Nicolson and Joanne Trautmann (New York, 1980), 159.

In this sense, *Three Guineas* both responds to what has occurred in Spain and builds on Woolf's earlier, direct experience of aerial warfare during the First World War.

Nor was Woolf alone in reflecting on the threat that air power posed, particularly to women. Like Woolf, Helena Swanwick had written of the influence of the Great War's raids on her thinking, although Swanwick's interwar writings (and actions) were far more overtly political. After the outbreak and destructive evidence of the Spanish Civil War, Helena Swanwick asserted again in her 1937 *The Roots of Peace* that "women's lives are and must be lived under conditions very different from that of men."[66] "Homes are theirs to make or mar," she continued, "but men can and do wipe them out with no more concern than they would kick over an ant-hill" (181). This kicking over of anthills was precisely what "the bomber" accomplished with his attacks on terrified women and children.

Air warfare, in Swanwick's account, evolved from men's "double infatuation with machines and with dominion" (181). Yet given the logic of how warfare has progressed, Swanwick also envisaged a "nightmare," in which she sees "women in the near future turning themselves into bombers, as they turned themselves into munition workers.... They can fly as well as men, they are as brave as men, and it would not take them long to learn the art of releasing bombs. That would release them from the hideous passivity of waiting until men had decided that enough 'women and children and homes' had been destroyed to warrant calling off the devil of war" (184). What would prevent this horror was what Swanwick saw dwelling in now-enfranchised women, whose "compensations" for the horrors of war, unlike those of men, are "few and fleeting ... [while] their sufferings are unspeakable and enduring" (184) and include witnessing the pain and devastation of their offspring.

Like other witnesses to the damage inflicted by one war and the potential for even more destruction in the methods of modern warfare unleashed in the 1930s, Swanwick was convinced that women, if only they would recognize it, had visceral reasons to oppose war collectively. Yet the changing nature of warfare had also given women new opportunities to be just like men. Women could now naturally become bombers as well as men, and this gave them access to "action," allowing them to avoid merely being victims of war. Still, Swanwick believed that women perceived war differently than men, with less enthusiasm. The danger

---

[66] Helena Swanwick, *The Roots of Peace* (London, 1938), 180. Further references are made parenthetically in the text.

remained that they would not allow themselves to act against the "herd" mentality of their fellow citizens.

Woolf also wanted to demonstrate how women responded to war differently than men, and the underlying effect of *Three Guineas* is a cohesive feminist critique of war. Woolf argued for the separateness of women in terms of their relationship to war and had earlier expressed a similar visceral reaction to the idea of women serving as bombers.[67] In *Three Guineas*, she carefully suggested that men can have a range of reactions to war, citing within a few paragraphs of one another both an "airman," who objected to peace and disarmament on the grounds that fighting produced vital "manly qualities," and Wifred Owen, who wrote of war's catastrophic effects on men (10). Given this disparity, how could women as a group have one overarching perspective? Yet she then turned to the photographs from Spain, calling them "a crude statement of fact addressed to the eye," but one provoking "horror and disgust" and the feeling that "war must be stopped at whatever cost.... For now at last we are looking at the same picture; we are seeing with you the same dead bodies, the same ruined houses" (14). The "we" here is implicitly women, but women responding as members of human society universally disgusted with the destruction of home life that these photographs represent. And this simple phrase, encapsulating the "horror and disgust" evoked by the air raid, runs like a refrain through the book: "dead bodies and ruined houses."

Despite the power of this image, Woolf continued, women's capacity to act on what they see – even if it is "dead bodies, ruined houses" – is limited. They cannot fight, they do not have political power, and they do not control the media. What they possess instead is the capacity to look disinterestedly at war, politics, and society precisely because of this lack of access, because of their difference. Unable to participate in the military, women can mock the outward emblems of militarism and patriotism such as uniforms; "we, who are forbidden to wear such clothes ourselves, can express the opinion that the wearer is not to us a pleasing or an impressive spectacle" (25). Woolf suggested that one way to promote peace was to support new forms of education, especially for women; another was to encourage women's economic independence in order to foster their ability to resist the lure of war and empire.

Aware of the tenuous links between the photographs from Spain and the underlying message that it was by promoting women's independence

[67] See, e.g., her diary entry for June 1918 in Virginia Woolf, *The Diary of Virgina Woolf*, Vol. 1: *1915–1919*, ed. Anne Olivier Bell (New York, 1977), 153, discussed in Chapter 3.

that war could be prevented, Woolf spent the final section of her work exposing women's fundamental status as outsiders. It was this status, available, she suggested, to all women but not to men that made their potential to work against modern war so powerful. Some of Woolf's claims for women seem strikingly similar to ones exposed in the previous discussions of interwar feminist pacifism: "[A]s fighting thus is a sex characteristic which she cannot share, the counterpart to some claim of the maternal instinct which he cannot share, so is it an instinct which she cannot judge" (123). Once again, soldiering and mothering are set as *the* fundamental gendered activities. Yet unlike earlier arguments, for Woolf, women's opposition to war was not based on maternity. Instead, the common experience of exclusion from the nation, women's alienation from public life, increased their critical distance from appeals to patriotism and militarism. As she famously put it:

> [I]f you [men] insist on fighting to protect me, or "our" country, let it be understood soberly and rationally between us, that you are fighting to gratify a sex instinct which I cannot share; to procure benefits which I have not shared and probably will not share; but not to gratify my instincts or to protect either myself or my country. "For," the outsider will say, "in fact, as a woman, I have no country. As a woman, I want no country. As a woman my country is the whole world." (125)

In addition to making this internationalist assertion, Woolf identified the common enemy, whose empowerment had led to the dead bodies and ruined houses inflicted by the air raid.

Once again, Woolf used a visual image, in this case of a man in uniform, sword in hand, to evoke a response: "He is called in German and Italian Führer or Duce; in our own language Tyrant or Dictator. And behind him lie the ruined houses and dead bodies – men, women and children" (162). Woolf then explained the importance of these interlocked images, for they suggested "that the public and the private worlds are inseparably connected; that the tyrannies and servilities of the one are the tyrannies and servilities of the other" (162). She continued:

> How essential it is that we should realize that unity that the dead bodies, the ruined houses prove. For such will be our ruin if you, in the immensity of your public abstractions forget the private figure, or if we in the intensity of our private emotions forget the public world. Both houses will be ruined, the public and the private ... for they are inseparably connected. (163)

Modern war exemplified by the air raid has crossed these borders – making the home the war zone. While Woolf was undoubtedly unaware of this particular link, her language here echoed the words of Ida O'Malley in 1917 that the realms of men and women, state and home had been mixed up. In 1938, on the eve of another war that would attack Britons in their houses and families, Woolf insisted that the concerns of men and women, of the public and private worlds, must be combined if humanity were to survive.

CONCLUSION

When air raids returned to Europe with a vengeance in the Spanish Civil War, a variety of British activists took note of the lessons for Britain. Despite the efforts to curtail or curb the use of air raids, and the power of some of these anti-militarist arguments, it was clear that the clock could not be turned back. Aerial warfare and its terrors would almost certainly return to British soil. While some could still draw on this insight to argue that any type of war under any circumstances was unacceptable, others became increasingly resigned to air war's inextricable arrival. The next chapter takes up the increased government measures developed to prepare civilians, including women and children, to face the bombs, perhaps even the chemical weapons, which could rain down upon them.

8

Preparing the Public for the Next War

Air Raid Precautions on the Eve of War

INTRODUCTION

In the aftermath of the failure of disarmament measures, the return of aerial warfare in Spain and elsewhere, and the increasing international tension, a new openness about air raid precautions emerged. Among a host of works on the subject in the late 1930s was Labour MP Dr. Leslie Haden-Guest's 1937 *If Air War Comes*, which was itself part of the effort to publicize what the state had been doing and would continue to do to protect the home. Haden-Guest was quick to acknowledge the government's own assessment of its inability to guarantee "absolute immunity from air attack" and that such attacks could push the civil population to the limits of endurance. Haden-Guest noted, however, that measures could be taken to encourage the possibility of survival and victory:

> Air war will be the war of heroic defence and terrible reprisals. It will be swift and fierce beyond comparison with anything known up to the present time. In that warfare the nation will be victorious which is best organized in advance to bear the terrible effects of an air attack and yet maintain order and moral discipline in its life.
>
> And because the civilian population will be attacked by an air enemy, then defeat or victory for the nation will depend on the endurance and discipline of the civilian.[1]

In orchestrating the preparations for its citizens, the state echoed this language by promoting ARP in anticipation that civilian behavior and

---

[1] Leslie Haden-Guest, *If Air War Comes: A Guide to Air Raid Precautions and Anti-Gas Treatment* (London, 1937), 5.

morale could well determine whether a coming war could be won. At the same time, the apparatus of ARP as it came into being relied on both gendered and class-based assumptions about the capacity of civilians to "hold on," even as it attempted to promote the kind of wartime civil identity that would transcend all other differences. Drawing upon years of internal debate, questions about methods and motives for ARP emerged into the public with new intensity in the middle and late 1930s. The question of how to protect home life by effectively militarizing the entire civil population remained a fundamental issue in discussions of these measures, as can be found in the internal workings of the government, its public announcements, and the parliamentary debates about ARP in the second half of the decade.

Most important, the expansion of civil defense reified the intermingling of state and home produced by aerial warfare that Ida O'Malley had discovered in her response to the London raids of 1917. Not only did government policies take for granted that the home had become a war zone, but they also acknowledged the key roles of men and women, and even children, as active participants in this new kind of war. While tracing the evolution of the measures that the government debated and enacted as "Air Raids Precautions" after 1935, this chapter seeks not so much to offer a narrative of how plans developed as to explicate the cultural, and often gendered, assumptions that undergirded the measures designed and now implemented bit by bit to protect civilians from the air war to come.

TAKING AIR RAIDS PRECAUTIONS PUBLIC

Public awareness of the work being done to prepare the nation for new threats to civilians and home life emerged forcefully with the release of the first ARP circular in July 1935, the moment when the work of ARP shifted from being under the purview of the Cabinet's Committee of Imperial Defence to that of the Home Office. While continuing to develop strategies for minimizing damage to civilian life and even to test protective measures under simulated attacks, the government also began to invite press scrutiny in order to call attention to what the state *was* doing to meet the potential threats posed if a new war should occur. The July 1935 ARP circular provoked some sustained critical responses, although the editors of *Flight* (the official organ of the Royal Aero Club) explained that

> curious reactions may follow the issue of the Government's circular ... on the subject of air raid precautions. Pacifists may well gloat over it, for

many of them believe that to emphasize the horrors of war is the best
way to make the world peaceable.... Another school of thought, which
we may call the extreme air school, rejoices in descriptions of the horrors of air bombardment as an argument for increasing our air forces.

This neatly summed up the absolutist positions regarding air power: one
must either reject or embrace it entirely. Instead, this article urged "calm
consideration" of the issues raised by the ARP circular and further noted
that while lacking in details, this first official government pronouncement
had exercised "common sense" by recognizing that in some future war
"some nation may be both brutal and unscrupulous."[2] As we have seen,
this was precisely the tone that the ARP planners had repeatedly invoked
in their own internal discussions.

The *Times* presented much of the circular in its entirety, highlighting,
by means of captions, several points. The most important was that there
was "no immunity from attack."[3] The circular was adamant that "the
need for these measures in no way implies a risk of war in the near future"
and went on to insist upon the government's commitment to international peace. Still, it emphasized, "the Government would be neglecting
their duty to the civil population – men, women and children – if they
failed to take these measures."

As far as the actual provisions, in keeping with the entire enterprise,
they remained modest and vague: the placement of an ARP Department
in the Home Office, the need to coordinate separate efforts against
chemical and explosive weapons, the decision that the widespread provision of shelter was "impracticable" but that instructions to safeguard
homes would be delivered to householders in the near future and that
the government would proceed to develop local arrangements for medical services and other needed procedures and equipment to deal with
the consequences of aerial warfare. What was also brought forward was
the idea that these were measures that had already been adopted elsewhere in Europe.[4]

Critics of the 1935 ARP circular, notably from Labour, made their
views public shortly after its release. In the House of Commons, Rhys
Davies attacked the procedures outlined in the circular as having become
necessary only because of the government's failed policies and labeled
it one of the "most terrible" statements "in its implications" that had

[2] "Air Raid Precautions," *Flight*, July 1935.
[3] The actual wording of the circular was that "it is impossible to guarantee immunity from
attack." See "Civilians in Air Attacks," *Times*, 11 July 1935.
[4] See the reproduction of the circular in "Civilians in Air Attacks"; see also "Safety During
Air Raids," *Times*, 11 July 1935.

ever been issued.[5] The coverage of this critique went even further in the *Manchester Guardian*, which echoed the opinions of ARP already discussed in Chapters 6 and 7, that instead of pursuing a policy of precautions that could never work, the government should be advocating the "abolition of military aviation and the control of civil aviation.... The circular was a clumsy and cowardly way of dealing with the issues of peace and war."[6] The editorial page of the *Manchester Guardian* was almost equally scathing in its attack on the government:

> The circular ... is as depressing a document as anyone has seen from this Government.... A British Government proposes in peace time to place this country on what is tantamount to a war basis.... There is no justification of this elaborate and costly scheme and the disarrangement of civilian life which it must entail, except on the assumption that war ... will be waged by the "indiscriminate bombing of civilians".[7]

In place of this, the editorial urged a renewed commitment to the internationalization of air power and to disarmament, an approach that had become increasingly unpromising.

The *Times* remained less critical, praising the circular for not being "alarmist" and providing detailed and useful information for the population about the potential threat. Its conclusion, however, shared one point with that of the *Manchester Guardian*, namely the need for some kind of bracing international stance against the bombing of civilians:

> Public opinion in all countries must come to regard any nation resorting to bombing as outlaw, and by a series of air conventions between neighbours aggression in the air must be rendered liable to such overwhelming retaliation as to become an act of self-destruction.[8]

The difference between this perspective and that of the *Manchester Guardian* is also marked; the agreements advocated by the *Times* are backed by the possession of air power and the threat of mutual destruction, not international mechanisms either to control air arms or to prevent war itself.

Other reactions were more open to the government's message. The *Daily Mail's* headline read, "Air Raid Measures: Plans Revealed at

[5] "Home Office and Air Raids," *Times*, 17 July 1935. See also "Air Raid Precautions" (Editorial), 27 Aug. 1935 below.

[6] "Air Raid Circular," *Manchester Guardian*, 17 July 1935. The paper also noted the WIL's condemnation of the circular later that summer; see "The Air Raid Circular: Women's Criticism," *Manchester Guardian*, 3 Aug. 1935.

[7] "The Air Raid Defence Circular," 11 July 1935.

[8] "Air Raid Precautions" Editorial, *Times*, 27 Aug. 1935.

Last." Describing the planned actions as both "long-delayed" and "still tentative," the paper began by again quoting the government memo's basic acknowledgment that "it is impossible to guarantee immunity from attack" and that ARP called for policies that were "wholly precautionary" and "not as yet compulsory."[9] At this initial stage, British citizens were being taught to accept their vulnerability and avoid despair, yet whether general panic in the face of air raids could always be avoided remained the great fear of government officials.

As other guidelines followed the first circular, commentators took note of exactly how Britons were meant to behave. In the summer of 1935, an article in the *New Statesman and Nation* suggested:

> [T]he unemotional pages of the Home Office's new handbook on Anti-Gas precautions ... turn what has hitherto been an horrific fantasy into a close and appalling reality.... Mr. Baldwin's famous and candid words remain the precise truth: 'The only defence is offence, which means that you have to kill women and children more quickly than the enemy if you want to save yourselves.' Mr. Baldwin's remark is terribly substantiated by this handbook. There is no defence.... The object of all air-raid precautions is ... to postpone panic until after the outbreak of war itself. Consequently the keynote of this handbook is discipline. The population is to be regimented before the war because it will be too late after war has begun. We are to be drilled in the use of gas masks.... We are to get into the habit of regarding this horror as inevitable; we are to show our British courage by not getting excited. If we display our characteristic ability to die more quietly than other people, they may surrender first.[10]

Such critics urged the rejection of all such policies, offering support for air disarmament as an alternative, but whatever the emotive punch of such responses, planning to safeguard civilians from aerial and gas attacks continued to expand.

The preamble to the 1936 draft report of the new Air Raids Precautions Department of the Home Office outlined the basic issues and difficulty of balancing civilian and military preparations for air war:

> Owing to the trend of modern warfare, air raid precautions have become an essential and almost universal complement to active defence....
>
> The purpose of air raid precautions is to enable the civilian institutions of the country and the individual members of its population to be organised and prepared against the effects of hostile air attack, since civil immunity from the direct operations of the enemy can unfortunately no longer be guaranteed. It is, therefore, essential that every step

---

[9] "Air Raid Measures," *Daily Mail*, 11 July 1935.
[10] "Air Raid Precautions," *New Statesman and Nation*, 17 Aug. 1935.

should be taken which would enable the life and war effort of the country to be sustained with the minimum of dislocation and interruption.

The organisation of air raid precautions is a task of magnitude, touch-
ing as it does almost every aspect of civilian activity. It must clearly
take a number of years to complete, and in certain respects, it would be
difficult, without grave, possibly permanent, and certainly undesirable
dislocation of normal social life, to attain in time of peace the immediate
degree of readiness which is expected from the active defence forces.[11]

Despite a sense of urgency, the issues raised here were not new. The insistence that both "life" and the "war effort" had to continue in the face of
attacks that could *not* be prevented against a civilian population underlay
a variety of schemes that had begun with the air raids of the First World
War. It is also not surprising that civil defense could not be directly equated
with "active" defense, an issue that figured in public government plans for
shaping every aspect of civilian life in anticipation of the next war.

Another of the public statements about the work that had been done
behind the scenes by the ARP planners came in an announcement on
1 October 1936. In a new booklet sent to householders, officials suggested that the real danger from air raids arose from civilians not knowing what to do. The key was education, both to alleviate panic and to
shore up a system of civil defense. As an article highlighting the arrival of
the 1936 manual explained, "[T]he Government ... suggested that each
householder should provide his own refuge in his own house ... [as] the
only public shelters would be for people caught in the streets."[12] This
remained the intent until 1938, although subject to debate. Among arguments mounted against the provision of larger, public shelters was the
idea that "if a large number of people are taking refuge in a public shelter,
the casualties caused by the collapse of the building are going to be so
much greater than from the collapse of an ordinary dwelling house."[13] It
was thus not until the mid-1930s that news of specific government proposals filtered into public forums and, with the passage of the Air Raids
Precautions Act, that these proposals took concrete shape.

LEGISLATING PROTECTION FROM AIR RAIDS

By the spring of 1937, the work of ARP had grown substantially, and the
government felt ready – nearly two years after issuing the first general

[11] Draft, First Annual Report of the A.R.P. Department, 1936, TNA HO 45/17218.
[12] "Advice on Air-Raid Precautions," *Times*, 1 Oct. 1936.
[13] See discussions in ARP minutes, TNA HO 45/17588.

circular on ARP in July 1935 – to present legislation to Parliament about protecting the population in case of aerial bombardment. In the internal discussions of what became the Air Raid Precautions Bill, the efforts to include civilians in preparing for the next war also revealed an aware-ness of the limits that any such measures could offer. For example, com-ments on draft legislation circulated in October took issue with the use of phrases such as "immunity," when the original suggested that local governments could exercise greater leeway over measures when a part of their district was likely to remain safe from attack.[14] Critics pointed out that no such assumption – that any place would be "immune" – should or could be made.

Even more startling were objections to the very word "protection." A sentence in the draft detailing the role of the state read that the bill's aim was "the protection of persons and property from injury or damage arising out of hostile attack from the air." A note in the margins of this initial draft reads: "This should be reworded. It is bad politically 'there is no protection' and anyhow most of these services are for amelioration once injury and damage have been done."[15] At the very moment that the government was getting ready to enact legislation to prepare for aerial warfare and offer relief to civilians, it acknowledged that mostly what it could do was respond to the disaster after the fact, admitting that this was not truly "protection."

In the fall of 1937, the prelude to the introduction of legislation in Parliament began with a series of announcements. On 14 October, the *Times* published a long editorial on air raid precautions, noting that it concurred with the prime minister's recent speech: "[T]he terror which flies by air is inseparable from modern warfare." Getting to the heart of the issue of who should fund and take responsibility for providing ARP measures, the editorial agreed with government proposals that this should be divided between local authorities and the central government, in contrast to Herbert Morrison, the Labour leader who had emerged

---

[14] This was in reaction to the following clause concerning local proposals for ARP: Clause 2 Section 6, "If the Secretary of State is satisfied that by reason of the probable immu-nity of the whole or any part of the area of a council from hostile attack from the air it is unnecessary that an air-raid general precautions scheme or an air-raid fire precautions scheme should be brought into force for that area or part, he may on the application of the council dispense with the ... submission of such a scheme for that area or part." Comments on initial drafts also focused on the role of local versus central authority in Scotland and Ireland; see Notes, First Draft of Air Raids Precautions Bill, 20 Oct. 1937, TNA HO 45/17608.

[15] First Draft of Air Raids Precautions Bill.

as the strongest advocate of funding coming entirely from Westminster. According to the *Times*, in order to do the work efficiently and cost effectively and to meet specific needs, local government had to have a direct stake in allocating funds. The *Times* praised the work that had already taken place, noting that the training of wardens and others in anti-gas, fire fighting, and first aid measures as well the process of provisioning gas masks had already begun. It concluded with this call to action without fear: "[A]ir raid precautions are ... a very serious business, requiring from now onwards all the drive that can be imparted to them. But to take them seriously does not in the least imply panic.... Air raid precautions in this country are no more evidence of panic than the construction of a line of defence along the frontiers of a continental power." What is once again being acknowledged is how aerial warfare had erased the safety of the sea as a frontier and made it necessary to adopt ARP to try to safeguard all of Britain and all of its inhabitants.[16]

The government officially presented the Air Raids Precautions Bill to Parliament on 4 November. The legislation aimed to formalize the financing and responsibilities for ARP measures, dividing them between local and national authorities, as well as to make a definitive public stance about what the next war would entail and how the state intended to ameliorate, even if it could not prevent, what would ensue. Although its preparation had been long in the making, the announcement of impending legislation coincided with the release of a guide for householders on ARP.[17] As the *Times* noted, while representatives of local authorities had voiced, and would continue to voice, their objections to funding ARP, they were committed to carrying out the safety measures suggested once they became law.[18]

It was upon the bill's second reading in the House of Commons that debate over its essence – the acknowledgment that the entire nation must now be considered to be potentially under attack – forcefully emerged. When introducing the second reading, the secretary of state for the Home Department, Sir Samuel Hoare, used the raids of the First World War as a starting point. The tonnage of bombs dropped over the duration of that war, he proclaimed, would now fall within the first full day of an attack in a new war. Thus, the danger the airplane posed to the security of the British Empire must be halted in its tracks. In addition to developing

[16] "Air Raid Precautions," *Times*, 14 Oct. 1937. The prime minister quoted is Neville Chamberlain, who had replaced Baldwin in May.

[17] See the overview in T. H. O'Brien, *Civil Defence* (London, 1955), 103–106.

[18] "Protection in Air Raids," *Times*, 6 Nov. 1937.

significant air power to repel such an attack, the purpose of the proposed
civil defense legislation was "to go far to guarantee the country against
panic and the stoppage of national life" in order to enable the fighting services to continue. Hoare was also quick to point out what the government
had already done; among other things, it had produced "a supply of gas
masks for the civil population which, I believe, is better than the supply
in any other country in Europe" and already enrolled some 200,000 men
and women as ARP volunteers. The bill proposed to increase the scale,
and thus effectiveness, of mass ARP efforts. Hoare further stressed that
not only was the task of ARP a civilian one – "the field of the householder,
of the father of the family" – but inherently a "local" one, to "be carried
out by civilian men and women."[19] Hoare may have seen it as natural to
equate "father of the family" and "householder," but his use of this language shows how the tasks required for civil defense offered men a new
way to enact the normative masculine role of defenders of the home.

Many of the details of the Air Raids Precautions Bill concerned the distribution and allocation of resources for detecting air raids; warning of
their arrival; mitigating the most deadly effects of high-explosive, incendiary, or gas bombs; and assisting in the recovery process after the raids.
Providing protective elements such as gas masks and shelters and relocating the population away from obvious targets were among the measures
to alleviate aerial attacks that came under closer scrutiny during these
debates. So too did the staffing of ARP services, with subsequent questions about the compensation for this labor.[20] The government stressed
its willingness to fund nearly 90 percent of the costs of ARP in order to
ensure that the necessary means of civil defense would be established.
However, those claiming to speak on behalf of local authorities, namely
Labour's Herbert Morrison, argued that the government should *fully*
fund ARP as it funded the army, navy, and air force, without request-
ing supplemental funds from local authorities. What was striking at this
juncture was the insistence that the bulk of those laboring under ARP
would be "volunteers" and that cooperation between the government –
at both local and national levels – and the "ordinary man and woman in
the street" was essential for the success of any ARP measures.[21]

[19] Sir Samuel Hoare, *Parliamentary Debates – Commons*, 15 Nov. 1937, vol. 329, cols.
41–43, quote on 43 and 44.

[20] Compensation for injuries or even deaths sustained in training for such services as
well as providing them in wartime was also taken up by Parliament; see *Parliamentary
Debates –Commons*, 30 Nov. 1937, vol. 329, cols. 2003–2010.

[21] Sir Samuel Hoare, *Parliamentary Debates – Commons*, quote from vol. 329, col. 49;
Herbert Morrison quote from col. 60.

This spoke to the desire to ensure that the civilian population would heed a call to duty and service, not compulsion; this language also downplayed the mainly financial aspects of the actual bill. In rhetoric that suggested a marked equivalence of military service and ARP work, the under-secretary of state for the Home Department late in the debate spoke of the essentially local nature of the work of ARP: "[T]he conception of an air-raid warden is that really he is a citizen who is specially marked out as one with knowledge and authority."[22] Much like the traditional wartime transformation of the citizen into one especially marked to wage war – the soldier – this new warfare demanded the transformation of both male and female citizens into civil defense workers waging another sort of war.

A certain wistful tone arose among the MPs negotiating this bill. Individual members spoke of feeling "indignation that we should have to contemplate this beastly business for the protection of the British people and British homes." Those in the opposition, such as Herbert Morrison, continued the Labour critique that blamed the government's failures in international politics for necessitating the proposed legislation, the implication being that following a program more committed to peace and disarmament would have eliminated the need for ARP.[23] Despite a new insistence on the ability to prevent aerial attacks so that ARP measures served as a backup, the infamous words of Stanley Baldwin in 1932, that the bomber would always get through, meant that this bill had become, even for those critical of the government, "a regretted Bill, but … a necessary Bill."[24]

Debates over the bill focused on all the elements that it left vague, notably the sheltering and/or evacuation of the population and the protection of civilians, especially women and children, from gas and aerial attack. Members of Parliament were willing to congratulate the government for its policy of providing gas masks but also to criticize it for the lack of clarity over providing shelters, compared with other nations such as France.[25] Wilfrid Roberts, MP for Cumberland, explicitly raised the

---

[22] Geoffrey Lloyd, Under-Secretary of State for the Home Department, *Parliamentary Debates – Commons*, 25 Nov. 1937, vol. 329, cols. 1494–1495, quote from col. 1495.

[23] Herbert Morrison, *Parliamentary Debates – Commons*, vol. 329, cols. 68–69.

[24] Herbert Morrison, *Parliamentary Debates – Commons*, vol. 329, col. 71. It is also telling over the course of the debate that the government was taken to task both for not working hard enough for peace, by those like Morrison, and for not keeping up with the civil defense planning of France or Germany, by Conservative MPs like Duncan Sandys; see vol. 329, cols. 75–77.

[25] Duncan Sandys, *Parliamentary Debates – Commons*, vol. 329, cols. 72–73; Wilfrid Roberts, Herbert Morrison, *Parliamentary Debates – Commons*, vol. 329, cols. 83–86.

question of what to do with "young children and their mothers," suggesting that such individuals must go somewhere safe, and that if officials did not plan for evacuation, they would surely face disorderly, unplanned evacuations once the bombing started. Such proposals were questioned by those who wondered where such "safe" locales might exist in a future, aerial war and by others who insisted that the government should determine what areas as well as what members of the civil population required removal (evacuation) before air raids occurred.[26]

In proposing the dispersal of the most vulnerable members of the population, the MP for North Islington, Dr. Leslie Haden-Guest, called for more advanced planning, for the "wholesale evacuation of certain populations" – children, the elderly, the disabled – during a time of national emergency. All of this was necessary because "[u]nder aerial warfare conditions the whole country will be at war." Later in the debate, he would go further, asserting that "the whole of this country would be in the active area of the conflict if it came along, and … must be treated as if it were, as indeed it is, part of the military problem."[27] Nor was he

---

[26] Wilfrid Roberts, *Parliamentary Debates – Commons*, vol. 329, cols. 86–87. Interestingly, Roberts also attacked government secrecy in ARP planning, stating that "there is far freer discussion in some of the dictatorial countries than there is in England on the question of air-raid precautions" (col. 88). Later in the debate, James Ede questioned how a planned evacuation could possibly be done without inciting panic, especially if raids preceded a declaration of war, as some predicted. Surely in that case, everyone "will all be making tracks for the open country." See Ede, *Parliamentary Debates – Commons*, 15 Nov. 1937, vol. 329, col. 126. Ede further made the case that given the scope of the problem, ARP should be entirely in the hands of the national government. Still later in the proceedings, William Kelly raised the question of whether the government would consider compulsion or even "military action" in restricting the free movement of the population in the event of air raids and the need for orderly evacuations "should a barbarous air raid ever take place." See *Parliamentary Debates – Commons*, 25 Nov. 1917, vol. 329, cols. 1468–1469.

[27] Sir Richard Meller, *Parliamentary Debates – Commons*, 15 Nov. 1937, vol. 329, col. 89; see also Viscount Wolmer [Roundell Palmer], *Parliamentary Debates – Commons*, 15 Nov. 1937, vol. 329, cols. 107–108, who also insisted that "it will be impossible to say that any town or village in England, Scotland or Wales will not be open to attack in the next war" (col. 108); Dr. Leslie Haden-Guest, *Parliamentary Debates – Commons*, 15 Nov. 1937, vol. 329, cols. 96–97 and cols. 105–106, quote from col. 106; and Dr. Haden-Guest, *Parliamentary Debates – Commons*, 25 Nov. 1937, quote from vol. 329, col. 1444. Haden-Guest stressed the dangers posed to London and especially the East End. In the continuation of the debate, Haden-Guest urged further consideration of the obstacles that made the idea of Londoners waiting out aerial attacks in household-based shelters as implausible as the full evacuation of any large city. Evacuation thus had to be more carefully laid out in any bill, lest a "panic evacuation" result; see cols. 1441–1444. In addition, other MPs from the north of England took issue with the focus on London. As David Adams, MP from Newcastle, put it, "We do not subscribe to the view that

alone in using such rhetoric. Sir Ralph Glyn stated plainly, in support of the bill, that "in the next war, if there is one, the people at home will be in the front line. There is anxiety in the country about this." For that reason alone, Parliament needed to take immediate action on what the debate had shown "very largely ... [to be] a psychological question."[28]

In contrast, Viscount Wolmer noted the difficulties of removing the civil population, especially since there would be "an enormous number of women ... whom it would not be possible to evacuate from London because they would be required to work in the munitions factories and to feed their husbands who would be working in various national services." Here it was women's seemingly irreplaceable domestic labor as much as their service in war factories that must be sustained. Moreover, Wolmer continued, a large number of small children would not be able to wear gas masks and thus would require gas-proof rooms; some means of sheltering the population of cities would thus have to be found.[29]

The difficulties of providing any effective protection under the proposed government measures for the bulk of the working class was emphasized by still other prominent MPs, including those opposed to anything that looked like preparation for war. As Philip Noel-Baker argued, the whole notion of asking the civil population to create "refuge rooms" inside their homes required both space and money to spare in peacetime. Such an in-home shelter had to be built before war broke out and, according to Noel-Baker, some 7 to 8 million Britons did not have access to a home with such a spare room to convert into one that could offer a safeguard against shells and even gas attacks. Explicitly bringing class differences to bear on his argument, Noel-Baker asserted that those most in danger of aerial attacks were the poor, because they lived near factories, power plants, and rail stations. Moreover, "it is in those regions [where bombs would fall] that the houses are weakest and will afford the least protection ... that population is the densest" and where, therefore, the most casualties would occur. The solution was for full control

London is necessarily the heart of the country, and we are of opinion that we live in a dangerous area as far as air warfare is concerned." This being the case, if the population was not to be systematically evacuated, "the statutory provision of bomb-proof shelters" was necessary. See David Adams, *Parliamentary Debates – Commons*, 25 Nov. 1917, vol. 329, cols. 1463–1464.

[28] Sir Ralph Glyn, *Parliamentary Debates – Commons*, 15 Nov. 1937, vol. 329, cols. 132–133.

[29] Viscount Wolmer, *Parliamentary Debates–Commons*, 15 Nov. 1937, vol. 329, cols. 110–111. Later in the debate, concern over the costs of providing such shelter also emerged; see Maxwell, *Parliamentary Debates – Commons*, 16 Nov. 1937, vol. 329, col. 284 among others.

over ARP to lie with the central government, one committed to making "collective security and real air disarmament the first of all the objects that they pursue."[30]

Like Noel-Baker, other MPs expressed their skepticism about all ARP measures. As Campbell Stephen asserted:

> What the government is trying to do is plain. They are trying to create a feeling of confidence in the minds of the people before war comes.... [T]he government think that they will be able to allay the feeling among the people of the country who are wholly opposed to the policy of the National Government and to the possibility of war.[31]

Since the possibility of war evoked horror, the government needed to reassure them that with the Air Raids Precautions Bill, they would now be "comparatively safe." And the problem with this was that any of the measures undertaken by the government were "largely an illusion." The correct alternative would come from government policies designed to promote peace and to expend resources on domestic reforms needed now. Emotively, Stephen continued, "This Bill contemplates an invasion by bombers from other countries. In the constituency which I represent there are hundreds, aye, thousands of houses which are already invaded by rats and bugs... Just as you have not provided shelter for the working class in my division for carrying on their ordinary business, I do not believe in the shelter that you will provide for them under this Air-Raid Precautions Bill."[32] Like Sylvia Pankhurst responding to the actual raids of the First World War by pointing out the horrific conditions that the poor faced under ordinary circumstances, Stephen suggested the need for the government to focus on alleviating existing fundamental problems instead of promising to solve future ones.

---

[30] Philip Noel-Baker, *Parliamentary Debates – Commons*, 15 Nov. 1937, vol. 329, cols. 151–157; quotes from col. 156. Noel-Baker also criticized government plans not only because of the presumed cost of a refuge room, but also due to its ineffectiveness, going on to dismiss the efficacy of gas masks in general as well as of refuge rooms in offering any protection against high-explosive or incendiary bombs. Mr. William Leonard, the MP from Glasgow, concurred, offering a detailed portrait of Cowcaddens, one of its worst neighborhoods, where the suggestion that inhabitants could shelter in their homes was laughable. Homes in the area could provide no safety in case of aerial warfare. See *Parliamentary Debates – Commons*, 16 Nov. 1937, vol. 329, cols. 257–258. Later in the debate J. J. Davidson raised the issue of Glasgow as a special case in terms of the cost of providing shelters, given the large number of inhabitants living in tenements. See J. J. Davidson, *Parliamentary Debates – Commons*, 30 Nov. 1937, vol. 329, cols. 1939–1941.
[31] Campbell Stephen, *Parliamentary Debates – Commons*, vol. 329, col. 114.
[32] Stephen, *Parliamentary Debates – Commons*, vol. 329, cols. 116–117.

Another MP representing a northern London district, Frederick Montague, pointed out other ways in which the proposed legislation overlooked basic aspects of ordinary life not only on class lines but also in terms of gender. Along with criticizing an overall failure to understand the "psychology" of those in "poverty-stricken districts," Montague spoke of how relying on the population to take shelter within their homes failed to consider that, as a rule, only the mother would be at home; other members of the family would be in more public spaces. If an air raid were to take place, "a mother would not seal herself in a gas-proofed room while her family was not there with her."[33] Instead, one could expect people to leave their homes, if only to gather their families together. Montague called, therefore, for both clear plans to evacuate the population and to make use of public shelters such as Tube stations in London as alternatives to what he characterized as impractical and largely useless home-based measures. The government representative, Geoffrey Lord (under-secretary of state for the Home Department) responded matter-of-factly that "in wartime the population will be living in the knowledge that air raids may occur" and, assuming the ability to call upon a new kind civil identity that would be required to face aerial warfare, asserted that all members of the household would adjust their behavior accordingly.[34]

Vociferous opponents of all ARP measures, notably George Lansbury, well-known Labour and pacifist MP, lambasted the bill and its acceptance of ARP even more forcefully. Dismissing the proposed legislation as madness, he argued that "this Measure is an infamy for which everybody is responsible."[35] Other opponents, such as William Gallacher, insisted that all protective measures were a sham; the aim of aerial warfare was to demoralize civilians as "an essential feature of modern warfare," and under these circumstances, with direct attacks on the civil population,

---

[33] See Frederick Montague, *Parliamentary Debates – Commons*, 30 Nov. 1937, vol. 329, col. 1934. In Montague's hypothetical example, a host of gendered assumptions appear; for instance, while the mother stayed home, "Annie" would be eyeing goods in the shops, "Johnny and Tommy" might be playing in the street, and the husband "may be at a trade union branch." See Frederick Montague, *Parliamentary Debates – Commons*, 30 Nov. 1937, vol. 329, cols. 1932–1933.

[34] Geoffrey Lloyd, *Parliamentary Debates – Commons*, 30 Nov. 1937, vol. 329, cols. 1949–1950.

[35] George Lansbury, *Parliamentary Debates – Commons*, 25 Nov. 1937, vol. 329, cols. 1540–1545, quote from col. 1545. James Maxton, representing Glasgow, strongly supported him, saying that no one could pretend after listening to the measures necessary for civil defense that the nation could go to war "lightly," or emerge unscathed; thus, the promotion of "effective peace efforts" was ever more necessary. See James Maxton, *Parliamentary Debates – Commons*, 25 Nov. 1937, vol. 329, col. 1550.

"no matter how much money you spend ... there will be terrible agony
and suffering."[36] Some members wanted to assign blame, stressing that
the majority of people did not want to have to prepare for aerial warfare, preparations that "the folly of governments, capitalist governments"
had made necessary.[37] Still other MPs like Cecil Wilson, who represented
Sheffield, if less suspicious of government plans, nonetheless called for
a new direction in policy, for movement toward "the abolition of air
warfare."[38]

One of the most notable supporters of building up air power, Winston
Churchill, forcefully argued that waiting for such an unrealistic outcome
as the abolition of aerial warfare was more than dangerous. Churchill
spoke at length during the debates and insisted on the necessity not only
of the passive forms of defense that the bill afforded, but also of aggressive counter-offensives. If an enemy felt that the other side could be forced
to "give in before the regular operations of war can get to work, then this
odious and frightful form of warfare comes much nearer to us, because
it is much more likely to be employed." If the aim of aerial attacks were
to undermine "the freedom of a great people by destroying their women
and children from the air," then this bill could help curtail this process.[39]
Like others active in the debates over ARP, Churchill pointed to the threat
against "women and children" as the core of what this new "odious" and
"frightful" form of war-making portended. Unlike those who attacked
ARP as futile, he saw these measures as part of an overall strategy, which,
along with the ability to utilize British air power offensively, was to safeguard the island nation and its freedom.

Moreover, Churchill was careful to argue that since totalitarian
regimes could instantly compel compliance with strict civil defense measures, "the only chance for defenders of liberty and democracy ... is to
substitute for the many advantages which despotic authority gains in

---

[36] William Gallacher, *Parliamentary Debates – Commons*, 25 Nov. 1917, vol. 329, col.
    1457. Samuel Silverman went so far as to suggest that "this whole question of protecting
    the civil population has in it an element of fraud," even if the fraud was "not deliberate,"
    since it relied on persuading people "that the adequate protection of the civil population
    from air attack is not only possible but far more than that." See *Parliamentary Debates –
    Commons*, 25 Nov. 1917, vol. 329, col. 1467.

[37] J. J. Davidson, *Parliamentary Debates – Commons*, 7 Dec. 1937, vol. 330, col. 298.

[38] Cecil Wilson, *Parliamentary Debates – Commons*, 15 Nov. 1937, vol. 329, col. 121.

[39] Winston Churchill, *Parliamentary Debates – Commons*, 16 Nov. 1917, vol. 329, cols. 247–
    249. Churchill went on to cite the examples already known from the First World War, the
    ongoing war in East Asia, and the first ARP circular of July 1935. He further expressed his
    shocked dismay at the delay between the summer of 1935 and fall of 1937 in the govern-
    ment's taking action via the ARP Bill; see col. 248 and, for this quote, col. 249.

the field of action a lively comradeship and association which enables them ... to produce not only an equally fine but a more flexible and more durable organisation."[40] Here, he perhaps unwittingly adopted the perspective of those planners who all along had urged that civil defense be constructed as a voluntary commitment of citizens to one another and to the state.

In contrast, in keeping with some of the internal discussion within the ARP planning committee, opposition MPs such as Noel-Baker suggested that the government needed to claim "compulsory powers" in order to control the movement of people and vital resources "if, unhappily, war should come."[41] Even MPs who concurred with Churchill's emphasis on voluntarism emphasized the State's need to generate public opinion in order to foster the civic ties and civil identity necessary for voluntary action. As Oliver Simmonds argued, the entire country needed "an entire change of mind" brought about by the careful manipulation of "all modern methods of publicity in order to bring home to the heads of households their responsibility to their families, because it is upon them that responsibility for protecting the women and children in their houses falls."[42] Once again "women and children" stood in for the most vulnerable segment of the population, the one most in need of protection by male heads of households and indirectly by a paternalist state.

These back-and-forth exchanges did little to derail the passage of the bill, but they revealed broad agreement – and not solely along party lines – over the kind of war that had long been feared and was now being solidly acknowledged.[43] Some MPs evoked the legacy of the First World War: "I shall never forget the scene in Sheffield when fellow citizens of mine were killed as a result of air raids," claimed Oliver Short, while Sir William Davison spoke of the notable lack of "panic" when bombs fell in the West End of London during the war.[44] Other MPs such as William

---

[40] Churchill, *Parliamentary Debates – Commons*, 16 Nov. 1917, vol. 329, col. 253.

[41] Philip Noel Baker, *Parliamentary Debates – Commons*, 16 Nov. 1917, vol. 329, col. 1431.

[42] Oliver Simmonds, *Parliamentary Debates – Commons*, 16 Nov. 1917, vol. 329, col. 268.

[43] The debate did become quite partisan at times, with MP Sir Gifford Fox attacking the socialist-controlled boroughs in London, where, he claimed, "no steps have been taken to protect the civilian population ... [T]hey do not mind what happens to British men, women and children. They are prepared to do nothing to help them if ... there should be an air raid against this great city." See Sir Gifford Fox, *Parliamentary Debates – Commons*, vol. 329, col. 140.

[44] Alfred Short, *Parliamentary Debates – Commons*, 16 Nov. 1917, vol. 329, col. 1473, and again on 30 Nov. 1937, cols. 1967–1968; Sir William Davison and Short, *Parliamentary*

Gallacher referenced the more recent carnage – "the new horrors of modern warfare" – displayed in China and Spain and the lessons to be learned
from both the damage sustained and the popular reaction to these attacks
on civilians.[45]

Over and over again, MPs stressed the blurring of the lines between
the fronts. Frederick Bellenger went so far as to declare that "there will
be no comparative freedom from danger, whether you be on the home
front or in the front-line trenches ... [the latter] possibly ... more immune
from danger than those who are left to man the home front."[46] The language of "immunity" here is reminiscent of the government directives
discussed earlier with their awareness that there was no longer such a
thing. Government representatives such as Sir Samuel Hoare responded
to criticisms of the measures by saying, "[W]hatever we may do, there
will be the risk of air raids, and if there are air raids, there will be almost
certainly loss of life and terrible destruction.... Let us not turn aside from
these horrors, let us realise that they exist ... and let us try to deal with
them as best we can." Hoare made "no higher claims for these provisions
than they will tend to diminish the loss of human life; that they will go far
... to avoid the risk of panic ... [and] to ensure that the essential services
of our civilised life will continue."[47] This in itself was enough for some
MPs such as Samuel Silverman to claim that the entire burden – including all its financial aspects – should fall upon the national state, as a
communal responsibility. If the state, in Silverman's view, failed to keep
the bomber from "our shores," the subsequent cost of defense should be

---

Debates – *Commons*, 30 Nov. 1917, vol. 329, col. 1930. Davison elaborated that "I have
seen no signs of panic on the occasion of an air raid. Of course, if one of these bombs
falls upon a house all the occupants will be 'done for' in all probability. The best thing to
do is to hope and pray that the bomb does not fall on your house; it is no good rushing
down the street to try to get into an air-raid shelter"; see cols. 1930–31. On the basis of
his anecdotal evidence of a lack of panic, Davison suggested that there was no need to
plan for evacuations.

45 For references to "the new horrors of modern warfare" in Spain and China, see William
Gallacher, *Parliamentary Debates – Commons*, 16 Nov. 1917, vol. 329, col. 1435–1436;
see also Philip Noel-Baker, *Parliamentary Debates – Commons*, 30 Nov. 1937, vol. 329,
col. 1908 and col. 1912, where he evoked the specters of the First World War, Canton,
Madrid, and Shanghai.

46 Frederick Bellenger, *Parliamentary Debates – Commons*, 15 Nov. 1937, vol. 329,
col. 135. See also J. J. Davidson, *Parliamentary Debates – Commons*, 25 Nov. 1937,
vol. 329, col. 1509. Davidson spoke, too, of the success of ARP being measured in part
by its ability "to prevent a general widespread panic among the people of the country";
see col. 1511.

47 Sir Samuel Hoare, *Parliamentary Debates – Commons*, 25 Nov. 1937, vol. 329,
col. 1563.

borne by the nation-state, not individuals or local authorities.[48] It also led
to an intense discussion that concluded that ARP service should count as
"a first line activity" in war, subject to similar rules and compensation as
any other military service.[49]

When calling for the final passage at the third reading of the bill, Sir
Samuel Hoare spoke of the mixed emotions that such measures heralded:

> Let us pass the Bill to-night; let us, however, mark the fact that what we
> are forced to do seems to run counter to most of the ideals, and most of
> the chief movements and tendencies of civilised life.... [H]ere, in 1937,
> we are making provision for setting the clock back thousands of years,
> and making men, women and children disperse over the country into
> the most remote districts, and to abandon all the amenities and necessi-
> ties of civilised life....
>
> [L]ook at clothing.... Under the provisions of this Bill we are making
> arrangements for dressing people up in gas-masks and gas-proof suits
> that make them look as if they were monsters out of the dark ages.
>
> These facts do genuinely depress me.... They are so depressing, so fan-
> tastic in face of the conditions of the modern world, that I cannot believe
> they are going to persist.[50]

Yet, Hoare continued, while the government worked to "re-introduce
sanity" to the world, the third line of national defense, air raid precautions, would be pursued vigorously. Despite the costs, both material and
psychological, there was no turning back. As Wilfrid Roberts summed up
the new realisation, "[I]f you are going to protect the population, you will
have to protect them everywhere."[51] Still others who agreed to support
this legislation, such as Joseph Westwood, did so while hoping "sincerely
for the time when it will be possible to wipe war from the midst of so-
called civilised nations."[52]

It was clear to all that the future had arrived, a future predicted
by H. G. Wells in 1908, realized, to a very real extent, during the First

---

[48] Samuel Silverman, *Parliamentary Debates – Commons*, 30 Nov. 1937, vol. 329, col.
1969; for the quote, see cols. 1979–1980.
[49] Walter Elliot, *Parliamentary Debates – Commons*, 30 Nov. 1937, quote from vol. 329,
col. 2013, debate from cols. 2003–2019.
[50] Sir Samuel Hoare, *Parliamentary Debates – Commons*, 7 Dec. 1937, vol. 330,
cols. 284–85.
[51] Wilfrid Roberts, *Parliamentary Debates – Commons*, 7 Dec. 1937, vol. 330, col. 299.
Roberts made this point in reference to the idea that if a bomber did not reach the desired
target, bombs could be unloaded essentially anywhere. The larger notion that all must
participate because all were now affected still applies.
[52] Joseph Westwood, *Parliamentary Debates – Commons*, 7 Dec. 1937, vol. 330, col. 302.

World War, and then remembered and imagined in a variety of interwar cultural media. This was a future in which the government had to shelter and protect its non-combatant population, contemplate the provision of gas masks for the *entire* nation, plan for the evacuation of some segment of the domestic population (most likely women and children), and know that deadly aerial fire power would be used against civilians. The Air Raids Precautions Bill, which easily passed both Commons and Lords in December 1937, heralded the future that was now at hand. Indeed, as coverage in the *Times* noted when royal assent was given to these measures, some 200,000 women and men had already enrolled as air raid precautions workers, doctors had been trained in anti-gas measures, and plans for distributing shelters and gas masks were already under way.[53]

ARP AFTER THE ACT

In the aftermath of the promulgation of the Air Raids Precautions Act in 1937, the organization of ARP services gained greater visibility. In late January 1938, the Home Office issued instructions to all local authorities on the construction of ARP schemes that including provisions for rescue, shelter, and fire brigades.[54] By early February 1938, the first ARP plan for an area of London was unveiled for Hornsey. An announcement in the *Times* listed an array of proposed services, including fire prevention, warnings, first aid, and public shelters to accommodate approximately 1 percent of the population who might find themselves "caught in the streets during air raids."[55] The reporting of plans for the county of Huntingdon a few days later was similarly matter-of-fact, although there was a striking difference in the provisions being made. In Huntingdon, the Air Raids Precautions Committee for Huntingdonshire chose to issue "a card of instructions" for each household and have the wardens who distributed such cards "ask permission to hang the card in the kitchen." Thus, in every hearth in Huntingdon, residents could learn "what to do now" (select a suitable refuge room), what to do "in the event of war" (construct the gas-proof room), and what to do once an air raid warning had been issued (proceed to the gas-proof room).[56] Protection in this case, while assisted by ARP staff, was basically left as the responsibility

---

[53] "Safeguards in Air Raids," *Times*, 23 Dec. 1937.
[54] "Protection in Air Raids," *Times*, 29 Jan. 1938.
[55] "Hornsey's A.R.P. Scheme," *Times*, 5 Feb. 1938.
[56] "A.R.P. in the County of Huntingdon," *Times*, 10 Feb. 1938.

of individual homes and families rather than the more elaborate public services of the urban district of Hornsey. This was part of the local aspect of ARP in the legislation passed in 1937, but it also underscored how, despite different assumptions based on geography and class, the expectation that air raids would come home was omnipresent.

Air raid drills also tested the readiness of the nation early in 1938. Beaminster, Dorset, which conducted such a drill on 9 February, represented "perhaps the first market town of 1,600 to 1,700 inhabitants to show how well it has organized its air raid precautions." On the note of a warning at 8:40 P.M., lights went out, and by 8:42, when wardens patrolled, all was in darkness. Approximately fifteen minutes later, a mock aerial attack began, with one "house" (i.e., pile of rubbish) set on fire to test the fire brigade. At 9:15 a gas drill commenced, and the decontamination squad set to work. A subsequent "attack of high explosive bombs" allowed for further treatment of mock casualties. The entire event was described as proceeding "smoothly" and "efficiently," and even the headline, "Beaminster's Big Night," suggested that it was something more lighthearted than a serious precursor of war to come.[57]

Elsewhere, provisions of the Air Raids Precautions Act slowly took shape. For instance, some localities tried to negotiate the costs associated with the new civil defense measures. On 11 February, the ARP Committee of the Cardiff Corporation voted to ask that the government bear the entire cost of the measures necessary rather than the 60 to 65 percent that they were required to do.[58] Despite continued arguments over costs, other trials of ARP measures went forward. On 8 March in Lichfield, the "first automatic blackout" occurred. In front of representatives from every large town, together with those from the Air Ministry and Home Office, witnesses observed how one individual was able to "extinguish and light the street lamps, call out the fire brigade, ambulance and wardens, and sound air-alarm signals." Local inhabitants participated by covering their windows and dimming lights on the road. The reaction of experts was positive, as the test revealed a flexible and inexpensive way to show how a community might be erased from the air and made safer.[59] Another test involving a thousand wardens took place in Southampton and in Paddington, the second large-scale London test, later that month.[60]

---

[57] "Beaminster's Big Night," *Times*, 10 Feb. 1938.
[58] "A.R.P. in Cardiff," *Times*, 12 Feb. 1938.
[59] "First Automatic Blackout," *Times*, 9 Mar. 1938.
[60] "Southampton's A.R.P. Test" and "Paddington Air Raid Test," *Times*, 25 and 31 Mar. 1938.

In an article accompanying the issuing of official instructions on what was now commonly called "ARP" in March 1938, the *Times* quoted Sir Samuel Hoare: "[I]f this country were ever at war the target of the enemy's bombers would be the staunchness of the people at home." The significance of such domestic participation in war preparedness was emphasized repeatedly: "[I]t is impossible to devise a scheme that will cover everybody unless each home and family play their part in doing what they can for themselves.... If the emergency comes the country will look for her safety not only to her soldiers and sailors and airmen, but also to the organized courage and foresight of every household."[61] What was being called upon here was something more than concrete measures; this was an acknowledgement of the necessity of a transcendent civilian morale, the foundation of a necessary wartime civil identity.

After sending out a draft version for comment, the government issued a set of basic instructions for ARP measures in a booklet entitled "The Protection of Your Home Against Air Raids," or, in its later incarnation, "Air Raid Precautions Handbook No. 1."[62] Still voiced in the conditional, the booklet suggested that "every home should have a refuge specially prepared in which the whole household could take cover in greater safety." Even here there was no promise of total security or safety. It encouraged people to ask for help from friends, neighbors, and officials; to consider where they might send children, invalids, and the elderly (if they lived in a large town); and to be well stocked before war broke out with the expensive materials necessary to change the home into a refuge. While explaining how to use gas masks, it also insisted that they provided a second line of defense, while ARP measures for the home were the first line.

Much of what the handbook mentioned was fairly straightforward, yet it contained multiple assumptions. After carefully illustrating how to choose which room to turn into a refuge, it stated that "you can still make a refuge-room even if you have no surplus room to set aside, in war-time, for the purpose." The manual stressed that even those living in one room could make this space safer and that being inside anywhere was better than being out in the open: "[D]o not think you have no protection."[63] Many of the instructions for the refuge room concerned how to make it gas-proof by sealing all cracks and windows with pasted paper and

[61] "A.R.P. in Each Home," *Times*, 10 Mar. 1938.
[62] For more on this pamphlet, including figures about distribution, see O'Brien, *Civil Defence*, 124–25, 148, 150, 163. For the booklet itself, see "Air Raids Precautions Handbook No. 1" (London, 1938), quotes from 4, 6.
[63] "Air Raids Precautions Handbook No. 1," 10.

by sealing doors with blankets. Regarding high-explosive bombs, the instructions were similar but had more to do with using posts or scaffolds to give extra structural support to a room. There was a long list of things deemed necessary to store in the room: tinned food, water, blankets, first aid material, chamber pots, bedclothes, and furniture, as well as books, cards, and toys for children. Everything about these measures, including the illustrations in the manual, suggested attacks against a family in a middle-class home were the model.[64]

A brief two-and-half-minute film, *Your Book*, underscored the message of the newly released ARP handbook.[65] Designed to demonstrate visually and reassuringly the instructions detailed in the leaflet, it featured a narrator intoning the various things that the book would teach a householder, while photogenic and middle-class women and children, for the most part, performed the tasks described. For instance, as the narrative voice declaimed, "It will tell you how to make your windows gas-proof," a mother and her son tape over the windows in what appears to be a well-maintained, middle-class home. An assertion that following these instructions would allow citizens to be "as safe from harm as possible" was accompanied by the sight of members of the ambulance brigade preparing an air lock entrance to a refuge room using blankets. The film introduced the gas mask by having an avuncular member of the brigade help a little girl in a floral dress with a ribbon in her blond hair and a doll in her arms deal with hers, while the narration prompted, "Just note how confident this little girl is with hers, both in putting it on and taking it off." As she removed the mask, her hair loosened and brushed her face; she was shown blowing it off and (seemingly prompted) turning to look directly at the camera and smile broadly, thereby undercutting the chilling sight of this personification of innocence in a device designed to protect her from chemical warfare.

The cinematic interpretation of these basic ARP instructions continued with the narration that "the ordinary householder helping women and children should the emergency ever arise will be of untold value." The visual image accompanying these words showed two women assisting three children in putting on their masks in a sunny, clean, decorated room. The final piece of advice explicated visually by the film had to do with the garden shelter; in this case it showed the diagram of such

---

[64] "Air Raids Precautions Handbook No. 1," 18.

[65] *Your Book* (1938), IWM Film and Video Archive, HOY 81. All quoted references are to this film. A revised version of the film was distributed in September 1938.

a structure from the booklet. The final statement suggested the strange state in which ARP planners found themselves at the end of the decade: "Although we hope that war will never come it is up to you to be prepared." The "we" of the government, or perhaps of the collective nation, hoped that a war involving gas and fire from the air would not come, but it was up to "you," the individual accustoming him- or herself to act in the calm and cheerful manner of the women and children in this film, to be prepared for the horrors of this modern war. This was literally an illustration of a universal wartime civil identity in action.

By the late spring of 1938, the Home Office was announcing new plans to recruit volunteers in order to hasten the spread of ARP measures. Home Secretary Sir Samuel Hoare in particular spoke of the urgent work of wardens conducting a local "house-to-house canvass … for the purpose of bringing home to all householders their own duties in regard to A. R. P." Yet even at this stage "the Government maintained their view that the proper policy should be based on dispersal" rather than risk a large number of civilians staying put and taking shelter.[66] Thus, at the same time that the government was emphasizing that every home had to be prepared for aerial attacks, it was continuing to avoid implementing a centralized shelter policy.

Meantime, during the spring and summer of 1938, tests of ARP measures continued, including one in Southend in early June.[67] Given increasing international tension, new criticism of the pace of such measures also continued. An editorial in the *Times* on air defense took up the issue not only of anti-aircraft services, but also of "the still newer and more immature service of air-raid precautions." Here the issue was not government inaction so much as "skepticism" among the general public that had to be addressed: "[T]he unanswerable justification of air-raid precautions is insurance against such a panic as might frustrate the whole of the national effort. It follows that those measures best calculated to avert panic should be taken first, and … in areas where panic is most likely." What was needed, according to the editorial, was a clear sense of how the government would address dispersing and sheltering the civil population. What was also once again made abundantly clear was the realization that cultural measures aimed at civilians – avoiding panic and accepting the possibility of danger and sacrifice calmly – served as the means to the end of winning a war now waged at home.[68]

[66] "The Urgency of A.R.P.," *Times*, 26 Apr. 1938.
[67] "A.R.P. in the Thames Estuary," *Times*, 1 June 1938.
[68] "Air Defence," *Times*, 1 June 1938.

CONCLUSION

As those reading in British newspapers about air raids in Spain or China in the spring and summer of 1938 came to realize, the threat of air war was very real. The bombs that fell abroad and the increasing threats to international peace from regimes in Japan, Italy, and Germany led to a new urgency in ARP measures. Cultivating the proper attitude toward such measures, as we have seen, remained a constant challenge. By the time the government was ready to take ARP public, two main ways of defining the status and role of the civilian in modern, total war had emerged.

One was to adopt a strategy to promote "business as usual," to rely on the steadfastness of a community of individuals informed and *willing* to be complicit in ARP schemes. The less desirable alternative was now to regard everyone as "fighting soldiers," a militarized population that might be subject to appropriate coercion. These became two dominant ways in which the wartime status of civilians could be understood. Both, however, demanded a new kind of civil identity, and at the core of this identity lay the transcendence of the individual, the family, and the local into something *all* belonging to the imperial state could embody, even if it remained the case that some seemed to naturally do this better than others.

In terms of specific measures, the national organization of ARP services through the 1937 legislation and its first implementations suggest how profoundly air raids had transformed the understandings of civilians and modern warfare. From the moment of their arrival in First World War, aerial attacks changed war into something that took place at home, and thus made its defense the potential concern of every man, woman, and child. By the end of the interwar period, that potential was realized and the domestication of home defense nearly complete. We will examine the ARP measure that arguably embodied the worst fears of the war to come, the infant gas mask, in the next chapter.

9

Protecting the Innocent

Gas Masks for Babies and the Domestication of Air Raids Precautions

INTRODUCTION

Is life on earth a viler thing
Than ever was known before?
Who shall we ask – the wise old man
Whose years have reached five score?

When we have questioned Church and State,
Is there anyone else to ask?
Is it the Baby, three weeks old,
That wears a gas-proof mask?

Is it the Infant armed to meet
A poisoned earth and sky –
A thing too weak to lift its hand
To rub a sleepy eye?[1]

This poem, "Armed for War," appeared in the autumn of 1937 in the literary journal *London Mercury*. It invoked the conflicts of the era and the new visibility given to Britain's own civil defense measures against the terrifying prospect of gas and aerial attacks, of a war of annihilation. At its heart, the image that suggested that life on earth was truly "viler" now than at any other moment in its history was the baby in a gas mask, the "Infant armed to meet / A poisoned earth and sky." Nothing, this poem suggests, should induce greater feelings of disgust and despair. That this representation should appear at the same time that the government was actively trying to develop such a device is telling, especially since it was by no means certain that such a form of protection could even be created.

[1] W. H. Davies, "Armed for War," *London Mercury*, Sept. 1937.

Other air raid precautions, such as evacuation and shelters, had acknowledged that aerial warfare would not discriminate between combatants and non-combatants. Evacuation planners looked at moving women and children to some place considered less dangerous, and shelters, especially the house-bound variety, such as refuge rooms, attempted to make the home and domestic space itself safer. Both of these measures reflected what had changed as a result of the First World War when civilians at home had come under fire in Britain and women and children had died from aerial attacks. However, the development of civilian anti-gas protection was a response not to actual experiences but to anticipated fears. As we have seen previously, many in the interwar period believed not only that war would come through the air, but also that it would involve chemical weapons. The decision to invest heavily in protecting civilians who could make no useful contribution to fighting the war makes sense when regarded as being as much about morale (of both combatants and non-combatants) as about military necessity. And of all the personal anti-gas protection developed by the British government, the creation of the infant gas mask offers a potent case study of the extent to which innocents, as well as innocence itself, had to be protected.

PLANNING FOR CIVILIANS TO FACE CHEMICAL WARFARE

From its inception, the CID Sub-Committee on Air Raids Precautions took seriously the threat of a chemical attack against civilians. It had agreed in principle in 1924 to establish "a defensive organisation designed to protect the civil population against the effects of gas," stressing that the public must be prepared well in advance due to the "serious effect that the employment of gas may have on the *morale* of a population ignorant of the subject."[2] One of the challenges facing ARP planners remained how to ensure the safety of those at home and of those quintessential civilians, women and children. In a variety of ways, as we have seen, the government had been caught short by aerial attacks in the British Isles during the First World War and had to improvise responses, from warnings to shelters to evacuation plans. Aids to combat other new features of war, such as chemical attacks, had similarly to evolve quickly. The prospect of gas attacks at home posed a new set of challenges in terms of safeguarding the civil population in the postwar world.

---

[2] Maurice Hankey, ARP Memo no. 11, TNA CAB 46/3. Emphasis added.

Discussing this matter in March 1926, the ARP Sub-Committee explored whether public buildings could be made "gas proof." In conjunction with information from a separate Chemical Warfare Committee, Frank Baines, representing the Department of Works and an expert on shelters, noted that "it was impossible to issue gas masks and provide shelters to all the population." Wing Commander Portal, director of intelligence for the Air Ministry, added that this ministry anticipated "that in the future gas attacks by night would take the form of spraying from aeroplanes rather than being released in containers. Against such attack any roof would provide an adequate shelter." In that case, Baines added, "something ought to be done in regard to shelters if the morale of the population was to be maintained."[3] Assuming such shelters might also be breached, civilian respirators would become a necessary second line of defense.

The creation of the 1924 Geneva Gas Protocol – in which "contracting parties, subject to reciprocity" undertook "to abstain from the use in war of asphyxiating poisonous or similar gases" – signaled more widespread international opposition to these weapons.[4] Once Britain had agreed to join this international agreement in 1929, the question remained, as Sir John Anderson put it to the ARP Sub-Committee, of "how much importance could be attached to pledges exchanged between the different nations in regard to the prohibition of gas warfare." Anderson concluded that "it would be a mistake to take these pledges at anything more than their face value, unless we had good grounds for thinking that the general international atmosphere had undergone a marked change from that in 1914."[5] Sir Maurice Hankey affirmed, however, that the prospect of gas warfare had become somewhat more unlikely due to the fact that the League of Nations was keeping a closer eye on such armaments, to the high costs associated with such weaponry, and to the belief that high-explosive bombs would cause sufficient damage. While urging the government not to abandon anti-gas efforts, he argued that such developments made planning for a chemical attack a lower priority than preparing for more conventional aerial bombardment.[6] Yet voices outside the

---

[3] Sir Frank Baines and Wing-Commander Portal, CID Sub-Committee on ARP, Minutes, 15 Mar. 1926, TNA CAB 46/1.

[4] And yet Britain was not a part of this initial agreement, although it became a signatory in 1929. See T. H. O'Brien, *Civil Defence* (London, 1955), 38.

[5] Sir John Anderson, CID Sub-Committee on ARP, Minutes, 13 May 1929, TNA CAB 46/7.

[6] Sir Maurice Hankey, CID Sub-Committee on ARP, Minutes, 13 May 1929, TNA CAB 46/7.

government, as we saw in Chapters, 4, 6, and 7, continued to highlight the particular dangers of this feature of modern war. As a result, ARP planners felt that they had to respond to "public outcry" for some form of protection, while debating whether the effects of such efforts were "likely to be more moral than material."[7]

The government also had to contend with a peculiarly visceral reaction from disarmament campaigners around the issue of chemical weapons. As we examined in earlier chapters, those public figures working against the "next war" were particularly agitated about this matter and insisted that there were no adequate protective measures that could be put in place for women and children. At the WILPF May 1929 conference on "modern methods of warfare and the protection of civil populations," Dr. Nestler, the expert on "collective and individual protection" from chemical weapons, pointed out the exorbitant costs involved in developing suitable civilian gas masks. He also insisted that additional psychological barriers to their effectiveness were nearly insurmountable. As he elaborated:

> To wear a gas-mask requires extraordinary discipline; people put them on with teeth clenched. If discipline is difficult for trained soldiers, how much more so with civilians. A mother could not endure to hear her child crying under its mask. Women and children will certainly not be able to make full use of protective apparatus; every gas attack would cause a panic.[8]

Such dire assumptions could help undergird the passion with which anti-militarists reacted to any preparations for this new kind of war.

However, unlike those campaigning actively for disarmament in interwar Europe or imagining the horrors of chemical attacks upon women and children in their fiction, government civil defense planners could not officially share Nestler's pessimism. They had to consider how to help women and children adapt to protective measures against chemical warfare. Indeed, despite the steps taken in the 1920s to restrict chemical (and bacteriological) weapons, those meeting to plan Britain's official response decided to prepare civilians for chemical warfare, while initially keeping such initiatives under wraps.[9]

Even before the collapse of disarmament efforts that had centered around the Geneva-based conference of 1932–1934, British officialdom

---

[7] CID Sub-Committee on ARP, Minutes, 17 June 1929, TNA CAB 46/7.
[8] Nestler, "Collective and Individual Protection," *Chemical Warfare* (London, 1930), 77.
[9] CID Sub-Committee on ARP, Minutes, 13 May 1929, TNA CAB 46/7.

began to orchestrate a plan to combat the "moral" as well as "material" effects of the next war's potential chemical air raids. The sub-committee had begun to plan for the development and distribution of a civilian respirator by the early 1930s. It agreed in April 1932, for instance, that anything required on the first day war broke out would have to be put in place beforehand, and thus "as a matter of principle, a start should be made to build up a reserve of respirators at once."[10]

While service respirators had been designed for soldiers during the First World War, such devices would have to be modified for civilian use. Furthermore, the question of who would manufacture and distribute – let alone fund – civilian gas masks was a subject of debate throughout the early 1930s.[11] Those meeting in secret under the auspices of the CID Sub-Committee on ARP continued to explore the variety of issues that would need to be addressed regarding the threat of chemical warfare throughout the 1930s. They seemingly concurred with public fears that aerial and chemical attacks could lead to a panic that would destroy the will to wage war – "the moral effect." In early 1934, members of the committee determined that "if only for the sake of mass psychology" and to avoid a general panic that might "decide the fate of the war," gas masks suitable for the entire population might have to be devised.[12] Another sub-committee was then created specifically to investigate the production of such devices.

The collapse of the Geneva Disarmament Conference prompted a variety of more public calls for the government to take action against the aerial and chemical threat posed by the next war. As an article in the *Saturday Review* in February 1934 put it: "Perhaps it is idle to ask how long it would take to equip the civilian population with even the crudest masks, because experts have already declared it impossible to attempt. If we leave ourselves vulnerable to poison-gas attack, we must just accept that we shall be massacred helplessly by the scores of thousands." Given the expansion of air power, "*every city in the kingdom is … liable to gas attack.*"[13] The article's author, Boyd Cable, exhorted readers to imagine the suffering and the sheer number of men, women, and children who would die without some form of protection. This was fearmongering with a purpose, to encourage the government to provide such protection.

---

[10] CID Sub-Committee on ARP Minutes, 13 Apr. 1932, TNA CAB 46/8.
[11] CID Sub-Committee on ARP, Minutes, TNA CAB 46/7, 46/8, and 46/9 (1929–1935).
[12] CID Sub-Committee on ARP, Minutes, 19 Mar. 1934, TNA CAB 46/9.
[13] Boyd Cable, "Poison Gas as *We* Knew It," *Saturday Review*, 24 Feb. 1934. Emphasis in original.

A few weeks later, Cable was once again urging a combination of protection and more active defense. He asserted, "In another war, 'the front' will be the limit of the long distance bombers' flights, the 'firing line' will be occupied by more women and children than men." Cable attacked as ignorant those who declared that they would not participate in another war, for no one would ask them to do so. Instead, "[t]hey'll probably go to bed one night ... and then wake to the crash of bombs, the clatter of collapsing masonry." Then the enemy will go after "the civilian population and civilian morale ... [T]he mass murder of civilians will be accepted as 'legitimate' war because by that, by driving others into panic, the military object would be achieved of bringing all mobilisation, munitions production, and communications into a state of chaos, and the 'will to war' be broken." At all costs, this must be prevented.[14]

Presumably unbeknownst to Cable, in April 1934, the ARP civilian respirator sub-committee took up the following question: "It is agreed that, should an emergency occur, there may arise a very big demand from the public to be provided with protection by the Government, and, if so, is it also agreed that a large percentage of the public concerned will not be in a position to provide themselves with such protection?" If that were the case, and given the problems that might arise if the government did not respond, was it then the responsibility of the state to provide "a cheap respirator, capable of rapid mass production and sufficient protection to enable persons to shop and carry out other necessary duties ... in case their homes become 'penetrated by gas'?" Concurring that such a scenario required an affirmative answer to this question, the ARP civilian respirator sub-committee determined that the government needed to acquire a sufficient reserve of gas masks in peacetime so as to enable distribution in the event of war.[15] It is worth noting that shopping – an activity gendered feminine – was one of the "duties" that the government expected its citizens to be able to perform, and it took responsibility for ensuring their ability to do so.

The ARP civilian respirator sub-committee concluded that urging the civil population to purchase a device of absolutely no use during peacetime would fail; thus, there was "no alternative" to the government taking responsibility for providing enough gas masks to meet "overwhelming public demand."[16] Some of the public demand responded

[14] Boyd Cable, "Air Attacks on Civilians," *Saturday Review*, 14 Apr. 1934.
[15] Quotes in this paragraph are taken from CID Sub-Committee on ARP Sub-Committee on the Production Policy with regard to the allocation of respirators, Draft report, 19 Apr. 1934, TNA CAB 46/30.
[16] CID Sub-Committee on ARP, Minutes, 18 July 1935, Comments of Wing Commander Hodsoll and E. H. Hodgson of the Board of Trade, TNA CAB 46/9.

directly to the issuing of the first general announcement of ARP plans in the July 1935 circular and the greater publicity thus given to ARP. Even a writer of fiction could claim this explicitly, as did Simpson Stokes in his 1935 *Air-Gods' Parade*, a bizarre book even by the standards of interwar "next-war" fiction. Stokes – the pseudonym of Frank Fawcett – wrote the novel very quickly and dedicated it to "the British Home Office, Air Raid Precautions Department, who have the most onerous task ever assigned to a Government Organization – that of creating adequate defensive measures for the men, women and children of the Realm."[17]

Not only did Fawcett dedicate this novel to the ARP, but he also ended it with an epilogue that engaged in direct dialogue with the July 1935 circular and other ARP publicity. His text referred explicitly to the "disconcerting" pamphlets distributed and published by the ARP Department that required the population to envisage protection against chemical and aerial warfare in time of peace. Yet he cited the pamphlets as provoking more fear than reassurance, taking issue with the government's decision "not to provide shelters" and instead offering instructions for how householders should safeguard their premises (151–152). Quoting details about different forms of poison gas and their effects, he stated that "those who wish to read further into this product of twentieth-century culture and illuminating sidelight on what religion, ethics, forbearance, and philosophy have failed to accomplish" need only consult "The Air Raids Precautions Handbook." What such preparations produce, according to Fawcett, is the following question: *"Does it begin to dawn on the mind that we, in common with other nations, are heading for hell? (168)"*[18]

As the frontispiece image labeled "twentieth-century culture" depicted it, hell was a world where a mother in a simian-like gas mask held her unguarded infant in her arms, beneath a primate mother and young. Hell was where – in one of the novel's most vivid and gut-wrenching scenes – a mother helplessly tries to save her dying infant as it asphyxiates:

> The baby in the pram started to scream ... and there was a certain note of pain in the screams that every mother knows and instinctively recognizes.

[17] Simpson Stokes, *Air-Gods' Parade* (London, 1935). Brief biographical information and a discussion of the novel can be found in Martin Ceadel, "Popular Fiction and the Next War, 1918–39," in *Class Culture and Social Change: A New View of the 1930s*, ed. Frank Gloversmith (Brighton, 1980), 179.

[18] Emphasis in original.

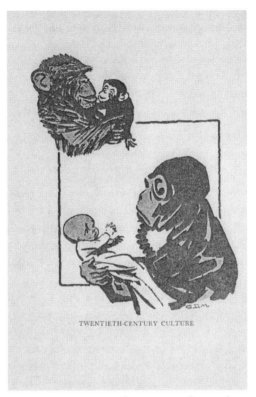

TWENTIETH-CENTURY CULTURE

FIGURE 9.1. Frontispiece to Simpson Stokes's *Air-God's Parade*, 1935. Reproduced by permission of the British Library.

The mother's heart suddenly contracted, as though an ice-cold hand had gripped it and was squeezing it tight. She unstrapped the infant, who was by now almost in convulsions, and saw on its neck and arms some strange red patches, with here and there white blisters visibly appearing. The child's eyes were tightly closed and thin trickles of yellow pus oozed between the lids.

From the little strip of green outside, and from every house in the row, came frantic crying and confusion....

By the time Mrs Prettyman had prepared a tepid bath in the bowl, the baby's body had broken out into sores and there were violent spasms of retching and coughing, followed by the vomiting of fearsome pieces of tissue, looking like blood-stained scraps of dirty rags. Then, as the child's body touched the water, the limbs stiffened. There was no life there now.

The mother, half comprehending, half crazy ... looked at the tortured body through eyes that had filled with smarting tears. Her lips, dry and

parched a moment before, began to burn, and went sticky with some running matter that dribbled from the corners of her mouth. (137–138)

It was just such a scenario that the ARP planners had to attempt to counter. Readers of interwar fiction could find multiple examples of what
chemical bombs dropped from the air might do to a civilian population;
the state had to find some measure of reassurance and, it hoped, basic
protection against this horror.

DEVELOPING INFANT ANTI-GAS PROTECTION

Thus, in July 1935, the ARP civilian respirator sub-committee concluded
that the production of 10 million respirators per year should be the goal;
this would ensure that "preparations should be complete by 1939."[19] Such
provisions had been hinted at in the July circular, but not in any detail;
the committee now took up the issue with renewed vigor. One prospect
hidden in these initial estimates was the decision that the provision of
such respirators to the estimated 8% of the population under five years
of age was not contemplated, as it was not deemed possible. Given the
pro-natalist climate of interwar Britain, it is hard to imagine that infant
and child casualties could be so easily written off. Quite soon, questions
of morale led the committee to decide that it must develop anti-gas protection for women and all children, including infants. Furthermore, extensive
plans to evacuate school-age children, infants, and their mothers were also
under way. Thus, the protection of the linked category of "women and
children" was two-pronged: combining evacuation of vulnerable populations from danger zones with measures to allow domestic and even family
life to continue under the heinous conditions of chemical warfare.

A few months after the public launching of ARP, participants at a
conference held on 30 September 1935 concluded that "it would be perfectly feasible to fit even the smallest infant with some form of facepiece."
Efforts to devise protection now therefore encompassed the entire population. Those participating in the meeting involved with adding anti-gas
measures to ARP also acknowledged that:

> Certain very important psychological factors have ... to be taken into
> account in considering this problem.... Experiments appear to show
> that children down to the age of four can wear a respirator without

[19] CID Sub-Committee on ARP Sub-Committee on the Production Policy with Regard to the
Allocation of Respirators, Minutes, 12 July 1935 and 17 Sept. 1935, TNA CAB 46/30.

difficulty or distress, though children of this age and possibly slighter older are rather inconvenienced by the weight of the container....

As regards tiny babies, it was unanimously accepted that it would be impossible on all grounds to propose the use of a respirator of an ordinary sort, and accordingly Porton [site of the Chemical Defence Research Department, CDRD] have been developing a cardboard box, covered with suitable material, with a window made of non-inflammable material, which is fitted with a hand pump at the bottom of which is an ordinary filtering container.

Such a box device could bridge the gap between babies and young children. Two members of the sub-committee, including the sole woman, Dame Louise McIlroy, argued that "it would probably be quite impossible to get women in the slums and poorer quarters to use anything of the kind by themselves." However "unreasoning this attitude," it must be considered, and efforts to promote "collective protection" that would not fail due to individual or class-based recalcitrance had to proceed. The conferees thus conceded that even if the government would soon be in position "to provide protection for babies as well as adults," there "may be a great number of people who, on the grounds of ignorance or for any other reason might refuse to use an apparatus of this kind." This made "collective arrangements," especially in poor communities, of paramount importance, and as the report concluded, "the faster the authorities push on with their housing and de-slumming schemes, so much the better from the point of view of protection."[20]

Here, various aspects of interwar state planning came together so far as those working to render the civil population safe from chemical weapons were concerned. According to some government experts, the welfare state reform of housing could have the unintentional consequence of aiding civil defense efforts, another example of the intertwining of state and home. In these discussions, class bias entered decisively into the shaping of this aspect of ARP, as planners assumed that the ignorance of slum dwellers and especially the unreasoning attitude of poorer *mothers* would prevent them from using this new civil defense technology. The two solutions to the problem addressed two fundamentally different approaches: the collective and individual. One was overwhelmingly a state prerogative – building safer dwellings – but the other rested on a belief that education and what might be deemed "character building," the

---

[20] E. J. Hodsoll, Report on Conference, CDRD, held 30 Sept. 1935, 1 Oct. 1935, TNA HO 45/17620.

active construction of an appropriate civil wartime identity, remained of profound importance.

An article in the *News Chronicle* on 10 December 1935 publicized the work being done to safeguard women and children under the headline "Gas Proof Cases Save the Babies: Mothers Will Pump in Air." The article went on to note that "anti-gas containers for babies, into which the mother will pump filtered air, and gas-proof tents for prams ... are two of the latest devices to protect civilians in the next war, when gas attacks will imperil combatants and non-combatants alike.... Free gas masks for all are to be provided by the Government.... While authorities think small children could wear these masks they fear that it will be impossible to persuade women to fit them on babies – hence the container device."[21]

Much of the discussion in 1936 concerned the proposed design of a device that would protect babies and small children, possibly some mechanism that would work with a perambulator. When the CDRD issued a memo on such protection in May 1936, it listed the following criteria as necessary for any protection for infants:

1) It must protect.
2) It must not cause distress to the baby.
3) It must be simple in operation so that the parent understands it and has *faith* in its efficacy.

Inspiring the belief that such a device provided protection was thus deemed consequently important to its functionality. The report elaborated that while protection was of primary importance, eliminating not only physical discomfort but also "mental distress due to such causes as separation from parent and unaccustomed environment or treatment" was also necessary. So, too, was overcoming the fear of parents that the failure of such a device "might either allow the baby to be gassed or cause it to be asphyxiated." Stressing that collective protection was still more important than individual mechanisms, the department saw such equipment as "required only for super-emergency measures." Thus, the most obvious way to make a device both safe and portable was to turn a perambulator into a gas-proof enclosure, to transform a household item deeply associated with middle-class domesticity into an object fit for wartime conditions of chemical battles.[22]

---

[21] "Gas-Proof Cases Save the Babies ..." *News Chronicle*, 10 Dec. 1935, TNA HO 45/17620.

[22] C. G. Trotman and J. A. Sadd [Chemical Defence Research Department, Porton], "The Protection of Babies and Young Children Against Gas," 11 May 1936, TNA HO 45/17620. Emphasis added.

The report went on to describe the many benefits of the gas-proof pram, ranging from the fact that it could offer babies a comfortable and familiar surrounding, carry young children up to the age of three, and allow for active toddlers and babies to be strapped in. Presumably, babies could also sleep and be protected in an undisturbed manner, and thus parents would feel reassured by the babies' presence in them. The report was accompanied by designs for a gas-proof cover, arguing for both its simplicity and effectiveness. What ended up being the report's most controversial statement was its assertion that "it may be assumed that for fully 90 per cent of babies a perambulator is possessed.... In slum areas, the proportion of suitable perambulators may be low, but for these cases, it is suggested that an inexpensive Government pattern of protective perambulator could be made available."[23]

The idea of providing "protective perambulators" was not a source of dissension, but the question of whether such a contraption would work became one. The elite and all-male team of civil defense planners had little idea what percentage of families with babies actually used prams. A response from the assistant under-secretary of state working with the ARP Department, E. J. Hodsoll, praised the initial design but found the assertion that it would work for all but 10 percent of the population "quite unjustified.... [I]t looks to me like protection for the rich and not for the poor." He continued: "They are basing the whole of their constructions on collective protection as a first line of defence, in other words you don't want anything more for the baby than you do for the individual unless the gas-proof room gets blown in.... [This] does not unfortunately help us one atom with your three quarters of a million slum problem." Writing to members of the air force for help, he asked them to interrogate "friends in the poorer metropolitan boroughs ... to what extent the population of these areas do in fact possess prams," adding, "I don't want to turn you into a maternity department, but this is a very important question."[24]

Eardley Wilmot took only a few days to comment and agreed that, on the basis of his observations of Poplar and then Gravesend, the idea that 90 percent of the population had access to perambulators was unfounded. On a journey from Aldgate to Poplar, he saw only three perambulators, in contrast to twenty-eight "push chairs," which could not be made

[23] Trotman and Sadd, "The Protection of Babies and Young Children Against Gas."
[24] E. J. Hodsoll to Wing Commander Steele Perkins and Flight Lieutenant Eardley Wilmot, 24 June 1936, TNA HO 45/17620.

gas-proof. He encouraged a further survey of Infant Welfare Centres in order to obtain more accurate figures.[25] A follow-up message on 6 July relayed that the medical officers of the boroughs of Poplar, Camberwell, Hackney, and Bermondsey had agreed to survey the number and variety of prams at children's clinics in their districts, and passed along observations made at the Guys Hospital Children's Out-Patients Department. During the visit, children arrived in forty-seven prams, only nineteen of which could possibly be made gas-proof; a full twelve consisted of "the ordinary wooden go-cart type with no canvas at all round the body," rendering them useless in case of attack.[26]

It was in light of this unscientific survey that, in October 1936, the government came up with a set of requirements for anti-gas protection for young children and babies. It agreed that the "gas-proof room" represented the first line of defense, with the gas mask serving as a backup in case of damage to such a shelter; the mask could also "enable the wearer to seek a place of safety." While it was already confident that instructions in the first ARP handbook for householders would suffice for adults, "preliminary training in the wearing of respirators, which is possible for adults, would be impracticable in the case of young children, and virtually impossible for babies."[27]

It then provided a list of desired features for infant anti-gas protection while noting that "it may be impossible to find a design which meets all these conditions satisfactorily." These conditions included offering protection against all known poison gas by means of a filter of activated charcoal, a non-flammable mask, and the ability to put the device on quickly. In addition, such an apparatus had both to "impose the minimum of discomfort on the child" and yet be "impossible for the child to remove;" it had to be "self-contained," that is, not dependent on the possession of a cradle or pram, as "different classes of society vary very much in equipment of this kind which they possess." It could not be attached to an adult's own device. Furthermore, it had to allow for visibility, an issue that was as much psychological as practical: "It is generally expected that the mother of the child will wish to see it continuously ... at least part

[25] L. Eardley Wilmot to Asst Under Secretary for State, Memo, 29 June 1936, TNA HO 45/17620.
[26] Memo to Asst Under Secretary for State, 6 July 1936, TNA HO 45/17620.
[27] "Anti-Gas Protection for Young Children," Report sent from Assistant Under Secretary of State to Chief Superintendent, CDRD, 26 Oct. 1936, TNA HO 45/17620.

of the child's face must be visible.... [T]his is also important from the point of view of the comfort of the child."[28]

This report offered a few examples of possible devices and objections to them, starting with a "cardboard box with a large window and a small pump to send air through the filter." With respect to this model, the report noted that "uneducated mothers would not be willing to let their child be treated in this fashion" and that it was not well suited for "rapid escape." Another suggestion involved some sort of device to cover a pram, but acknowledged that pram use was related to class and would exclude, for instance, 80 percent of babies in the East End. It then offered the example of the Russians, who were said to be experimenting with a device that would protect an adult and child together. This, however, raised objections that if such a method of dual protection failed, the result would be two casualties instead of one.[29]

By the spring of 1937, the ARP sub-committee was putting additional pressure on the CDRD to come up with a workable form of protection. E. J. Hodsoll complained that "questions are continually being raised all over the place" and that "the protection of babies is a very big and important gap in our protection proposals." It was time, he urged, for the matter to be resolved, especially since "I understand only too well the difficulties, which I think are really more *psychological* than practical."[30] One result of such pressure can be seen in a set of designs offered for the protection of children and infants against gas in June 1937; these included a cot made of gas-proof material with a cover, a pram cover, and two devices that could protect "the child while in physical contact with the mother." This last criterion proved key.

This preliminary account also noted that the testing of these devices had begun at the Babies' Hotel in Clapham Park, where "there was no difficulty in getting the children to co-operate, but this should not be taken to mean that there is no psychological problem, because they are very exceptional children apparently being brought up by exceptionally sound methods."[31] Once again, government planners were concerned primarily with the potential psychological effects of air warfare; in this case, they demonstrated their belief that obtaining the necessary correct

---

[28] "Anti-Gas Protection for Young Children."
[29] "Anti-Gas Protection for Young Children."
[30] E. J. Hodsoll, Letter to N. K. Johnson, 16 Mar. 1937, TNA HO 45/17620. Emphasis added.
[31] Report for the Assistant Under Secretary of State, 22 June 1937, TNA HO 45/17620.

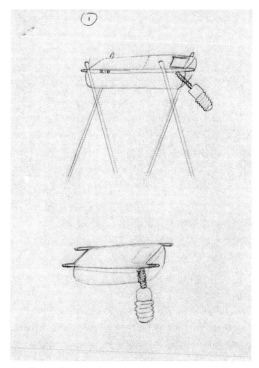

FIGURE 9.2. Design for infant anti-gas protection, June 1937 – cot. Reproduced by permission of the National Archives.

"attitude" from the children was something that only "exceptionally sound methods" could do. If class (presumably) and education resulted in cooperation with civil defense aims, these "sound methods" might need to be more widely adopted.

Certainly by the start of 1938, in addition to designing civilian respirators of various sizes to fit women and older children, government officials had definitively concluded that any device that could protect a mother and child together, such as a gas-proof tent to enclose both, was impractical.[32] However, the government found it difficult to launch trials for the newly devised "baby anti-gas helmet," for they had trouble locating volunteers. As E. J. Hodsoll complained, "Trials have been carried out to a limited extent with babies belonging to the staff at Porton but the supply is not sufficient." ARP planners encountered resistance as they sought more extensive trials of the practicality of gas masks for both

[32] Report concerning protection of young babies and children, 5 Jan. 1938, TNA HO 45/17620.

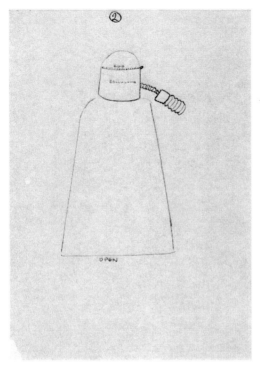

FIGURE 9.3. Design for infant anti-gas protection, June 1937 – suit. Reproduced by permission of the National Archives.

mothers and babies. The London County Council expressed reluctance to support conducting the tests, and as word of air raid precaution planning became public, critics continued to raise concerns about the psychological consequences of gas mask testing for the children under study.[33]

Enlisting outside aid, the CDRD was able to conduct a number of tests at maternity and child welfare clinics during the spring, summer, and fall of 1938, and it is worth emphasizing that all such experiments employed either a less than well-to-do clientele or one that could be said to be under some form of compulsion, the offspring of those working at Porton or members of the armed forces. For instance, the CDRD conducted trials for the protective baby bag (a bag of "thin rubberized material with a transparent cellulose acetate window" for use by infants too small for even a child-sized respirator) at the Army Welfare Centre on 21 February 1938, using the babies of families of non-commissioned officers and men of the Brigade of Guards.

[33] For a further discussion of such protests, see Chapter 6.

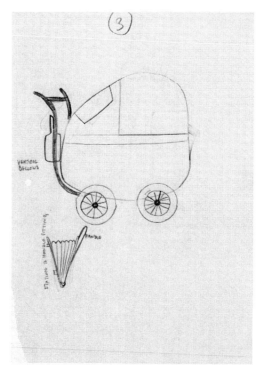

FIGURE 9.4. Design for infant anti-gas protection, June 1937 – pram. Reproduced by permission of the National Archives.

As the report on this trial noted, their military affiliation meant that "they did not represent the undisciplined and unthinking type on which it is most advisable to carry out tests," but for the present, they were the only "type" available. It was clearly a small sample, consisting of babies of three months, ten months, and three years of age, and involved mothers "placing the baby in the bag, nursing it, and moving about for a period of about 15 minutes." The end results revealed "no difficulty or reluctance by the mothers" – there was no mention of the attitude of the babies. Plans thus proceeded for taking the tests "a stage further by the mothers wearing Civilian Respirators and simulating the use of the bag under the conditions of an air raid."[34]

In late May 1938, the most extensive trial to date compared two similar devices at a test conducted on eleven babies at the New Health Clinic

[34] CDRD, Chief Superintendent, to Deputy Under Secretary of State ARP Dept., 7 Mar. 1938, TNA HO 45/17620.

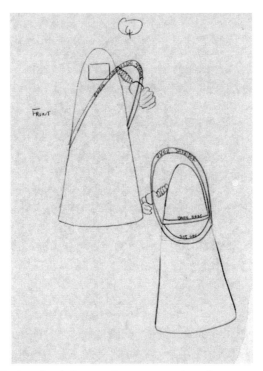

FIGURE 9.5. Design for infant anti-gas protection, June 1937 – baby bag. Reproduced by permission of the National Archives.

in Bristol. Observers noted the challenges of a "baby bag" that required the mother to pump clean air continuously into a gas-proof bag that completely encased the child. This test showed that the pumping required by the mothers for the device to work did not live up to the sixty strokes per minute estimate but that even at a slower pace, the children did not seem to suffer from a lack of air. Those conducting the test further found that the time it took to place the child in the bag varied from twelve seconds to two and a half minutes; the latter case involved a child "who struggled determinedly … having to be retrieved by mother from the door through which she was trying to escape; yet the mother, appealed to imagine that gas was entering the room and the bag offered the only hope for the child, succeeded – *and the child's resistance ceased immediately she was in the bag.*"[35] This example reinforced the conclusion that

[35] "Report on Trial of 'Baby Bag: Mark I-DMDS' at Bristol," May 1938, TNA HO 45/17620. Emphasis in original.

once placed in the bag, even struggling children were reduced to "quiet resignation ... in almost every case." It also demonstrated the manipulation of the worst maternal fears even to allow the test to take place.

Eager to obtain more information, the committee made arrangements for further tests in late June. In a letter sent to Medical Officers of Health, the government stressed that anti-gas protection for babies had now reached a crucial stage and that "the object and scope of the trial is not only to observe the working of the baby bag in action but to afford a practical demonstration of it throughout the country." Promising a delivery of the bags by 27 June, the letter outlined the findings so far, including the claim that "the bag was found to be psychologically satisfactory for any age up to two years" for at least half an hour and required the full attention of only one adult. The adult in question was explicitly the mother, as the letter continued, "the scope and object of the trial ... the working of the bag and the method of use should be explained to individual mothers."

The baby bag trials required a mother to put her infant in the bag, close it up while wearing her own gas mask, manipulate the pump attached to the baby bag, and hold the child in her arms while sitting or moving about. The designers were particularly eager to learn if there was any difficulty with use, and they offered special tips for "fractious" children, recommending that they could "be persuaded into the bag if tact and firmness are employed." Moreover, they noted that in previous trials mothers were able to pump throughout the test, control the situation, and communicate with the child in the bag, even to the extent of passing them biscuits "from the skirt of the bag."[36] Here was another responsibility that would be assigned to women as mothers in a coming war; they would have to take charge of the anti-gas protection of their babies.

Yet the reluctance of "actual" mothers to participate in these trials also continued. The Medical Officer of Health for Southampton noted that he was trying to arrange "to have five babies with foster-mothers from the Hollybrook Babies Home as it would be difficult to persuade

---

[36] Letter to Medical Officers of Health for Baby Bag Trials, undated c. June 1938, TNA HO 45/17620. Explicit instructions for how mothers were to behave at the trials were also contained in a 14 June memo. After receiving "adequate simple instructions" about the device and its uses, a mother would put the baby in the bag at the word "gas," quickly put on her own gas mask, and begin pumping while holding the child in the most comfortable manner that still allowed for pumping at about sixty strokes per minute. See "Notes on Trials of the Babies Protective Device," 14 June 1938, TNA HO 45/17620.

outside mothers to consent" to the tests.[37] This was further evidence of
the difficulty of persuading mothers to cooperate and the class component of those babies who indeed became guinea pigs. Several trials of the
"Baby Protective Device" nonetheless proceeded in July, including a test
in Southampton on 4 July performed on seven babies, several of whom
seemed particularly dismayed by the experience. Officials reported that
a girl of six and a half months "cried practically the whole time and
appeared to be somewhat distressed. The psychological effect of this on
the mother was very marked and by the end of ten minutes she was herself in tears." The mother of a four-month-old boy who was "agitated
and crying" made the mother "obviously upset," so much so that "she
was inclined to forget to pump." A ten-month-old girl "cried most of the
time" and seemed to resent being in the confined space, while another
nine-month-old girl "cried rather a lot," although "the mother in this case
was not greatly affected." In only one case of a mother "who appeared
very intelligent" did a six-month-old girl seem "quite amused and until
the last 5 mins. did not seem at all distressed." Once again, government
representatives stressed the correlation between maternal fitness and
the ability of babies to endure these trials, but the detailed observations
and the bureaucratic language cannot mask the profound discomfort of
mothers and babies.[38]

Another test of the baby bag on six infants took place at Holborn
Town Hall on 8 July, and this report offered general rather than individual observations. For five out of the six infants tested, the bag was
deemed a success, but several modifications were proposed. Babies, it
seemed, preferred to be held while "in a sitting position on the mother's
knee," and altering the design to allow this to be more easily accomplished was encouraged. The current form not only was uncomfortable
for two of the mothers, but also meant that the head of the baby was
positioned in such a way that it prevented him or her from seeing out.
The comfort of the baby was of more concern than that of the mothers, whose complaints are noted in handwritten comments on the original report. The report also stated that the "head part of the bag" was
too small to allow children to move their arms in front of their faces,
and this lack of room "frustrates the child and makes it unruly," urging
another modification of the design in order to placate the baby. Finally,

---

[37] Memo on "Baby Bag Trials," 30 June 1938, TNA HO 45/17620.
[38] Report concerning protection of young babies and children, Bristol, 20 May 1938, and
Southampton, 4 July 1938. Quote is from latter report, TNA HO 45/17620.

it noted that "the mothers required a good deal of instruction before they could satisfactorily manipulate the bag," thus casting doubt on the ability both of air raid wardens to provide sufficient instruction and of mothers to understand how to use the devices after the one lesson now proposed.[39]

The testing of similar devices occurred at the New Eltham Infant Welfare Centre in Woolwich later that month. This time around five babies endured two trials, with the latter designed to determine whether "they had any unpleasant recollections of the previous occasion." The Medical Officer of Health for the Borough, John Macmillan, provided extensive details on each subject tested, noting that the sole four-month-old baby "cried continuously," while another boy of ten months "struggled a good deal," as "the bag was much too small to allow him full freedom of movement." When removed, he was very hot and dripping with perspiration, and the officer concluded that all of the children became overheated. This remained a serious problem with the device that made it satisfactory for only about fifteen minutes of use, rather than the thirty minutes for which it was intended. As far as the second test was concerned, only one child seemed to react, a one-year-old girl who "appeared to recognise the bag five days later – clutched on to her mother very tightly and cried the moment she saw it."[40]

Unusually, Macmillan provided reactions from the mothers of the babies tested in Woolwich in his report. The mother of the most distressed baby suggested that the bag be widened at shoulder level: "I am sure my baby would have been happier if she could have moved her arms more freely." Nonetheless, she also "was most agreeably surprised by the simplicity of both gas mask and bag. I had imagined something far more complicated." Another mother voiced similar surprise that "neither the gas mask or bag are as clumsy as I imagined they would be." The mother of the four-month-old saw the baby bag as "a very good idea" that left little room for improvement, "unless something can be done to keep the temperature down a little." She further commented that she was pleased to help with the tests and "to see what was being done … as it inspires confidence when one has practical demonstrations of the precautions being taken." One other mother echoed this: "I am happy to know that such precautions are being taken to protect our babies," although

---

[39] "The Report on the Trial of Infants' Anti-Gas Protective Device (Baby Bag)," Holborn, 8 July 1938, TNA HO 45/17620.
[40] John MacMillan, Report, 20 July 1938, TNA HO 45/17620.

she added that she had doubts about the child's mask: "[T]he colour ... and the features of two eyes and nose makes it more frightening than the adults mask." The final mother suggested that two sizes be made, "as babies are so varied as to size up to two years old," and concluded, "may we never have to use them!"[41] These mothers thus demonstrated that one of the goals of ARP was being realized, for they found it reassuring that their government was making plans to protect the civil population and their children. However, the specter of putting gas masks on one's children also brought forth the fervent (and understandable) wish that such devices would never need to be utilized.

A further test was held in August using a variety of devices simultaneously in order to determine the preference of mothers and, to some extent, of the babies as well. As was the case with most of these experiments, the sample was not particularly large, testament no doubt to the "psychological effects" of the idea of gas protection for infants itself and the continued problem of locating volunteers. At Holborn Town Hall on 17–18 August, eighteen babies tested three devices. Seven were put into a "Baby Bag," five in a "protective stretcher," and six tried the "Protective helmet." The final report noted that "the fact that most of the babies cried during the test must not be given undue weight since this is to be expected to some extent with any device." Nonetheless, it also observed that the mothers preferred the protective helmet to the other options. One baby was described as "completely terrified in the bag and was removed in 4 minutes by the mother," something that would certainly defeat the purpose of this form of protection. The report's conclusion concurred with the mothers' choice of the helmet, mentioning the following advantages of this design: because of its window "the mother can hold baby and see baby and vice versa," and the child could be more easily carried and placed inside, in contrast to the "baby bag" device, which totally encased an infant. The report also noted that this made it easier to change a nappy and keep the baby comfortable. As a result, child-sized respirators and baby anti-gas helmets became part of the provisions that the state could potentially offer to a public facing the full brunt of chemical warfare during a future conflict.[42]

---

[41] See appendix to John MacMillan, Report, 20 July 1938, TNA HO 45/17620.

[42] As late as March of that year, members of the House of Commons were still seeking clarification as to the provision of gas masks, although the role of local authorities in distributing the masks (free of charge) was part of the ARP Act, see *Parliamentary Debates – Commons*, 10 Mar. 1938, Vol. 332, cols. 2129–2130.

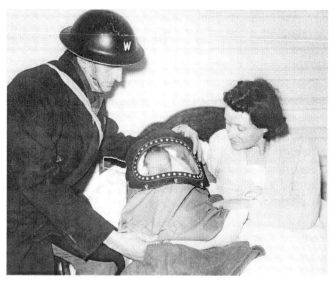

FIGURE 9.6. The baby anti-gas helmet, 15 November 1939. Reproduced by permission of the Imperial War Museum.

The development of the baby anti-gas helmet created another role
for women in wartime, that of administering and monitoring the anti-
gas protection of their infants. When the babies' protective helmet was
finally ready to be launched in December 1938, officials from the ARP
Department agreed that the training of "*mothers* in the use of the babies'
device" required careful consideration, and "for obvious reasons the
demonstrations [of how to use the device] should be given by an individual in the Medical offices of Health Department, accustomed to handling
babies, and not be one of the local A.R.P. instructors."[43] Once again,
the operation of these devices was to fall to mothers, although officials
remained aware of the challenges – both practical and psychological –
this posed. By the end of January 1939, three samples of the baby helmet
were available for demonstrations, but spreading the word to ordinary
mothers remained a challenge for the ARP bureaucracy.

   In May 1939, Wing Commander A. J. Brown, the medical adviser
for ARP, wrote to Lady Denman, chair of the National Federation of
Women's Institutes (NFWI) asking for her organization's assistance. He
noted: "We have had some difficulty in deciding the best means of having

---

[43] See Memorandum from E. J. Hodsoll, Dec. 1938, and Letter from G. H. Findlay to
   Porton, 6 Jan. 1939, TNA HO 186/980. Emphasis added.

the new Baby Protective Helmet demonstrated to mothers throughout the country, who would not attend demonstrations at clinics and welfare centres." Such mothers might include middle- and upper-class women who would not frequent "clinics," but another advantage of Women's Institutes was their presence in rural districts as well as population centers. The secretary general of the NFWI responded that they were already cooperating with the Women's Voluntary Services as far as ARP and would certainly encourage any individual institute that wished to do so to arrange for a demonstration.[44] Like the proposed gas-proof pram, turning the Women's Institutes – with all of their associations with comfortable, domestic life – into spaces for training women to prepare for aerial and chemical warfare displayed the incredible transformation of the meaning of "home defense."

In the tense atmosphere of July 1939, when war with Germany seemed imminent, in addition to having commenced demonstrations of sample baby helmets, the ARP Department was ready to issue a pamphlet entitled "Anti-Gas Protection of Babies and Young Children." Officials wanted it made clear that "these respirators will not be issued in peace time except in so far as an issue is necessary for fitting purposes." Meanwhile, the leaflet provided a brief explanation of how both the small child's respirator (for two- to five-year-olds) and protective helmet (for newborns to two-year-olds) worked and how to determine what device was best for one's child. It offered instructions on coping with recalcitrant children, suggesting that for those small children who refused to wear a respirator, the infant protective helmet could serve as a recourse. Ignoring the contradictory evidence of the baby anti-gas protection trials discussed earlier, it claimed that "most babies and children quite readily take to the Helmet.... [I]n fact it is common for them to go to sleep." When this did not occur, "it is possible for one adult quickly to place the child in the Helmet and thus to protect it from gas in spite of its resistance. Once inside, such children usually ... appear contented." Moreover, it informed mothers that "it may be possible to remove the child's fear by persuasion.... [T]he sight of other children wearing respirators will often inspire confidence in nervous children."[45]

---

44 See Letter, Wing Commander A. J. Brown to Lady Denman, 5 May 1939, and the response in Letter, Frances Farrer, Secretary General of NFWI, to A. J. Brown, 12 May 1939, TNA HO 186/980.

45 See "Revised Draft of Memorandum on Anti-Gas Protection of Babies & Young Children," June 1939, TNA HO 186/980.

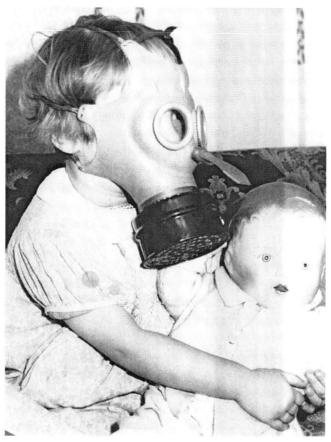

FIGURE 9.7. Anti-gas protection for children. A girl in the small child's respirator holds her doll, 19 October 1940. Fox Photos; courtesy of Imperial War Museum.

Yet shortly after the outbreak of the Second World War, in mid-September 1939, the medical profession continued to seek solutions to the problem of young children's resistance to anti-gas protective measures. Writing to the ARP Department, E. A. Hardy, the assistant medical officer of health for the city of Westminster, offered an improvement over the suggestion of "tying a child's hands behind it" if it refused to stop struggling when faced with his or her gas mask. Hardy's associate, Dr. Christine Thompson, had found that "all the mothers she has asked have refused to consider this suggestion." Although Hardy pointed out that tying a child's hands and, if necessary, feet behind its back remained

FIGURE 9.8. Training session at Kensington Town Hall on the use of the baby gas mask, c. 1939. Reproduced by permission of the Imperial War Museum.

an effective and fast method of subduing a child, Hardy passed along to officials Dr. Thompson's "pillow case method," whereby the child was secured within a pillowcase before being placed in the gas mask.[46]

CONCLUSION

Whatever children's or infants' individual responses to these objects designed for their protection, the commitment of the state to such devices, with its acknowledgment of the new horrors of this type of war, was irrefutable. Nor did the government cease trying to persuade British mothers of the significance of accepting their new status as full participants in modern war. We can see this in the image of women being trained to use infant anti-gas protection. The state needed women to accept their expanded civic role as much as the civil defense measures such as gas

[46] See Letter, E. A. Hardy to Kirwan, and Memo, "Small Child's Respirator – Method of Securing Child Suggested by Dr. Christine Thomson (Pillow Case Method)," 15 Sept. 1939, TNA HO 186/980.

mask wearing that it had prepared both for them and for their children.[47] As we will see in the chapters ahead, the real test of ARP was still to come. At the same time, the development of the baby anti-gas helmet reveals how much the state had already domesticated the air raid.

[47] By February 1941, more than 2 million children's respirators and 1,680,000 babies' helmets had been produced. Another fascinating aspect of this largely unknown story is the number of devices sent to British colonies and the discussions over who should receive gas masks, when and where. All ARP measures had an imperial dimension that I hope to address in future work. For more on the British Empire and the Second World War, see Ashley Jackson, *The British Empire and the Second World War* (London, 2006). See Memorandum of 18 Feb. 1941, TNA HO 186/1358, for details of numbers listed here.

10

Responding to Air War's Return

The Militarized Domestic Sphere from September '38 to the Blitz

INTRODUCTION

The Czechoslovakian crisis of September 1938 provided a dress rehearsal for ARP, and its accompanying distribution of gas masks and of shelters offered the civilian population an opportunity to recognize fully what could be expected in the war to come. That war was averted at this point did little to reassure those enacting ARP. When war broke out nearly a year later, the same sets of measures were again put in place, although the so-called Phony War meant that complacency about gas mask carrying and other protective measures soon became evident. When the war became more "active," and certainly by the outset of the long-anticipated aerial onslaught, "the Blitz," which began in the fall of 1940, both material and psychological ARP measures would finally be tested as never before. This chapter examines personal, official, and cultural responses to impending and actual aerial warfare in Great Britain from the crisis of September 1938 through the beginning of the Second World War's aerial attacks as a culmination of the thorough intermingling of state and home that began with air raids a generation earlier.

While numerous studies – dating from the war years themselves – have discussed the extensive aerial attacks on Britain during the Second World War in great detail, the following exploration offers a somewhat different perspective on these events by placing them at the end of a rather longer story about civilians and war in the air.[1] This, then, provides not a new

[1] There is an enormous literature on Britain during the Second World War. See, in addition to Angus Calder, *The Myth of the Blitz* (London, 1991) and Sonya O. Rose, *Which People's War? National Identity and Citizenship in Wartime Britain, 1939–1945* (Oxford,

history of the Blitz or of the well-documented British civilian responses to the Second World War, but instead an investigation of how the legacy of the air raids of the First World War, the cultural work of interpreting these raids, the failure of efforts at air disarmament, and the return of aerial devastation to European soil in the mid-1930s all contributed to the climate in which Britons faced air war in 1940. It argues that the cultural work necessary to prepare the civil population for a war of "terror," one in which success would be measured by psychic damage and blows to morale as well as by material effects, had been concluded long before the first bombs fell again on British soil. It finds striking similarities in the reactions to air raids during the two world wars, and it recovers the renewed call to a civil identity of shared sacrifice and stoicism under fire that (re)emerged in the latter conflict.

MORALE, THE CRISIS IN CZECHOSLOVAKIA, AND THE DRESS REHEARSAL FOR ARP

The emphasis on maintaining morale through psychological and material preparedness loomed large during the crisis of September 1938 that led to the signing of the Munich Agreement. The schematics of this crisis, now taken to be the quintessential moment of "appeasement," are not difficult to trace. In light of the Nazi takeover of Austria in the Anschluss of mid-March, the status of Czechoslovakia's Sudentenland German population became a critical issue. A German nationalist movement in the region, actively fostered by the Nazis, began to make demands in April 1938 that included autonomy for German-speaking areas, and the region almost erupted into conflict in May of that year. Although war was forestalled, Adolf Hitler was now seemingly determined to crush the Czechoslovakian government, using the alleged grievances of its minority German population as an excuse, and the situation escalated into a crisis

2003), the following studies as starting points: Winston S. Churchill, *Their Finest Hour* (Boston, 1949); Peter Clarke, *Hope and Glory: Britain, 1900–2000* (London, 2004), ch. 6; Tim Clayton and Phil Craig, *Finest Hour: The Battle of Britain* (New York, 1999); Mark Donnelly, *Britain in the Second World War* (London, 1999); Juliet Gardiner, *Wartime Britain, 1939–1945* (London, 2004); Tom Harrisson, *Living Through the Blitz* (London, 1976); Robert Mackay, *The Test of War: Inside Britain, 1939–45* (London, 1999); Clive Ponting, *1940: Myth and Reality* (Chicago, 1991); Peter Stansky, *The First Day of the Blitz: September 7, 1940* (New Haven, CT, 2007); Peter Stansky and William Abrahams, *London's Burning: Life, Death and Art in the Second World War* (London, 1994); Charles Whiting, *Britain Under Fire: The Bombing of Britain's Cities, 1940–45* (Barnsley, 1999). For a key study of its memory and gendered legacy, see Lucy Noakes, *War and the British: Gender, Memory, and National Identity* (London, 1998).

after Hitler gave a speech on 12 September that set off rioting in the Sudentenland and led Czechoslovakia to declare martial law.[2]

The height of this crisis, which spawned the conviction that the long anticipated next war would immediately become a reality, took place over the next two weeks. Neville Chamberlain, Britain's prime minister, sought to negotiate a solution to this crisis on three separate occasions, 15 September, 22 September, and ultimately at the four-power summit in Munich on 29 September that produced the infamous Munich Agreement. It was in the interim between the failed negotiations of 22 September and the end of that month that Britain began to mobilize for war. This is the context in which the public launching of ARP services took place. And while the order to mobilize the British navy on 27 September provides one vivid reminder of just how close Britain came to war, the event hailed by the press as "Gas Mask Sunday" (25 September) offers an even starker indication of just what type of war – a total war involving all civilians – Britons were being prepared to accept.

It was in the crisis-laden atmosphere of this month that a flurry of articles on ARP appeared in major newspapers. Like the handbook that had been issued in March, all of these articles contained government-approved instructions for turning domestic spaces into ones associated with war. They called upon civilians of all ages and both sexes to participate in civil and home defense.[3] September 1938 thus provided a public test of what civil defense planners had been struggling to achieve for more than a decade.

When war seemed imminent in Europe in the late 1930s, governments had already prepared appeals to "ordinary" citizens, including women. As we have seen in previous chapters, the British government had laid the groundwork for how to instruct the civilian population to respond to

---

[2] There are a number of studies of so-called appeasement and of the crisis of 1938; see, among others, R. J. Q. Adams, *British Politics and Foreign Policy in the Age of Appeasement, 1935–1939* (Stanford, CA, 1993); Geoffrey K. Fry, *The Politics of Crisis: An Interpretation of British Politics, 1931–1945* (Basingstoke, 2001), ch. 4; James P. Levy, *Appeasement and Rearmament: Britain, 1936–1939* (Lanham, MD, 2006), which defends Chamberlain; Gaines Post, Jr., *Dilemmas of Appeasement: British Deterrence and Defense 1934–1937* (Ithaca, NY, 1993); and the useful comparative study, Talbot Imlay, *Facing the Second World War: Strategy, Politics, and Economics in Britain and France, 1938–1940* (Oxford, 2003). For more general accounts of interwar Britain that contextualize the events of 1938–1939, see Peter Dewey, *War and Progress: Britain, 1914–1945* (London, 1997); Charles Loch Mowat, *Britain Between the Wars, 1918–1940* (Chicago, 1955), as well as the studies by Kent and Overy previously cited.

[3] See as examples "Kitchen as Air Raid Refuge," *Times*, 22 Sept. 1938; and "Volunteers for A.R.P.," *Times*, 23 Sept. 1938.

future wars during the 1920s and 1930s, including plans for providing shelters from air raids in both private homes and public spaces and for protecting civilians from chemical weapons by issuing gas masks. They made plans for evacuating children and mobilizing men and, wherever possible, women as well. Along with these practical preparations, they tried to ensure that these actions would proceed calmly and not unduly upset the civil population.

There were a number of visible signs of the "speedup" of ARP as the sense of urgency deepened. In London's parks, men from the Office of Works dug seven-foot trenches, while "children on Primrose Hill, Hampstead, played 'king of the castle' on the rubble thrown up from excavations for similar shelters."[4] Nor was activity restricted to London. The Manchester City Council held a special meeting on 23 September to discuss its accelerated ARP preparations. It talked not only about the distribution of gas masks, but also about the need to undertake a survey of basements to determine their suitability as shelters within the city and to appeal for more ARP volunteers.[5] Another sign of the ubiquity and importance of these precautions can be seen in a short article announcing that every member of the royal household, including potentially the king and queen, would soon be fitted for civilian respirators, a task that was the responsibility of the Westminster City Council as part of its duty to fit all residents for such masks.[6]

As one of the most noticeable signs of ARP and of the type of war that might be expected, the distribution of gas masks provoked a range of responses in the media and among the British civilian population. News of a "gas mask wedding" showed the extent to which those involved with new forms of civil defense adapted to these measures. A short notice in the *Manchester Guardian* announced the marriage of two volunteers for the local ARP organization in Gillingham, Kent, on 21 September. What made their wedding noteworthy was that the bridal party wore "A.R.P. clothing, with gas masks and steel helmets and carr[ied] incendiary bomb scoops" to form a guard of honor over the newlyweds.[7]

A longer account in the *News Chronicle* featured a slightly different photograph than the one above, while it, too, clearly showed the

[4] "A.R.P. Speed-Up," *Reynold's News*, 23 Sept. 1938.
[5] "Speeding Up A.R.P. Schemes in Manchester," *Manchester Guardian* 24 Sept. 1938.
[6] "Gas Masks for Royal Family," *Daily Telegraph*, 24 Sept. 1938. An article several days later indicated that a number of vaults in Buckingham Palace had been made "gas-proof"; see "Gas Mask Issue Begins," *Daily Telegraph*, 27 Sept. 1938.
[7] "Gas Masks at a Wedding," *Manchester Guardian*, 22 Sept. 1938.

FIGURE 10.1. "The Gas Mask Wedding." Hulton Archive, Fox Photos, September 1938. Reproduced by permission of Getty Images.

bridesmaids and groomsmen in gas masks; in this version, the happy couple was obscured by smoke from a small bomb. The article continued by noting that both the bride, Dorothy Treacher, and the groom, William Clements, worked for Gillingham's main ARP office, as did the bride's father, the town's former mayor. The meaning behind the smoke bombs that exploded in the road as the couple left the church, and the fact that the bridegroom and his best man wore "gas masks while the wedding cake was cut," was left to the reader's imagination. The display could have been didactic, thoroughly domesticating this wartime garb and turning it into something to be used in "normal" life. Or it could have been a way to show off and attract attention. Whatever the motives, this wedding clearly incorporated items associated with war and devastation into a ritual associated with domesticity, family, and peace.[8]

The response to the photo and article was decidedly hostile. Two letters to the editor denounced both the couple's behavior and the newspaper for publicizing it. A. E. Palmer of Taunton found the photo "revolting" – "a scene which should surely never have been allowed by the

[8] "Arrayed for a Wedding," *News Chronicle*, 22 Sept. 1938.

officiating parties." Palmer decried as "sacrilegious and impious" the idea of setting off bombs on consecrated grounds and further suggested that Gillingham's ratepayers would like to know "who authorised the use of the A.R.P. clothing, gas masks, and steel helmets, which are intended for use in a national emergency, and not for private entertainment purposes."[9] H. W. Earthrowl was even more outraged, asserting that "it would be difficult to measure the degree of disgust expressed at the wedding picture published in your paper last Thursday." Earthrowl took special exception to the fact that a cross was clearly visible behind the display of the gas-mask-attired wedding party, noting that "most of the spectators stand [in the photo] with their backs to the Cross – indicative of the mental attitude of many today."[10] Whatever the mental attitude of the participants, the distribution of gas masks beyond ARP workers was one additional outcome of the crisis.

Various news outlets publicized the work being done, as one put it, to enable "protection of the home."[11] Some announced the imminent arrival of further instructions on using the covered backyard trench as a shelter and on the gas masks that the public would need to carry at all times; one stated that "when a state of national emergency is proclaimed by the Government," masks would then by distributed by ARP wardens to every home based on the "fittings now being taken."[12] These fittings coalesced into the well-publicized actions of 25 September 1938.

"This Was 'Gas Mask' Sunday," read the headline in the *Daily Express* on 26 September 1938, which compared the gathering of everyone from "titled people" to "telephone girls" for "Chelsea's first face-to-face meeting with gas masks" to a "church social." As the reporter wondered "how the average family acts in times of crisis" and looked for "reports of hysteria, of emotional upset to the smooth machine that collected nearly a quarter-million face sizes, issued cards worth a mask each 'in case of need,'" he found instead that "[e]verywhere they told me – 'no excitement; we've had no fuss.'" Typical of those who adopted this no-fuss attitude was one Mrs. John Briggs; with "her youngest in her arms" and "the other three children beside her ... [she] ordered the children, 'Pay attention, now. This has to fit, so you can use it – just like a pair of shoes.'" Nor was Chelsea unique, for in this account calm queues for gas masks

9   A. E. Palmer, Letter to the editor, *News Chronicle*, 26 Sept. 1938.
10 H. W. Earthrowl, Letter to the editor, *News Chronicle*, 26 Sept. 1938.
11 "Protection of the Home," *News Chronicle*, 23 Sept. 1938.
12 "Protection of the Home."

formed all over London, from Westminster to Camberwell to Croydon, Harrow to Poplar, Leyton to Hendon and Stepney.[13]

Gas Mask Sunday was preceded by the appeals of London's local authorities, using such public venues as cinemas and football pitches, to families to take the time to be fitted for gas masks. As an article entitled "Gas Masks for Londoners" noted, a similar message would be heard from many pulpits on the day itself.[14] Akin to the scene in the 1936 film *Things to Come*, Londoners "followed advice flashed on cinema screens, messages blared from loud-speakers on cars in the streets, or leaflets displayed in cafés, restaurants and hotels" calling upon them to visit "A.R.P. centres throughout the metropolis ... to be fitted with gas masks." For more than twelve hours, fittings took place in every corner of the teeming metropolitan area. The *Daily Sketch* reporter found five thousand men, women, and children being fitted for the masks on a visit to Battersea Town Hall, where the overwhelming mood was "cheerful." As one representative of an "average" family, Mr. W. J. Elsbury, waiting with his wife and two children, put it: "I haven't been at all worried.... Maybe it's an English trait not to worry, but it's good to see that the Government are taking care of us in the event of anything so terrible as a gas attack."[15]

Press coverage of Gas Mask Sunday itself was nearly unanimous in its emphasis on the calm that prevailed as families lined up for gas masks. It pointed out that some London "children were fitted while in Sunday school," and others in the care of their parents were fitted in outlets across the metropolis.[16] It told of similar reactions throughout the nation, where almost "half the population of the main cities and towns had been fitted with gas masks by a late hour" in a quiet and cooperative manner. Articles insisted on the bridging of class lines: an "astonishing collapse of social barriers which turned the whole horrible performance into a picnic."[17] Other reports emphasized that women were suited to participate fully in all such preparations, extolling female ARP wardens for not

---

[13] "This Was 'Gas Mask' Sunday," *Daily Express*, 26 Sept. 1938.

[14] "Gas Masks for Londoners," *Observer*, 25 Sept. 1938. Hodsoll was quoted in this article as stating that the demand for respirators "has increased since the international emergency arose" and the government had produced about 40 million respirators, 30 million of which it hoped to distribute.

[15] "ARP Day in Masks," *Daily Sketch*, 26 Sept. 1938. This article was accompanied by a page of photographs showing ordinary folks being fitted for masks and crowds waiting in line to be so fitted.

[16] See "Families Queue to Fit Gas Masks," *Daily Herald*, 26 Sept. 1938; and "A.R.P. Day in Masks," *Daily Sketch*, 26 Sept. 1938. Quote is from the latter.

[17] "Trying It On," reprinted from the *News Chronicle* in the *Star*, 27 Sept. 1938.

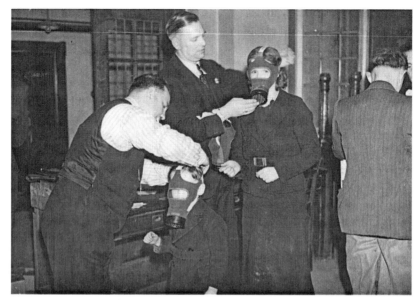

FIGURE 10.2. A mother and child being fitted on Gas Mask Sunday. Hulton Archive, J. A. Hampton, September 1938. Reproduced by permission of Getty Images.

having shown "the slightest sign of nerves, hysterics, or fainting."[18] When nerves were displayed, assurance was quickly offered, as was the case with nine-year-old Gladys Alwin, who took three tearful girls to be fitted in Caxton Hall; her response to their tears was to take them by the hand: "'Come on sillies.... Don't be frightened.'"[19]

Photographs accompanying such articles also made certain to turn this extraordinary day into a statement about the fortitude of the entire population. A patient crowd of families waiting outside a school in Finsbury or a family grouping from Penge wearing gas masks thus revealed "a typical English family taking precautions and taking them calmly – with faith in Britain prepared and Britain strong." An image in the *Star* showed a mother fitting a mask on the youngest of her eight children.[20] A photograph in the *Daily Mail* showed a calm and crowded queue outside the Brixton Town Hall, with three young boys and a mother holding a baby

[18] Sheila O'Callaghan, "Women's Work," *Star*, 30 Sept. 1938
[19] "Families Queue to Fit Gas Masks."
[20] "Families Queue to fit Gas Masks"; and "Britain Queues Up in Millions on Gas Mask Sunday," *Daily Mirror*, 26 Sept. 1938. Quote is from caption to photo accompanying the latter. "Trying It On," *Star*, 27 Sept. 1938.

in the foreground, as an illustration of the thousands of "mothers, fathers, sisters and brothers" who "were flocking to centres all over London to be fitted for their respirators."[21]

The *Daily Mail's* coverage continued a day later with the sweeping statement that "civilian Britain squared up sensibly and practically throughout yesterday and last night to face the menace that might come from the skies." While reports that the "ready-made plans for safe-guarding, to the limit of human ingenuity, the millions who may be subject to air raids" acknowledged the fundamental idea that nothing like safety could be guaranteed, such accounts continued to stress the prevailing sense of calm. While people were digging trenches and shelters across London, and major provincial centers were preparing to issue gas masks, then above all, British men, women, and children demonstrated that they were prepared to face a war truly waged against them.[22] That, anyway, was the public message.

The illustrations accompanying the coverage of the day after Gas Mask Sunday again underscored exactly whom this new war threatened, in one case with a heartrending photograph of a mother carrying a baby in the background while a very young boy in short pants cradles a gas mask in the foreground. The caption is quite matter-of-fact: "[M]others and children among the crowds receiving and being fitted with gas-masks in London yesterday." However, the look on the boy's face and his carrying an object designed to protect him from poison unleashed above his home belie the tension this activity must have generated.[23]

The *Daily Herald* began its coverage by pointing out the obvious: "[Y]esterday, all over London, A.R.P. passed from plan into practice." It featured visually the fundamental distinction of ARP under the caption "Families Queue to Fit Gas Masks," as a crowd seeming to consist mainly of women and children waited outside the Amwell Street School in Finsbury.[24] In keeping with the dominant tone of the media, the reporter noted that "for the most part there was calm and good humour" but added that "here and there a child sobbed and turned away from the respirator. A mother laughed nervously at her husband as she slipped on the black facepiece." Given that the *Daily Herald* was a paper of the Left that had been highly disparaging of the government's failure to support

---

[21] "England's Call to Gasmasks," *Daily Mail*, 26 Sept. 1938.
[22] "All Britain Digs Air Raid Trenches," *Daily Mail*, 27 Sept. 1938.
[23] "His Gas-Mask," *Daily Mail*, 27 Sept. 1938.
[24] "Families Queue to Fit Gas Masks."

disarmament, this unusual note of nerves and sobs may itself be taken as a kind of criticism of the government's failure to prevent war.

As predicted by ARP planners, the lack of anti-gas protection for infants and young children was mentioned in a number of articles, and families were told to register the presence of such infants when the rest of the family was fitted, because "the production of a protective device and of a respirator for very young children is in hand." If gas masks for those under four were not immediately available, the Home Office was quick to publicize the expectation that such devices would soon be "perfected."[25] In the meantime, officials advised parents to wrap small children in blankets and head for the nearest gas-proof room or shelter.[26] It may have been less encouraging to the parents of such children that gas-proof kennels for dogs and cats were apparently already available, although under the auspices of the People's Dispensary for Sick Animals rather than the government. One then wonders how British animal lovers responded to the news that while their domestic pets might be thus kept safe, ARP plans at the London Zoo included provisions to shoot any large animals that might escape during a raid.[27]

In the *Daily Telegraph*, an unnamed ARP officer hailed the fitting of gas masks throughout London as a success, describing the public's behavior as "magnificent." Reports from across the metropolis highlighted the sheer number of those who had been fitted – more than 75 percent of the borough population of Finsbury and sixty thousand in Islington. In Poplar and Wandsworth the response was more descriptive, respectively "great" and "excellent."[28] Exemplary volunteers, including Boy Scouts as well as ARP wardens, helped spread the word of the ARP measures across local communities and assisted the nearly non-stop process of starting to equip the population for aerial and chemical warfare. The paper emphasized, too, that this was the work of the government, adding that it was asked "to stress that no charge is made either for fitting or masks."

The *Times* was notably more restrained in its coverage of what it deemed "A.R.P. Sunday." "Yesterday was used to press on vigorously, though calmly," it reported, "with preparations for passive defence in the event of an emergency" as "thousands of citizens attended at depots

[25] "Gas-Masks: Babies Must be Registered," *Daily Mail*, 28 Sept. 1938.
[26] "Respirators Soon for Babies?" *Daily Herald*, 28 Sept. 1938. See the preceding chapter for a full discussion of anti-gas protection for children and babies.
[27] See "Gas-Proof Kennels Ready," *Daily Mail*, 28 Sept. 1938; and "A.R.P. at the Zoo," *Times*, 29 Sept. 1938.
[28] "Week-End Gas Mask Drive All over London," *Daily Telegraph*, 26 Sept. 1938.

to be fitted for their gas masks." Like other newspapers, this one noted the length of both queues and the hours during which depots remained open, as well as the "motor-vans equipped with loud-speakers which cruised slowly around London" urging folks to go their nearest depot and be fitted with a mask. As another indication of the domestication of civil defense, the reporter described how at Caxton Hall, "on Saturday a newly married couple went straight from the office of the registrar of marriages there to another part of the building to be fitted for gas masks." Unlike the "gas mask wedding" that provoked such outrage, here was simply a case of calm efficiency or an acknowledgment of marriage truly for better or worse.[29]

A more emotive reflection appeared in the *Evening Standard*, whose reporter contrasted the posters appearing in the West End bearing the words "Fitting of Gas Masks" with a scene beside the Tomb of the Unknown Warrior in Westminster Abbey. In the latter, "two candles burn steadily ... there is no sound save footsteps. Some of the women are in black; some are weeping."[30] This scene of women mourning the war dead offered a reminder of the costs of the last war, one where warriors fought and died while those at home were left to grieve. In contrast, the new war for which everyone will need a gas mask will affect men and women, combatants and civilians alike.

One reporter even tried to humanize the expected enemy by comparing the reactions of Londoners with those of Germans living in the Rhineland. Writing in the *Daily Express*, Hilde Marchant described driving through the countryside to the Belgian frontier, finding Rhinelanders "tense and uneasy ... they don't want war." In contrast, "London was reassuring – quietly assembling the A.R.P. scheme, yet still keeping a sense of humour. There is none of the stamping and saluting, but more efficiency." Marchant ended her article with the headmaster of St. Peter's School, a Mr. Hardingham, trying to engage in a more personal act of reassurance to the mothers who were crying over the idea of sending their children away, by insisting that "I have a child myself.... I was in the last war. I know what air raids are. They must be away from the town.... Don't be afraid – it may never happen but we must be ready."[31] It was this mixture of knowing past horrors and pretending that such recurrences

---

[29] "A.R.P. Sunday," *Times*, 26 Sept. 1938.
[30] "How London Looks to Its Safety," *Evening Standard*, 27 Sept. 1938.
[31] Hilde Marchant, "And Mr. Hardingham Advises Mothers," *Daily Express*, 27 Sept. 1938. She also insisted that in London "the atmosphere is easier and more confident than in Germany."

might still be in doubt that captured the paradox of this moment, with its need to create a cultural climate in which fear could be manipulated into action but not panic.

A few discussions of evacuation plans and other ARP measures such as the digging of trenches and the provision of shelters also acknowledged that what was happening here was a repetition of what had been seen in the last war. Another report in the *Times* noted that "although London looked much as usual and her citizens went calmly about their business – though eager for news and, unlike the citizens of Berlin, for instance, informed of developments in the international situation ... there was much to be seen that has been unfamiliar for a quarter of a century."[32] The living memory of air raids could thus shape responses to the return of air war in 1938.

Along with being fitted for gas masks, civilians were expected to prepare their homes for aerial war. On 26 September, William Astor, the parliamentary private secretary to the home secretary, urged "anyone who has a garden to start building a shelter to-day" and not to waste time.[33] Meanwhile, Herbert Morrison appealed for more ARP workers in London to help with the increased pace of preparations, delivering a special message to the general population: "I ... urge all those who have no other task to discharge to see to it that London maintains its reputation in civic order."[34] During the crisis, the ARP Department also ran advertisements for volunteers under the heading "Why Wait until They Are on the Way?" The stark black letters that make up this question are set against planes in the background. The advertisement further stressed the need for five thousand women to register as car drivers and twenty-five thousand men and youths to train as auxiliary fire fighters.[35]

This appeal to the new civil identity required to face air war was evident as well in an editorial in the *Manchester Guardian*. Developing the theme of the "civilian task," it argued:

> If the worst should come this autumn, there will be considerably less scope for genial catch-cries like, "Business as usual," or "Keep the home fires burning"; everyone will be aware that courage and fortitude on

---

[32] "Passive Defence," *Times*, 28 Sept. 1938.
[33] "Do Not Waste Time," *Daily Mail*, 27 Sept. 1938.
[34] Quoted in "All Night Digging of A.R.P. Trenches in London Parks," *News Chronicle*, 27 Sept. 1938.
[35] "Why wait until they are on the way?" Advertisement in the *Evening News*, 28 Sept. 1938.

the home front ... will mean just as much to the safety of the realm as do the same qualities when displayed on any fronts that may be aligned elsewhere.... [T]he "shock tactics" that were so largely stifled in the combatant areas under the muddled sullen weight of trench warfare will be transferred by those who have again made blood their argument, in new and hideous forms to the cities ... that are far behind the fighting fronts.

If war comes our frontier will not be on the Rhine. It will be in the air and over London, Birmingham, Sheffield, Manchester, and other centres where hostile aircraft might hope to spread a disabling burden of panic and dismay among closely dwelling populations.[36]

Much as was the case during the First World War, this emphasis on the stalwart ability of those at home to control panic and mitigate despair called upon civilians to perform their active wartime role. Damage cannot be contained but, the editorial continued, "if we can avoid disorder we can deal with destruction and thereby rob the new shock tactics against the civilian front of the[ir] disabling effect." In part this had to be done, by removing "certain women" and "as many children as possible" from crowded locales likely to become targets. Beyond this, there would be vital tasks left to perform by both men and women; "the steady example of those who have work to do ... will play no small part in maintaining public spirit and confidence at the level we should expect from the people of this country through any hour of trial."[37]

The reaction to such instructions, however, could not be controlled. Writing in her diary just a few days before the Munich Agreement halted the crisis, Vivienne Hall commented:

God, how I hate this business of fighting for life against something we can't understand or can't even see! A vast and efficient defence organisation is moving – books are delivered to everyone on the simplest forms of self-protection against gas, incendiary bombs, splinters, fire, water, the pathetic preparations of thousands of ants against the unknown horror of an aerial boot poised above our heads![38]

This was not the voice of confidence that civil defense planners hoped to inspire.

Neither was the response of Helena Britton to the directive to be fitted for a gas mask. Her account of Gas Mask Sunday in a letter of 30

---

[36] "The Civilian Task," *Manchester Guardian*, 28 Sept. 1938.
[37] "The Civilian Task."
[38] IWM, Department of Documents, Papers of V Hall (DS/Misc/88), Vivienne Hall, Diary, 28 Sept. 1938.

September 1938 to her daughter Florrie in California offered an alternative perspective:

> On Sunday just as we were having tea, a car with a loud speaker, came round and said, everyone was to go to the nearest school to be fitted for a gas mask, you can guess how we felt, at first I said I wouldn't go, they were useless, but Dad said we *must* do what we can to protect ourselves and he would go, so I thought, well if a war does comes, Dad will be giving me his & that won't do, so I must go.
>
> We had to line up men, women and children, I had never seen so many pregnant women before, my heart ached for the young mothers & fathers....
>
> We were fitted & given a card, which we had to take, when the gas masks arrived.[39]

The opinions within this one couple ranged from thinking the anti-gas protection "useless" to being willing to "do what we can." What is also clear in these private accounts is how gut-wrenching it could be to witness, let alone take part in, this process of preparing for a war to be waged against pregnant women.

As if to reassure Londoners that they could survive the aerial threat, on 28 September the *Daily Mirror* ran the headline "Bombing of Protected Cities Fails." The point of this piece by a special correspondent was to demonstrate that the experience of cities and towns "which have been bombed incessantly in the past two years, ha[s] proved that when adequate protective measures are taken, attacks from the air are a dismal failure." Spain provided the most obvious examples, as the reporter claimed that Madrid and Barcelona "still function as cities – none has been destroyed." Instead, "the civil population" of all bombed locations "has either redoubled its grim determination or has assumed an attitude of indifference."[40] Taking the British public to task a bit for not being better prepared, the same issue of the *Daily Mirror* also ran a lengthy explanation of the fitting, use, and care of gas masks under the heading "before it's too late ... the page that teaches you to be STRONG so that Britain will be STRONG too." Its concluding line, after encouraging readers to

---

[39] IWM, Department of Documents, Papers of G Britton (Con Shelf), Letter, Helena Britton, Walthamstow, UK, to Daughter Florence Elizabeth Britton Elkus in Berkeley CA, USA, 30 Sept. 1938. Enclosed with this letter are several Labour pamphlets, "This Dishonour Will Not Bring Us Peace" and clippings from the *Daily Herald*.

[40] "Bombing of Protected Cities Fails," *Daily Mirror*, 28 Sept. 1938. The other examples were Chinese: Hankow, Canton, and Nanking, cities that also endured intensive bombardment.

cut out the page and discuss its contents with their families, was "[T]here is nothing to be afraid of if you know what to do!"[41]

Despite the years of preparation, there was a sense of urgency in the flurry of information conveyed through newspapers in late September. It was on 29 September that the *Times* described for its readers the official audible warning of an aerial attack; in the case of both the warning and the all clear, a two-minute siren blast would sound.[42] Under the heading "Do It Now," the paper also reprinted the ARP Department's "20 precautions against air raids." It began with the fitting of gas masks, went on to describe procedures for the blackout, and the construction of a "refuge room" (noting that this should include "something to do – books to read, games to play"), and closed with the ways to reduce the risk of serious fires. In keeping with the overall message of ARP during this grave test, its final advice was to "keep calm" and "do all you can in an emergency to help your neighbours, particularly those who are aged or who have children."[43] This appeal for the creation of a community of stalwart civilians – looking after those whom air war would not spare, the elderly and the young – was entirely in keeping with the desire of most ARP planners to foster a sense of willing commitment rather than coercion to adopt what might seem to be terrifying or at least intrusive measures.

Publicly it seemed that the attitudes cultivated during the long process of developing ARP came to fruition. In the immediate aftermath of this crisis, one reporter affirmed that:

> the people of London displayed to the full the qualities that they do have. They took up the duty to their land in the 'decent and dauntless' spirit of which one American has spoken, and which, in the words of another, makes Englishmen, faced by emergency, 'melt into one family.' ... It has been shown something of what war means now that the air has become its chief theatre, and of the transformation that it enforces upon every branch of ordinary life.[44]

Others congratulated Britain for showing the Europe of dictators that "in the hour of crisis Britain was not found wanting."[45]

Perspectives that were more critical of the British response also appeared in the aftermath of September's crisis. The *Sunday Express* felt

---

[41] "Have You Found Out How to Use This Yet?" *Daily Mirror*, 28 Sept. 1938.
[42] "Siren Warnings Against Air Raids," *Times*, 29 Sept. 1938.
[43] "'Do It Now': Home Office Advice to Householders," *Times*, 29 Sept. 1938.
[44] "London in the Crisis," *Observer*, 2 Oct. 1938.
[45] "How the Country Faced the Prospect of War," *News of the World*, 2 Oct. 1938.

that the weeks of turmoil had indeed shown how ill-prepared Britain was
for war, commenting about ARP services that "rightly or wrongly, the citizens take the view that the gas masks they have been given are of doubtful value," let alone that the supply was limited. This article also took
the government to task for overlooking the most vulnerable members of
the population, noting that "no form of anti-gas protection was ready
for infant children up to four years of age."[46] As criticism of state efforts
emerged after the crisis, some press accounts not only castigated the government for the lack of masks and information, but also condemned some
civilian responses to ARP protective devices such as gas masks, using the
example of mothers who "looked on these vital protectors as an easy way
of amusing the children. In Notting Hill, children played with them in the
streets and were seen trying them on the dog."[47] The cultivation of the
proper attitude – the appropriate civil identity blending duty, calm, and
optimism – was not accomplished overnight.

Nonetheless, at the end of October, the changed atmosphere created
by the threat of war in September was evident in a brief article on a
drill conducted by the St. John Ambulance Brigade in a playground off
of Commercial Street in East London on 28 October. After two "smoke
bombs" were set off, nurses in gas masks flocked to aid those "scattered
on the ground," offering first aid in a "vivid picture of what may happen
during a bomb attack on London."[48] Such practices suggest a recognition that the Munich Agreement had granted a reprieve from, but not
a solution to, the coming air war against the civil population, including
children.

Popular culture also took ARP measures as a theme. One example of
this could be found in the pages of Jan Struther's popular column for the
Times, "Mrs. Miniver."[49] Mrs. Miniver – a privileged, highly domestic
and good-natured woman – provided an example of how to face a world
preparing its families for war. Struther's version of ARP Sunday finds

---

[46] "Where Were the Guns?" *Sunday Express*, 2 Oct. 1938
[47] "Huge A.R.P. Crisis Blunders," *Reynold's News*, 2 Oct. 1938.
[48] "Children 'Bombed,'" *Sunday Dispatch*, 29 Oct. 1938.
[49] Jan Struther's columns were then collected and published in book form in 1939. See Jan
Struther, *Mrs. Miniver* (1939, rpt. London, 1989). In her important critical study, *Forever
England*, Alison Light places *Mrs. Miniver*, the book, in the context of the domestic conservatism of the 1930s, but she, like others, pays scant attention to its foreshadowing of
war. Alison Light, *Forever England: Femininity, Literature and Conservatism between
the Wars* (London, 1991).

Mrs. Miniver waiting in line with her two young children, their nanny, cook and parlor maid, and reflecting on the stack of masks "covering the floor like a growth of black fungus." "It was for this ... that one had boiled the milk for their bottles, and washed their hands before lunch." The inability to protect one's children was part of what this new warfare would bring, and yet Struther pointed out through Mrs. Miniver that women also had the responsibility to guard against blind nationalism and hatred: "[T]hat was the most important of all the forms of war work which she and other women would have to do: there are no tangible gas masks to defend us in war-time against ... [the] slow, yellow, drifting corruption of the mind."[50] When the danger of imminent war was seemingly past, Mrs. Miniver recounted that while her family was "poorer by a few layers of security," it was nonetheless enriched by a sense of "looking at each other, and at their cherished possessions, with new eyes ... by a sudden clarifying of intentions."[51]

The crisis had also brought forward another new role for women that seemingly built upon their domestic and civic responsibilities: that of air raid wardens. Writing about this new task under the headline "Women's Work" in the *Star*, Sheila O'Callaghan made much of the fact that during the crisis "no woman warden has shown the slightest signs of nerves, hysterics or fainting." Instead, these women performed vital tasks, in addition to working regular jobs. O'Callaghan detailed how two women whom she interviewed spent the night assembling gas masks, then the next morning went to their retail or office jobs, and returned after work to help fit the masks. In other depots, she found women wardens hailing from "the stately homes in Grosvenor-square" similarly working through lunch breaks and committed to doing this bit of public service. She noted that their work would continue, as the wardens would have to make a round of visits to ensure that residents fully embraced ARP measures. O'Callaghan ended by praising the ability of women of different classes and ages to perform this work – "influence and moral persuasion go a long way in helping them to perform their duties successfully" – adding that "although women of all ages up to 70 are welcomed as recruits, no 'frivolous types' need apply." This message is perhaps belied by the fact that the photograph accompanying the article shows a women's ARP

---

[50] "The Minivers and Gas Masks: Thoughts in a Queue," *Times*, 28 Sept. 1938. This is also a chapter in Struther, *Mrs. Miniver*.
[51] "Back to Normal: The Afterthoughts of Mrs. Miniver," *Times*, 6 Oct. 1938. Also in Struther, *Mrs. Miniver*.

squad trying to fit a dog with a gas mask.[52] That said, publicity continued to extol the value of women's ARP work.[53]

Another consequence of the Munich crisis can be seen in more public debates about whether any ARP measures could really work in a true emergency. Home Office personnel themselves admitted that the nation was "unprepared" for the crisis and that one of the aims of both conventional and gas bombs was to destroy the "hearts and courage" of the people. ARP had to be seen not as a political statement but a necessity.[54] The Labour Party tried to pass a motion condemning the government for this admission in Parliament and was defeated, with Herbert Morrison calling the lack of adequate protection for civilians "tragic and wicked." Sir John Anderson, newly appointed as minister of civil defence, responded by affirming "his faith in the possibilities of voluntary organization under our democratic system – both for A.R.P. and for national service generally" but accepted that "there was an enormous inertia to be overcome."[55]

An early November article in the *New Statesman and Nation* turned to Mass Observation, the recently established organization to collect sociological information, for data on how the population was responding to the introduction of ARP schemes. It quoted a report from an unnamed female warden of what it took to be a troubling conversation among a group of wardens:

> Someone remarked sarcastically that he was sure that all the wardens who were supposed to be on duty at specified places would all be taking cover at home if there really was a raid. Far from being annoyed by this all the wardens agreed that that is just where they would be and that they all considered that their first duty was to their homes and families and that you could not do much good wandering round the streets anyway.

It described such "typical" attitudes as conveying that "our society was not in a position to take the strains of modern war," since neither ARP propaganda nor training had been able to "break down the ordinary

---

[52] Sheila O'Callaghan, "Women's Work," *Star*, 30 Sept. 1938.
[53] See "Women's Voluntary Services," *Times*, 21 Oct. 1938.
[54] See "Unpreparedness in A.R.P.," *Times*, 27 Oct. 1938. The official was C. W. G. Eday, deputy under-secretary of state, Home Office, speaking at the Royal United Services Institute.
[55] "A.R.P. in the Commons," *Times*, 4 Nov. 1938; and "Civil Defence and A.R.P.," *Times*, 4 Nov. 1938.

man's feeling that his home comes first."[56] Thus, in addition to "Calm" "Stout-heartedness," the ability to "avert panic" – non-gender-specific traits at the core of civilian identity during a new kind of war – came altruism and the ability to see beyond the protection of the individual home to that of both the local and national communities. This, then, was the larger notion of wartime civil identity that had to be forged. The article concluded by concurring with Sir John Anderson's earlier assertion that ARP could succeed only on a voluntary and not compulsory basis.[57]

The Munich Agreement was not taken as a decisive end to the threat of war, and ARP measures and public attention to them continued throughout the remainder of 1938. Trenches were not filled in, and October saw the launching of a massive call for ARP volunteers, including appeals made at football matches.[58] Letters to the editor of the *Times* demonstrated an acceptance of many of these changes. The deputy mayor of Hendon, Arthur Reynolds, wrote that the crisis had shown that "we must be forearmed with protection for the non-combatant.... [P]ermanent shelters and defences against attack from the air are as essential for the future as are our battleships." On the other hand, Lennox Russell of Surrey railed against the evacuation of "victims of dirt and vermin, of consumption, alcoholism and venereal disease," as well as criminals from the city and their forced imposition "on English homes." Russell proposed the creation of a kind of "civic passport" testifying that the bearer was not disqualified from taking refuge in such a home. The imposition of dirt and disorder from urban England to a rural ideal, too, was something that the government should be protecting its citizens from, according to Russell.[59]

The issue of government sponsored refugees and evacuation may have provoked outrage and consternation, but it could also become a cause for mirth. Harold Brighouse quickly penned "Air-Raid Refugees: A Face of the Crisis," which detailed the travails of an upper-middle-class couple, Arnold and Thisbe Watson, forced to cope with a string of refugees

---

[56] "Sociology of A.R.P.," *New Statesman and Nation*, 5 Nov. 1938.

[57] This was even more complicated when it came to the colonies – where assumptions about race and gender influenced debates about who could perform civil defense and under what circumstances.

[58] See "Completing the Defences," "A.R.P. Campaign This Week," and "A.R.P. Recruiting Campaign," *Times*, 1, 3, and 5 Oct. 1939.

[59] Arthur J. Reynolds, Letter to the editor, *Times*, 3 Oct. 1938; and Lennox Russell, Letter to the editor, *Times*, 6 Oct. 1938.

evacuated from danger zones who come to take shelter in their country cottage. When before their arrival Mrs. Watson tries to reassure her husband that the refugees would probably all be women, he churlishly comments, "This gets worse ... so my contribution to ... the crisis is to preside at a mothers' meeting in session for the duration." The refugee that the couple takes on instead is a criminal on the run – shades of Russell's fears above – and they experience endless aggravation. In the end, the couple decides to return to London, where "we shan't get anything worse than air-raids."[60]

In anticipation of the air raids that civilians would face, on 21 December 1938, Sir John Anderson, on behalf of the ARP Department of the Home Office, announced the government's plans for sheltering the civil population. He highlighted the imminent arrival of a new kind of household protection, a steel shelter that could offer "protection, *in their own homes*, of occupants of small houses against blast and splinters from bombs and falling debris from damaged buildings."[61] Under the heading "Home Air Raid Shelters," the *Times* elaborated on the scheme in January 1939, pointing out the advantages to a range of industries of the initial order for 400,000 of these shelters.[62] In the aftermath of the Munich crisis, the stakes were that much clearer; as Anderson elaborated: "[I]t was not sufficient to provide something which theoretically might give a certain degree of protection. They had to take into account the risk of panic."[63]

By the end of 1938, a two-part series in the *Times* was ready to assess the state of ARP. It began by stating that only at that moment was "A.R.P. policy ... catching up with public opinion" and reminding readers that "the official precautions effort is still only 10 months old." Given that, the flurry of activity since September had nearly resolved the problem of recruiting volunteers, while a sound evacuation and shelter policy remained to be worked out. Solving the one – evacuation – would also potentially alleviate the latter; once it was clear that vulnerable dependents like schoolchildren would be evacuated from London, the provisioning of shelters for the remaining population could be more easily addressed.

[60] Harold Brighouse, *Air-Raid Refugees: A Farce of the Crisis* (New York, 1939).

[61] See summation of this in the *Times*, 17 Jan. 1939. Emphasis added.

[62] "Home Air Raid Shelters," *Times*, 17 Jan. 1939. Criticism of these shelters began as soon as they were announced and continued throughout the fall of 1938 and into 1939. See "Half-Way Anderson," *New Statesman and Nation*, 31 Dec. 1938, and "Planned A.R.P.," *New Statesman and Nation*, 25 Mar. 1939.

[63] "A.R.P. After Munich," *Times*, 2 Mar. 1939.

The reporter criticized the prevailing view that "mask distribution is just a bluff to reassure people," pointing out not only that "it is better to be on the safe side" but, more important, that "no local authority can distribute gas masks without finding out the gaps in its organization." Thus did the distribution of masks serve as both the symbol and test of ARP. Despite obstacles and the need for a firmer sense of camaraderie among ARP workers, the article concluded on an optimistic note: "[T]his army of nearly 1,500,000 volunteers is an impressive example of the vitality of our traditions of public service in every class of the nation."[64] This quite explicitly validated the need not to coerce or militarize the population but to use cultural means to create and sustain a shared sense of responsibility, of obligation to the state – a new civil identity – in the face of shared danger.

The difficulties, perhaps, of evoking this sense of shared duty can be seen in the irate response to one piece of ARP recruitment propaganda in January 1939. At the annual conference of the National Union of Women Teachers, Mrs. Fisher, the Union's vice president, complained about placards displayed in London that claimed "it was a man's job." She continued: "A man was shown as a fine, healthy, and strong specimen. But there was a placard with a woman on it. The woman looked depressed; she had a pale face and lank hair, and looked like a refugee." The image was "an insult to the women of the country, and should be taken away."[65] The aim of such posters was to recruit men, of course, by showing that there was nothing unmanly about ARP, but in this case it seemed to have alienated precisely the type of women that the government was eager to have volunteer.

A further sign perhaps of the uneven efforts at ARP outreach was evident in the February 1939 contest to provide a "name" for the ARP sanctioned steel-roofed, earth-fortified backyard refuges announced in December of the previous year. Handwritten on postcards, a flurry of entries mainly played off the initials "ARP" – suggestions along these lines included calling them "arps" or "ark angels" or "Arcaids," spelled

[64] "A.R.P. To-day: I. The Symbol of the Gas Mask," and "A.R.P. To-day: II. The Active North," *Times*, 19 and 20 Dec. 1938.
[65] "A.R.P. Poster as Insult to Women," *Times*, 4 Jan. 1939. One aim of ARP propaganda was to make this work desirable for men and women. Posters asked them to choose between "Chaos" and "Security," and one depicted a large man with a shield labeled "ARP" sheltering a cowering woman and child above the motto "Serve to Save," appealing to the more traditional male's wartime role of safeguarding passive dependents by his active efforts. See poster by Frank Gardner, "Serve to Save," IWM, Department of Art, PST 0720.

FIGURE 10.3. A family carrying gas masks enters their Anderson shelter during a drill, c. 1939. Hulton Archive. Reproduced by permission of Getty Images.

"Arkaids" as well or, even more popularly, "arks" – some amplifying that this evoked the story of Noah and the sense of refuge, and others adding that the initials in ARK could stand for "Air Raid Kiosk" or "Air Raid Kover," with a "K." A variety of suggestions incorporated the idea of the "umbrella" – that tidy and ubiquitous item of British life – turned now into such phrases as "Chambrella" (from Chamberlain and umbrella), "Umbombellas," "Gunbrella," "Tinbrellas," or "Steelbrella." Other proposals included "Air Haven," "Bunkholes," "Stealaways," "Divin (dive ins)," "Panicure," "Hideout," "Jitterbox," "Wardens," "Goodintent (good tin tent)," and "Cromwells because they are protectors." A final set of proposed names linked the shelters with Sir John Anderson as the public figure most associated with their development. These included "Jimmies," "Johnsons," "Andechambers," "Undersons," "Andeshel," "[H]andy Hut," "Handy," and "Andies" or "Andy" (because "also they will be so 'andy for housing the chickens").[66] In the end, as

---

[66] See postcards for ARP shelter competition, Feb. 1939, in Mass Observation Archives (henceforth MOA), TC 55.

we saw earlier, they became known as "Andersons". As most of the suggestions sent in to this contest indicate, it was a name associated with the public figure most identified with ARP – Sir John Anderson – but came from one of the three engineers – David Anderson – who had designed it for the government. The extent to which such shelters could be used or even could prove useful remained to be dealt with in the next piece of ARP legislation.

CIVIL DEFENSE IN 1939

The international situation worsened in the spring of 1939 with Germany's rapid violation of the Munich Agreement in March. This caused many to predict the outbreak of war in the near future and to put into action the further expansion of ARP. Even while these policies were being anticipated and enacted, the extent to which British civilians accepted the measures that sought to contain fear and domesticate the aerial threat remained unknown. In an effort to gauge popular reaction, Mass Observation conducted surveys on ARP while the government was preparing a Civil Defence Bill. For instance, a series of questions posed to residents of Fulham in March 1939 asked respondents to evaluate local efforts and their own intentions regarding taking part in ARP work as volunteers. Most declared some variation of "I haven't thought that much about it" when asked about local ARP work, and as for volunteering, few expressed any great enthusiasm.[67] ARP had not yet engaged much of the population.

Responding to the increased likelihood of war after March, the government quickly debated and passed a further elaboration of the many measures, including the provision of shelters, which would be required to protect civilians in the event of war. Parliamentary debates over the Civil Defence Bill in April 1939 were, perhaps understandably, less intense than those that accompanied the Air Raids Precautions Bill of 1937. Indeed, as Sir John Anderson put it when introducing this legislation in the Commons, it was a bill reflecting "the anxious times in which we live" with provisions that might be regarded as "quite intolerable in normal times" but not under present circumstances. Anderson emphasized the voluntary nature of many of the provisions of this legislation, which sought to "capitalize [on] the great volume of good will and readiness to collaborate which exists in all sections of the community.... We

---

[67] Survey in Fulham, 25 March 1939, "What Do You Think of Local A.R.P.?" MOA, reel 118, part 1.

aim at defining duties, and by offering guidance, and where necessary financial assistance, to make it as easy as possible for those concerned to carry out their duties." By focusing on the "business as usual" and voluntary rather than coercive aim of ARP, Anderson insisted that this was not a bill about "war-time powers"; rather it was "concerned solely with powers required in normal times if, indeed, these may be called normal times."[68] Like appeals to volunteer for ARP work, this stressed that it was a job for all.

The bill regularized governmental responsibility for all ARP measures. It delegated some to the Ministry of Health; endowed local authorities with further powers, including the right to requisition space to prepare public shelters and first aid posts; obliged employers to provide shelter in factories or places of business – turning this from a "moral" to a "legal" necessity; provided rules concerning household (backyard) steel shelters; put forward ARP measures that public utilities would have to adopt; and elaborated procedures for the blackout and evacuation.[69] Debate over the bill began with criticism that it had taken the government so long to enact this vital legislation, as well as concern with the haste with which the bill was now being put forward.[70] Herbert Morrison, for example, also made reference to the context of the debate, another week of "days of anxiety" for the British people, one in which they exhibited less calm than they had during the crisis of September 1938. If the aim of dictators was to coerce governments that opposed them by threatening, "Bend to my will or I will bomb your civilian population," the only correct response of their government was "to stand up and tell them to go to the devil. But they will find it difficult to do that if in fact the civilian population feel that they have no effective protection from enemy aircraft."[71] Thus were effective shelters, which Britain currently lacked, according to Morrison, as vital to meeting the challenge of facing down dictators and fascism as any branch of the military. This once again elevated the protection of the home and the family within it to the level of military defense measures in waging war.

---

[68] Sir John Anderson (Lord Privy Seal), *Parliamentary Debates – Commons*, 4 Apr. 1939, vol. 345, cols. 2633–2634.

[69] See Sir John Anderson (Lord Privy Seal), *Parliamentary Debates – Commons*, 4 Apr. 1939, vol. 345, cols. 2633–2653, where he presents the bill to Commons on its second reading. See also the Civil Defence Bill 1939, parts I–IX, *Parliamentary Papers* (1939).

[70] See the comments of Herbert Morrison, *Parliamentary Debates – Commons*, 4 Apr. 1939, vol. 345, cols. 2654–2666.

[71] Herbert Morrison, *Parliamentary Debates – Commons*, 4 Apr. 1939, vol. 345, col. 2667.

One subject of heated discussion during debates over the bill remained the issue of what sort of shelter could be offered to all. The Anderson shelter would, in the words of Sir Percy Harris, be appropriate in "the backyards of the smaller houses in suburbs and places where the houses are scattered" but not in "towns like London, Liverpool and Manchester." How were such urban dwellers to be protected? Was the only solution "deep shelters," and how were these to be constructed and maintained? The seeming lack of concern over the urban population, short of evacuation, agitated many involved in the debate. A further criticism of the proposed shelter policy invoked the lessons of Spain and even of the First World War, asserting that the lack of protection against the noise of continual night bombing was something that the government needed to consider:

> [W]hen we remember the large numbers of people who during the War suffered from shell shock and other kinds of shock, and whose lives were completely shattered by it, and when we remember also that one of the main purposes of aerial bombardment is to break the resisting power of the civil population, we must count this shock which will inevitably come as a very definite element against which some kind of protection must be provided, but certainly is not provided by what is called the Anderson shelter.

Evacuation policy would not resolve this problem completely, as dense urban and industrial areas, such as Coventry and Greater London, would surely be targets of such attacks.[72]

The government plan to have employers provide shelters for factory workers was challenged for unrealistically assuming that women workers would not want to be with their families when attacks came. According to Sir Ralph Glyn, representatives of factory women "all said, with one voice, that the first thing that they wanted to do was to run home and see if their families were all right." A factory filled with such workers engaged in work of national importance needed a solution other than the mere provision of onsite shelters for workers. This echoed concerns voiced in the course

---

[72] Sir Percy Harris, *Parliamentary Debates – Commons*, 4 Apr. 1939, vol. 345, col 2671. For further criticism of the shelter policy, see Miss Lloyd George, cols. 2817–2822; quote is from col. 2818. For other MPs who brought up the issue of deep shelters, see Sir Arthur Salter, cols. 2835–2838; Sir Robert Tasker, cols. 2851–2852; Mr. Ridley, col. 2854. See further questions on this issue from Morrison, col. 2864. For an overview of the public criticism of the shelter policy in the late 30s, which this debate echoes, see Joseph S. Meisel, "Air Raid Shelter Policy and Its Critics in Britain before the Second World War," *20th Century British History* 5:3 (1994), 300–319.

of planning these measures about the special problem of how women, and especially women with children, would respond. Glyn also spoke of the value of training everyone to respond to raids, calling "remarkable" and "amazing" the way "in which workers of both sexes" had already immersed themselves in such things as learning basic first aid.[73]

Other members of Parliament were even more explicit about the need to rely on "the spirit of the people" in a war to come. Leading Labour politician Arthur Greenwood asserted that "our Maginot line was ... our system of Civil Defence. The new factor of terror from the air means that, as in all war, it is the spirit of the people that in the last resort makes victory possible." The danger was that "this Bill has not yet provided the people of this country with the outlines of a scheme adequate to meet what may fall upon this country at any moment." Recalling September 1938, when, in his view, there was "panic," Greenwood was confident that the people – especially of his native Yorkshire – "will be brave when the hour comes, but they are deserving of a good deal more adequate protection" than the government had hitherto provided.[74] That the spirit of the people would respect the need to take particular care of certain categories of people was asserted by Elliot, on behalf of the government: "I hope that the phrase 'women and children first,' with which we are all familiar in times of danger, will be accepted by the people as a whole."[75] Elliot referred directly to evacuation plans and the fear of "self-evacuation" disrupting more official measures, but the implication for the entirety of civil defense shows the ongoing tension over the whole civil defense scheme. On the one hand, appeals had to be made to a transcendent civic participant, and on the other, the specific requirements of those deemed most in need of protection – by gender or age – contradicted this overarching message.

Despite the criticism of the delay in and inadequacy of the government's proposals, the bill passed by a comfortable margin. Whatever the scope of the powers that it now granted the state and whatever its limits in terms of not specifying how all members of the civil population would gain access to equal measures of security, the government had established the ARP program that it would take into the war. This indicated that even if times were not, as Anderson suggested, "normal," the expectation that air raids would come was seen as such.

[73] Sir Ralph Glyn, *Parliamentary Debates – Commons*, 4 Apr. 1939, vol. 345, cols. 2824–2825.

[74] Arthur Greenwood, *Parliamentary Debates – Commons*, 4 Apr. 1939, vol. 345, cols. 2855–2856. As we saw earlier, the news media for the most part insisted on the calm and cheerfulness with which Britons faced the crisis.

[75] Elliot, *Parliamentary Debates – Commons*, 4 Apr. 1939, vol. 345, col. 2875.

DO IT NOW: ARP AT WAR

The Second World War began on 1 September 1939; the collapse of the Munich Agreement and mounting tension over German claims to Poland increased the preparations for war, including those for the civil population up until the war's outbreak. While the early months of the war gave rise to the phrase "Blitzkrieg," or "lightning war," to describe the rapidity of the German conquest of Poland, the term "Blitz" as a way to refer to aerial bombardment and particularly to the aerial attacks on Britain would not emerge until nearly a year later. The period between September 1939 and May 1940 came to be known as the "Phony War," as both Allied civilians and combatants mobilized for a conflict that remained, for the moment, geographically removed. In particular, the attempted aerial knockout blow, which ARP planners had anticipated as *the* initial step in a new war, failed to materialize. Nonetheless, the government sought both to assure the civil population that everything was being done for their safety and to urge them to remain vigilant and calm.

As war came closer, the government hastened its efforts to spread information about ARP through a variety of channels. A new wave of literature from both official and unofficial sources appeared in the summer of 1939, most stressing "everyone has now a part to play, and national security depends on the willingness and ability to play it correctly."[76] As had been discussed fairly early on among ARP planners, one popular means to spread the word and offer guidance was through the cinema. By August 1939, the GPO Film Unit of the Home Office had produced a short instructional film, *If War Should Come*. By the time the film was ready for release, war had come. So in September 1939, the film unit put forward *Do It Now*, virtually identical to *If War Should Come*, save for an altered introduction and the inclusion, at the end, of text from Prime Minister Chamberlain's September declaration of war.[77]

---

[76] William F. Deedes, "A.R.P.: A Complete Guide to Civil Defence Measures" (London, 1939), 5. Deedes was described as the ARP correspondent from the *Daily Telegraph*, which issued the leaflet in August. See also S. Evelyn Thomas, *Handy War-Time Guide for the Woman at Home and the Man in the Street* (St. Albans, [1939]), and the official Public Information Leaflets from the Office of the Lord Privy Seal issued in July 1939, including "Some Things You Should Know if War Should Come," "Your Gas Mask: How to keep It and How to Use It," "Your Food in Wartime," and "Fire Precautions in Wartime," as well as its *Air Raid Precautions* (London, 1939).

[77] See *If War Should Come* (1939) and *Do It Now* (1939). All references in the text are to the latter; both films held as COI 849 and COI 850, respectively, in the IWM, Film and Video Archive.

Do It Now begins with a narrator putting on a steel helmet, with a warden's armband and the strap of his gas mask case across his uniform, stating firmly that "now war has come, things appearing in the film as possibilities are now facts and the film intended as a warning for the future becomes advice for the present, advice to be heard and taken here and now." At both its start and conclusion, a single line encapsulates the message of the film: "No one in this country wants war"; nonetheless, "don't be alarmed, keep a good heart, Britain is a nation prepared." The film intersperses scenes in which the only sound is the music of Elgar with a narrative consisting almost entirely of declarative statements such as "Do so at once," "Avoid panic buying," "Have buckets of water and sand on every landing," and "Do not be alarmed by noise in an air raid." It is the visual elements accompanying such messages that give the film its resonance. Shot in recognizable parts of London, from the city center to residential areas, the film shows ordinary folks – young and old, men and women – enacting civil defense calmly and orderly. For example, the construction of a backyard shelter is depicted as a family affair and as no more strenuous than a bit of gardening. While a matter-of-fact voice intones, "First, dig a pit four feet deep," "Dad" is seen shoveling in his shirt sleeves. As layers of corrugated metal are placed across the pit, the whole family pitches in, dappled in sunlight – mother, son, daughter – all helping to pile dirt against its walls.

A few types of bad behavior shown by wealthy and frivolous women – to comic effect – underscore the heroic actions of the others depicted in the film. The first woman wears furs and pearls and seems completely flustered as she harasses a shop clerk to provide her with ever more tinned goods; she illustrates the opposite of the instruction "Avoid panic buying." Later, when warning viewers not to misuse the telephone, which might be needed for vital communications, the film shows a young woman eating chocolates and obliviously chatting away. In contrast, when the narrator intones, "Always keep your gas mask handy in the house; never go out without it," we see a feminine hand clearing a space for a gas mask box beside a framed photograph on top of a desk. When the well-dressed middle-aged (and middle-class) woman goes out her front door, her gas mask box dangles beside her handbag. While informing the audience about how to respond to air raid warnings and warnings of a gas attack, the film shows a woman efficiently putting on her mask and a mother quickly leading her daughter (both in masks) to the previously constructed backyard shelter. Subtly but unmistakably – given the lack of men behaving badly – the film delivers a message primarily to women of the significance of their role and their assumption of responsibility for civil defense.

Indeed, in one of the few instances in which the images belie the calm narration, we hear a voice commanding, "Do not be alarmed by noise in an air raid, much of it will be the noise of our own guns." Yet the close-up of a woman in a gas mask, shadowed against a backdrop of corrugated steel (the inside of the garden shelter), reveals a face far more anxious than serene. Again, this contrasts with the scene documenting what to do when a gas attack is over – signaled by the ringing of what looks like a handbell – when the mother and daughter seen earlier emerge from the shelter and take off their masks. The images that close the film – of "Britain prepared" – are sweeping vistas of the city and then of a factory, an office, a shipyard, and a farm. Across occupation, class, region, and gender, the implication is clear: ARP will work so long as people (all civilians) "keep a good heart."

When war broke out in September 1939, many in Britain did not need the bombs to start falling on British soil to condemn the savagery of the war. On 3 September 1939, Elaine Cheverton reflected in her diary that "for the second time in 25 years, men will fight with a barbarity that hundreds of years of 'civilisation' has only made a hundred times worse."[78] Vera Brittain, who had spent the interwar period as an active feminist and peace campaigner, wrote in response to the outbreak of war that "we may weep for ourselves as individuals. Not one of us now is free from peril. As husbands, as wives, as parents, as children, we must bear the intolerable burden of unceasing apprehension, not only for those on the battlefield, but for one another."[79] That this would be a devastating war upon civilians was in no doubt.

A few months after the official outbreak of war, an editorial in the literary periodical *Life and Letters To-day* commented on the "strangeness" of this new type of war:

> War is waged, no longer by surprising the enemy, but by gradually accustoming him to a strangeness, which he must finally accept as the

---

[78] IWM, Department of Documents, Papers of E P Cheverton (02/26/1), Elaine P. Cheverton, Diary, 3 Sept. 1939.

[79] Vera Brittain, "Lift Up Your Hearts," *Peace News*, 8 Sept. 1939; reprinted in *Testament of a Generation: The Journalism of Vera Brittain and Winifred Holtby*, ed. Paul Berry and Alan Bishop (London, 1985). Brittain would continue to write as a "peace lover" during the war, notably an account of England under fire, *England's Hour* (London, 1941). In 1944, she published one of the most devastating critiques of the Allied aerial bombardment of Germany, "Seeds of Chaos: What Mass Bombing Really Means," (London, 1944).

normal order of things. War came because for years we had been put under a process of accustoming ourselves to it.... The hurried distribution of gas-masks last September caused consternation; this year far more startling measures were accepted calmly.[80]

Authorities and individuals alike worried about how the ordinary folk facing this strange type of war – primed for terror or action but not experiencing either – would adapt when the bombs fell.

In order to assess this, the government and Mass Observation launched inquiries into popular reactions to civil defense. In October 1939, Mass Observation issued a study based on interviews with 980 adults from Fulham in London and Bolton in Lancashire in order to determine how well the public had absorbed the lessons imparted by ARP propaganda. It found little difference between the understanding of working- and middle-class people about basic measures to deal, for instance, with incendiary bombs that fell on a home. Most respondents had little knowledge about everything from air raid sirens to blackouts; their feelings about any ARP measures, however, were not revealed.[81] As a sign of further concern about attitudes toward the war, in December 1939 the Civil Defence Committee presented a draft report to the War Cabinet on "the attitude of the Public towards Civil Defence Preparedness." The report began with the statement that since the outbreak of war, there had been a "deterioration in morale" that had to be counteracted. It suggested that this had occurred because the government had prepared for a devastating aerial blow – particularly against London – at the outset of war. Presumably since this had not in fact taken place, the public was confused as to how to respond. The report outlined the three methods chosen to address aerial warfare: dispersal of the vulnerable population through evacuation; protections such as blackouts and shelters; and services to deal with damages after the raids. Insisting that all such measures were important, the report admitted that "the common knowledge proved wrong in the matter of timing ... [and] has undoubtedly tended to unsettle the public mind." The true danger was that the "populace ... [now] regard the possibility of large scale and indiscriminate air attack as remote."[82]

The report continued that the government had to be wary of those who used the "numerous disagreeable restrictions and prohibitions" associated

[80] *Life and Letters To-day*, Nov. 1939.
[81] "A.R.P. Instructions: The Public Information Leaflets," 18 Oct. 1939, MOA.
[82] Civil Defence Committee, "Draft Report to the War Cabinet on the Attitude of the Public towards Civil Defence Preparedness," [Dec. 1939], TNA HO 186/371.

with ARP to encourage a relaxing of these standards or even to challenge the continuation of the war itself – singling out the Communists' "Stop the War" campaign in this regard. The committee thus urged "a vigorous bracing up of public opinion" and the need to sustain all aspects of the war effort. It recommended that someone – preferably the prime minister – "make it clear that the whole defence policy is based on the assumption that sooner or later this country may be subjected to heavy air attack" and must remain vigilant and ready.[83]

When the War Cabinet discussed the report on 21 December, it suggested the issuing of a public declaration that "an examination of all the factors involved had led to the conclusion that there was no case for modifying the policy previously adopted." The air minister was adamant that measures had to continue, given that there was "no assurance that they [heavy air attacks] could be completely prevented." The "spirit of false optimism" engendered by the lack of actual attacks to date had to be countered; a notable lack of enthusiasm for the shelter program was indicated, as was the return of most of the children who had been evacuated from northern towns and about a third of the children from London.[84]

Some of the work of keeping the public informed and inspired for action came through the instructions in booklet and book form that ARP officials continued to produce and distribute. The 1939, second edition of the "concise, fully illustrated and practical guide" to ARP was even more explicit than earlier versions about the stakes of such preparation: "[O]ur security as a nation may depend on the security of the home.... [T]herefore it is the common sense duty of every householder or head of a family ... to learn now how to protect his own people and himself in war time."[85] This was far from a gender-inclusive sense of ownership; appeals and instructions to "households" implicitly assumed that such households were headed by men and included women and children in need of protection.

Later versions of instructions to homeowners undergirded the emerging gendered division of labor and pointed out the significant roles to be played by those quintessential civilians, "women and children." This can be found notably in other ARP guides, such as the "Handy War-

---

[83] Civil Defence Committee, "Draft Report to the War Cabinet on the Attitude of the Public towards Civil Defence Preparedness."

[84] War Cabinet 121 (39), Meeting, 21 Dec. 1939, TNA HO 186/371.

[85] E. J. Hodsoll, "Introduction," *Air Raid Precautions: A Concise, Fully Illustrated and Practical Guide*, 2d ed. (London, 1939).

Time Guide for the Woman at Home and the Man in the Street," which
began as follows:

> War conditions in the past have been nothing like those that now con-
> front us....
>
> [A] nation's safety and success in war now depend very much on the
> safety of the home and on the courage and co-operation of those who
> have to carry on with their daily round of common tasks. When enemy
> attacks can reach our very homes, ultimate victory is no longer only a
> matter of arms and of men. It is also a matter of women and even of
> children. Victory or defeat may depend ultimately on the steps we have
> taken to protect our homes and our families, on the way in which we
> tackle our domestic problems and discipline ourselves to face the perils
> that may beset us.[86]

Instructions on home defense proposed turning homes into shelters so
as to reassure the population that everything was being done for victory
and that even their "passive" defense was a kind of resistance. Manuals
continued not only to offer instructions for finding a secure space within
the home – in a cellar or beneath stairs – but also to list "essential items"
to be placed in a "small inner refuge or shelter of concrete or steel." These
included, in addition to such obvious practical items as adequate supplies
of water and tinned foods, things like "flasks for hot tea, coffee ... or an
electric kettle" and "books, cards, toys." The implicit idea that one would
need entertainment in a refuge did little to obscure the larger intent of
these handbooks.[87] To wit, "the civilian's best weapons against air attack
are intelligent foresight and preparedness, and full *confidence* in all forms
of protection."[88] Confidence in ARP measures, like morale, proved tricky
to measure, especially where the individual aspects of protection were
concerned: home-based or backyard shelters and gas masks. The longer
the phony war endured, complete with media coverage of damage overseas but not in Britain, the more lax the civil population appeared to
become.

   For example, if the construction of a shelter were to be treated as a
private and homebound act, the state then took on the role of instructor
trying to ensure that "A.R.P. in each home" could become a reality. Yet
once the Andersons were made available, how did the civilians meant to
be reassured as much as protected by them respond? Writing from her

---

[86] Thomas, *Handy War-Time Guide*, 3.
[87] *Air Raid Precautions*, 33.
[88] Hodsoll, "Introduction," 1. Emphasis added.

home in Bromley, Kent, Mrs. R. G. Cottrell described her preparations for a domestic shelter in August 1939 as consisting as yet of only "a series of deep holes" in the backyard. With the actual declaration of war on 1 September, she noted that she was now "steadily preparing and finishing our gas proof room, getting blankets down" and otherwise following the instructions designed to make her and her family feel safe at home. This included foraging to find "planks of wood" for seats in the interior of the Anderson being constructed in the yard; although by October, she was noting that the "trench" fills with water and, during warnings, "Mum much prefers to stay indoors."[89] Nellie Carver had voiced similar sentiments in her diary in August, noting that "Mum doesn't want us to have an Anderson in the garden.... [B]etter to be bombed in the warm than to get pneumonia."[90] It was mothers in these accounts who resisted leaving home to take shelter anywhere else, even that extension of domestic space and presumably feminine domain, the back garden. The reasons may well have been practical ones, but the emotional implications seem evident as well.

George Britton, a resident of Walthamstow, expressed a similar sense of female heads of households resisting the Anderson but offered a more cynical take on the feelings elicited by the new shelters. As he wrote to his daughter in August 1939:

> Our aid-raid shelter arrived yesterday and made Mother feel quite ill for a time, but she has quite got over it now. Yesterday and to-day three men are in the garden digging a hole three feet deep to put it in. My personal opinion is that the whole performance is merely a dodge to put the population in a complacent vein and so save them getting out of hand.[91]

Britton's sense of the ultimate futility of such gestures was echoed by his wife. Her subsequent letter to their daughter describing the arrival of the shelter amplified some of this skepticism:

> It took 3 men from Friday midday till 5:30 from 7:30 next morning till 12:30 then Monday morning, it did one good to hear the views of those

[89] IWM, Department of Documents, Papers of R G Cottrell (04/40/1), See R. G. Cottrell, Letters to Patricia, 30 Aug. 1939, 1 Sept. 1939, 3 Sept. 1939, 10 Sept. 1939, and 25 October 1939.
[90] IWM, Department of Documents, Papers of N V Carver (90/16/1), N. V. Carver, Diary, 28–31 Aug. 1939.
[91] IWM, Department of Documents, Papers of G Britton (Con Shelf), George Britton, Letter to Florence Britton Elkus, 12 Aug. 1939.

men, they talked of the different MP's who had interests in the firms
who made the shelters.[92]

Once war was officially under way in September, it found Mrs. Emmerson
describing Edinburgh, where shelters were "now being placed in almost
every available open spot. There are no parks or gardens left unspoiled
by these refuge huts." She noted in particular some neighbors who had
"their own air-raid shelter in the back yard, and so each night they have
their clothing in readiness as the shelters are deep and damp!"[93] After all,
the Anderson was, fundamentally, a fortified hole in the back garden and,
as such, a reminder that war would come home.

Whether reflecting the reluctance to make use of these structures, their
failure to alleviate anxiety, or their inherent lack of comfort, photographic
images of Andersons – whether interior or exterior shots and whether
found in the mass media or government-issued instructions – highlighted
their *domestic* as much as *protective* aspects, their aesthetics as much as
function. The Ministry of Home Security's popular and oft-reprinted *Air
Raids: What You Must Know, What You Must Do!* featured a photograph of "a completed Anderson shelter" that blended almost completely
into the landscape. It was covered by plants and grass, and only the corrugated doorway hinted that this was a manmade structure at all, let
alone a space for a family to take refuge from indiscriminate bombing
against the civil population. Many wartime images depicted the Anderson
in a similarly tranquil, rural mode. Publicity photographs, for instance,
showed a family happily entering their shelter; another featured a woman
watering the garden growing atop the family's backyard shelter. In shots
of an Anderson's interior, calm domesticity prevailed. A photo taken for
the *Daily Mirror* in 1940 shows a Mrs. Shepherd in Kent with her seven
children in a double Anderson shelter; the children are all tucked in and
their mother reads to them.[94] Such images contrasted sharply with the
military purpose of these shelters, but at least they showed the population
making use of them.

---

[92] IWM, Department of Documents, Papers of G Britton (Con Shelf), Helena Britton, Letter
to Florence Britton Elkus, 22 Aug. 1939.

[93] IWM, Department of Documents, Papers of G Emmerson (67/289/1), Mrs. G Emmerson,
Letter to Margaret and Wirt, Sept. 28, 1939. She noted that she would rather "take my
chance outside, but they [shelters] are supposed to give protection." Her journey to the
United States was interrupted when her ship, *Athenia*, was torpedoed.

[94] Photo labeled *Daily Mirror*, IWM Photography Archives (henceforth PA) ZZZ 9182C;
garden photo, IWM PA HU 63827A.

The widespread distribution of gas masks was also accompanied by messages stressing that the masks would serve no useful purpose if not in the constant possession of their owners, who might be caught in a gas attack at any moment. During the Phony War from September 1939 through the spring of 1940, Mass Observation conducted a survey of "gas mask carrying" to determine the extent to which Britons of all ages and in all locations took seriously this aspect of ARP. It tried to establish who was likely to do so, when, and why, thus attempting to trace the rise and fall of its use during this period. An initial report from London on 4 September 1939 noted that of one hundred men and one hundred women observed, sixty-two men and seventy-one women carried their masks; breaking this down by age, forty-seven men older than forty but only fifteen women in the same age cohort had masks with them. The tendency of women and of younger women in particular to be more likely to carry masks remained notable, although a marked drop-off occurred as the war continued without air raids taking place. An overview in May 1940 summarized the previous eight months, noting that gas mask carrying rose steadily, peaking at about 6 September 1939, when two-thirds of the population consistently (and visibly) carried their masks with them. This fell to 50 percent in October and 33 percent in November, reaching about 10 percent in mid-January and falling well below 5 percent in March. Not until the news of the invasion of Holland and Belgium reached the country in May did the carrying of masks rise to about 20 percent of the observed population, according to these records.[95] Even the commencement of heavy raids pushed gas mask carrying up to only 35 percent by late September 1940.[96] Maintaining the appropriate actions (such as obeying strictures always to have one's gas mask), let alone the correct emotions (calm and fortitude), required by civilians facing indiscriminate bombardment would also prove challenging once aerial warfare did return to Britain in 1940.

UNDER FIRE AGAIN

As we have clearly seen throughout this book, from the First World War on, there was little the government could forcibly do to control the responses, practical as well as emotional, of the civilian population to being under attack. Careful instructions about "how" to behave were one

[95] Gas Mask Carrying Report, 28 May 1940, MOA, TC 55, box 2, file A.
[96] Gas Mask Carrying Report, 17 Sept. 1940, MOA, TC 55, file A, box 2.

thing, individual reactions quite another. Nonetheless, from the Great War forward, a main aim of all official and many unofficial endeavors was to minimize panic and shore up civilian morale. The diversity of experiences and the tension between the projected ideal of a unified domestic front of a rock-steady nation and the range of individual responses have been explored in many recent accounts of Second World War Britain, but most have not highlighted the continuity between the two air wars.[97] Both public and personal reactions to the return of aerial bombardment clearly echo the voices of the First World War discussed in Chapters 2 and 3.

The tone of press coverage describing the onslaught of aerial attacks in September 1940 is starkly reminiscent of that of the First World War. A headline quoted the official communiqué describing the "Blind Savagery of Night Attacks" and informed Londoners of the damage that had been inflicted upon the city in the raids of the first week of September and of the ability of its citizens to meet such barbarity with "admirable courage and resource."[98] On 20 September, the *Times* spoke of London carrying on its daily life despite "destruction wrought by the blind and wanton night attacks of German bombers," pointing out that the bombs had fallen on "humble suburban homes" and "a maternity hospital." Reports of attacks on Merseyside focused on the heartrending story of a four-month-old who survived in a drawer for twenty-five hours amid the wreckage of a home where the rest of the family had been killed by falling debris.[99] Once again, the media focuses on showing a stricken population what sort of enemy it faces: one that wages savage aerial warfare wantonly on innocence – on humble homes and infants being born. Once more, calm, failure to panic, perseverance, and sacrifice will enable Britain to survive. The scale is new, but so too are the measures that have been put in place to prepare for air raids.

[97] Rose, *Which People's War?*; Calder, *The Myth of the Blitz*; Helen Jones, *British Civilians in the Front Line: Air Raids, Productivity and Wartime Culture, 1939–45* (Manchester, 2006). For an account of how the Second World War allowed for the enactment of the antipathy to the kind of civil identity being called for in public, see Donald Thomas, *An Underworld at War: Spivs, Deserters, Racketeers and Civilians in the Second World War* (London, 2003).

[98] "'Blind Savagery' of Night Attacks," *Times*, 10 Sept. 1940. Unlike the situation during the First World War, separate articles praised the work of civil defense, and readers were reminded of the importance of their refusal "to be rattled by these deliberate attempts to lower their spirit and fray their nerves." This claim could be made at the outset, quite unlike what occurred during the First World War. On the preceding day, the *Times* had discussed the "indiscriminate bombing" of the raids of September 7 and 8.

[99] See "Damage in East and West End," "Wanton Attacks on Houses," and "Heavy Raid on Merseyside," *Times*, 20 Sept. 1940.

One notable difference between the air raids of the First and Second World Wars lies in the type of media that conveyed the devastating effects of air power and the stoicism with which raids were faced. Short newsreel films like *London Can Take It* showed Londoners carrying on with daily life as well as heroically fighting fires and coping with the aftermath of destruction. After scanning a line of men, women, and children waiting patiently to take shelter, the film's narrator intones, "Do you see any fear on these faces?"[100] This is clearly a rhetorical question. If the aim of air power was to "terrorize," then to admit to terror was to concede victory, but fear was understandably rampant, and the measures that the government had provided could do only so much to alleviate anxiety.

As ARP planners eventually decided, the evacuation of children was intended both to reassure parents and to remove "bouches inutiles" from more likely danger zones. A few days into the Battle of Britain, a mother and father in East London were writing to relatives in Kent asking them to let their children come and stay:

> We are writing on behalf of our children for whose safety we feel most anxious, due to the recent happenings here in the way of air raids. It is our intention to get them, at least temporarily, out of London.... This week-end wouldn't be any too soon to get them away from here. Only those living here can tell what it is like.[101]

And what those in London told about their experiences reflected their central perception that this war was against civilians. Writing to his sisters in the United States in mid-September 1940, sixty-three-year-old Melville Preston Troy began:

> This is not a gentlemen's war. I think I would perfer the old chivalrous kind, when a commander arriving on the field and finding the enemy not yet in battle array waited for them to line up before he attacked.[102]

This resonates with Helena Swanwick's interwar remarks that air power's attacks on women and children meant that there was no longer anything chivalrous about war. Under bombardment, Troy reaches a similar conclusion, noteworthy, moreover, because it indicates a change from a letter dated 22 August describing the searchlights and occasional flashes in the

---

[100] *London Can Take It* (1940).

[101] IWM, Department of Documents, Papers of E A Wood (05/33/1), Mr. and Mrs. Wood, Letter to Mrs. Wood, 11 Sept. 1940.

[102] IWM, Department of Documents, Papers of M P Troy (95/25/1), Melville Preston Troy, Letter to Allah Balfour Troy [eldest sister], 16 Sept. 1940. Spelling left uncorrected.

sky: "[N]o aurora borealis or music of the spheres could have afforded a more magnificent entertainment, although they might have been appreciated more."[103] Once bombs began to fall, the entertainment value of the "ungentlemanly" war waged on London dropped significantly.

Melville Troy was old enough to have lived through the raids of the First World War and contextualized a press cutting of a Londoner sleeping through a raid that he enclosed with his letter as follows:

> [T]he reason I cut it out is that this is the same station where we took refuge in the first daylight raid in the last war. We were on top of a bus in the Strand, with Corona then three years old, when we looked up and saw the sky full of airplanes, and hurried across the street (with shaking knees I must confess) to the Aldwich station.
>
> We are not yet immune to such sensations, though somewhat hardened.[104]

If the first raids induced knocking knees, the older and more experienced father and grandfather claims no privilege of immunity but a tougher external response when he next encounters them.

In writing about the Blitz, Troy noted that it was extraordinary "how quickly devastated streets are put right – completely out of business one day and carrying on as usual a day or two later, and how normal a great part of London looks in spite of the many disasters to individual localities. It might be much worse than it is, and in fact, when we hear the planes pulsating overhead in the mist and darkness, there seems no reason why they could not drop a thousand instead of a few scattered every night. Our guns roar and thunder away in the darkness, but it looks like shooting at echoes."[105] Troy refused to leave London, and defended his choice to his American relatives, but was clearly affected by the strain and sleeplessness of insistent bombardment, as were many during the less deadly but still terrifying raids of the First World War.

Writing home to her mother, Yvonne Green, French Canadian in origin and British by nationality, also tried to offer reassurance via a comparison with the last war and with the notion of international protection for open cities. She suggested in June 1940 that London was most likely safer than any other place in England and explicitly stated that she felt

---

[103] IWM, Department of Documents, Papers of M P Troy (95/25/1), Melville Preston Troy, Letter to sisters, 22 Aug. 1940.

[104] IWM, Department of Documents, Papers of M P Troy (95/25/1), Melville Preston Troy, Letter to Lota Lee Troy [Lota, sister], 8 Oct. 1940.

[105] IWM, Department of Documents, Papers of M P Troy (95/25/1), Melville Preston Troy to Arthur Troy [brother], 26 Sept. 1940.

London would, like Paris, be declared an "open town."[106] Mrs. Green joined the Auxiliary Fire Service (AFS) and served as a volunteer driver; by August 1940, she was again trying to cheer up her mother by noting that putting on the uniform of a civil defense worker made her feel as if she were part of a greater community.[107] When the Blitz hit, Yvonne Green wrote a long, evocative letter to her mother describing how proud she was of the work of the AFS, and while admitting in mid-September to being a bit shaken up by the first night of bombing, she insisted that she didn't want to leave others to do her work. When her husband made her evacuate London temporarily, she chose to return rather than face what felt to her like crushing boredom away from the city.[108] Green later became a "fire watcher" in the winter of 1941, and she died at the age of thirty on April 17 of that year when a bomb exploded while she was on duty – one of the thousands of civilians killed by aerial bombardment in this war.

Personal accounts underscored the government's fears (and insistence in public) that there was no place that could be made absolutely safe and no category of persons who remained impervious to the consequences of air war. Queenie Shepperd, who lived in Eltham in East London, recounted in mid-September 1940 that the door on her son-in-law Victor's "Andersons shelter blown off but none hurt there. Windows in our road smashed" after one raid, but more tragically, "the Vicarage shelter underground was bombed and seven people killed there on Wednesday night."[109] As was the case with the last war's raids, neither being in a house of God nor being underground guaranteed safety. Nurse G. Thomas wrote in her diary in mid-September that "the raids are more severe. We are beginning to receive some of the casualties, women and children, of course, are amongst Hitler's victims." It is the "of course" that emphasized her disgust with the way in which the war was being conducted; it was only the little babies who, "blissfully ignorant ... happier then ever," slept through the raids. For herself, "I think as long as I can keep my nerve, I will. I fear if I saw too much havoc, I would lose it, and become a coward." She

---

[106] IWM, Department of Documents, Papers of Y Green (99/9/1), Yvonne Green, Letter to mother, 20 June 1940.

[107] IWM, Department of Documents, Papers of Y Green (99/9/1), Yvonne Green, Letter to mother, 30 Aug. 1940.

[108] IWM, Department of Documents, Papers of Y Green (99/9/1), Yvonne Green, Letter to mother, 14 Sept. 1940, 23 Sept. 1940, and 8 Oct. 1940.

[109] IWM, Department of Documents, Papers of A Shepperd (95/13/1), Anne Walker Shepperd, Diary entries listed as Wednesday evening and Friday afternoon, [18 and 20] Sept. 1940.

found it more harrowing to treat those she knew and the injured young. Yet while she wrote in late September, "Now the night is approaching again with all the terror it brings," fear did not stop her from doing an increasingly difficult job.[110]

Those who had commented on the destructive potential of air power in the years leading up to the war, such as Virginia Woolf, also reflected on the meaning of the air raid's return. Woolf's poignant "Thoughts on Peace in an Air Raid" reiterated themes from both *Three Guineas* and her reflections, found in her diary entries, on the First World War's raids.[111] She underlined the effect of the sound of the attack – the "queer experience [of] lying in the dark and listening to the zoom of a hornet which may at any moment sting you to death" (243). Woolf went on to note that this war was being fought by men as both "attackers" and "defenders" and to ask what women could then do. She argued that women could "fight for freedom without firearms" by making "ideas that will help the young Englishman who is fighting up in the sky to defeat the enemy" (244). Juxtaposed with Woolf's musings on how to achieve true disarmament and how women must participate in this came her matter-of-fact evocations of a raid: "A bomb drops. All the windows rattle.... At any moment a bomb may fall on this very room. One, two, three, four, five six ... the seconds pass. The bomb did not fall. But during those seconds of suspense all thinking stopped. All feeling, save one dull dread, ceased" (245–246). Woolf ended with a plea to America – "to the men and women whose

---

[110] IWM, Department of Documents, Papers of G Thomas (90/30/1), G. Thomas, Diary, 9–10 Sept., 13 Sept. (blissfully ignorant), 17 Sept. (havoc), and 26 Sept. 1940. In the summer of 1944, her witnessing of the direct aftermath of an attack near Lewisham would prompt her to write, "[T]his was hell with all its fury let loose, no battle-field could be worse, or more bloody." See Diary, 28 July 1944. For a discussion of civilians and fear, see Joanna Bourke, *Fear: A Cultural History* (London, 2005; rpt. 2006), 227–232. Much of Bourke's discussion of the phenomenon of "civilians under attack" focuses on the deadly events at the Bethnal Green underground station, where many were killed by a panicking mob seeking shelter in 1943. For an official contemporary perspective on this event, see *Tragedy at Bethnal Green: Report on an Inquiry into the Accident at Bethnal Green Tube Station Shelter* (1945, rpt. London, 1999).

[111] Virginia Woolf, "Thoughts on Peace in an Air Raid," August 1940; reprinted in *The Death of the Moth and Other Essays* (London, 1942). Further references are made parenthetically in the text. Virginia Woolf committed suicide in March 1941. In the aftermath of her death, Vera Brittain reflected on her death (occurring as it did in the midst of the bombing war against civilians) that "her end was perhaps a kind of protest, the most terrible and effective that she could make, against the real hell that international conflict creates for the artist." See Vera Brittain, "Letter to Peace Lovers," 24 Apr. 1941, in *Testament of a Peace Lover: Letters from Vera Brittain* (London, 1988), 69–70.

sleep has not yet been broken" – from "the shadowed half of the world" to help rethink a world freed from the struggle for domination, the desire for military glory, and the power of the machine (248).

Such lofty thoughts were not the province of celebrated writers alone. On the eve of the Blitz in London, Isabelle Granger offered in a letter the following reflections on increased risk to civilians:

> The amazing courage of the people in the streets are things to rejoice in. I do want to live till after the war if it can only be arranged, but since there must be a war I am happy to live dangerously in the midst of it, to risk the future. This war against civilians is a foul thing but I think war against anyone is a beastly thing. I can feel a certain satisfaction that its being waged against everyone: it will make the thoughtless think twice before they embark on adventures of this sort again or before they let things get to the pitch of its having to be endured by them again. Up to now there has been too much heroic talk by some people about "giving" sons & young people in the cause of war. When its brought home to the "giver" what its like to be part of the great sacrificed I am not sorry.[112]

Despite admitting regularly in her correspondence that raids frightened and disturbed her, she continued to embrace the idea of shared danger and sacrifice as just.[113] She evoked this particularly when contrasting her current state of mind with her emotions during the Great War:

> Its odd that in thinking of 1914–18 I can always feel unutterably sad, they seem years of unbearable unhappiness. This war isn't especially sad – it's annoying, frightening, time-wasting (I spend hours weekly doing silly things like pulling curtains and turning off gas at the main & hurrying home before the barrage begins!) ... but I find it such an excellent thing that it has come to England & to everyone in England – we can't "offer" a few hundred thousand young men: they are safely tucked away in camps now & it falls on us all equally which is quite right.[114]

This again hearkens back to how some civilians and soldiers felt about air raids of World War I: that there was something just and right about shared danger and sacrifice in a total war.

---

[112] IWM, Department of Documents, Papers of I H Granger (94/45/2), Isabelle Granger, Letter to Harrison Brown, 1 Sept. 1940; original spelling has been retained.

[113] IWM, Department of Documents, Papers of I H Granger (94/45/2), Granger to Harrison Brown, 8 Sept. 1940. Enclosed with the letter is a list of her possessions in case she is killed in the Blitz.

[114] IWM, Department of Documents, Papers of I H Granger (94/45/2), Granger to Harrison Brown, 5 Nov. 1940.

Some tried to joke about the altered status of non-combatants, as did Mrs. R. G. Cottrell in one of her letters, which she used as a kind of diary for recording her experience of the Blitz. In late October 1940, she noted that "so long as Londoners especially can see the humour in everything they will come through." She continued to recount an article in the paper that read:

> "The current joke is about the comparative safety of the Army, whose task this winter, Londoners suggest, should be knitting socks and scarves for civilians." Then she added her own comments, "[T]he Army is just dug in, and the civilian front is getting it at the moment, where before it was the other way round. In the last war it was exceedingly difficult for men to keep out of the Army, now it is exceedingly difficult for them to get *in*. In fact Snook [a co-worker] ... told me this morning of a girl whose man went in to the Army, and she handed him a white feather. However all sorts of these jokes are going the rounds. It really is a most peculiar war.[115]

The "white feather," the classic and controversial emblem that a few women infamously bestowed on "shirkers" and "cowards" out of uniform in the First World War, had now become something to bestow on men in the military who were "safe" from aerial attacks aimed at civilians.[116] While participants could thus describe the raids of 1940 as representing a peculiar war or an ungentlemanly war, it was certainly a war confusing the borders between civilians and the military that had long been anticipated.

But what of the war that did not occur – the dreadful specter of chemical weapons and asphyxiated babies? Despite the lack of chemical attacks, the government continued to develop and remind its citizens to carry and care for their gas masks. When modifications to the civilian gas mask were ready for distribution in late May of 1940, Mass Observation again sent informants to report on reactions to this at various points in London and elsewhere. An observer in Stratford Road described "a constant flow of elderly men and women," where the chief warden reported that "there had been no nervousness except in the case of one or two elderly ladies who complained that they could not breathe in their masks and were inclined to be hysterical."[117] At Queen's Gate, the observer saw

---

[115] IWM, Department of Documents, Papers of R G Cottrell (04/40/1), Mrs. R. G. Cottrell, Letter to Patricia, 23 Oct. 1940.

[116] For the most significant discussion of the white feather campaign in the First World War, see Nicoletta F. Gullace, "White Feathers and Wounded Men," *Journal of British Studies*

[117] Stratford Road W8 Report, 24 May 1940, MOA, TC 55, Box 1, file A.

"chiefly women ... and scarcely any under seventy," while the warden commented that "people were quiet and brought their babies with their cases. The babies were not frightened but the children were inclined to be and needed a lot of coaxing."[118] Overall, reports singled out two groups for behavior that belied the overall suggestion that there was "no panic": children and elderly women.

As the raids of the first sustained aerial onslaught abated in 1941, the government continued to remind civilians that they needed to be prepared for the potential use of chemical weapons. A new pamphlet from the Minister of Home Security, which appeared in April 1941, warned that "other counties lost their freedom in this war because they allowed the enemy to create confusion and panic among their civilian population.... It won't happen here if we are all on our guard, prepared to meet anything the enemy might do. He may use gas. THE DANGER IS NOT SERIOUS if you do the right thing.... If you do, this weapon will have failed and you will have helped to beat it." Among other specific recommendations, the leaflet advised making sure that "your own and your children's gas masks fit and are in working order" and that all members of the family practice putting on the masks and "wearing them with confidence."[119]

Shortly after the appearance of this pamphlet, Mass Observation set out to determine if it had had any effect on the actual carrying of gas masks and what further links could be found between the carrying of masks and "good morale." In May 1941, it reported that while the majority of those who had seen the government's latest instructions felt "considerable if mild approval" of them, they had little effect on the main message (i.e., carry your gas mask), noting that only 20 percent of Londoners were doing so. Despite this, "almost half of Londoners, for instance, expect some new gas to be used and feel some doubt about the efficacy of their masks and other measures in such an emergency."[120] When attempting to assess the connection between gas mask carrying and morale in June of that year, a report concluded that while "any difference between the cheerfulness of gas mask carriers and non-carriers is small," still in times of bad news, "female gas mask carriers became more depressed than female non-carriers."[121]

---

[118] Queen's Gate Report, 24 May 1940, MOA, TC 55, Box 1, File A.
[119] "What to Do About Gas?" (London, 1941); copy in MOA, TC 55, Box 2, File A.
[120] Reaction to "What to Do About Gas?" 1 May 1941, MOA, TC 55, Box 2, File A.
[121] "Morale and Gas Mask Carrying," 11 June 1941, MOA, TC 55, Box 2, File A.

The longer that war continued without British civilians coming under attack from chemical weapons, the less likely civilians were to carry gas masks or to take the other anti-gas precautions advised. This was hardly surprising news. Even before the official start of World War II, civilian women such as Helena Britton were already skeptical about such measures. So much, then, for the underlying ideas of both planners and critics that what truly mattered about air raid precautions, and the gas mask as an emblem of this, was the psychological effect, that giving a tangible means of protection, however inadequate, was necessary to maintain morale. The impressions left by both public and private reactions to the carrying of gas masks and other civil defense measures suggest that they neither greatly reassured nor deeply alarmed the population. The anecdotal evidence of a gendered split over gas mask carrying may say more about rule abiding than morale, but putting in place visible, material emblems to safeguard women and children calls attention (once again) to how fully integrated they and the entire so-called home front had become into the calculations required of the long planning for modern and total war.

CONCLUSION

Personal reactions to ARP measures and then to the raids themselves varied. In private, some Londoners drew upon their experiences of the First World War as they tried to make sense of this new war, but many seemed to think that something genuinely unprecedented was occurring. Whether or not they acknowledged Britain's previous experiences of aerial bombardment, many also articulated a sense of shared danger, responsibility, and sacrifice. These were precisely the virtues enshrined in the new civil identity fostered by official voices ever since the air raids of the First World War. To some extent, the Blitz was but a more intensive, and deadly, version of the bombardment suffered by Britain during 1914–1918. Moreover, because poison gas was expected and yet not used, it was also less horrific than some of the worst imaginings of either planners or pacifists. The ways in which issues of morale and character, especially for non-combatants personified by women, remained at the forefront of wartime representations of war at home will be taken up in the next chapter.

11

Representing the New Air War

Morale, the Air Raid, and Wartime Popular Culture

INTRODUCTION

By the time that aerial warfare returned to Great Britain, its civilian population had seemingly had decades to adjust to the idea that war would be waged against them. Nonetheless, propaganda addressed to women, and also created by some of them, took special note of this feature of war – the attack on homes and families – as it returned to Europe. By not only mobilizing women, but also focusing on them as key components of sustaining the war effort, the British government both in the prelude to the Second World War and its duration followed patterns previously established during and after the First World War. State agents linked a variety of behaviors and qualities – serenity, steadfastness, cheerfulness, self-sacrifice – that could perhaps be best exhibited by women (and should be expressed by all) with the maintenance of good, civilian morale and the civil identity necessary for the successful outcome of the war.

A 1940 Mass Observation report took note of the particular challenge of women's morale:

> The word 'morale' has been used widely by press and Government propaganda to describe the state of the public mind about the war and the principles for which we are fighting. An official definition of morale has yet to be given.... Though many of them are now doing a man's job, sharing with men danger and hardship, the morale of women cannot be judged by the same standards as that of men and soldiers. The housewife, though she has not the direct leadership and discipline that the soldier experiences, may have to undergo *more* danger and put up with *more* inconveniences than her husband. It is the propaganda of her

everyday life which determines whether she accepts war and sacrifice willingly or not.[1]

After spending some time illustrating how women across Britain were facing the war, the report concluded that "the majority are accepting the inevitable, not with a fervour that accepts sacrifice as a duty, but with a quiet endurance and passivity that conserves their energies for the hum-drum, everyday tasks necessary for holding together what remains of ordinary life and habit."[2] The Mass Observation report further noted

[1] "M-O Report No. 520: Women and Morale, December 1940," in *Wartime Women: A Mass-Observation Anthology, 1937–45*, ed. Dorothy Sheridan (1990; rpt. London, 2000), 110–111. Emphasis added. Robert Mackay, *Half the Battle: Civilian Morale in Britain during the Second World War* (Manchester, 2002), offers an overview of civilian morale but does not analyze women as a group. Like others studying the war, he looks at the effects of film on maintaining morale. For other work on wartime morale in Britain using Mass Observation records, see Brad Beaven and John Griffiths, "The Blitz, Civilian Morale and the City: Mass Observation and Working-Class Culture in Britain, 1940–41," *Urban History* 26:1 (1999), 71–88. For studies examining wartime film, see H. Mark Glancy, *When Hollywood Loved Britain: The Hollywood "British" Film, 1939–45* (Manchester, 1999); Christine Gledhill and Gillian Swanson (eds.), *Nationalising Femininity: Culture, Sexuality and British Cinema in the Second World War* (Manchester, 1996); Antonia Lant, *Blackout: Reinventing Women for Wartime British Cinema* (Princeton, NJ, 1991); S. P. MacKenzie, *British War Films 1939–1945: The Cinema and the Services* (London, 2001); and Neil Rattigan, *This Is England: British Film and the People's War, 1939–1945* (Cranbury, NJ, 2001). For a contemporary example of British women and the Second World War, see *British Women at War* (London, 1944); for some useful historical perspectives, see James Hinton, *Women, Social Leadership, and the Second World War: Continuities of Class* (Oxford, 2002); Alison Oram, "'Bombs Don't Discriminate!' Women's Political Activism in the Second World War," in *Nationalising Femininity*, ed. Gledhill and Swanson; Sonya O. Rose, *Which People's War? National Identitiy and Citizenship in Wartime Britain* (Oxford, 2003); Harold Smith, "British Feminism in the Second World War," in *Gender, Labour, War and Empire: Essays on Modern Britain*, ed. Philippa Levine and Susan R. Grayzel (Basingstoke, 2009); Penny Summerfield, *Women Workers in the Second World War: Production and Patriarchy in Conflict* (London, 1984); *Reconstructing Women's Wartime Lives: Discourse and Subjectivity in Oral Histories of the Second World War* (Manchestser, 1998), and with Corinna Peniston-Bird, *Contesting Home Defence: Men, Women and the Home Guard in the Second World War* (Manchester, 2007). For more on the use of other media to promote women's morale, see Becky Conekin, "'Magazines Are Essentially About the Here and Now. And This Was Wartime': British *Vogue's* Responses to the Second World War," in *Gender, Labour, War and Empire*, ed. Levine and Grayzel; Lucy Noakes, *War and the British: Gender, Memory and National Identity* (London, 1998), ch. 3; and Janice Winship, "Women's Magazines: Times of War and Management of the Self in *Woman's Own*," in *Nationalising Femininity*, ed. Gledhill and Swanson. For some useful studies of women and wartime fiction, see Jenny Hartley, *Millions Like Us: British Women's Fiction of the Second World War* (London, 1997); Phyllis Lassner, *British Women Writers of World War II: Battlegrounds of Their Own* (Basingstoke, 1998); and Gill Plain, *Women's Fiction of the Second World War: Gender, Power and Resistance* (Edinburgh, 1996).

[2] "M-O Report No. 520: Women and Morale, December 1940," 122.

that while air raids did upset women at first, there were "recorded very few instances of women's morale being seriously affected by raids."[3] Women's ability to sustain morale and the home despite the hardships imposed by the air war thus appeared to be something actively cultivated, and this can be seen in various examples of wartime popular culture. As we have seen by now, this should *not* have been necessary or novel but continued to be treated as such in the mass media. The message that the unthinkable – attacks on women, children, and home life – had to be made bearable resonated in imaginative works produced in the immediate aftermath of the Blitz. The analysis of civilian morale and civil identity in the context of air raids that follows thus focuses on the cultural work of delivering this state-sponsored message, mainly by analyzing two of the most popular and successful 1942 films that represented the Blitz to its contemporary audience: *Mrs. Miniver* and *In Which We Serve*.

WOMEN AND CHILDREN IN THE LITERARY BLITZ

As was the case with fictional representations of aerial warfare that appeared during the First World War, such as "Mary Postgate" and *The Pretty Lady*, the contemporaneous literature of the bombing of Britain in the Second World War focused on how civilians responded to the war at home. Whether wartime novels were published extremely close to the time of the heaviest initial raids, such as *The Little Doves of Destruction* (1941), *Blitz Kids* (1941), and *London Pride* (1941), or shortly thereafter, such as *House in the Dust* (1942), *Blitz Hero* (1942), and *The Hour of the Angel* (1942), they repeatedly emphasized the "front line" nature of the civilian experience of war and the significance of civilian morale, especially among women and children.

George Wolfenden insisted upon this in the dedication to his *Little Doves of Destruction*:

> This is a story of Britain to-day.... All I have been able to do is to intro-duce as many aspects of our besieged island as possible, all the things we know about but don't read about in the papers, the everyday lives.... I want to dedicate this book to the young mothers I know.... [T]hey are not part of the war effort nor yet has anyone ... extolled them in a Sunday postscript. They are too busy bringing up a nation.[4]

---

[3] "M-O Report No. 520: Women and Morale, December 1940," 118.
[4] George Wolfenden, *The Little Doves of Destruction: A Romance of England under the Blitz* (London, 1941), 6.

Precisely because he claimed that fiction was only a step removed from journalism and that journalism focused on obvious heroes, Wolfenden was able to assert that the job of "bringing up" children (the nation's future) was a vital part of the "war effort." This became, as his rather conventional tale of wartime love, marriage, and family revealed, even more difficult when the bombs were falling upon you.

Both *Blitz Kids* and *London Pride* focused on the resourcefulness of the family under fire, but not on mothers. Rather it is the children who must face air raids, whose humor and ability to cope with the destruction of their environment and home lives exemplify the changing nature of warfare. What remains striking about these books is their matter-of-fact way of putting children in the firing line.

Blitz Kids's narrator is a nine-year-old South Londoner, Nancy, who along with her many siblings refuses to leave London under attack. In her version of the war's air raids, they sneak up suddenly: "It was a queer go, when it did happen. One morning we were all out in our street, that is called the Cut ... when what they called 'the sirens' started screaming." However, she soon becomes accustomed to the raids: "The sirens were always going after that, like mad cats yowling. A great many children got evacuated, which is different from vaccination, though many of them didn't know it, and means being sent away down to the country. But none of that for us Healeys. There we were and we stuck together." Despite plenty of descriptions of Nancy and the other Healeys flagrantly disregarding the measures provided for their safety like evacuation, the children's spirit in the face of being bombed out is summarized by a fellow Londoner's reaction to Nancy caring for baby Grace, who laughs through an air raid in a public shelter: "[T]he other people in the shelter [say,] 'Look at that there kid; there's the true blue British spirit for you right enough, and no mistake about it either.'"[5] This was one version of the myth of the Blitz enacted at the moment of its creation.

The heroic action of children during the Blitz is seen from a somewhat less comic perspective in *London Pride*, where the first night of air raids in East London finds Ben Barton acting like the real-life Violet Buckthorne of the First World War. Young Ben is alone with his baby sister, Mabel, and despite blood dripping down his head, he carries her off to shelter and safety:

> Ben didn't like the darkness, or the roaring sounds; and still less, the strange hard things flying by him through the heavy air; but he plodded resolutely on; and no one tried to stop him – or to help him.

[5] Elinor Mordaunt, *Blitz Kids* (London, 1941), 13–14, 94.

This was the first air raid in the neighbourhood; and people still thought first of themselves and their children.[6]

The black-and-white illustration accompanying these words demonstrated the helplessness and isolation of the small boy, while the text vocalized the fear expressed throughout ARP planning that few would look beyond their own homes and families.

However, Ben does not remain isolated for long; over the course of the novel, he joins forces with a neighborhood girl, Emily, taking part in looting and gathering goods from bombed-out homes, until all three children get buried under a house. Then the hospital where they take refuge suffers a direct hit. It is after this catastrophe – and after a bomb wipes out Emily's family – that the concern of the outside world, in the form of hospital workers and a larger family, actively intervenes in Ben's life. An uncle living in Yorkshire offers to take in baby Mabel:

Mr. Brattle had suddenly developed a fixed idea, and this was that he didn't hold with bombs being dropped on babies ... and informed his wife that she *must* invite her sister's youngest for the duration of the war. Apparently, Mr. Brattle *did* hold with bombs being dropped on small boys, for when his wife suggested to him that Ben might accompany Mabel, he said, 'Certainly not!' and flew into a passion.[7]

This desire to protect babies as the emblem of "innocence" – which we saw most profoundly in the development of the infant gas mask – extended into the war, despite circumstances and family ties that might elicit a wider sympathy. Not all victims of the Blitz were equal.[8]

While London remained central to stories of the Blitz, the air war in the northeast of England also received its due in John Owen's *Blitz Hero*, a tale that, as the author explained in his preface, aimed to explore the nature of courage, "a virtue so complex in its manifestations as to be found in the strangest places – in the heart of a coward or in a mind that draws its vitality from another mind."[9] This idea of the transfer of courage (vitality) from one person to another was itself a hallmark of many wartime love stories from the First World War, in which the love or faith

[6] Phyllis Bottome, *London Pride* (London; rpt. Boston, 1941), 56.
[7] Bottome, *London Pride*, 243. Ben eventually joins the ranks of evacuated children when he is sent off to be with his younger twin siblings.
[8] Another sign of this may be perhaps one of the most famous photographs of the war, Cecil Beaton's portrait of a Blitz victim, Eileen Dunne, a little girl with a bandage around her head, in the London Hospital for Sick Children, 1940. See copy, IWM PA, MH 26395.
[9] John Owen, *Blitz Hero* (London, 1942), v.

of a good woman redeems the slacker.[10] Owen's story was quite melo-dramatic; a young couple, Ruby and Morrow, are living with their young son, Geoffrey, in a northeast town when war breaks out. Unfit for the army and fearful of his cowardice, Morrow becomes an air raid warden. He is mistakenly identified as a hero, even receiving a medal, but fears being found out and is indeed blackmailed, until Ruby prods him to act. Due to her encouragement, during the height of a devastating air raid, he saves five lives, including that of the head warden, and is then him-self gravely injured. The book contains very typical war romance novel elements; masculinity and bravery under fire are distinctly tied up in the novel and the feminine task of inciting heroism could be found in almost any conventional wartime romance.

However, the presumed difference of this war against home life is underscored by Ruby as she reflects on the danger that her five-year-old must face:

> I'm always wondering about Geoffrey.... I can't see how I could bear his being killed in a raid.... Lots of folks have shown how they can make do with the sort of personal tragedy that can never have invaded people's lives in quite the same way in the last war. I imagine if you heard your son or husband was killed in France then, you were supported by your sense of sacrifice: you told yourself that you could not do less than he.... Today, mothers may have to look at their children after they've been smashed up, mutilated, killed horribly. When you think of the historic simplicity of children, it's odd to have to see them standing with adult soldiers. Yet soldiers they are, if Home Guard rather than Coldstreamers or Royal Welsh. If they don't know they may have to die for their coun-try, they still may have to.[11]

This sober analysis of air war ignored any parallel experiences of the last war, but it echoed the refrains of those who commented on both the loss of life and innocence in that war's air raids. What was different about the new war was the scale and, with it, the inability to ignore the ways in which sacrifice and service to the nation had expanded across age, gender, and class borders. The ability of women in particular to serve, sacrifice, and die for their nation came across vividly in two popular 1942 films that show how air raids destroy home life but the homeland endures.

---

[10] See Susan R. Grayzel, *Women's Identities at War: Gender, Motherhood, and Politics in Britain and France during the First World War* (Chapel Hil, NC, 1999), ch. 2, and Ruby Ayres, Richard Chatterton, V.C. (London, 1915), as a prime example.

[11] Owen, *Blitz Hero*, 18–19.

MARTYRED WOMEN AND CIVILIAN MORALE
IN WARTIME FILM

Two films appeared in 1942 that resonated deeply with wartime audiences. The first of these, *Mrs. Miniver*, was a Hollywood production based on Jan Struther's transatlantic best-selling book. Its entire focus was on the war at home as experienced by its steadfast titular wife and mother. The second was homegrown in Britain, written and directed by Noel Coward, and celebrating equally men at sea and women at home. Both films offered important and deliberate evocations of how air war endangered women and children and showed their ability to stoically endure, even if they did not always survive the war waged against them.

First appearing, as we have seen, as the title character in a column by Jan Struther, the pseudonym of Joyce Maxtone Graham, in the *Times* in the late 1930s, "Mrs. Miniver" went on to achieve iconic status as a transatlantic image of stoic womanhood in the face of the traumas of the Second World War. The Hollywood adaptation of the book, *Mrs. Miniver*, opened in June 1942 in the United States and a month later in Britain, and it went on to win the Academy Award for Best Picture. Such acclaim for a story about war (both anticipated and then experienced) that focuses mainly on family life and the so-called home front offers a culminating vision of the domestication of aerial warfare. By providing an emblematic heroine who faces the hardships of war at home without flinching, it offered a model to its female audiences – to wives and mothers rather than mobilized single women – of how to react to the exigencies of World War II.

In the 1939 book version, Kay Miniver, after describing her willingness to take as many evacuated children as possible into the family's home in Kent, satirizes a titled woman complaining about the entire scheme and recounting her command to the billeting surveyor that "'if the worst does come to the worst, you must make it quite clear to the authorities that I can only accept Really Nice Children.'"[12] Then, in London in August, she meets a woman in a park practicing knots for first aid, and she takes in the fact that "the ever-present contingency of war" has some positive effect: "[A]lmost everybody you meet is busy learning something" (261). There is an idealism in Mrs. Miniver's desire to see good and reject bias, whether it is based on class or national distinctions. A kind of simplified internationalism

---

[12] Jan Struther, *Mrs. Miniver* (New York, 1940), 206–207. Further references appear parenthetically.

emerges when she describes the similarities between children, regardless of their nationality, and thinks of what could be accomplished if "all governments would spend the price of a few bombers on exchanging for the holidays, free of charge, a certain number of families" so that they could get to know one another as people first and foremost (271).

The transatlantic best-selling book – and its selection by the Book-of-the-Month Club attests to its middlebrow appeal in the United States – ends with a "letter" from Mrs. Miniver dated 25 September 1939, with Britain now officially at war. She describes her husband's battery quartered in a girls' school, and her own children adjusting to "our seven tough and charming évacuées." She then summarizes the mood: "[W]e're all so buoyed up just now with the crusading spirit, and ... burningly convinced of the infamy of the Government we're fighting against (this time, thank goodness, one doesn't say 'the nation we're fighting against')" (286). Kay Miniver makes a broadly humanitarian appeal to her fellow citizens: "[I]t oughtn't to need a war to make a nation ... give all its slum children a holiday in the country... to make us ... live simply, and eat sparingly, and recover the use of our legs, and get up early enough to see the sun rise" (286).

In a critical review of the book, novelist Rosamond Lehmann claimed to speak for a minority who found that Mrs. Miniver, despite her tact, kindness, tolerance, humor, and contentment, "exercises an oppression of spirits" upon her audience. Her delightful life with its gleaming home and charming children belied "sentimentality masquerading as sensibility." And now that "war is upon Mrs. Miniver, as it is upon all of us," she concluded, "whoever is defeated, she'll come through ... she will be adaptable, and come up, shaken but intact, whatever new society emerges."[13] Lehmann seemed to suggest that such an apolitical domestic woman could survive as easily under fascism or democracy. In contrast, a short review in *Punch* noted that the last chapter "has something to say about the things that it has needed this war to teach us and that no peace must make us forget, which are very well worth saying."[14]

It would take a film version of Mrs. Miniver both to broaden her audience and change her into a more political creature, whose belief in transcending differences among people clearly does not blind her to the horrors of Nazi Germany. Meanwhile, Struther would continue to represent British women as possessing an ability to hold onto essential values

[13] Rosamond Lehmann, "A Charming Person," Review of *Mrs. Miniver*, *Spectator* 163 (1939).
[14] "The Promotion of Mrs. Miniver," *Punch*, 197, 15 Nov. 1939.

by writing the introduction to a collection of letters, entitled *Women of Britain*, published in the United States in 1941. In it, she hoped to help provide "a true picture of wartime life in Great Britain" and began by acknowledging what was different about this new war, "in which the entire domestic life of one of the most domesticated countries in the world [has been] turned inside out and upside down.... In war, our upbringing had led us to suppose, the men would go away to fight in order to defend their homes.... We certainly never imagined a war in which the homes themselves would be changed almost beyond recognition."[15] Yet it was precisely this type of war that the government – and its harshest critics among pacifists – had been envisaging throughout the interwar period. Like other commentators seeking to highlight how well civilians had responded to the Blitz, Struther found that something new had occurred, and not merely the devastation of the "comparatively few homes which have been physically destroyed by fire or high explosive," but also the nearly universal way in which those occupying homes from villas to tenements have "been forced to change the whole rhythm and pattern of ... daily life" (6). She explained further:

> [W]hen a nation has already had the greater part of its home life disrupted, transplanted or indefinitely suspended, and it still goes on fighting and enduring, then we know that it is fighting for something more precious then bricks and mortar, more precious even than its own home life-that is, it is fighting for the *idea* of home life, for the right of all human beings to live how and where they like. (10)

Yet the positive lessons to be learned from all such changes, in family and home life, are what Struther ultimately underscored, trying to show her audience not only what Britons fight for – the very idea of home life – but also what they too might learn by fully participating in the wartime world.

By the fall of 1941, four screenwriters, including George Froeschel, an Austrian refugee, along with William Wyler, were working on a film adaptation of Struther's *Mrs. Miniver*, the film itself being the brainchild of Hollywood producer Sidney Franklin. Between the American publication of the book in 1940 and the appearance of the completed film in mid-1942, a great deal had changed. Britain had faced the Blitz and, by the time of the film's release, the United States had experienced the

---

[15] Jan Struther, *Women of Britain: Letters from England* (New York, 1941), 6–8. Further references appear parenthetically.

attack on Pearl Harbor. Thus, while the original intent may have been to show Americans (especially American women) how to respond to the possibility of a war that might directly affect their home lives, the film ended up being avidly consumed by a wartime audience both American and British.[16]

In transforming the literary figure of Mrs. Miniver into a cinematic emblem of women at war in the 1942 film, her heroism took on both more inspirational and practical forms. Interestingly, the military war experiences of men, both Mr. Minivers (Clem, the husband, and Vin, the eldest son), take place offscreen (the father goes to Dunkirk to rescue stranded troops after the fall of France; the son joins the RAF). It is the Mrs. Minivers (the mother and eventual daughter-in-law) who are portrayed as engaging the enemy directly. First and foremost, however, the story presents this idealized English family as one now facing blackouts, bombs, and, ultimately, the death of loved ones.

The film begins by establishing a portrait of the Minivers and their deceptively simple life in suburban England, where the inhabitants are preoccupied with growing roses, buying hats, and indulging in the domestic pleasures of an idyllic home life. Unlike the book, the film depicts war occurring without warning (something for which British reviewers would be quick to take it to task). We witness some of the wartime adjustments with comic effect (an air raid warden – and grocer – inspects the family's precautions and tries to sell provisions at the same time), but gradually war transforms the family. Vin achieves a purpose in life by becoming a pilot, and, as mentioned earlier, Clem Miniver joins a group of local men to voyage by sea to an unknown location. We see his boat join others in a huge flotilla – and we see his disheveled appearance upon his return – but of the actual rescue at Dunkirk, we see nothing.

Instead, while Clem is away, in one of the film's most well-known scenes, the unarmed Kay Miniver confronts and ultimately defeats a downed German pilot. However, in keeping with the tone of the written

---

[16] For other studies of the film *Mrs. Miniver*, see Michael Druxman, *One Good Film Deserves Another* (South Brunswick, NY, 1977); Roger Manvell, *Films and the Second World War* (South Brunswick, NY, 1974); Michael Anderegg, *William Wyler* (Boston, 1979); and Andrea Walsh, *Women's Film and Female Experience, 1940–1950* (New York, 1984). For information about the film's popularity in America, see Susan Hartmann, *The Home Front and Beyond: American Women in the 1940s* (Boston, 1982), 191, which describes audiences "flocking" to it in 1942; and for British popularity, see the appendix entitled "British Box Office Information, 1940–1950" in Lant, *Blackout*, 231, which lists *Mrs. Miniver* as having the biggest box office sales in 1942. All descriptions and direct quotes are taken from *Mrs. Miniver* (1942), dir. William Wyler.

Mrs. Miniver and quite opposite to World War I's Mary Postgate, who as we saw in Chapter 2 kills the pilot she encounters, Mrs. Miniver attempts to minister to her fallen enemy. She assures him that he'll be well looked after in the hospital and that, after all, "the war won't last forever." The German pilot instead swears revenge: "You will see ... we will come. We will bomb your cities." And, he continues, England will be like other places that have fallen to the Reich. When Mrs. Miniver protests that the war has thus far entailed the bombing of "innocent people" and "women and children," he declares that there will be "the same thing here." At this, Kay Miniver turns from the maternal every-woman to the female patriot and slaps him across the face. The police and a doctor then arrive to take the airman away, and the scene closes with her reassuring the doctor that she's perfectly "all right." If the enemy has been in her home, she has protected it, her family, and herself from harm.[17]

Shortly thereafter, the film re-creates the Blitz in miniature, highlighting the danger posed to the entire family as it endures an air raid from within the backyard Anderson shelter. By focusing on the family, and particularly by foregrounding Mrs. Miniver, the camera allows the audience vicariously to witness the raid in all its noise and fearful uncertainty. The film offers a sentimental yet highly effective portrait; the mother has just finished reading *Alice in Wonderland* and tucking in her two small children. The father goes out to have a last smoke on his pipe, and both parents watch distant explosions as if they were fireworks before settling themselves into the shelter for the night. While she is knitting and he has his tea and biscuits, they discuss the return of their elder son, Vin, from his Scottish honeymoon with his new, aristocratic wife, Carol. All of this is so seemingly far removed from war. Then, the sound of planes and bombs grows louder and louder, but the camera never leaves the cramped interior of the shelter. The walls shake, and objects fall off shelves. As if to remind us of more deadly possibilities, the camera pans across the shelter to reveal gas mask containers for the entire family; the explosions grow louder, the door swings open – flames vaguely appear outside – the children awaken, and the mother tries to comfort them over the deafening sound of the aerial onslaught. The camera focuses tightly on Mrs. Miniver throughout; she remains the centerpiece as the child in her arms

---

[17] Mark Glancy points out that this scene was changed from its original version, in which the pilot was much less threatening, due, in part, to America's entry into the war. See Glancy, *When Hollywood Loved Britain*, 147–148.

cries out the scene's last line, "They nearly killed us this time, Mummy."
Yet once again, the emotions of Mrs. Miniver are displayed on her face,
not in any panic-stricken words or gestures. She holds her child close,
offers comfort, and does not express fear even under fire.

It is not until the next morning, when Mr. and Mrs. Miniver return
from picking up the newlyweds at the train station, that we see the material effects of the previous night's raid. The house has been hit directly;
war has literally come home, and yet Mrs. Miniver carries on as if a hole
in her roof were only a minor inconvenience. The scene in the shelter also
underscores the words of the downed pilot, lest we have forgotten. More
enemy fliers have come, and they have bombed "women and children."
Yet if Kay Miniver cannot deliver a literal slap in the face to those who
have wrecked her home, she can deliver (and, implicitly, so too can all
women) a metaphorical slap in the face by ignoring the devastation and
carrying on.

Yet more destruction awaits the Minivers. In the film's denouement,
the younger Mrs. Miniver is killed during an air raid as her mother-in-
law tries to drive them both to safety. Once again, the film portrays war
intruding without warning, disrupting the annual flower show. The perspective of the two women in the car becomes ours as they watch a flam-
ing plane sink to the ground, followed by another that sprays gunfire
across the roadway. Carol Miniver is hit; an innocent civilian, female
victim of the war, and we feel the sense of horror and violation as the
camera focuses again on Kay Miniver's face. Yet even in this instant and
its immediate aftermath, the film shows us the strength of those waging,
as the minister's sermon in his bombed-out church reminds us, "a people's war." The enemy may attack these ordinary people and kill women
and the young, but they will not surrender.

It is the main character's actions after the culmination of these traumatic events that are meant to rivet us. Despite the intensity of these
experiences, Mrs Miniver exudes calm, stoic acceptance, and certainty
that in the end Britain will prevail – in other words, the essence of good
morale. While the final words of encouragement are left to the minister
to deliver at the funeral service, the film made clear the essential heroism
of its (and potentially all) women.

As an Anglo-American production, the film received a interestingly
varied critical reception, while the popular reaction was largely positive.
The film was a success in the United States and Britain; a survey con-
duced by Britain's Mass Observation found that it was the most popular

box office film of 1942.[18] Popular opinion and critical opinion, however, diverged, largely along national lines. The *New York Times*'s Bosley Crowther began his response to the film as follows:

> It is hard to believe that a picture could be made within the heat of present strife which would clearly but without a cry for vengeance, crystallize the cruel effect of total war upon a civilized people. Yet that is what has been magnificently done in... 'Mrs. Miniver.'... For this is not a war film about soldiers in uniform.... This is a film about the people in a small, unpretentious English town on whom the war creeps up slowly, disturbing their tranquil ways of life, then suddenly bursts in devastating fury as the bombs rain down and the Battle of Britain is on. This is a film of modern warfare in which civilians become the front-line fighters and the ingrained courage of the people becomes the nation's most vital strength.

From the outset then, the film was seen as revealing the transformation in modern war that "turned" civilians like Mrs. Miniver into "front-line fighters." This was the startling aspect – after all, there was nothing unusual about turning male civilians into "front-line fighters." Yet as we have seen, Mrs. Miniver is a particular kind of "front-line fighter," defined primarily as a wife and mother. In expanding her domestic role to national caretaking perhaps, she responds to crises without betraying either her essential feminine domesticity or displaying the most outward emblems of fear.

Other American responses in the mass media tended to concur with Crowther's positive assessment. "Whether or not the screen story was contrived as propaganda for our side, the Metro-Goldwyn-Mayer release happens to pack a more persuasive wallop than half a dozen propaganda films pitched in a heroic key," stated the review in *Newsweek*.[19] The *New Yorker*'s reviewer described the film as "stupendous ... the final say on the superb and hellish struggle of English families from the beginning of the war until today." *Time*'s critic celebrated "that almost impossible feat, a great war picture that photographs the inner meaning, instead of the outward realism of World War II.... With reticence, good taste, and an understanding of events, [director Wyler] reflects the war's global havoc without ever taking his cameras off the Minivers' quiet corner

---

[18] Janet Thumim, "The Female Audience: Mobile Women and Married Ladies," in *Nationalising Femininity: Culture, Sexuality and British Cinema in the Second World War*, ed. Christine Gledhill and Fillian Swanson (Manchester, 1996), 248.

[19] "Mrs. Miniver's War," *Newsweek*, 15 June 1942.

of England." It made some of the implied messages of the film obvious to Americans, by singling out the scene where the war is "reduced to the compass of an Anderson shelter when the Minivers and their well-scrubbed youngsters ride out an air raid in their own backyard. It is anybody's backyard, anywhere."[20]

Several British critics had a slightly different response. The *Times* of London began its reflection after the film's British debut, a month later, by noting the differences between the book and the film, seeing the latter as using the Minivers as "a means of illustrating to America the way in which the English behave under the impact of war." Yet "the picture of England at war suffers from that distortion which seems inevitable whenever Hollywood cameras are trained on it. It is absurd to show an English village ... caught unprepared for the news of the declaration of war." Even if such mistakes are tangential to the film, they "nag at the natural sense of gratitude for an American film which is generous and whole-hearted in its desire to offer tribute to the courage and character of ordinary people attacked by a force they are determined to resist."[21]

Other British critics had even harsher things to say about how "their war" had been reinterpreted by Hollywood. Several reviews brought the class biases of the film to the forefront. Writing in the *New Statesman and Nation* in July 1942, William Whitebait commented, "Most American films about England ... at war have a blithe inaccuracy that soars at times into fantasy." While noting that some aspects of the film are less "calamitous" than one might imagine, he assails the film for at most achieving "an easy pathos; sentimentality (and class sentimentality at that) takes on a tone of holiness, of smug simplicity, which personally I found it rather difficult to bear. 'This is a people's war,' says the vicar delivering a sermon in his bombed church; but it isn't, it is only (look round at the faces, look back over the story!) the best people's war."[22] Nor can Whitebait resist a dig at Mrs. Miniver's creator: "[T]he fact that Miss Jan Struther ... saw the Blitz from America probably also accounts for the grace with which her heroine weathers the war." In a similar vein, the reviewer in the *Documentary News Letter* of August 1942, described it as in many ways "just repulsive." Yet a viewer "can sit in the Empire [theater] and hear practically the whole house weeping – a British audience with three years of war behind it, crying at one of the phoniest war films that has ever

[20] "Cinema: New Picture," *Time*, 29 June 1942.
[21] "Mrs. Miniver," *Times*, 8 July 1942.
[22] William Whitebait, "The Movies," *New Stateman and Nation*, 18 July 1942.

been made."[23] This suggests something of the film's appeal – as its critics stated over and over again – being based on emotion and sentimentality despite what an audience might know about the "real" nature of warfare and, in particular, about the effects of the war on those without the class privileges of the Minivers.

Edgar Anstey began his response in the *Spectator* by describing the first half hour of the film as "intolerable." If the Minivers are supposed to represent "'ordinary' people whose fortitude in luxurious adversity" is meant to be "symbolic of the British war effort," then only one conclusion can be drawn "by the transatlantic victims of such well-meaning but unconsciously pro-fascist propaganda – that the world revolution which is visible to the people of every other country in the world has manifested itself in Britain only as a defence of bourgeois privilege."[24] Anstey refused to let the "Hollywood" origins of the film excuse such inaccuracies. As he pointed out, the physical details of the Anderson shelter are accurate, so why couldn't "the historical and psychological milieu" be presented in a similarly authentic manner? Although he saw the film as being fundamentally about "puppets," not "people," Anstey did find some redeeming moments – "the frightened family in the shelter, each member suppressing or communicating terror in the most convincing manner" – and went on to assert that there is no doubt the film will be popular.

Other popular films reflected the contributions of women in realms more usually associated with "war work." Few, however, highlighted the "quiet" heroism of wives and mothers under the threat of aerial bombardment as effectively as *Mrs. Miniver*. Although the title character lives a life made easier by her class status, her situation as a wife and especially as a mother – of a son in uniform – who nonetheless faces war in the form of aerial bombardment full on is meant to transcend these differences and speak to a very widespread female audience. As a model for the women watching her exploits in the dark theater, Kay Miniver does all she can to protect those she loves and to maintain the essence of domestic well-being despite the war. She comforts her children, supports her husband, runs her household, and does not let material losses bother her. That she is unable to safeguard her family entirely speaks to vulnerability of "all of us" under the conditions of modern (aerial) warfare.

The same year that *Mrs. Miniver* was released to such mixed acclaim, Noel Coward's *In Which We Serve*, a homegrown British war movie also

---

[23] "Film of the Month: Mrs. Miniver," *Documentary News Letter*, Aug. 1942.
[24] Edgar Anstey, "The Cinema," *Spectator*, 17 July 1942.

appeared. Focused on the navy and with much of the story told in the form of flashbacks by sailors clinging to a life raft in the Mediterranean after their ship has gone down, the film also demonstrated an explicit awareness of the heroism of those on less active front lines. *In Which We Serve* also presented an idyllic England, very much the island nation, which confronts the onslaught of aerial warfare. Although the film claimed to be (and to a large extent is) "the story of a ship," the *HMS Torrin*, and its crew led by Coward's Captain Kincross, it also told a story – like *Mrs. Miniver* – of Britain facing total war. The bulk of the narrative conveys the experiences of those waiting to be rescued from the *Torrin* through flashbacks of the homes and women left on shore.[25]

Again as was the case with *Mrs. Miniver*, we watch as war encroaches upon a peaceful England. For instance, during a scene in which a British couple watches newsreel footage in a darkened theater, the audience learns that France has fallen. The scene immediately shifts to a family picnic in a countryside that looks "so sweet and green and peaceful," as Alix, the upper-class wife of the ship's captain puts it. The camera focuses our attention on Captain Kincross, Alix, and their children in this idealized landscape only after showing us the vapor trails of planes overhead. When the camera swoops down on where the family is picnicking, the young son corrects the father about the identification of the plane they are watching (another sign of how children have adapted to war), and then the wife asks if "it's so dreadfully wrong to forget the war now and again?" Her husband replies, "I think it's very clever of you with all hell breaking loose immediately over our defenceless heads." But his calm demeanor belies any sense of "hell" being present at all, even as Alix Kincross says that she gives herself comfort by imagining the planes are "toys having a mock battle just to keep us amused." Here was a vivid portrayal of lightheartedness in the face of death from the air.

The film provides several other scenes of iconic wartime moments – women seeing their men off in a train station and a domestic portrait of Alix Kincross reading Lewis Carroll to her children dissolving into a

---

[25] S. P. MacKenzie suggests that "it rapidly became clear that intertwining the private lives of three members of the crew – specifically the women they love – with the story of the ship made it wildly popular." See MacKenzie, *British War Films*, 73–82; quote on 79. In another assessment of the film, Neil Rattigan observes that it is among the most class bound and therefore honest films of the war; see Rattigan, *This Is England*, 75–94. Antonia Lant notes that the film's scenes are evenly divided between the fronts; see Antonia Lant, *Blackout: Reinventing Women for Wartime British Cinema* (Princeton, NJ, 1991), 46.

sweep of bombs exploding into the water. The setting fades out on the war at sea to fade in on the war at home. The lens returns the viewer to Plymouth under fire, where Freda, the new wife of *Torrin*'s seaman Shorty Blake, has taken refuge with her aunt. We have seen the quick courtship between Shorty and Freda when she was on route to visit her aunt Kathleen, who is the wife of the *Torrin*'s chief petty office, Walter Hardy. Now pregnant, Freda is living with Kathleen Hardy and Kathleen's mother-in-law, Mrs. Lemmon.

An aerial attack interrupts an ordinary and highly domestic evening at home for three generations of women. While the youngest and oldest women present knit, the air raid sirens go off. Freda refuses to go to a shelter – it "makes me feel sick" – although she is clearly getting nervous. Meanwhile, Mrs. Lemmon states that "my nerves won't stand much more of this" and continues what is clearly a long-running conversation with her daughter, urging her to leave the area under attack and take safety in the countryside. Kathleen Hardy – making her case against the backdrop of increasingly loud explosions and the ongoing wail of the sirens – firmly rebuffs her mother: "This is Walter's home and he expects to find me in it when he comes on leave." She insists that her duty is to maintain the home (front), and to leave it seems to her equivalent to abandoning her man and her nation at war.

Immediately after this dialogue, even louder explosions fill the sound track, while Kathleen ushers Freda into a rocking chair placed under the stairs for greater safety. Almost predictably, the women look up, the screen fades to black, only to have the camera fade in on a scene of total devastation. The house has suffered a direct hit; first aid workers carry the women out on stretchers. With her last breath, Kathleen Hardy whispers to the nurse, "Tell Walter I didn't want to leave the house." Freda survives unscathed, but the other women are dead, and the scene ends by focusing on Freda closing her eyes as the sirens continue to scream.

The deeply emotionally and resonant death of Kathleen Hardy clearly shows her as a victim of the war. The three main male naval characters – Kincross, Hardy, and Blake – all survive the sinking of the HMS *Torrin*, rescued from the life raft by another British ship, and at film's end, they are presumably able to take up their lives and duties. The film depicts a calm and orderly, even bored group of sailors receiving word of the tragedy in Plymouth when the post arrives. At first, Shorty Blake is overjoyed to hear from Freda and learn of the birth of his son, but as he explains to his shipmates, his son was born "in the middle of a Blitz." He heads off soberly to try to find Hardy and tell him the devastating news – raising

the question of why there are no next-of-kin telegrams to send to service-
men when their civilian beloveds have been killed. The camera pans over
Hardy's head as he writes a letter to his "old darling" and is interrupted
by Blake, who delivers the news that Hardy's home suffered a direct
hit, killing his wife and her mother. His reaction is eerily calm, "Oh I
see ... Thanks son, much obliged," and he heads on deck, crushing the
letter home that no longer needs to be sent. He throws it into the sea. It
becomes part of the flotsam that leads our eyes to another sea, and this
time to the end of the flashback, to the men clinging to the life raft watching the *HMS Torrin* finally sink.[26]

Critical reaction to *In Which We Serve*, which opened on 23 September
1942 in London, was highly sympathetic on both sides of the Atlantic.
The *Times* proclaimed that "what it lacked in cumulative power it makes
up for in the vividness of its individual scenes."[27] William Whitebait
described it as "good, nearly very good," although he complained about
its length and about the humorlessness of Coward's character.[28] Edgar
Anstey, who had such devastating things to say a few months earlier
about *Mrs. Miniver*, hailed the film: "[T]here can be no doubt that *In
Which We Serve* is the best film yet made about the war in any country."
Anstey was impressed by "the ingenuity of its transitions, moving from
present to past in a moment of delirium, or through a lingering phrase,
the film combines into a rounded whole the home-lives of members of the
'Torrin's' crew with the war-story of the ship." He was especially pleased
by "scenes of home life. Here at last on the screen in a war-film are working-class men and women with integrity, wisdom and humanity," who, he
might have added, unlike the characters in *Mrs. Miniver*, more accurately
represent the kind of civilians who had lost their lives and possessions in
air raids at home.[29]

The film was less a work of propaganda aimed at an American audience than was *Mrs. Miniver*, but its value as a sympathetic portrait of
the travails of wartime Britain resonated in the United States when the
film was released in December. Before American audiences could view
the film, they were alerted to its significance by a short notice in the
New York Times in October of a "slap-up premiere – or as slap-up as
you can expect at 6:30 on a Sunday evening in wartime" – of the film,
attended by high-ranking American and British naval officials as well as

---

[26] All references are from *In Which We Serve* (1942), dir. Noel Coward and David Lean.
[27] "In Which We Serve," *Times*, 24 Sept. 1942.
[28] William Whitebait, "The Movies," *New Statesmen and Nation*, 24 (1942).
[29] Edgar Anstey, "The Cinema," *Spectator*, 2 Oct. 1942.

Foreign Secretary Anthony Eden, in London. The reporter, while eschewing any attempt to evaluate the film, commented that "from the reviews, the packed houses and the extraordinary demonstrations at the close of each show it would appear to be very much to London's taste."[30] In addition, before the film could be released in the United States, it had to win a battle with the Hays Office responsible for movie censorship, which asked that the terms "God, hell, damn and bastard" be deleted from the film before its distribution could be allowed. American critics such as the reviewer for *Time* magazine commented that "only an evil-minded ear could have detected anything profane in *In Which We Serve*," adding that British censors had allowed not only the four offensive words, but also " 'bloody' (to Britons a much more shocking term than 'bastard')."[31]

Mainstream media reactions to Coward and Lean's film in United States further revealed an enthusiasm for the film's portrait of Britain at war, not just of military action but also of the lives of "wives and sweethearts" at home. *Newsweek* praised it as "far and away the finest film to come out of the war.... [I]t is also one of the screen's proudest achievements at any time and in any country."[32] *Life* similarly described it as "one of the greatest war films yet to appear."[33] Calling it "the first really great picture of World War II," the reviewer for *Time* found that while the film is about a ship, "the most moving sequence is not her sinking but the scene in which Shorty breaks the news to Hardy that during a heavy bombing of Plymouth Shorty has gained a son and Hardy has lost his wife."[34] Clearly for this critic and for others, profanity lay in the heartless killing of civilians at home rather than in the terms sailors might utter in the midst of war. Critic Manny Farber summed up the power of the "movie of the year" by noting that Coward had "made a picture of average people in war instead of the exclusively *Harper's Bazaar* set of "Mrs. Miniver."[35] Like Anstey in Britain, Farber compared the two films and found the version of only an upper-crust Britain at war lacking.

Taken together, these films conveyed to their wartime audiences a vision of a world at war that acknowledged and even commemorated the deaths of civilians from air raids at home as a core war experience. The reactions to such losses – the stoic grief portrayed by men who had to mourn their

[30] C. A. Lejeune, "Noel Coward Presents –," *New York Times*, 25 Oct. 1942.
[31] "The New Pictures, *Time*, 28 Dec. 1942.
[32] "Entertainment: H.M.S. Torrin: Chap. 1," *Newsweek*, 21 Dec. 1942.
[33] "Movie of the Week," *Life*, 21 Dec. 1942.
[34] "The New Pictures."
[35] Manny Farber, "Movie of the Year," *New Republic*, 28 Dec. 1942.

women killed in such domestic circumstances as knitting in a rocking chair or driving along a country road – offered a powerful message about morale and about the essential inhumanity of this form of warfare. No matter that, as we have seen, Britons had decades in which to imagine and thus prepare for a future where everyone would come under fire. The emotions evoked by these films and their representations of "Blitzed Britons" suggested the need to cultivate a fresh sense of outrage, not an acceptance of what was, after all, a fairly long-standing threat.

CONCLUSION

By the end of 1942, the image of grace under fire as *the* desired response of everyone to total war became once more enshrined in popular culture. Even if such responses were as much fictive as real, they represent the culmination of the acceptance that modern war destroyed civilian lives that began with World War I. Viewed alongside the personal reflections on the Blitz discussed in the preceding chapter and the fictional accounts briefly examined in this chapter, both *Mrs. Miniver* and *In Which We Serve* firmly presented the kind of civil identity that valued stoicism, calm, and acceptance of danger and sacrifice across geographic, class, and gender lines. They also were in keeping with representations of air war dating back to the raids of the Great War that used attacks on emblems of innocence – women and children – to expose the horrors of this form of warfare. Air power had wrought this fundamental change in the role of civilians at war, and now its full effects were being felt and depicted as never before.

12

Conclusion

Air Raids and the Domestication of Modern War

Air raids fundamentally redefined the civilian experience of warfare. Part of the story we have just traced is about how men – the overwhelming majority of state agents and war planners – came to terms with the fact that they could never make women and children immune to direct attack during wartime.[1] If, as Jack Mudd put it in 1917, it was difficult for a man to go off to fight knowing his "wife and children cant be safe," then a state could now mobilize for war only by assuming a broader paternalistic role in protecting his family and home life in his stead. However, the state could not act alone; it needed civilians to accept a new kind of civil identity that embraced qualities usually associated with combatants: stoicism, steadfastness, and a willingness to endure many of the hardships and risks associated with battle, including death.

As we have seen, this story began with the air raids of the First World War. The death and destruction from those raids forced a recognition of the harsh reality of modern war. The survival of the state and the home now relied on the joint efforts of combatants and non-combatants. The key work of preparing Britain to accept this transformation was cultural, played out in a variety of settings and with a good deal of resistance and discomfort throughout the interwar period.

Indeed, the central and local expansion of the state in order to protect the civil population from attack during wartime was something that William Beveridge made clear several years *before* the start of the Second

---

[1] There has been a good deal of recent work on masculinity and war; for a useful account of British men and air power, see Martin Francis, *The Flyer: British Culture and the Royal Air Force, 1939–1945* (Oxford, 2008).

World War.[2] Drawing upon his experiences mobilizing civilian resources during the Great War, Beveridge authored a prominent series of articles in the *Times* in February 1937 entitled "The Home Front in War." As information about British civil defense planning in the form of ARP was increasingly publicized after 1935, Beveridge clearly drew the stakes for the nation:

> In the last War families waited for bad news about their fighting men in the trenches; in a new war fighting men may wait for bad news about their families at home.... If we prepare at all for a new war, we must prepare completely, not on the military front alone.
>
> [W]ar, like other misfortunes of mankind, is now totalitarian.
>
> If we prepare for war at all, we must prepare for it completely.[3]

Beveridge stressed that "in a new war the civilian population may be subject to direct attack from aircraft, to an extent unparalleled in the past and the issue of the conflict may turn on the extent to which this direct attack on homes can be foiled."[4] This first article, subtitled "Security and Progress," and its companion pieces acknowledged that attacks on civilians were not new, something made evident both by the First World War and by the return of air raids to European soil in Spain, although the articles predate the devastating attacks on Guernica. What these articles acknowledged as different was the *extent* to which damage could now be done. Given this transformation, the state needed to take direct action but so, too, did those at home. Unless Britain prepared "completely" – a term that Beveridge repeated more than once – it would lose the next war, perhaps before it even started.

Moreover, Beveridge asserted that "many ... of the civilian measures now needed to make us safer in war are measures already overdue for

---

[2] For key works on the development of the welfare state, see Peter Baldwin, *The Politics of Social Solidarity: Class Bases of the European Welfare State, 1875–1975* (Cambridge, 1990); Gisela Bock and Pat Thane (eds.), *Maternity and Gender Policies: Women and the Rise of the European Welfare States, 1880s–1950s* (London, 1991); and Susan Pedersen, *Family, Dependence and the Origins of the Welfare State: Britain and France, 1914–1945* (Cambridge, 1993). For the Beveridge Report itself, see William H. Beveridge, *Social Insurance and Allied Services, Report by Sir William Beveridge* (London, 1942). For more perspectives on the political context of the report, see Kevin Jefferys, *War and Reform: British Politics during the Second World War* (Manchester, 1994).

[3] Sir William Beveridge, "The Home Front in War," three-part series, *Times*, 22–24 Feb. 1937.

[4] Sir William Beveridge, "The Home Front in War," *Times*, 22 Feb. 1937.

making us happier in peace."[5] Beveridge concluded his series by again insisting that measures to safeguard the civil population in war should be thought of as desirable in their own right. For instance, instead of the prospect of evacuation from major cities being viewed with horror, it could be seen as effectively giving a population room to breathe away from ever more crowded urban areas. Unlike other overtly military war preparations, the process of making the homeland "less vulnerable threatens no man and raises no doubts."

An editorial in the *Times* entitled "The Home Front" buttressed Beveridge's remarks. Appearing the same day as Beveridge's final article, it too laid out the particular stakes for Britain as a democracy facing the threat of modern warfare. The nation needed to take advantage of the opportunity provided by war planning, "for war simplifies the problems of constructive thought in the very act of making them more urgent." Among the urgent tasks were "the transition from an individual to a coordinated economy" and addressing the balance between authority and liberty. The editorial asserted that for democracies "either the outward tokens of a free life must be sacrificed or freedom itself will be imperiled, for in the modern world improvisation in support of the best of political causes will fail against organized and mechanized tyranny." Freedom itself has to be redefined: "[T]o be free, as twentieth-century thought is beginning to see it, is so to organize that the gains of freedom shall not be precarious but shall be wrought into the very texture of a people's life." Thus, "an adequately protected home front" becomes not "one huge national dug-out, but a healthier and more evenly prosperous England."[6] Here we see not only an echo of the 1917 feminist vision of the state and home "mixed up," but also the growth of military expenditure – including that on civil defense – justified as improving domestic life. We see the warfare and welfare states mixed up, expanding in tandem in interwar Britain.

An issue underlying state expansion remained. If all were at risk and had to contribute to safeguarding the state completely, how was such total preparation to proceed? In public and private, many conceded that it had to *start* with civilians, with their character, morale, and fitness. It thus

---

[5] Beveridge, "The Home Front in War," *Times*, 22 Feb. 1937. The second article was devoted to the food supply, and the third to transportation and labor, and in both instances, Beveridge argued for greater regulation to secure the well-being as well as safety of the nation at home. See *Times*, 23 and 24 Feb. 1937.

[6] "The Home Front" (editorial), *Times*, 24 Feb. 1937.

both relied on gendered and class-based assumptions about the capacity of civilians to endure aerial bombardment and attempted to fix a new kind of civil identity that would transcend all other differences. In recent work, David Edgerton has argued that Britain after the First World War is better understood as a "warfare" state than a welfare one.[7] While this book concurs with Edgerton that technology – such as air power – drove transformations in politics and culture, the state that developed was a welfare *and* warfare state because warfare itself came to attack domestic rather than solely military life. Once air raids as a primary instrument of war attacked civilians at home, centralized state intervention into the home could be (and was) justified to secure the survival of home life and thus the state itself.

And so in 1942 the Committee on Social Insurance and Allied Services under the leadership of Sir William Beveridge issued what became known as the "Beveridge Report," a plan for comprehensive social insurance that made the state responsible for, among other things, a national health service, family allowances, and full employment. Such a model took the family as the unit by which to guarantee "freedom from want." By 1944 many had embraced its planned redistribution of resources in order to reward citizens for their shared wartime sacrifices. A bargain that historians of the welfare state have traced between the willingness of citizens to be subjected to state intervention and the state's alleviation of fundamental wants (hunger, shelter, education, health) thus resonates with the story of an emerging "civil defense" state that we have seen outlined in this book.

This study has begun to recover this complex story. It has provided an account, hitherto largely overlooked, of one of the Great War's most enduring legacies, one that decisively altered the expectations for, and even experiences of, the Second World War. This book has thus also had a larger aim: to show how the domestication of the air raid was both shaped by and helped to transform understandings of how the state and the home together confronted total war; for after 1914, the history of civilians at war became an essential aspect of military history.

From the moment that civilian lives were lost and homes destroyed in the Great War, witnesses spoke of a changed world. In 1917 Ida O'Malley wrote of the "strange times" in which it was no longer possible to "think of the state as separate from the home, of men as separate from women." This perhaps gets at the meaning of total war, an oft-used and debated

---

[7] David Edgerton, *Warfare State: Britain, 1920–1970* (Cambridge, 2006).

concept.[8] War was *total* when the distinction between combatant and non-combatant ceased; when babies in cradles in London fell victim to bombs deployed from enemy planes; when states had to plan to ameliorate, while admitting they could never prevent, catastrophic damage inflicted potentially on all civilians. Throughout the interwar period, pacifists and war planners, government officials and novelists, men and women, repeatedly predicted that in the war to come *all* would be at risk, and *all* would be called upon to suffer and sacrifice.

There are many things still to say about the devastating bombing campaigns of the Second World War and, of course, about the Blitz itself, but one thing is clear: there was nothing fundamentally *new* about this war's air raids. Even the scale – dreadful as it was – was not as great as had been predicted or imagined. If, as Cicely Hamilton put it, everything had altered on that "red wicked night" when she first witnessed the unleashing of aerial warfare in 1918, she was far from the only one to reach such conclusions. Throughout the interwar era, the dead schoolchildren of Poplar could haunt the imagination as much as the crowds fleeing the bombing planes. Those entrusted with planning for ARP and those insisting on disarmament at all costs shared – and indeed helped to produce – a set of cultural assumptions: war had changed; war would kill the innocent; no one and no place was safe. All the anxiety about protecting "women and children" could not erase this fundamental transformation. The question remained, to what kind of imagined war would the next war be compared? The war only of the air, devastating enough, or the war of the air and the laboratory, unleashing a kind of hell upon civilians not yet seen in modern war? If the worst visions of full-scale chemical warfare unleashed on helpless populations were then mediated by the state provision of gas masks for men, women, and children of all ages, gas mask drills could not fully disguise the prospect of domestic life laid waste. In the end, although not for those living in Britain, the Second World War produced an even more potent example of the scientific annihilation of entire cities from the air.

At the conclusion of World War II, the citizens of Britain and of most other participant states could begin the long process of recovery and remembrance. They had confronted the destruction of their homes and

---

[8] See the introduction to Roger Chickering and Stig Förstser (eds.), *The Shadows of Total War: Europe, East Asia, and the United States, 1919–1939* (Cambridge, 2003), and to Roger Chickering, Stig Förstser, and Bernd Greiner (eds.), *A World at Total War: Global Conflict and the Politics of Destruction, 1937–1945* (Cambridge, 2005).

witnessed the deaths and injuries inflicted by seemingly indiscriminate aerial bombardment. Counting all of that war's losses, in the end total civilian deaths outnumbered those of combatants, although this was not the case for Britain, where civilian casualties were estimated at around 50,000 out of 350,000 overall.[9] But numbers, as we have seen, are not the reason to focus on those who experienced this war under fire at home. Nor, as this work has shown, was this a story that began in 1939.

Renewed interest in the damage inflicted on bombed civilians as a category worthy of study has become a hallmark of late-twentieth- and early-twenty-first-century studies of war. From Sven Lindqvist's meditative *A History of Bombing* and Yuki Tanaka and Marilyn B. Young's recent edited collection, *Bombing Civilians*, to the work of political scientists such as Hugo Slim's *Killing Civilians* and Alexander Downes's *Targeting Civilians in War*, to the philosophical inquiries into the Second World War's aerial campaigns, including A. C. Grayling's *Among the Dead Cities* and W. G. Sebald's *On the Natural History of Destruction*, as civilians, and especially women and children, continue to suffer from the bombs unleashed in our contemporary wars, we seek to understand how the once unthinkable has become acceptable, an "ordinary fact of war."[10] Collectively, such works help us appreciate the new stakes that

---

[9] See the chart under the heading "Demography of the War," in *The Oxford Companion to World War II*, ed. I.C. B. Dear (Oxford, 1995), 290.

[10] Sven Lindqvist, *A History of Bombing*, trans. Linda Haverty Rugg (New York, 2001); Yuki Tanaka and Marilyn B. Young (eds.), *Bombing Civilians: A Twentieth-Century History* (New York, 2009); Hugo Slim, *Killing Civilians: Method, Madness, and Morality in War* (New York, 2008); Alexander Downes, *Targeting Civilians in War* (Ithaca, NY, 2008); A. C. Grayling, *Among the Dead Cities: The History and Moral Legacy of the WWII Bombing of Civilians in Germany and Japan* (New York, 2006); and W. G. Sebald, *On the Natural History of Destruction*, trans. Anthea Bell (New York, 2004). For other studies of the bombing campaigns of the Second World War, see the controversial Jörg Friedrich, *The Fire: The Bombing of Germany, 1940–45*, trans. Alison Brown (2002; rpt. and trans., New York, 2006), and responses to this by Mary Nolan, "Germans as Victims during the Second World War: Air Wars, Memory Wars," *Central European History* 38:1 (2005), 7–40 and Robert G. Moeller, "On the History of Man-made Destruction: Loss, Death, Memory and Germany in the Bombing War," *History Workshop Journal* 61:1 (2006), 103–134 and the expanded version of this, "The Bombing War in Germany, 2005–1940: Back to the Future?" In *Bombing Civilians: A Twentieth-Century History*, ed. Yuki Tanaka and Marilyn B. Young (New York, 2009); Tami Davis Biddle, "Dresden 1945: Reality, History and Memory," *Journal of Military History* 72 (2008), 413–449; Marshall De Bruhl, *Firestorm: Allied Airpower and the Destruction of Dresden* (New York, 2006); and Stephen A. Garrett, *Ethics and Airpower in World War Two: The British Bombing of German Cities* (New York, 1993). For more on the general history of air power, see Stephen Budiansky, *Air Power: The Men, Machines, and Ideas That Revolutionized War from Kitty Hawk to Gulf War II* (New York, 2004); the strategic

air power raised, and some of the consequences of our collective failure to halt those beautiful and deadly sights of machines "dripping death" from the sky.

This study has traced the air raid from its unleashing in the first great war of the preceding century through the cultural work of those imagining – in the space between the wars – how it might be possible to prevent, or prepare civilians for, this new feature of modern conflict. When a government war planner can suggest that it is time to ask H. G. Wells, a writer of science fiction, to help him and his colleagues to visualize what war might do, it is clear that both are engaged in a *cultural* effort. This effort continued through the Second World War, and this book has ended with what was new in *scale* but not in *kind* when air power inflicted damage anew on British homes and lives. This book has not provided another account of the Blitz or of the British population under attack during the Second World War, but rather a history necessary to understand fully both of these. In part, it has traced the story of the forging of a kind of civil identity between 1914 and 1939 that evolved before the onset of the bombing campaigns of this later war and of the growth of a state that had to encompass the protection of all civilians at home as part of its war making.

Helena Swanwick, one of the protagonists of the story of failed but nonetheless compelling efforts to stop the devastating effects of aerial warfare, wrote in 1935 that air power threatened to make the home "the most dangerous of all places" (or perhaps more accurately as dangerous as any place). In the air raids of the First World War and of all the wars that have followed, every space was now a potential battleground, and every citizen-subject faced choices that could determine whether both the home and the state endured.

study, Robert A. Pape, *Bombing to Win: Air Power and Coercion in War* (Ithaca, NY, 1996); and Biddle Davis, *Rhetoric and Reality in Air Warfare: The Evolution of British and American Ideas about Strategic Bombing, 1914–1945* (Princeton, NJ, 2002). The phrase "ordinary facts of war" comes from a 1916 article describing French air raids in *Le Petit Parisien* and is quoted in my article " 'The Souls of Soldiers': Civilians Under Fire in First World War France," *Journal of Modern History*, 78:3 (2006), 588–622. Feminist theorist Cynthia Enloe has suggested the use of "womenandchildren" as a compound noun in reference to wartime; see Enloe, "The Gendered Gulf," in *Collateral Damage: The "New World Order" at Home and Abroad*, ed. Cynthia Peters (Boston, 1992).

Bibliography

Archival Sources

Imperial War Museum, London
  Department of Art
  Department of Documents
  Film and Video Archive
  National Inventory of War Memorials
  Photography Archive
Mass Observation Archives, Sussex
National Archives, London
  Records of the Air, Admiralty, Foreign, Colonial, and Home Office on Air Raids
  Records of the Air Raids Precautions Department, Home Office
  Records of the Committee of Imperial Defence, Sub-Committee on Air Raids Precautions
Women's International League British Section, British Library of Political and Economic Science, London

Periodicals

Bookman
Common Cause
Commonwealth
Daily Express
Daily Herald
Daily Mail
Daily Mirror
Daily Sketch
Daily Telegraph
Daily Worker
Documentary News Letter
Evening News

Evening Standard
Illustrated London News
Lancet
Life and Letters To-day
London Mercury
Manchester Guardian
Nation & Athenaeum
Nature
New Statesman
New Statesman and Nation
New York Times
News Chronicle
News of the World
Pall Mall Gazette
Punch
Reynold's News
Saturday Review
Spectator
Star
Tatler
Times
Times Literary Supplement
Weekly Dispatch
Women's International League Monthly News Sheet

Printed Primary Sources

Air Raid Precautions: A Concise, Fully Illustrated and Practical Guide, 2d ed. (London, 1939).
   "Air Raid Precautions Handbook No. 1" (London, 1938).
Baker, Philip Noel. "The International Air Police Force." In Storm Jameson (ed.), *Challenge to Death* (London, 1935).
   "A National Air Force No Defence." In Storm Jameson (ed.), *Challenge to Death* (London, 1935).
Bennett, Arnold. *The Pretty Lady* (London, 1918).
Beveridge, William H. *Social Insurance and Allied Services, Report by Sir William Beveridge* (London, 1942).
Bottome, Phyllis. *London Pride* (1941, London; rpt. Boston, 1941).
Brighouse, Harold. *Air-Raid Refugees: A Farce of the Crisis* (New York, 1939).
Brittain, Vera. *Chronicle of Youth: War Diary, 1913–1917* (1981, rpt. New York, London, 1982).
   England's Hour (London, 1941).
   Honourable Estate (London, 1936).
   "Seeds of Chaos: What Mass Bombing Really Means" (London, 1944).
   Testament of a Peace Lover: Letters from Vera Brittain (London, 1988).
   Testament of Youth (London, 1933; rpt. London, 1977).

Burroughs, E. A. "The Lambeth Series: The Christian Church and War" (1931; rpt. Milwaukee, WI, 1931).

Butler, Elizabeth. *An Autobiography* (London, 1923).

Cambridge Scientists Anti-War Group, *The Protection of the Public from Aerial Attack* (London, 1937).

Charlton, L. E. O. *War over England* (London, 1936).

Charlton, L. E. O., G. T. Garratt, and Lt-Com. R. Fletcher. *Air Defence of Britain* (Harmondsworth, 1938).

Chemical Warfare: An Abridged Report of Papers Read at an International Conference at Frankfurt am Main (London, 1930).

Clausewitz, Carl von. "On the Character of Modern War." In *On War* (1832; rpt. and trans. Harmondsworth, 1982).

Cornwallis-West, G. *The Woman Who Stopped War* (London, 1935).

Deedes, William F. "A.R.P.: A Complete Guide to Civil Defence Measures" (London, 1939).

Douhet, Guilio. *The Command of the Air.* Translated by Dino Ferarri (1921, rpt. and trans. New York, 1942).

Foster, Arnold. *The Disarmament Conference* (London, 1932).

Gibbs, Philip. *Realities of War* (1919; rev. ed., London, 1929).

Haden-Guest, Leslie. *If Air War Comes: A Guide to Air Raid Precautions and Anti-Gas Treatment* (London, 1937).

Haldane, J. B. S. *Callinicus: A Defence of Chemical Warfare* (London, 1925).

Hamilton, Cicely. *Lest Ye Die: A Story from the Past or of the Future* (New York, 1928).

   Life Errant (London, 1935).

   Theodore Savage (London, 1922).

   William: An Englishman (London, 1918).

Harris, Lilian. "Disarmament and Security" (London, 1931).

Hazeltine, Harold. *The Law of the Air* (London, 1911).

Head, Alice M. *It Could Never Have Happened* (London, 1939).

Heald, Stephen. "Memorandum on the Progress of Disarmament, 1919–1932" (London, 1932).

Hirschfield, Magnus. *The Sexual History of the World War* (New York, 1934).

Hodsoll, E. J. "Introduction," *Air Raid Precautions: A Concise, Fully Illustrated and Practical Guide,* 2d ed. (London, 1939).

Home Forces General Headquarters, Section I. *Air Raid Secret Circulars,* 1914–1916.

Hyde, H. Montgomery, and G. R. Falkiner Nuttall. *Air Defence and the Civil Population* (London, 1937).

Innes, C. A. "A.B.C. of Air Disarmament: An Account of the Efforts Made to Abolish Military and Naval Aircraft" (London, 1935).

James, Winifred. *Out of the Shadows* (London, 1924).

Kendall, James. *Breathe Freely: The Truth about Poison Gas* (London, 1938).

Lacroix, Pierre. *Le Domaine Aérien et la Guerre: Essai sur les hostilités et la neutralité aériennes dans le conflit de 1914–1918* (Toulouse, 1919).

Langdon-Davies, John. *Air Raid: The Technique of Silent Approach, High Explosive Panic* (London, 1938).

Liddell-Hart, Basil H. *Paris: or the Future of War* (London, 1925).

Liepmann, Heinz. *Death from the Skies: A Study of Gas and Microbrial Warfare.* Translated by Eden and Cedar Paul. (rpt. and trans. London, 1937).

Linklater, Eric. *The Impregnable Women* (London, 1938).

Mee, Arthur. *Arthur Mee's Hero Book* (London, 1921).

"Miles." *The Gas War of 1940* (London, 1931).

"Minutes of the Air Commission," *Records of the Conference for the Reduction and Limitation of Armaments*, series D, vol. 3 (Geneva, 1936).

MacFie, J. W. S. *An Ethiopian Diary: A Record of the British Ambulance Service in Ethiopia* (London, 1936).

Mordaunt, Elinor. *Blitz Kids* (London, 1941).

Moseley, Maboth. *The War upon Women* (London, 1934).

Mr. Punch's History of the Great War (London, 1919).

Mumford, Philip S. *Humanity, Air Power and War* (London, 1936).

Munich, P. "Preface," *What Would Be the Character of a New War?* (London, 1931).

Orwell, George. *The Collected Essays, Journalism and Letters of George Orwell*, vol. 1. Edited by Sonia Orwell and Ian Argus (New York, 1968).

Keep the Aspidistra Flying (1936; rpt. Harmondsworth, 1975).

Review of *Spanish Testament* by Arthur Koestler, *Time and Tide*, 5 Feb. 1938. In *The Collected Essays, Journalism and Letters of George Orwell*, vol. 1. Edited by Sonia Orwell and Ian Argus (New York, 1968).

Owen, John. *Blitz Hero* (London, 1942).

Paget, Henry Luke, Bishop of Stepney. *Records of the Raids* (London, 1918).

Pankhurst, E. Sylvia. *The Home Front: A Mirror to Life in England during the First World War* (London, 1932; rpt. London, 1987).

Parliamentary Debates – Commons.

Parliamentary Debates – Lords.

Pethick-Lawrence, Emmeline. *My Part in a Changing World* (London, 1938).

Public Information Leaflets, Nos. 1–5 (London, 1939).

Records of the Conference for the Reduction and Limitation of Armaments, series D, vol. 3 (Geneva, 1936).

Rhonnda, Lady. *This Was My World* (London, 1933).

Richardson, Ethel. *Remembrance Wakes* (London, 1934).

Ross, Albert Henry [pseudonym of Frank Morison]. *War on Great Cities: A Study of the Facts* (London, 1937).

Royden, A. Maude. *Women's Partnership in the New World* (London, 1941).

Royse, M. W. *Aerial Bombardment and the International Regulation of Warfare* (New York, 1928).

Rudkin, Mabel S. *Inside Dover, 1914–1918: A Woman's Impressions* (London, 1933).

Salmond, Monica. *Bright Armour: Memories of Four Years of War* (London, 1935).

Sayers, Dorothy. *The Letters of Dorothy L. Sayers, 1899–1936: The Making of a Detective Novelist.* Edited by Barbara Reynolds (New York, 1996).

Schreiner, Olive. "Women and War." In *Woman and Labour* (London, 1911).

Shute, Nevil. *What Happened to the Corbetts* (1939; rpt. London, 1961).

Spaight, James. *Air Power and the Cities* (London, 1930).

Air Power and War Rights (London, 1924)

Steer, George Lowther. *Tree of Guernika* (London, 1938).

Stern, G. B. [Gladys]. *Monogram* (London, 1936).

Stokes, Simpson. *Air-Gods' Parade* (London, 1935).

Strang, Herbert. *The Air Scout: A Story of National Defence* (London, 1912).

Struther, Jan. *Mrs. Miniver* (New York, 1940).

Women of Britain: Letters from England (New York, 1941).

Swanwick, H[elena] M. "Frankenstein and His Monster: Aviation for World Service" (London, 1934).

I Have Been Young (London, 1935).

The Roots of Peace (London, 1938).

Thomas, S. Evelyn. *Handy War-Time Guide for the Woman at Home and the Man in the Street* (St. Albans, 1939).

Times Diary & Index of the War (London, 1919).

Tragedy at Bethnal Green: Report on an Inquiry into the Accident at Bethnal Green Tube Station Shelter (1945, rpt. London, 1999).

Von Metzsch, Lieut-General. "The New Tendencies of Development in Warfare." In *What Would Be the Character of a New War?* (London, 1931).

Wells, H. G., *The Shape of Things to Come* (New York, 1933).

The War in the Air. (1908; rpt. Lincoln, NE, 2002).

Wintringham, T. H. *Air Raid Warning* (London, 1934).

The Coming World War (London, 1935).

Woker, Getrud. "Chemical and Bacteriological Warfare." In *What Would Be the Character of a New War?* (London, 1931).

Wolfenden, George. *The Little Doves of Destruction: A Romance of England under the Blitz* (London, 1941).

Woolf, Virginia. *The Diary of Virginia Woolf*, vol. 1: *1915–1919*. Edited by Anne Olivier Bell (New York, 1977).

The Letters of Virginia Woolf, vol. 6: *1936–1941*. Edited by Nigel Nicolson and Joanne Trautmann (New York, 1980).

"Thoughts on Peace in an Air Raid" (1940). Reprinted in Jenny Hartley (ed.), *Hearts Undefeated: Women's Writing of the Second World War* (London, 1994).

Three Guineas (1938; rpt. Harmondsworth, 1982).

The Years. (1937; rpt. New York, 1965).

Films

Do It Now (1939).

If War Should Come (1939).

In Which We Serve, Directed by Noel Coward and David Lean (1942).

London Can Take It (1940).

Mrs. Miniver, directed by William Wyler (1942).

Things to Come, directed by W. Cameron Menzies (1936).

Your Book (1938).

Secondary Sources

Alberti, Johanna. *Beyond Suffrage: Feminists in War and Peace, 1914–1928* (Basingstoke, 1989).

Allen, Ann Taylor. *Feminism and Motherhood in Western Europe, 1890–1970: The Maternal Dilemma* (New York, 2005).

Anderegg, Michael. *William Wyler* (Boston, 1979).

Audoin-Rouzeau, Stéphane, and Annette Becker. *1914–1918: Understanding the Great War*, Translated by Catherine Temerson (New York, 2002).

Baldwin, Peter. *The Politics of Social Solidarity: Class Bases of the European Welfare State, 1875–1975* (Cambridge, 1990).

Bazin, Nancy Topping, and Jane Hamovit Lauter. "Virginia Woolf's Keen Sensitivity to War: Its Roots and Its Impact on Her Novels." In Mark Hussey (ed.), *Virginia Woolf and War: Fiction, Reality, and Myth* (Syracuse, NY, 1991).

Beaven, Brad, and John Griffiths. "The Blitz, Civilian Morale and the City: Mass Observation and Working-Class Culture in Britain, 1940–41." *Urban History* 26:1 (1999), 71–88.

Bell, David A. *The First Total War: Napoleon's Europe and the Birth of Warfare as We Know It* (Boston, 2007).

Beer, Gillian. "The Island and the Aeroplane: The Case of Virginia Woolf." In Homi K. Bhabha (ed.), *Nation and Narration* (London, 1990).

Berry, Paul, and Alan Bishop (eds.). *Testament of a Generation: The Journalism of Vera Brittain and Winifred Holtby* (London, 1985).

Bialer, Uri. *The Shadow of the Bomber: The Fear of Air Attack and British Politics, 1932–1939* (London, 1980).

Biddle, Tami Davis. "Air Power." In Michael Howard, George J. Andreopoulos, and Mark R. Shulman (eds.), *The Laws of War: Constraints on Warfare in the Western World* (New Haven, CT, 1994).

"Dresden 1945: Reality, History and Memory," *Journal of Military History* 72 (2008), 413–449.

Rhetoric and Reality in Air Warfare: The Evolution of British and American Ideas about Strategic Bombing, 1914–1945 (Princeton, NJ, 2002).

Bock, Gisela , and Pat Thane (eds.). *Maternity and Gender Policies: Women and the Rise of the European Welfare States, 1880s–1950s* (London, 1991).

Bourke, Joanna. *An Intimate History of Killing: Face to Face Killing in Twentieth Century Warfare* (London, 1998).

Fear: A Cultural History (London, 2005; rpt. 2006).

Buchanan, Tom. *Britain and the Spanish Civil War* (Cambridge, 1997).

The Impact of the Spanish Civil War on Britain: War, Loss and Memory (Brighton, 2007).

Budiansky, Stephen. *Air Power: The Men, Machines, and Ideas That Revolutionized War from Kitty Hawk to Gulf War II* (New York, 2004).

Bussey, Gertrude, and Margaret Tims. *Pioneers for Peace: Women's International League for Peace and Freedom* (London, 1980).

Caesarini, David. "An Embattled Minority: The Jews in Britain during the First World War." In Tony Kushner and Kenneth Lunn (eds.), *The Politics of*

Marginality: Race, the Radical Right and Minorities in Twentieth Century Britain (London, 1990).

Calder, Angus. *The Myth of the Blitz* (London, 1991).

Ceadel, Martin. *Pacifism in Britain, 1914–1945: The Defining of a Faith* (Oxford, 1980).

"The Peace Movement between the Wars: Problems of Definition." In Richard Taylor and Nigel Young (eds.), *Campaigns for Peace: British Peace Movements in the Twentieth Century* (Manchester, 1987).

"Popular Fiction and the Next War, 1918–39." In Frank Gloversmith (ed.), *Class Culture and Social Change: A New View of the 1930s* (Brighton, 1980).

Chickering, Roger, and Stig Förstser (eds.). *Great War, Total War: Combat and Mobilization on the Western Front, 1914–1918* (Cambridge, 2000).

The Shadows of Total War: Europe, East Asia, and the United States, 1919–1939 (Cambridge, 2003).

Chickering, Roger, Stig Förstser, and Bernd Greiner (eds.). *A World at Total War: Global Conflict and the Politics of Destruction, 1937–1945* (Cambridge, 2005).

Churchill, Winston S. *Their Finest Hour* (Boston, 1949).

Clarke, I. F. *Voices Prophesying War*, 2d ed. (Oxford, 1992).

Clarke, Peter. *Hope and Glory: Britain, 1900–2000* (London, 2004).

Clayton, Tim, and Phil Craig. *Finest Hour: The Battle of Britain* (New York, 1999).

Conekin, Becky E. " 'Magazines Are Essentially About the Here and Now. And This Was Wartime': British *Vogue*'s Responses to the Second World War." In Philippa Levine and Susan R. Grayzel (eds.), *Gender, Labour, War and Empire* (Basingstoke, 2009).

Davin, Anna. "Imperialism and Motherhood." *History Workshop Journal* (1978), 9–35.

De Bruhl, Marshall. *Firestorm: Allied Airpower and the Destruction of Dresden* (New York, 2006).

Dear, I. C. B. (ed.). *The Oxford Companion to World War II* (Oxford, 1995).

Dillingham, William B. *Rudyard Kipling: Hell and Heroism* (Basingstoke, 2005).

Donnelly, Mark. *Britain in the Second World War* (London, 1999).

Downes, Alexander. *Targeting Civilians in War* (Ithaca, NY, 2008).

Druxman, Michael. *One Good Film Deserves Another* (South Brunswick, NY, 1977).

Dwork, Deborah. *War Is Good for Babies and Other Young Children: A History of the Infant and Child Welfare Movement in England, 1898–1918* (London, 1987).

Edgerton, David. *England and the Aeroplane: An Essay on a Militant and Technological Nation* (Manchester, 1991).

Warfare State: Britain, 1920–1970 (Cambridge, 2006).

Ehrman, John. *Cabinet Government and War 1890–1940* (Cambridge, 1958).

Enloe, Cynthia. "The Gendered Gulf." In Cynthia Peters, (ed.), *Collateral Damage: The "New World Order" at Home and Abroad* (Boston, 1992).

Firchow, Peter E. "Kipling's 'Mary Postgate': The Barbarians and the Critics." *Études anglaises* 29:1 (Jan.–Mar. 1976), 27–39. Reprinted in Harold Orel (ed.), *Critical Essays on Rudyard Kipling* (Boston, 1989).

Francis, Martin. *The Flyer: British Culture and the Royal Air Force, 1939–1945* (Oxford, 2008).

Fraser, Ronald. *Blood of Spain: An Oral History of the Spanish Civil War* (New York, 1979).

Fredette, Raymond H. *The Sky on Fire: The First Battle of Britain, 1917–1918* (1966, rpt. Washington, DC, 1991).

Friedrich, Jörg. *The Fire: The Bombing of Germany, 1940–45*. Translated by Alison Brown (2002, rpt. and trans., New York, 2006).

Fritzsche, Peter. *A Nation of Fliers: German Aviation and the Popular Imagination* (Cambridge, MA, 1992).

Gardiner, Juliet. *Wartime Britain, 1939–1945* (London, 2004).

Garrett, Stephen A. *Ethics and Airpower in World War Two: The British Bombing of German Cities* (New York, 1993).

Geyer, Michael. "The Militarization of Europe, 1914–1945." In John Gillis (ed.), *The Militarization of the Western World* (New Brunswick, NJ, 1989).

Gillis, John (ed.). *The Militarization of the Western World* (New Brunswick, NJ, 1989).

Glancy, H. Mark. *When Hollywood Loved Britain: The Hollywood "British" Film, 1939–45* (Manchester, 1999).

Gledhill, Christine, and Gillian Swanson (eds.). *Nationalising Femininity: Culture, Sexuality and British Cinema in the Second World War* (Manchester, 1996).

Grayling, A. C. *Among the Dead Cities: The History and Moral Legacy of the WWII Bombing of Civilians in Germany and Japan* (New York, 2006).

Grayzel, Susan R. "Across Battle Fronts: Gender and the Comparative Cultural History of Modern European War." In Deborah Cohen and Maura O'Connor (eds.), *Comparison and History: Europe in Cross-National Perspective* (New York, 2004).

"'Fighting for the Idea of Home Life': *Mrs Miniver* and Anglo-American Representations of Domestic Morale." In Philippa Levine and Susan R. Grayzel (eds.), *Gender, Labour, War and Empire: Essays on Modern Britain* (Basingstoke, 2009).

"'The Souls of Soldiers': Civilians Under Fire in First World War France," *Journal of Modern History*, 78:3 (2006), 588–622.

Women's Identities at War: Gender, Motherhood, and Politics in Britain and France during the First World War (Chapel Hill, NC, 1999).

Gregory, Adrian. *The Last Great War: British Society and the First World War* (Cambridge, 2008).

Gullace, Nicoletta F. *The Blood of Our Sons: Men, Women, and the Renegotiation of British Citizenship During the Great War* (New York, 2002).

"Friends, Aliens, and Enemies: Fictive Communities and the Lusitania Riots of 1915." *Journal of Social History* (2005), 345–367.

"Sexual Violence and Family Honor: British Propaganda and International Law during the First World War." *American Historical Review* 102:3 (June 1997), 714–747.

"White Feathers and Wounded Men: Female Patriotism and the Memory of the Great War." *Journal of British Studies* 36:2 (1997), 178–206.

Hagemann, Karen. "Home/Front: The Military, Violence and Gender Relations in the Age of the World Wars." In Karen Hagemann and Stefanie Schiller-Springorum (eds.), *Home/Front: The Military, War and Gender in Twentieth-Century Germany* (Oxford, 2002).

Harrisson, Tom. *Living Through the Blitz* (London, 1976).

Hartley, Jenny. *Millions Like Us: British Women's Fiction of the Second World War* (London, 1997).

Hartmann, Susan. *The Home Front and Beyond: American Women in the 1940s* (Boston, 1982).

Haslam, Beryl. *From Suffrage to Internationalism: The Political Evolution of Three British Feminists, 1908–1939* (New York, 1999).

Hesse, Carla. "Silences and the History of Representations of War: Comment on Peter Paret, 'Justifying the Obligation of Military Service.'" *Journal of Military History*, Special Issue, 57 (1993), 143–144.

Hinton, James. *Women, Social Leadership, and the Second World War: Continuities of Class* (Oxford, 2002).

Holton, Sandra. *Feminism and Democracy: Women's Suffrage and Reform Politics in Britain, 1900–1918* (Cambridge, 1986).

Hull, Isabel V. *Absolute Destruction: Military Culture and the Practices of War in Imperial Germany* (Ithaca, NY, 2005).

Hyde, Andrew. *The First Blitz: The German Bomber Campaign Against Britain in the First World War* (Barnsley, 2002).

Jackson, Ashley. *The British Empire and the Second World War* (London, 2006).

James, Lawrence. *Warrior Race: A History of the British at War* (London, 2002).

Jefferys, Kevin. *War and Reform: British Politics during the Second World War* (Manchester, 1994).

Jones, Helen. *British Civilians in the Front Line: Air Raids, Productivity and Wartime Culture, 1939–45* (Manchester, 2006).

Julius, Anthony. *Trials of the Diaspora: A History of Anti-Semitism in England* (Oxford, 2010).

Kennett, Lee. *The First Air War, 1914–1918* (New York, 1991).

Kent, Susan Kingsley. *Aftershocks: Politics and Trauma in Britain, 1918–1931* (Basingstoke, 2009).

  Making Peace: The Reconstruction of Gender in Interwar Britain (Princeton, NJ, 1993).

Kitching, Carolyn J. *Britain and the Geneva Disarmament Conference: A Study in International History* (Basingstoke, 2003).

Kramer, Alan. *Dynamic of Destruction: Culture and Mass Killing in the First World War* (Oxford, 2007).

Krebs, Paula M. *Gender, Race, and the Writing of Empire: Public Discourse and the Boer War* (Cambridge, 1999).

Lant, Antonia. *Blackout: Reinventing Women for Wartime British Cinema* (Princeton NJ, 1991).

Lassner, Phyllis. *British Women Writers of World War II: Battlegrounds of Their Own* (Basingstoke, 1998).

Laurence, Patricia. "The Facts and Fugue of War: From *Three Guineas* to *Between the Acts*." In Mark Hussey (ed.), *Virginia Woolf and War: Fiction, Reality, and Myth* (Syracuse, NY, 1991).

Levenback, Karen. *Virginia Woolf and the Great War* (Syracuse, NY, 1999).

Liddington, Jill. *The Long Road to Greenham: Feminism and Anti-Militarism in Britain since 1820* (London, 1989).

Light, Alison. *Forever England: Femininity, Literature and Conservatism Between the Wars* (London, 1991).

Lindqvist, Sven. *A History of Bombing*. Translated by Linda Haverty Rugg (New York, 2001).

Mackay, Robert. *Half the Battle: Civilian Morale in Britain during the Second World War* (Manchester, 2002).

The Test of War: Inside Britain, 1939–45 (London, 1999).

MacKenzie, S. P. *British War Films, 1939–1945: The Cinema and the Services* (London, 2001).

Manvell, Roger. *Films and the Second World War* (South Brunswick, NY, 1974).

Mayhall, Laura E. Nym. "The South African War and the Origins of Suffrage Militancy in Britain, 1899–1902." In Ian Christopher Fletcher, Laura E. Nym Mayhall, and Philippa Levine (eds.), *Women's Suffrage in the British Empire: Citizenship, Nation, and Race* (London, 2000).

Meilinger, Phillip S. "Clipping the Bomber's Wings: The Geneva Disarmament Conference and the Royal Air Force, 1932–1934." *War in History* 6:3 (1999), 306–330.

Meisel, Joseph S. "Air Raid Shelter Policy and Its Critics in Britain before the Second World War." *20th Century British History* 5:3 (1994), 300–319.

Moeller, Robert G. "The Bombing War in Germany, 2005–1940: Back to the Future?" In Yuki Tanaka and Marilyn B. Young (eds.), *Bombing Civilians: A Twentieth-Century History* (New York, 2009).

"On the History of Man-Made Destruction: Loss, Death, Memory and Germany in the Bombing War." *History Workshop Journal* 61:1 (2006), 103–134.

Morrow, John H., Jr. *The Great War in the Air: Military Aviation from 1909–1921* (Washington, DC, 1993).

Noakes, Lucy. *War and the British: Gender, Memory, and National Identity* (London, 1998).

Women in the British Army: War and the Gentle Sex, 1907–1948 (London, 2006).

Nolan, Mary. "Germans as Victims during the Second World War: Air Wars, Memory Wars." *Central European History* 38:1 (2005), 7–40.

O'Brien, T. H. *Civil Defence* (London, 1955).

Oram, Alison. " 'Bombs Don't Discriminate!' Women's Political Activism in the Second World War." In Christine Gledhill and Gillian Swanson (eds.), *Nationalising Femininity* (Manchester, 1996).

Omissi, David E. *Air Power and Colonial Control: The Royal Air Force, 1919–1939* (Manchester, 1990).

Overy, Richard. *The Twilight Years: The Paradox of Britain Between the Wars* (New York, 2009).

Panchasi, Roxanne. *Future Tense: The Culture of Anticipation in France between the Wars* (Ithaca, NY, 2009).

Pape, Robert A. *Bombing to Win: Air Power and Coercion in War* (Ithaca, NY, 1996).

Pedersen, Susan. *Family, Dependence and the Origins of the Welfare State in Britain and France, 1914–1945* (Cambridge, 1993).

Pisano, Dominick, et al. *Legend, Memory and the Great War in the Air* (Seattle, 1992).

Plain, Gill. *Women's Fiction of the Second World War: Gender, Power and Resistance* (Edinburgh, 1996).

Ponting, Clive. *1940: Myth and Reality* (Chicago, 1991).

Powers, Barry D. *Strategy without Slide-Rule: British Air Strategy, 1914–1939* (London, 1976).

Proctor, Tammy M. *Civilians in a World at War, 1914–1918* (New York, 2010).

Pugh, Martin. *Electoral Reform in War and Peace, 1906–1918* (London, 1978).
  Women and the Women's Movement in Britain, 1914–1959 (Basingstoke, 1992).

Rattigan, Neil. *This Is England: British Film and the People's War, 1939–1945* (Cranbury, NJ, 2001).

Rose, Sonya O. "Sex, Citizenship, and the Nation in World War II Britain." *American Historical Review* 103:4 (1998), 1147–1176
  Which People's War? National Identity and Citizenship in Wartime Britain, 1939–1945 (Oxford, 2003).

Rupp, Leila. *Worlds of Women: The Making of an International Women's Movement* (Princeton, NJ, 1997).

Saint-Amour, Paul K. "Air War Prophecy and Interwar Modernism." *Comparative Literature Studies* 41:2 (2005), 130–161.

Saler, Michael. *The Avant-Garde in Interwar England: Medieval Modernism and the London Underground* (Oxford, 1999).

Satia, Priya. "The Defense of Inhumanity: Air Control and the British Idea of Arabia." *American Historical Review* 111:1 (2003), 16–51.

Sebald, W. G. *On the Natural History of Destruction*. Translated by Anthea Bell (New York, 2004).

Sheehan, James. *Where Have All the Soldiers Gone? The Transformation of Modern Europe* (Boston, 2008).

Sheridan, Dorothy (ed.). *Wartime Women: A Mass-Observation Anthology, 1937–45* (London, 2000).

Slim, Hugo. *Killing Civilians: Method, Madness, and Morality in War* (New York, 2008).

Smith, Harold L. "British Feminism in the Second World War." In Philippa Levine and Susan R. Grayzel (eds.), *Gender, Labour, War and Empire: Essays on Modern Britain* (Basingstoke, 2009).

Southworth, Herbert Rutledge. *Guernica! Guernica! A Study of Journalism, Diplomacy, Propaganda, and History* (Berkeley, CA, 1977).

Spiers, Edward M. "Gas Disarmament in the 1920s: Hopes Confounded." *Journal of Strategic Studies* 29:2 (2006), 281–300.

Stansky, Peter. *The First Day of the Blitz: September 7, 1940* (New Haven, CT, 2007).

Stansky, Peter, and William Abrahams. *London's Burning: Life, Death and Art in the Second World War* (London, 1994).

Summers, Anne. *Angels and Citizens: British Women as Military Nurses, 1854–1914* (London, 1987).

Tanaka, Yuki. "British 'Humane Bombing' in Iraq during the Interwar Era." In Yuki Tanaka and Marilyn B. Young (eds.), *Bombing Civilians: A Twentieth-Century History* (New York, 2009).

Tanaka, Yuki, and Marilyn B. Young (eds.), *Bombing Civilians: A Twentieth-Century History* (New York, 2009).

Tate, Trudi. "HD's War Neurotics." In Suzanne Raitt and Trudi Tate (eds.), *Women's Fiction and the Great War* (Oxford, 1997).

Modernism, History and the First World War (Manchester, 1998).

Taylor, Richard, and Nigel Young (eds.), *Campaigns for Peace: British Peace Movements in the Twentieth Century* (Manchester, 1987).

Thomas, Donald. *An Underworld at War: Spivs, Deserters, Racketeers and Civilians in the Second World War* (London, 2003).

Thomas, Gordon, and Max Morgan Witts. *Guernica: The Crucible of World War II* (New York, 1977).

Thomas, Hugh. *The Spanish Civil War* (London, 1961).

Thumim, Janet. "The Female Audience: Mobile Women and Married Ladies." In Christine Gledhill and Gillian Swanson (eds.), *Nationalising Femininity: Culture, Sexuality and British Cinema in the Second World War* (Manchester, 1996).

Walsh, Andrea. *Women's Film and Female Experience, 1940–1950* (New York, 1984).

Whiting, Charles. *Britain Under Fire: The Bombing of Britain's Cities, 1940–45* (Barnsley, 1999).

Winship, Janice. "Women's Magazines: Times of War and Management of the Self in *Woman's Own*." In Christine Gledhill and Gillian Swanson (eds.), *Nationalising Femininity: Culture, Sexuality and British Cinema in the Second World War* (Manchester, 1996).

Wohl, Robert. *A Passion for Wings: Aviation and the Western Imagination, 1908–1918* (New Haven, CT, 1994).

The Spectacle of Flight: Aviation and the Western Imaginaion, 1920–1950 (New Haven, CT, 2005).

Index

CPSIA information can be obtained at www.ICGtesting.com
Printed in the USA
LVOW060749080213

319001LV00003B/5/P

9 780521 874946